Europea: Ethnomusicologies and Modernities

Series Editors: Philip V. Bohlman and Martin Stokes

1. *Celtic Modern: Music at the Global Fringe,* edited by Martin Stokes and Philip V. Bohlman, 2003.
2. *Albanian Urban Lyric Song in the 1930s,* by Eno Koço, 2004.
3. *The Mediterranean in Music: Critical Perspectives, Common Concerns, Cultural Differences,* edited by David Cooper and Kevin Dawe, 2005.
4. *On a Rock in the Middle of the Ocean: Songs and Singers in Tory Island, Ireland,* by Lillis Ó Laoire, 2005.
5. *Transported by Song: Corsican Voices from Oral Tradition to World Stage,* by Caroline Bithell, 2007.
6. *Balkan Popular Culture and the Ottoman Ecumene: Music, Image, and Regional Political Discourse,* edited by Donna A. Buchanan, 2007.
7. *Music and Musicians in Crete: Performance and Ethnography in a Mediterranean Island Society,* by Kevin Dawe, 2007.
8. *The New (Ethno)musicologies,* edited by Henry Stobart, 2008.
9. *Balkan Refrain: Form and Tradition in European Folk Song,* by Dimitrije O. Golemović, 2010.
10. *Music and Displacement: Diasporas, Mobilities, and Dislocations in Europe and Beyond,* edited by Erik Levi and Florian Scheding, 2010.
11. *Balkan Epic: Song, History, Modernity,* edited by Philip V. Bohlman and Nada Petković, 2012.
12. *What Makes Music European: Looking beyond Sound,* by Marcello Sorce Keller, 2012.
13. *The Past Is Always Present: The Revival of the Byzantine Musical Tradition at Mount Athos,* Tore Tvarnø Lind, 2012.
14. *Becoming an Ethnomusicologist: A Miscellany of Influences,* by Bruno Nettl, 2013.
15. *Empire of Song: Europe and Nation in the Eurovision Song Contest,* edited by Dafni Tragaki, 2013.

EUROPEA: ETHNOMUSICOLOGIES AND MODERNITIES

Series Editors: Philip V. Bohlman and Martin Stokes

The new millennium challenges ethnomusicologists, dedicated to studying the music of the world, to examine anew the Western musics they have treated as "traditional," and to forge new approaches to world musics that are often over-looked because of their deceptive familiarity. As the modern discipline of ethnomusicology expanded during the second half of the twentieth century, influenced significantly by ethnographic methods in the social sciences, ethnomusicology's "field" increasingly shifted to the exoticized Other. The comparative methodologies previously generated by Europeanist scholars to study and privilege Western musics were deliberately discarded. Europe as a cultural area was banished to historical musicology, and European vernacular musics became the spoils left to folk-music and, later, popular-music studies.

Europea challenges ethnomusicology to return to Europe and to encounter its disciplinary past afresh, and the present is a timely moment to do so. European unity nervously but insistently asserts itself through the political and cultural agendas of the European Union, causing Europeans to reflect on a bitterly and violently fragmented past and its ongoing repercussions in the present, and to confront new challenges and opportunities for integration. There is also an intellectual moment to be seized as Europeans reformulate the history of the present, an opportunity to move beyond the fragmentation and atomism the later twentieth century has bequeathed and to enter into broader social, cultural, and political relationships.

Europea is not simply a reflection of and on the current state of research. Rather, the volumes in this series move in new directions and experiment with diverse approaches. The series establishes a forum that can engage scholars, musicians, and other interlocutors in debates and discussions crucial to understanding the present historical juncture. This dialogue, grounded in ethnomusicology's interdisciplinarity, will be animated by reflexive attention to the specific social configurations of knowledge of and scholarship on the musics of Europe. Such knowledge and its circulation as ethnomusicological scholarship are by no means dependent on professional academics, but rather are conditioned, as elsewhere, by complex interactions between universities, museums, amateur organizations, state agencies, and markets. Both the broader view to which ethnomusicology aspires and the critical edge necessary to understanding the present moment are served by broadening the base on which "academic" discussion proceeds.

"Europe" will emerge from the volumes as a space for critical dialogue, embracing competing and often antagonistic voices from across the continent, across the Atlantic, across the Mediterranean and the Black Sea, and across a world altered ineluctably by European colonialism and globalization. The diverse subjects and interdisciplinary approaches in individual volumes capture something of—and, in a small way, become part of—the jangling polyphony through which the "New Europe" has explosively taken musical shape in public discourse, in expressive culture, and, increasingly, in political form. Europea: Ethnomusicologies and Modernities aims to provide a critical framework necessary to capture something of the turbulent dynamics of music performance, engaging the forces that inform and deform, contest and mediate the senses of identity, selfhood, belonging, and progress that shape "European" musical experience in Europe and across the world.

Empire of Song

Europe and Nation in the Eurovision Song Contest

Edited by Dafni Tragaki

*Europea: Ethnomusicologies
and Modernities #15*

The Scarecrow Press, Inc.
Lanham • Toronto • Plymouth, UK
2013

Published by Scarecrow Press, Inc.
A wholly owned subsidary of The Rowman & Littlefield Publishing Group, Inc.
4501 Forbes Boulevard, Suite 200, Lanham, Maryland 20706
www.rowman.com

10 Thornbury Road, Plymouth PL6 7PP, United Kingdom

British Library Cataloguing in Publication Information Available

Library of Congress Cataloging-in-Publication Data
Empire of song : Europe and nation in the Eurovision Song Contest / edited by
Dafni Tragaki.
    pages cm.— (Europea: ethnomusicologies and modernities ; 15)
    Includes bibliographical references and indexes.
    Summary: "The Eurovision Song Contest (ESC) is more than a musical event
that ostensibly "unites European people" through music. It is a spectacle and
performative event, one that allegorically represents the idea of "Europe."
In "Empire of Song: Europe and Nation in the Eurovision Song Contest,"
contributors interpret the ESC as a musical "mediascape" and mega-event that
has variously performed and performs the changing visions of the European
project. Through the study of the cultural politics of the ESC, essayists discuss
the ways in which music operates as a dynamic nexus for making national
identities and European sensibilities, generating processes of 'assimilation' or
'integration,' and defining the celebrated notion of the 'European citizen' in a
global context."
    ISBN 978-0-8108-8699-5 (cloth : alk. paper)—ISBN 978-0-8108-8817-3 (electronic)
    1. Eurovision Song Contest. 2. Music—Competitions—Europe. 3. Music—
Social aspects—Europe. 4. Music—Political aspects—Europe. I. Tragaki, Dafni,
editor.
    ML76.E87E47 2013
    780.794—dc23   2013002017

∞™ The paper used in this publication meets the minimum requirements
of American National Standard for Information Sciences—Permanence of
Paper for Printed Library Materials, ANSI/NISO Z39.48-1992.

Printed in the United States of America

Contents

Foreword

War without Tears
European Broadcasting and Competition

FRANCO FABBRI

The perception of the term "Eurovision" varies with time and place. Fans, journalists, and scholars alike, in many European countries and in other continents, seem to have adopted it—at least in the past ten/fifteen years—as a shorter form for "Eurovision Song Contest" (ESC). But it hasn't been so forever. For decades, even after the early mass success of the ESC in the late 1960s, "Eurovision" has been associated mainly with international television broadcasts of various kinds under the heading of the European Broadcasting Union (EBU), and especially with the visual and musical identifiers of Eurovision network transmissions: the Eurovision logo and Charpentier's *Prelude* to the *Te Deum* respectively. From sports events (Olympic Games and world championships for athletics, swimming and other Olympic sports; football matches in the FIFA World Cup or in European championships, or in international club competitions; the alpine ski World Cup and winter Olympics; bicycle races like Tour de France and Giro d'Italia; the Davis Cup and other tennis championships, etc.) to cultural events (especially the *Neujahrkonzert* from Vienna) and "light" entertainment (for a while Italy's Sanremo Festival, and of course the ESC since its inception), Eurovision broadcasts used to be opened by the identifier, with the logo changing from the one of the local broadcaster to the one of the remote transmitter, and the *Prelude* repeating accordingly. Among my peers, when I was a teenager, it was common to refer to an important football match we were waiting for by singing the last phrase of the *Prelude* and then imitating the sound of the stadium's crowd applauding and shouting: "Hhhhhhhhh . . ." And then, the commentator would start with his welcome to TV watchers. The ritual had also technical reasons, giving TV engineers from both sides of the connection enough time to establish and check it, before airing the actual broadcast. In fact, an equivalent procedure is still in use in EBU's Euroradio circuit, where concerts are preceded by the *Ouverture* from Monteverdi's *Orfeo*. On television, the move from ground microwave repeaters to satellite connections and computer-controlled switching procedures put an end to the usage of the identifiers, which steal precious time from advertising inserts: so, the ritual only remained for those broadcasts which are especially prestigious for the EBU. After the mid-1990s, Charpentier's *Prelude* has been associated mostly with the New Year Concert and the ESC.

Place is also relevant. Many countries (or, to be precise, nationwide broadcasting companies) adhered to the EBU before—even long before— they started participating in the ESC, as shown in table 1.1 on the next page.

Generally, it can be seen that for many countries in Western Europe (but also for Albania, Turkey, and Greece) "Eurovision" was for a while (a long while, in those instances) mainly the public name for EBU services and broadcasts, which might include the ESC (in some cases, with *other* participating countries), along with sports events of any kind and other entertainment programs. On the contrary, most countries in Eastern Europe became EBU members in 1993 (or soon after), and started participating in the ESC almost immediately, just around the time when the "Eurovision" identifier was dropped from regular international broadcasts, with the exceptions of the ESC and the New Year Concert. The ESC didn't become largely popular, even in the participating countries, before the late 1960s, so an articulated pattern can be observed: (1) countries that adhered early to the EBU and soon participated in the ESC, before the ESC became largely popular (Belgium, Denmark, Finland, France, Ireland, Italy, Luxembourg, Monaco, Netherlands, Switzerland, United Kingdom, Germany, Austria, Sweden); (2) countries that adhered early to the EBU and possibly received the ESC as one of EBU's offerings, but started participating later (Norway, Portugal, Spain, Yugoslavia); (3) countries that adhered to the EBU later and started participating in the ESC when it was already popular, but before the Eurovision identifier was discontinued (Israel, Greece, Turkey, Iceland, Cyprus, Morocco); (4) countries that adhered to the EBU and started participating in the ESC when it was already popular, in coincidence with or after the discontinuation of the Eurovision identifier (all remaining countries in the table, i.e., Eastern European countries, with few exceptions). Albania (1962–2004) and Malta (1970–1971) cannot easily be included in the above categories, although Albania can be assimilated to other Eastern European countries.

Every country has its own EBU and ESC history, of course. Italy is one of the examples of a distinctive position. RAI, Italy's state-owned broadcasting company, launched in 1948 (two years before the EBU was founded) the Prix Italia, a prize for radio programs—that later incorpo-

Table 1.1. EBU Membership and ESC Participation: Time Lapse by Country

Country	EBU	ESC	Years lapsed
Belgium	1950	1956	6
Denmark	1950	1957	7
Finland	1950	1961	11
France	1950	1956	6
Greece	1950	1974	24
Ireland	1950	1965	15
Italy	1950	1956	6
Luxembourg	1950	1956	6
Monaco	1950	1959	9
Netherlands	1950	1956	6
Norway	1950	1960	10
Portugal	1950	1964	14
Switzerland	1950	1956	6
Turkey	1950	1975	25
UK (BBC)	1950	1957	7
Yugoslavia	1950	1961	11
Germany	1952	1956	4
Austria	1953	1957	4
Spain	1955	1961	6
Sweden	1955	1958	3
Iceland	1956	1986	30
Israel	1957	1973	16
Albania	1962	2004	42
Cyprus	1969	1981	12
Morocco	1969	1980	11
Malta	1970	1971	1
Belarus	1993	2004	11
Bosnia & Herzegovina	1993	1993	0
Bulgaria	1993	2005	12
Croatia	1993	1993	0
Czech Republic	1993	2007	14
Estonia	1993	1994	1
Hungary	1993	1994	1
Latvia	1993	2000	7
Lithuania	1993	1994	1
Macedonia	1993	1998	5
Moldova	1993	2005	12
Poland	1993	1994	1
Romania	1993	1994	1
Russia	1993	1994	1
Slovenia	1993	1993	0
Ukraine	1993	2003	10
San Marino	1995	2008	13
Montenegro	2001	2004	3
Serbia	2001	2004	3
Andorra	2002	2008	6
Armenia	2005	2006	1
Georgia	2005	2007	2
Azerbaijan	2007	2008	1
Slovakia	2011	1994	n/a

rated television as well—aimed at promoting quality in broadcasting. The idea of a prize as a stimulus for artistic creation, obviously, wasn't new. Just to name a few truly international or national precedents: the Prix de Rome (France, 1663, for fine arts and architecture, and—after 1803—music), the Concorso canoro di Piedigrotta (Naples, 1839, songs), the Prix Goncourt (France, 1903, literature), Academy Awards (USA, 1929, cinema), Peabody Awards (USA, 1940, radio, and 1948, television), Tony Awards (USA, 1947, theater). Later, Emmy Awards (USA, 1949, television) and Grammy Awards (USA, 1959, records) would follow. After the Second World War, and Fascism, it was important for Italy and its public broadcasting company to be perceived internationally as promoting cultural exchange and quality in the field of modern, technically advanced media. Three years later, in 1951, RAI launched the "Festival della canzone italiana," to be held in Sanremo (on the Riviera, not far from the French border). It was initially broadcast over the radio, and from 1955 on television (regular TV broadcasts started in Italy in 1954). Not surprisingly, the festival was aimed at "promoting quality in Italian song." Here is an excerpt of the semiofficial presentation of the festival's guidelines in RAI's house organ:

> The influx of Afro-American and Latin-American popular music—whose main streams, i.e., jazz, Cuban, and Brazilian music, branch out almost infinitely [. . .] and grow turbidly passing across Broadway and Hollywood and providing material for the big international popular music market—this influx became more and more relevant and in the past few years imprinted an exotic physiognomy on songs from various European countries, weakening their original features and their coherence with the ethnic and sentimental substrate of the peoples from which they originate. Italian song, which springs from Neapolitan song and *romanza* and is related to operatic tradition (a celebrated one, but devoid of recent developments), has been exposed to such an influx, and has been lacking an original and lively character. With a series of initiatives, RAI is trying to promote the rebirth of a truly active spirit and of distinctive individuality in Italian song, providing directions for authors and music publishers. (Anon. 1951, my translation)[1]

Such an amazing mixture of literary and bureaucratic language evokes the style and content of similar comments published in the same magazine twelve years earlier, in 1939, when an anonymous contributor (possibly, the broadcasting company's director of programming) explained EIAR's policy regarding "light music" (Anon. 1939). After the collapse of Fascism, the company's name had been changed (from EIAR to RAI), but the director of programming, Giulio Razzi, remained the same. In that capacity, he also became the artistic director of the Sanremo Festival (see Fabbri 2008: 84–86). In fact, the festival was launched in the wake of the right-wing turn that followed the beginning of the Cold War and the exclusion of left parties from Italy's government, with the consequence of a strict conservative control over the state-owned RAI. During the festival's first decade, Sanremo's stage was monopolized by authors, singers, and conductors whose careers had started in the 1930s or 1940s. The winning songs in 1955 and 1957, "Buongiorno tristezza" and "Corde della mia chitarra," were composed by Mario Ruccione, the author in 1935 of "Faccetta nera," one of the most famous Fascist battle hymns (Fabbri 2008: *ibid.*); if Ruccione's new songs were traditional sentimental ballads, other pieces presented at the festival in the fifties were clearly nostalgic of war times ("Vecchio scarpone," 1953) or close to the patriotic themes agitated by conservative parties ("Vola colomba," winner in 1952).

So, the fact that the ESC was shaped in the mid-fifties according to the model of the Sanremo Festival, within an EBU where Italy acted as one of the most prestigious members—thanks to the Prix Italia, which wasn't an EBU event but inevitably influenced EBU broadcasters—suggests that the origins of the ESC (approved at an EBU meeting held in Rome) be considered carefully also in the context of the Cold War, in the framework of political and strategic alliances of the time, in the light of shared ideologies about the political and educational functions of broadcast entertainment and "light music" that had been, most unfortunately, developed by totalitarian states in the thirties (see Fabbri, forthcoming). Initial participations of countries that didn't belong to the early Western European core are telling: non–Warsaw Pact member Yugoslavia (1961), Franco's Spain (1961), Salazar's Portugal (1964), Israel (1973), and NATO member Turkey (1975). Of course, the development of both the EBU and the ESC parallels that of the European Economic Community (Rome, 1957) and, later, the European Union (Maastricht, 1993), against a very similar ideological, political, and strategic backdrop. It is symbolic and not purely coincidental that crucial dates (and even places) in the history of contemporary Europe be so close (or identical) to those that mark the ESC's history, and that the expansion of ESC participation follow the same geographical patterns of European economic and political expansion.

In its way, the ESC is "war without tears," as Peter Gabriel put it in his 1980 hit song "Games without Frontiers." Not surprisingly, that is actually the name of another EBU broadcast (*Jeux sans frontières*, JSF; the English title was actually *It's a Knockout*): it was very popular between 1965 and 1982 and again between 1986 and 1999. With the exceptions of Wales and Tunisia, which took part in JSF but not in the ESC, the list of participant countries is a subset of that of the ESC, with a core group of eight countries that participated more than ten times (Italy, France, Switzerland, Belgium, Germany, United Kingdom, Portugal, Netherlands), and eleven that won at least once (Germany, Portugal, Italy, United Kingdom, France,

Hungary, Belgium, Switzerland, Czech Republic, Spain, Czechoslovakia). With varying formats and rules, the broadcasts were based on circus-like competitions ("silly games," in Gabriel's words) among teams coming from towns representing all participating nations. Until 1995 the number of towns per nation would be equal to the number of nations, and they would compete in eliminatory contests hosted in turn in each country and broadcast over the EBU network. The best-placed towns representing each nation would then take part in the final. So JSF enjoyed a much larger exposure than the ESC in terms of broadcasting time, although it probably never became as popular as the ESC. It was Eurovision, and competition (even with more direct confrontation between countries, as sometimes teams had to struggle against each other), and it lasted for weeks (months, actually), but it missed something, and it didn't make it until the age of the World Wide Web. Like with the ESC, however, its relevance varied from country to country. The Nordic countries—so important in the ESC—never participated in JSF, and after 1993 very few Eastern European countries got involved. On the other hand, Italy took part in JSF thirty times (all editions), while participating in the ESC only thirty-seven times (in fifty-six editions until 2011). As RAI is the organizer of the Sanremo Festival, and as in the Italian music industry there is a widespread conviction that "Sanremo" (as it is abbreviated by people in the business) be a truly international event (broadcast live in Eurovision, though by fewer and fewer countries in the past decades), the ESC is undervalued by the Italian media and music industry: after 1997 RAI decided not to participate in the ESC and even not to broadcast it. The ban ended in 2011, after negotiations that Italy, as one of the larger contributors to the EBU, should be one of the "big five" countries, and as such admitted automatically to the contest. As can be clearly seen, participation in the ESC is intertwined with matters of politics, economy, and power, probably more than just "bloc voting." It is also true that Sanremo occupies in Italian popular culture and semiosphere a similar (although not identical) position as that of the ESC elsewhere in Europe (again, with differences): it is where serious matters and kitsch meet, overlap, and get confused; it is at the origin of futile and profound discourses on the value of music, that almost inevitably (with few exceptions) are focused on songs that will not succeed in the market or last in the memories of listeners; it is based on strict rules (the three-minute format, the prohibition or allowance for languages or dialects) that engender controversies and at the same time create a special music-semantic space, which incorporates and translates genres, but is anyway different from all of them (no rock piece really rocks on that stage, no singer-songwriter can actually be him/herself, no folk song can arguably be traditional: song contests function as genre benders). There are, of course, ESC fans in Italy, and there may be more if future editions are broadcast live, but the gigantic weeklong Sanremo Festival is bound to remain as an inevitable hindrance to a larger ESC popularity in Italy. And this may also be an explanation for the larger Italian success of JSF, which condensed aspects of international curiosity and rivalry and stereotypes absent in Sanremo, and quite remarkable in the ESC.

As an Italian and European citizen who grew up in the 1950s, my interest for the ESC has been shaped by the presence of the Sanremo Festival. Born in Brazil, one of my earliest memories of Italy is when, at the age of three, I listened to the 1953 edition of the festival on the radio, with my parents. I liked "Vecchio scarpone" without understanding its political undertones (twelve years later I found that the flip side of the Rolling Stones' "Satisfaction," titled "The Under Assistant West Coast Promotion Man," had a very similar melody: but it wasn't about nostalgia for the Fascist army's victories). In 1960 my father, a journalist and former radio director, was assigned the task to organize Sanremo's tenth edition, but had to resign because record companies and publishers opposed his proposal of a demographic voting system; before he resigned, I had the chance to attend with him a festival of Italian song organized in Zurich, one of the many Sanremo clones that sprang up in those years (another one was in Barcelona). I saw Gigliola Cinquetti's victory at the ESC in 1964 (she had won the Sanremo Festival even if she had scored second, as the winner was eliminated for using playback; mimicking was allowed only later): in that occasion I first learned the ritual of the ESC's voting procedures. I must have seen other editions, but the next one I remember is only in 1985: I was in Gothenburg, guest of Philip Tagg's, attending a meeting of IASPM's Executive, but I had a terrible stiff neck and couldn't participate in the celebration by all other attendees, who went somewhere else to watch the final. I was sincerely impressed by the enthusiasm of my colleagues: Alf Björnberg may have been one of them. Aching and alone, I watched Alice and Franco Battiato score fifth. Those were the years when I started writing about genre: festival rules and regulations, and unwritten conventions agreed upon in that context, were a continuous source of theoretical interest (I read a paper on the subject at Gothenburg's University, holding sheets above my head because that was the only position that hurt a little less). However, while I never missed a single edition of Sanremo, it became more and more difficult to attend the ESC, as it wasn't broadcast live in Italy, newspapers didn't announce or cover it, and at some point it disappeared from Italian television—until I entered a Bier Keller in Berlin after another scholarly meeting, in 2010, just in time to see Lena and her "Satellite" triumph in Oslo. But before then I had already been asked to write a foreword for this book.

As it should be clear now, and will be even clearer after reading all chapters, I was pleased both by the invitation and by the content of the individual essays. A subject like the ESC is bound to generate the kind of multidisciplinary and multidimensional approach that I like and try to promote in music studies: having been exposed to the Sanremo Festival and the ESC for nearly sixty years (I can't believe it . . .) I learned a lot from reading the pages that follow. That's why I decided not to make any individual comment, but to provide in this text some complementary information, that I hope will contribute to place each chapter in its right perspective, against the backdrop of European spectacle and politics. Enjoy the reading.

NOTES

1. L'influsso della musica popolare afro-americana e ispano-americana—le cui correnti principali, quella jazzistica e quella cubana e brasiliana, si ramificano in una infinità di filiazioni [. . .] e si intorbidano, ingrossandosi, al passaggio per Broadway e per Hollywood, fornendo così il materiale al grande mercato internazionale della musica leggera—questo influsso è divenuto via via più rilevante e col trascorrere degli ultimi anni ha impresso una fisionomia esotica alle canzoni dei diversi paesi europei, attenuando sempre più i caratteri originali di queste e l'aderenza al substrato etnico e sentimentale dei popoli da cui scaturiscono. La canzone italiana, che discende dai canti napoletani e dalle romanze e si collega a una tradizione lirica insigne ma scarsa di evoluzioni recenti, è andata particolarmente soggetta a questo influsso ed è venuta a mancare, negli ultimi anni, di un carattere originale e vivo. Con una serie di iniziative, la Rai cerca appunto di promuovere la rinascita di uno spirito veramente attivo nella canzone italiana e l'acquisizione di una individualità spiccata, indirizzando in tal senso gli autori e gli editori musicali.

REFERENCES

Anon. 1939. "Ancora della musica leggera," *Radiocorriere*, anno XV, n. 10, 5.
Anon. 1951. "Il Festival della canzone italiana a Sanremo," *Radiocorriere*, 28 gennaio-3 febbraio, 18–19.
Fabbri, Franco. 2008. *Around the clock. Una breve storia della popular music*. Turin: Utet Libreria.
Fabbri, Franco. forthcoming, "Il Trentennio: 'musica leggera' alla radio italiana, 1928–1958," paper presented at the conference *Radio e musica. Storia, effetti, contesti*, University of Parma, December 2, 2009. To be published in the proceedings (ed. by Angela Ida De Benedictis, Rome: Bulzoni).

Introduction

Dafni Tragaki

I am not a Eurovision fan. I have never been a fan of anything, indeed. Yet I enjoy the mediated phantasmagoria of the annual Eurovision song Grand Prix that attracts millions of scopophiles elsewhere on the globe, who share the "passion for the real" and "the spectacular effect of it" (Žižek 2002, 11).[1] For all us viewers, Eurovision has the power to arrest our attention, to "suspend our perception" (Crary 1999). It is a mediatic fiesta that transforms the experience of European modernity/-ies and their afterlives to an astonishing musical entertainment: the entertainment of Europe that is annually created, contested, and celebrated in music. In Eurovision Song Contest (ESC) Europe "is musicking" in the global public sphere (Small 1998, 9),[2] where year after year we are invited to engender and reflect upon our European/national selves in the performances of songs we find either arresting, or clichéd, eccentric, sentimental, kitsch, or camp.

Yet we take pleasure in participating in the scopic/sensual regimes of Europeanness constituted in the contested sounds of the Eurovision song, whether we like them or not. Most possibly because, as Crary has noticed, what is significant about spectacle is not so much *what* we see, as *that* we see (see Crary 1999). While we are watching Europe, Europe is also watching us. Perhaps, with the remote gaze that Jean Francois Mattéi termed as "le regard vide" ("the empty look"): the gaze of supremacy that has the self-acquired privilege of capturing the universality of the world that Europe hosts on stage, Europe's own world, its homemade universe. The gaze of a restless Europe, the Europe of inquietude, now fatigued to the point of exhaustion by being simultaneously in search of its own heritage and the need to overcome it (see Mattéi 2007). Seen in

1

those terms Eurovision becomes a technique both for the European self and for the virtual Europe that is made possible on our TV screens as long as it lasts—at least before we forget it. Yet more than a "regime of seeing," ESC suggests "ways of seeing" and sensing music in the technologically sophisticated, overwhelming mediascapes of the European Broadcasting Union which spectacularly pose the question: what it is to be European.[3]

The Eurovision empire of song is shaped in the context of a cultural institution that serves the raising of "a common European awareness" (Shore 2000, 45), one of the prime goals of the European Commission and the EU elites who, since the 1990s (and especially the Maastricht Treaty), have been striving to promote the European idea through the medium of "culture" to the absent demos of Europe—what Shore described as "the 'people's Europe' campaign" (Shore 2000, 44). Audiovisual policy has been one of the key sites for creating Europe as a popular master narrative, and television has been capitalized as a powerful field for the invention of new symbols. In the sounds of Marc-Antoine Charpentier's *Te Deum*, the EBU's march-styled music signal, we feel the idea of *Europe sans frontières*. The "bright and warlike" prelude coming from the European aristocratic musical tradition invests the ESC broadcast with the magnificence of the imperial ceremony, the splendor of the royalty, and the absolute order of the monarchy (see Fornäs 2012, 188).[4] As such, it becomes a sonic window to "our," "virtual Europe" that the pan-European television brings straight into our everydayness; we are all connected (Abélès 2000, 31). At the same time, it also reminds us that the ESC as an institution is part of the cultural policy of the Brussels officials and their top-down approach to the creation of Europe as more than a common market of goods, workers, and services. How much control, however, could they have over the kind of Europe that is constantly invented in the ESC? To what extent is it possible to market European and national utopias in music? And finally, what is the relationship between the Europe(s) created in Eurovision songs and the Europe idealized by the EU?

These are questions that address the complexities defining the ways Europe is sung on the ESC stage as well as the performativity of the European/national self in music year after year. Although ESC as an institution is part of the policy for bringing Europe closer to its citizens, a ritual in the service of the EU's political visions for a union among the people of Europe, it is doubtful whether it is an effective instrument for forging a common "European identity" and manipulating the "European consciousness" from above (see Shore 2000, 26). As the various case studies discussed in the present volume suggest, it is the greatest musical contest of the so-called supranational state, where the supranational state constantly projects its geopolitical anxieties, at the same time the nation plays with its boundaries and positioning in the global cultural industry.

ESC itself embodies these contrasting dynamics by supposedly being both an event where European community is constantly brought to life and a contest among nations.[5] As Bohlman and Rehding put it, the Eurovision entries dance "the European two-step" in the negotiation of the emerging frictions between the national and the European levels of the contest.[6] Like Europe, ESC needs thus to be studied as a process, not as a product (see Borneman and Fowler 1997): it is an institution that refers to the future of a harmonized Europe that is endlessly in question (see Abélès 1996).

It is important to bear in mind that, perhaps more than anything else, ESC is about music mediated by people; about performances framed in history. Despite its ritualistic norms, every ESC is unique and highly unpredictable. As a musical performance it is a level of reality where European subjectivities are constantly emerging, while established worldviews are negotiated, contested, inverted, or reaffirmed *in song*. Song becomes a site for branding Europe and the nation, on and off stage. Eurovision song, following Bohlman, should be taken seriously as the creative, mobile, mediated, embodied, ritualistic, performative, narrative unit that encapsulates and generates memories, histories, nations, and collectivities. History and politics in ESC *sound* in music: in the song structure, style, the lyrics, the composers and producers, the singers, the listeners, the Eurovision connoisseurs and the several media networks where the song acquires new lives.[7] Music thus matters, despite the tendency of recent Eurovision-inspired scholarship "to stimulate interest in the Eurovision Song Contest *in spite of* the word 'song' at its center."[8] The present volume stands against the cliché that "ESC is not really about music." It questions Eurovision song as the "one that articulates the historical moment" (Bohlman 2004, 9; Solomon 2007).

For the authors of this book, Europe in ESC is experienced, felt, and imagined primarily in singing and dancing, where the interplay of tropes of being local and/or European is enacted. Song is thus understood as the shifting realm where old and new states imagine their pasts, question their presents, and envision ideal futures. On this basis, the present volume encourages novel perspectives addressing the ways local, glocal, and supranational cultural politics are projected and negotiated in performances and discourses surrounding the mega-event. Exploring questions such as who is included or excluded, how and why, who is cherished, and who is disregarded in the media ritual of the ESC can provide an insightful perspective to the poetics of Europeanness, now and in the past. Through the music-cultural study of the ESC we come to know about the ways in which the song becomes a dynamic nexus for encapsulating processes of "assimilation" or "integration," as well as for defining European "identity" and "difference" in a global context.

Moreover, the popularity and the scale of the media-event invite us to situate the study of the ESC phenomenon in the network of musical and political realities emerging in Europe and outside it. One of the main concerns of this book is moving beyond the tendency to demarcate "European music culture" as a generic category to which the institution of the ESC is attached and, hence, to avoid theorizing the ESC as a special field of knowledge. Accordingly, we depart from panoramic views which tend to provincialize Europe, or regions of Europe, by reinforcing geopolitical distinctions, such as East/West, communist/capitalist, Mediterranean/North, oriental/occidental, that serve as normative categories for analysis. Rather than essentializing the study of the ESC as a *sui generis* phenomenon, the multiangled perspective proposed here suggests the framing of interpretations in association with theoretical explorations broadly discussing the concepts of popular music, nationalism, modernity, and postcolonialism, among others. Through an exploration of the ESC in these terms, this book critically readdresses the axiological distinction between "high" and "low" musical cultures by questioning the discourses that redefine, legitimize, mitigate, erase, or reinforce it.

WHAT IS "EUROPEAN MUSIC"?

But, it might be objected, Eurovision is not about European music. "European music" and, consequently, the essence of European "civilization," is to be found in the great works of the genius composers that brought the noble art of music to its highest degree of sophistication. This "European music" is both timeless and transcendental, a fixed canon of masterpieces that survives history as it is superior to it and has the power to reaffirm continuity with the past; it is, indeed, an almost organic part of the glorious imperial past. As such, it invests the imaginary of a European community born in music, a European community united by a common cultural heritage where the contribution of "others" remains invisible.[9] Instead, ESC is, for many of its critics, a triumph of bad taste, a foolish spectacle of light entertainment, a pathological symptom of a corrupting mass culture that serves the interests of the music industry. As "bad" popular music, it cannot be thought of as genuinely "European," because it fails to serve the "high" spiritual values and humanistic ideals embedded in the "true" art of music as this has been formed in the spirit of its shared Graeco-Roman and Christian heritage. Nonetheless, ESC involves a world of people, such as the members of the various fan clubs (OGAE), who follow enthusiastically the annual pilgrimage to the capital city that hosts the contest, Web bloggers and journalists, TV panels and talk shows that eagerly uncover exciting or scandalous details about the personal life of the contestants or the hidden politics and unknown conspiracies of the "big event," and millions of viewers who love to watch the mediated ritual of the singing European nations. Not to forget the major sponsor of the event, the European Broadcasting Union (EBU), that founded ESC as a European cultural institution.

The controversial landscape of discourses and popular evaluations of the ESC institution (including those that mitigate the apparent polarity) may perhaps be seen as a contemporary repercussion of what Andreas Huyssen has called, a while ago, "the Great Divide" (Huyssen 1986)—"the kind of discourse which insists on the categorical distinction between high art and mass culture" (Huyssen 1986, viii). Elsewhere, he extensively discusses Adorno as the master theorist of the Great Divide.[10] This divide is much more important for a theoretical and historical understanding of modernism and its aftermath "than the alleged historical break which . . . separates postmodernism from modernism" (Huyssen 1986, viii). However, the "Great Divide" is increasingly challenged by recent developments in the arts (among other creative domains)—in other words, we live, as Huyssen puts it, in the era "after the Great Divide."[11] This challenge to the canonized high/low dichotomy goes by the name of postmodernism and is associated with the increased blurring of the boundaries between "high art" and "mass culture" (this was also underlined by Fredric Jameson, among others, in his *Postmodernism and Consumer Society*). Such a blurring can be experienced, for instance, in the participation of opera singers in the Eurovision Song Contest, such as Malena Ernman, who represented Sweden in 2009, performing what was referred to as a "pop-opera" song that combined operatic singing flowing against a repetitive electronic beat.[12]

Yet the boundaries of genres have always been fluid and permeable. In the 1960s, for instance, one of the most renowned Greek composers, Mikis Theodorakis, experimented with the invention of a hybrid musical genre, the so-called *entehno-laiko* ("art-folk" song) that combined elements of the sophisticated "art" song (a Western European–oriented song style that was closely associated with achieved poetry) with that of rebetiko, a musical style that was charged with the stigma of an underworld of drug addicts and vagabonds and was perceived as the heritage of the Greek "oriental" past. His—then avant-gardist—experiment, one that destabilized the high/low opposition from within, generated a series of debates that articulated and reaffirmed, among other things, the uneasy relationship between "high art" and "popular" culture.[13]

The making of Greek "art-folk" song, or of the "pop-opera" genres, are only a couple among the plethora of examples exemplifying that although the "high-low" dichotomy was variously challenged throughout the twentieth century, "it has remained amazingly resilient over the decades"

(Huyssen *ibid.*). This has also been underlined by several contemporary critics of mass culture theory, who point out how influential it still remains as a grand narrative, one that was devised to examine and critique the "popular" in terms of commodity production for the culture industries and global capitalism.[14] The persisting notions of "bad" popular music today paradigmatically represent the lasting effects of the elitist resentment for certain forms of the "popular" (here the one identified with the mass-mediated music) as harmful for the ethos of the people, one that threatens to debase the "real" culture, as a genre that fails to meet the requirements of the genuine "art" of music and as a marketable product made for profit that serves the interests of the music industry. The ESC is thus denounced as a spectacle of mass production and mass consumption—according to a certain Marxian discourse—that the recent technological advancements have made ever more attractive, ever more arresting, and have thus given it the power to disorientate and distract spectators from matters of social injustice and inequalities. It drives the "people," considered as an inert crowd, away from the spiritual refinement promised by the "real" art.[15] The "real" art of music is thought to be a force of social change, it is an agent of progress—here the leftist discourse encounters a rather avant-gardist notion of music thought to be at the vanguard, beyond the everyday. Or, according to neoliberal ideals, the "real" art of music distances listeners from the deplorable and frustrating realities of the mundane;[16] it is a postpolitical product that exists for "its own sake," a "fine" art that should be an agent of hope and positivity "bringing people together," no matter where the harsh political and cultural realities are taking them. All these discourses are to be read and heard today in several variations and combinations in the context of critiques of musical taste—critiques that perhaps in turn imply critiques of cultural "identity," "heritage," and, perhaps more so, an enduring fear of the loss of the "European spirit."[17] In all cases, "bad" popular music is considered to be dangerous for the moral order of the society. Contemporary hostility to it can, therefore, be seen as a repercussion of the modernity's disapproval of the mass culture, an enduring teleological narrative that embodies the fear of contamination by alienating cultural forms.

Ironically, the current neoliberal revisiting of the notion of music as being beyond the political is also echoed in the rules set by the ESC organization according to which "no lyrics, speeches, gestures of a political or similar gesture shall be permitted during the ESC."[18] Following Teixeira and Stokes in this volume, the ESC itself sustains the neoliberal vision for a European political utopia and the belief in a transnational civility made possible in song. At the same time, ESC songs may have unpredictable political lives, notwithstanding EBU's official resentment of the political. The 1974 Portuguese entry, for instance, "E Depois do Adeus," acted as a signal for the Carnation Revolution (see Teixeira and Stokes in the present volume). Nonetheless, the "purely musical" narration of the ESC history is particularly cherished by its fans and the institution itself. Such a "denial of history," as Bohlman puts it in his contribution to this book, is also a proof of commitment to the organization by its fans.[19] Politicized entries often tend to escape the memory of the Eurovision lore and are marginalized as embarrassing reminders of the entanglement of the historical moment in the event itself.[20] Politics is a source of discomfort; they are improper for the kind of civility advocated by the ESC. Yet what many consider to be the "political bias" of the voting process, such as the traditional exchange of *douze points* between Greece and Cyprus, the so-called voting blocs,[21] or the biases of the juries are often discussed as evidences of the corrupted nature of a contest which, it is claimed, is not really about music at all.[22]

THE POLITICS OF THE "POPULAR" IN THE POSTCOLONIAL WORLD

At the same time the ongoing increased and unprecedented blurring of genres, as already mentioned above, suggests the weakening of the "Great Divide" and seriously questions the validity of its rigid dichotomies.[23] The making of the so-called hyphenated genres (such as "pop-opera," or "ethnic-jazz," or "ethno-beat") negotiate an "identity-in-between" which defines and is defined by the encounters of postcolonial musical worlds (see Bhabha 1994; Holt 2007). The "in-between" identity of Malena Ernman's "pop-opera" song, for instance, performs a sonic osmosis that takes place in the liminal space between and beyond the opera and the pop, in "the emergence of interstices" (Bhabba 1994, 2). Given the rapid spread of the genres which are constantly inverting and questioning the legacy of "the Great Divide," we are left with the obvious question: Does this mean that the "popular" hitherto defined in opposition to the "high" art is a category that irreversibly belongs to the past? Moreover, does the emergence of hybrid genres within a globalized postcolonial Europe (which is also the case with several Eurovision entries) suggest that the modernist differentiation between "high" and "low" music has today been erased?

Even when opera singing, for instance, becomes "pop" (by entering the domain of ESC) and, thus, transgresses the distinction between "high" and "low," its new perception as "popular" differentiates it from what is perceived as "not popular." The production of the hyphened genre described as "pop opera" still involves a process of categorization—the making and/or remaking of the "popular" as a category.[24] And the naming of a category, of a genre, presupposes and implies the perception of

difference: the invention of the term "pop-opera" is the invention of a
novel "popular" genre, which—its various meanings withstanding—is at
once inclusive and exclusive. It involves the making of new taxonomies
of the "popular," however transitory and fleeting, emerging through its
blending with other genres.

Naming, therefore, something as "popular" suggests difference, although not a bipolar (high/low), nor an unbridgeable one (a "Great
Divide"), but at least a conceptual one that engenders the demarcation of
the "popular" against or beyond what is not. To that extent, describing
a genre as "popular" is more than a way of identifying the properties of
the music itself—as the biological metaphor inherent in the etymology of
the term "genre" may suggest; it is primarily a political discourse. The
politics of who says what is "popular," what it means, and against what
it is defined, and of course when, where, and for whom, reproduce the
"popular" as an ideologically pregnant category, which although it is
constantly rediscovered, remains a category—I might say, a "soft" category, one that defines a postcolonial global "popular."[25] To that extent,
the endurance of the term "popular"—and its various ramifications—implies the existence of a conceptual distinction (in Bourdieu's terms; see
Bourdieu 1984) that underlines current conceptual mappings of the world
of musics (to which new genres are constantly added). This is a world
of music in which the popular as a genre is reinvested with notions of
place, ethnicity, race, religion, gender, class, nation—new distinctions, in
other words, embodied in the translocal, transnational, interracial nexus
of realities performed in the "European popular," the Eurovision song,
today. This "European popular" emerging on the ESC stage, is destined to
colonize the world, or at least the music market, in a process where genres
from all over the globe are rediscovered and transformed into signs of a
liberating diversity made in Europe. All the while, ESC brings to life its
internal "others," either as insular, stereotyped localities, as cynical and
thus delinquent ethnicities, or as peripheral, archaic, and thus Europeans
by definition who are nostalgically reinvented as eternal symbols of the
empire within.[26]

Whereas, therefore, the modernist "Great Divide" has nowadays collapsed, it seems that it is still haunting so-called "postmodern" tropes
of making sense of the world of musics; we can trace its shadow, for
instance, in the current discourses on the ESC.[27] A shadow that is now
encapsulated in differentiated or contested "structures of feeling" about
music that emerge in the context of the contemporary problematic and
perception of "otherness" (the subaltern, the non-Western, the racial,
the gendered, the East-European, the oriental, the American/capitalist,
home and the past as "otherness").[28] It becomes an "otherness" that is
variously negotiated (or ignored) in the musical phantasmagorias of the

ESC, whether it is silenced or implied or performed spectacularly.[29] By entering into a playful encounter with the Eurovisionist stereotypes of the European/global selfness, it participates in the blurring of so-called europop genres, even as it is essentialized, nationalized, legitimized, and celebrated as a popular "otherness" (see Bohlman 2004).[30]

To that extent, the blurring of the genres, and the subsequent emergence of new categories next to older typologies of the popular, is more than a postmodern phenomenon of musical democratization and free experimentation where "anything goes," where difference is understood as diversity. And it is more than a phenomenon of what might be described from a neoliberal perspective as the integrative multiculturalism of the "new" ecumenical, enlarged Europe, one accommodating a blissful pluralism (as in the case of the ESC). Although it suggests that older dichotomies are now obsolete, still it embodies and produces asymmetries that are nurtured in the constant emergence of new fields of power. In the blending of genres featuring Eurovision song difference becomes a spectacle that counterpoints a European sameness supplying Europeanness with new meanings.[31] It is a difference produced in discourses of distinction both within the generic term "popular" ("bad"/"good" popular music) and beyond its contested and open-ended domains.

EUROVISION'S EUROPES

Euro neuro don't be dogmatic, bureaucratic,
You need to become pragmatic

—from the lyrics of "Euro Neuro,"
Rambo Amadeus, 2012 ESC, Montenegro

The music-cultural study of the Eurovision song thus challenges us to pose the question: where does Europe begin and end? The victory of Azerbaijan in 2011, for instance, with Ell/Niki singing in English what has been described as a "pop ballad" which left out any reference to the Azeri (or any other) "local" music genres, invited us to expand our perception of Europeanness far beyond its continental boundaries toward the Middle East/post-Soviet and the Muslim world, the so-described hybrid entity represented by the land of "Eurasia."[32] Azerbaijan's victory, the victory of the borders—Europe's ever-shifting borders—relocated them as new centers;[33] Baku fast transformed itself into a Eurocity at least for a couple of weeks in May.[34] For the construction of the ESC German-built Crystal Hall hundreds of people were evicted from their apartments and residential areas were demolished, giving way to a vast construction site for the hosting of the media mega-event.[35] Despite the evident involvement of the European cultural institution with the global politics in the region, Sietse Bakker, the event supervisor, denied any association of the Eurovision organizers with "political goals," although he stressed that media attention will "contribute to improvements" in the country.[36] EBU's general director, Ingrid Delterne, explained that "evictions are taking place everywhere . . . it is more about proper procedures." Besides, Delterne argued, there were also evictions when the Olympic village was built in London.[37] Once more, Eurovision song was supposed to be disengaged from any connection with the political or with power. Any such symptoms ought to be treated as inappropriate in a cultural institution intended to serve the "common good" (the concept most often referred in Brussels's discourse in relation to the European project) and "community interest." Nonetheless, the need for harmonization, at least on stage, is pushed to the limit. Besides, European political and social consensus is urgent.

The 2011 Azerbaijani triumph thus animated images of a ubiquitous and all-pervading Europe in the global order, images that were invested with the fantasy of a shared past. At the same time, despite the fact that the Azerbaijani entry was sung in English, a language supposed to discharge any aura of locality, the song still had the power to reinforce national feelings.[38] At the winner's press conference Ell/Niki sung an Azeri song saturated with national affect.[39] Moreover, the EBU's peripheral partner—a "subsidiary" in the EU's political language—and especially its oil-fed economic elite anticipated the event as a chance to boost the country's international profile, to market Azerbaijan in the world of tourism and trade as a successful and prosperous state. After all, the country was considered as a promising energy supplier for continental Europe. Yet the temporarily centralized—at least in the regime of the EBU network—and exploitable Caucasian borders continued to be a source of anxiety for the ESC organizers as sites of instability defining a volatile and incomplete Europeanness.[40] Following the killing of an Armenian border guard by an Azeri sniper in February 2012 the Armenian delegation declared that they refuse to participate in the contest.[41] Moments like this project Europe as what Abélès and Bellier described as a "bizarre universe," an entity deprived of a fixed territory yet consisted of rather disconnected nation-states in search for harmonized coexistence (see Abélès and Belier 1996), no less because of the oxymoronic nature of a European musical competition taking place in a country where EU travelers required a visa. Europe's musical fiesta was hosted by what many describe as a corrupt state whose authorities have repeatedly been accused of ruthless authoritarianism and human rights abuses.[42] The oxymoronic quality of the event became more and more pressing: how was the Europe of democracy and humanitarianism going to ignore that its most popular musical institution will be accommodated in a country ruled by dictators?[43]

Questions like this raise doubts toward the project of unification. They bring forward the notion of "virtual Europe," the perception of Europe as an increasingly deterritorialized space of uncertainty and indeterminacy that is perpetually self-generated as a future creation (see Abélès 2000; 2010). Once more we are faced with the contradiction inherent in the poetics of the European identification. The ESC, which supposedly invites every voice to be heard on stage in the name of a polyphonic Europe, was hosted by a country that has been muting voices of dissent in the name of an imposed unisonality. Or is this perhaps Europe too?[44] Is this Europe defined in relation to its partners? And finally, which is today's Europe: the Europe of "euphoria" sung by Loreen of the 2012 Swedish entry or the "Euro neuro" described in the satirical lyrics of Rambo Amadeus representing Montenegro?[45] When asked what she knows about Azerbaijan, Loreen replied that she initially thought that "Baku was in the Caribbean."[46] After returning home from Düsseldorf in 2011, I was often asked the question: what is Azerbaijan doing in Eurovision? And what is Eurovision doing in Azerbaijan? Is it a token of the ESC's democratic and tolerant nature that it provided such generous space for its nondemocratic yet-to-be-Europeanized Eurasian periphery? To that extent, the staging of so-perceived "pan-european"/"global" styles (such as pop, electronica, hard rock, or hip-hop) next to songs that incorporate references to "tradition" and "national heritage," or "exotic" genres, and the various hybridities featuring Eurovision songs, whether in the form of a parody, an homage to the memorable past, or a promise of the zeitgeist, suggest less polyphony and more a kind of a musical Tower of Babel.[47]

At the same time, more and more entries are being performed by singers of "mixed origin." In the various media texts presenting the profile of the ESC 2012 singers, "origin" matters, particularly when it is "mixed," *almost* European, such as in the case of the "Afro-Ukrainian" Gaitana or when it is non-European at all but with a global/postcolonial appeal, as is the case of the Indonesian-born Anggun representing France in 2012, bringing an "Asian sensation" to the contest.[48] The winner Loreen, singing for Sweden, was described as "Swedish of Moroccan-Berber descent"; on top of that, her choreography and costume incorporated references to Japanese *butoh* dance and minimalist fashion design.[49] This rationalized, mediatic identity of the singers, the flesh and blood of the nation on the ESC stage, often becomes a site on which neoliberal European values of belonging are performed.[50] While Gaitana, for instance, was voted to represent the country as the dark-skinned R and B diva singing for European inclusiveness, she was disapproved of in racial terms by the Ukrainian far right as "non-organic," neither of Ukraine nor of Europe.[51] In Gaitana's story the notion of fortress Europe converges with that of the Europe of assimilation: together they constitute a regime of debates and discourses over notions of "identity" driven by cultural essentialism and cultural anxiety (see Grillo 2003, 158). At the same time, both Gaitana's and several "mixed-origin" singers' Eurovision mediatic profiling was empowered by representing them as well-intentioned appropriated alterities, as Europeans "at heart" able to become *more* European and thus entitled to perform *as* Europeans.[52] They may stand as a musical metaphor for EU's managerial notion of democratic accountability, where the singers manage their identities as if they are corporate organizations in order to market themselves in the name of the "free movement" of goods, in this case Eurovision song.[53] Likewise Europe, ESC performs itself today as an open and transparent media event that is increasingly decentralized, offering the opportunity for everyone to participate and everyone to vote. Not surprisingly, in 2008 EBU announced its plans to license Eurovision-like song contests in the Arab World, the Middle East, Asia, South America, and the United States, exporting and further commoditizing the musical show. While thus supposedly embracing difference in Europe, EBU's broadcasting neoimperialism is reconstructing a cartography of popular musics that is constituted of different musical peripheries: it globalizes and unifies the world by identifying and reaffirming its fragments as EBU's network provinces.[54] No surprise here. Since 2000 ESC, one of the longest-running TV programs, has been live-streamed on the Internet and televised extensively outside Europe.[55] Eurovision is everywhere.[56]

Overall, ESC entries may be understood as performances of various modalities of "commitment," to use a term from the Brussels jargon, that project a musical "culture of compromise" (Abélès and Bellier 1996). In this sonic laboratory of Europeanness we may detect the ongoing emergence of several Europes, all in a process of negotiation, if not bargaining, where integration is perpetually sought and continually postponed. The EU, after all, where the ESC locates itself, is said to be unique as a union that has never achieved unification (see Abélès 2004, 5).[57] Likewise EU, ESC cherishes the idea of a Europe that is destined to move ahead, a work in progress that must avoid looking backward. "What counts is that the presence of the future models and contextualizes the experience of the presence" (Abélès 2010, 79). Nonetheless, the Europes contested in the ESC remind one of an orchestra constantly tuning up.

It remains open to question whether this staging of invented localities and affinities may represent the ideal of a peaceful intercultural and supranational community, if this is the Europe desired by the ESC institution. It seems that the early twenty-first-century ESC provides the space for reinventing fundamentalist and essentialist notions of music "culture," which in the context of the EU's multiculturalist agenda is valued as a set of identified properties defining a community, or a nation, considered as the carrier of that "culture." Such culturalist perceptions of music develop alongside an idiom of cultural alienation and estrangement that involves the development of a consciousness of belonging to a cultural milieu, what Holmes described as "integralism" (Holmes 2000, 3). Against the backdrop of the advanced European integration project ESC's integralist sensibilities could hardly be disassociated from the pressing dislocations generated by fast capitalism and the concomitant broad-based social and political transformations dictated by the international financial markets today (see Stolcke 1995). After all, this is Eurovision entering a period, as Žižek puts it, "in which a kind of economic state of emergency is becoming permanent: turning into a constant, a way of life" (Žižek 2010, 86). It is perhaps a post-European ESC that emerges in the desperate struggle of the European project to survive, still carrying what appears now as the timeworn yet persistent promise of unity within a confused, tired, and fragile Europe. "It's cold, cold, cold, cold when the music dies."[58]

ABOUT THE BOOK CHAPTERS

The idea for this book has its roots at an international conference entitled "Singing Europe: Spectacle and Politics in the Eurovision Song Contest" organized by the Department of History, Archaeology and Social Anthropology of the University of Thessaly, at Volos, Greece, in 2008. The fourteen authors who contribute to the present volume provide insights to particular aspects of the ESC phenomenon, bringing together ethnomusicology, music studies, history, social anthropology, feminist theory, linguistics, media ethnography, postcolonial theory, comparative literature, and philosophy. The cross-disciplined perspective suggested here explores theoretical approaches from the broader area of humanities and social sciences (a by-now well-established interdisciplinarity in the area of music studies) while keeping its focus on the study of the sound itself as a site of history and politics.

This is an idea exhaustively explored by Philip Bohlman in the opening chapter, *"Tempus Edax Rerum: Time and the Making of the Eurovision Song."* Bohlman provides a theory of Eurovision song by addressing the issue of temporality, pointing both to the internal time of the song and its temporal context. As a start, he brings to our attention the so-called postcard of the ESC broadcast, the musical portal which bridges the fragmented Europe with the Europe of a potential sameness. With ESC postcards, argues Bohlman, we enter to the temporal groove of the Eurovision world. His theoretical analysis is framed by the Bakhtinian notion of chronotope, more specifically aiming to reestablish the validity of an analytical hermeneutics to the study of ESC. Bohlman's song chronotopes are constituted around six different types of temporality: musical time, historical time, ritual/mediated time, cyclical time, performative/embodied time, and monumental/epic time. All the six types of temporality interact in the making of the temporality of the ESC, the structure and meaning of the national song defining the ways song narrates the nation and Europe itself. He investigates Eurovision song in the context of his longstanding concern with nationalism and music, suggesting that national song is both a product of fragmentation and of a process of creating wholes. His detailed exploration of the various types of temporality concludes by bringing to our attention the return of the Eurovision song that is the return of Eurovision's original agency, the creator of the song, "the return to the past and the search of the lost time," as he puts it.

In the following chapter, Andrea Bohlman and Ioannis Polychronakis take us on a kaleidoscopic tour of the mega-event in the complex nexus of mediatic spaces and places where they have lived the contest both as scholars and as fans. Their chapter thus provides a critical contribution to the study of the ESC as a lived experience of the contest at home; the Internet fan culture and social networks; and the ESC in the vast arenas, in the Eurocities, and in the press. The suggested multiangled approach is intended to illustrate the diverse and multilayered modalities and meanings of ESC as an annual ritual that takes place everywhere. Their discussion of this omnipresent, ever-changing phenomenon is based on ethnographic reflections upon their fieldwork trip in Belgrade and Moscow, in 2008 and 2009 respectively, and their ongoing involvement with ESC organizations. The various sections of the chapter represent the multiplicity of the event in the discourses of the friends and fans that they met in the streets of postsocialist Belgrade and the former Cold War capital, Moscow, both now places of New Europeanness; in the branding of the Eurocity that becomes a kind of a temporary European cultural capital; in the multiple "lives" of the event in the various digital media networks; and in the ethnographic experience of the spectacle that opened the ESC in the Beogradska arena.

Chapter 3 by Annemette Kirkegaard critically addresses the notion of Nordic brotherhood based on observation of two TV programs that promote the idea of the "Nordic unity" and of the alleged "Nordic sound." First, in the "Before ESC" programs, which become niches of discourses on Europe and its nations, the stereotyping of "others" aims at sustaining the public awareness of a Nordic cultural cohesion, which in turn promotes, for the author, Nordic buddy-voting. Kirkegaard stresses that "there never was—as particularly seen in the Nordic area—a truly national form" in the ESC entries. Secondly, she shows how the fiftieth anniversary of the ESC in Denmark, titled "Congratulations—Eurovision at 50," placed the North at the heart of ESC. She notes that the Nordic countries are united by a peripheral position in Europe that inspires an emotional understanding of the region encapsulated in the slogan "we are small." However, Kirkegaard concludes, the claim of a specific Nordic musical sphere is a political construction. The Nordic countries are caught in the tensions between regionality and homogenization, the particularities of "national identity," and the universality advocated by the notion of European citizenship.

In chapter 4 Goffredo Plastino draws our attention to the theme of corruption featuring popular representations of the Sanremo Festival. His point of departure is the ongoing disenchantment expressed in discourses about the Sanremo Festival, which served as a model for ESC, and is thus a vital, if often neglected, point of reference for our discussion about Eurovision. Now and in the past Sanremo generated a public debate over the value of Italian music that embodied notions of Italian cultural identity. Plastino explores the popularity of the perception of Sanremo as a fraud in contemporary Italian cinema and literature. To that extent, he is concerned with the ways Sanremo, especially in the crime fiction, is represented as a place of obscure plots, the place of the death of Italian song and of music in general. He stresses that the festival is a metaphor for questions of Italian identity; the fraudulence of the event reaffirms the corruption of Italy and music itself. For Plastino the contrast between the official rules and the hidden mechanisms of the festival that generates simultaneous enjoyment and disapproval of the Sanremo at the same time. In the end, the festival "appears as an ideological/musical apparatus" where arcane power games are mirrored in the musical game itself.

"Where do songs happen?" questions Karin Strand in her chapter that addresses the representations of place in the lyrics of the entries of the Swedish national preliminaries (Melodifestivalen). In the light of the Bakhtinian concept of chronotope, Strand explores the fictional places generated by the singing voice by stressing her consideration of the mode of lyrics as more dramatic than poetic. The lyrical topos, she argues, sets the dramaturgical frame for the production of content and meaning in song. By focusing on songs characterized as "topical" she designates two recurrent types of milieus, the "international" and the "national." The first represent cosmopolitan places "out there" which are promising sites for risk taking, erotic adventures, and challenging opportunities. The second refers to the native home, often nostalgically depicted as the beloved ground of the ancestors, a landscape of organic belonging and tradition unaffected by modernity. The representation of the "national," argues Strand, contrasts with that of the "international" topos, as the latter is the essentially "modern" experience. Moreover, the contrasted topoi are often associated with binary gendered meanings: the social and geographical mobility of modernity is represented as masculine, while home, roots, and tradition are represented as feminine. Ultimately, Strand's analysis on the lyrical chronotopes is triggering the question of belonging: "how long have we traveled from our imagined past, how far have we come in the promised land of modernity?" she asks. "Where do we want to be?"

Moving from the topos of the Eurovision song to the Eurobody, Apostolos Lampropoulos examines corporeality in Eurovision narratives in ways that raise challenging questions about ESC fandom. These body-related fictions cherished by ESC fans contribute to the making of the Eurovision community, while they protect the integrity of Eurovision moments and the consistency of the contest's history. Lampropoulos addresses the Eurobody as one that incorporates the founding fictions of the contest and explores the ways corporeality is fictionalized in specific Eurovision narratives. He discusses particular episodes connected with the issue of corporeality and the fans' reactions to Eurovision narratives and myths, which were traced on various websites. The episodes are intended to exemplify the quasisanctification of the Eurobody and its perception as a timeless holy corpus that should remain unharmed by politics and history. Lampropoulos stresses that the Eurobody's reluctant politicization is understood by ESC fans "as a proof of loyalty to its supposed essence." He finally suggests that the only kind of politics perceived as inherent—and thus nonthreatening—to the Eurovision phenomenon is queerness, which needs to be interpreted in association with the fans' denial of politics and history. Queerness, argues the author, is the main portal for understanding ESC; it is a different kind of politics inherent in the Eurovision phenomenon that define the shared cultural experience shaping the collectivities identified in the name of the contest.

The oriental Eurobody on stage and the production of Turkish cultural identity is the focus of Tom Solomon's chapter. The controversy surrounding the orientalist imagery of the winner of the 2003 ESC Sertab Erener (that incorporated familiar orientalist tropes, such as the *harem*, the *hammam*, the hookah, the belly dance) is interpreted as part of the longstanding concern in Turkey with Turkey's image in Europe. Staging Turkey in ESC is a way of marketing the country both for export and for internal consumption. Drawing on Stuart Hall's ideas on the production of cultural identity (see Hall 1990), Solomon argues that the public debates over Sertab's orientalist promotional video clip, material and performance are rooted in the yearlong discussion over Turkish cultural identity, which is dominated by two master narratives: one is associated with the Kemalist secular modernization project looking toward the West; the other, described as neo-Ottomanist, advocates an alternative modernization that is coupled with a reclaiming of the Ottoman past. Sertab performs the neo-Ottoman fantasies that feed the European gaze with the orientalist stereotypes that Europe itself has created. Following anthropological approaches, Solomon suggests that Sertab embodies a gendered image of the nation as the feminized and exotic object waiting to seduce and to be seduced, while her performance touches upon sensitive issues in Turkey regarding the articulation of gender, class, and race. At the same time, Sertab's victory in the ESC validates the neo-Ottoman discourses and practices back at home, offering space for the nation to reinvent its "oriental" heritage.

The representation of the nation is also the topic of Alf Björnberg's chapter that addresses the question of what is perceived as typically Swedish in ESC and how the notions of Swedishness changed over time vis-à-vis other possible national or transnational identities. Swedish ESC entries are explored in the context of the public service media in Sweden and their relation to the Swedish music industry and popular culture. Björnberg's question is grounded on the argument (following Bohlman 2004) that there are few, if any, musical signifiers which denote or connote a Swedish cultural specificity. The shifting representations of the nation are discerned in different musical/stylistic phases of the Swedish ESC entries and the Swedish preliminaries. First, the "continental aspirations" lasting up until the early 1970s: despite a degree of artistry in songs during this phase, they were considered provincial in relation to the continental entries. Then there was the commercial "dance-band" music that dominated the 1980s in opposition to the politically aware "progressive music movement" bringing confidence to Swedish people who developed a sense of pride in their victories in the ESC in that era. Third, "self-consciously 'ethnic' styles" emerging in the 1990s, resulting in multicultural "musical pastiches." Björnberg brings to our attention the growth from the 1980s onward of what came to be described as "the Swedish music-export miracle," raising a public awareness of Sweden being a significant international agent in the field of popular music industry. Swedishness in ESC, he concludes, is represented by "the nation's music-industrial know-how"; sounding Swedish is sounding highly professional in the production of popular music.

Luisa Pinto Teixeira's and Martin Stokes's chapter investigates the so far largely ignored question of Eurovision's relations with the Iberian dictatorships, that of Franco in Spain and of Salazar in Portugal. They start with, and critique, Ulrich Beck's neoliberal vision for a European political utopia, one that is also, they suggest, sustained by ESC. Their historically situated analysis of the complex significations of the Spanish and Portuguese entries of the 1970s undermines what is today the dominant ESC narrative: one of Western versus Eastern Europe. It brings to the fore the rather embarassing, and now largely forgotten, accommodation of Western authoritarianisms by Western European democracies during the early years of the contest. Portugal's Eurovision entries are explored in the context of the broader picture of Portugal's popular music culture of that era, in order to provide a more nuanced analysis of the complex intersections of music and cultural anxieties of the moment framed by the colonial wars and the overthrow of the Estado Novo. "E Depois do Adeus," a cosmopolitan Eurovision pop song, became the signal for the Carnation Revolution alongside the revolutionary ballad "Grândola, Vila Morena." The two songs, although of apparently contrasting genres, "moved in musical worlds that often overlapped," constituting "mutually intertwined practices of resistance to the Portuguese regime." However, Portugal in the official ESC narrative authored by fans and the institution itself is, as Teixeira and Stokes notice, largely marginalized. This marginalization is interpreted on one hand as the failure of Portugal to adopt a successful Eurovision sound and image, while, on the other hand, it is the product of its rather uncomfortable, at least for ESC, entanglement with serious political and historical moments. The banishment of the historical and the political from ESC official history discards those, like Portugal, who "have stepped beyond the bounds of a certain kind of civility." To that extent, Teixeira and Stokes use the Portuguese case to critically question the self-congratulating histories of "democratic Europe."

The fantasy of the European empire within is brought forward in chapter 10 by Dafni Tragaki, which discusses the "extraordinary" triumph of the heavy-metal monstrous Finnish band Lordi in 2006. Lordi are explored as a phenomenon of "fantastic neomedievalism," here spectacularly reenacted on the ESC stage (Eco 1986, 63). Lordi's "barbaric" Dark Ages are explored as a performance of modernity's "other" that is itself a product of modernity. Their neomedieval horror-glam spectacle suggests an escape from the everydayness of global capitalism, even a way of dreaming that our subjectivity exists against something eternal, something that has been always there. It challenges us to think about the ways history is experienced, fabricated, and reappropriated in the realm of Eurovision song. The performance of Homo Monstrous embodies one of the many counternarratives to hegemonic conceptualizations of Europeanness that has been invented and recounted now and then in opposition to its various inner and external "others." Yet along with the monsters, the poetics of those alterities are altogether products of the European imagination. They invite us to think of the monsters as a metaphor for Europe; a monstrous, enlarged Europe greedy for power, yet troubled, if not frightened, by its own monstrosity that is ontologically sounded in the grain of the monster's voice. The song's bridge is where the monster's de-monstration takes place, constituting the monster as the double of our European subjectivity. At the same time, by participating in ESC, and by screaming in favor of Europe, Tragaki argues, the savagery of heavy metal sounds is domesticated and gentrified. "Hard Rock Halle-lujah" becomes an "arockalyptic" prayer for the neoliberal, multicultural EU-topia that sings Europe into a state of aporia, if not crisis, as it faces its own return.

Tony Langlois's chapter explores the Irish ESC history in association with the so-called "Celtic Tiger" phenomenon that involved the dramatic transformation of the Irish economy from 1993 to 2008. The Irish eco-nomic boom brought together a number of sociocultural changes, demo-graphic shifts, a reconceptualization of Irishness, and the repositioning of the country in relation to greater Europe. Providing statistical evidence, Langlois points to the correlation between Ireland's most productive and confident Eurovision years with the era's capitalist prosperity that transformed a once marginal nation—as performed in Dana's passive and childlike Eurovision song—to a European success story. At the same time, he associates the fate of Irish entries on the ESC stage with a change in cultural discourses about Ireland within Europe and the concomitant attitudinal changes on the part of the Irish toward Europe and EU in particular, as they have been manifested in the initial rejection of the Nice and Lisbon Treaties. The Ireland of Eurovision, Langlois argues, shifted from an early phase of naïve enthusiasm to a successful middle period of mature professionalism recently resorting to the cynicism of Dustin the Turkey that addressed both the ESC politics and the country's national representations. The analogies between the course of Ireland in Eurovi-sion and the changing attitudes to the EU, Langlois concludes, are not accidental. It would be interesting to trace similar correlations in other participating countries, especially in the context of the current crisis of the Euro-currency. And it will also be worth investigating Ireland's cultural relations with the rest of Europe and its impact on its Eurovision entries now that the "Celtic Tiger" era has come to an end.

In the final chapter, Andrea Bohlman and Alexander Rehding examine the complexities that define the interaction between the national and the international levels of the competition, looking at the multivalent signification of Eurovision song that emerges in the interstices between the two levels. This "European two-step" takes place in the areas of fric-tion between the national and the European performance contexts and is considered as an integral part of the "soft politics" of the ESC ritual. National selection encapsulates ways of imagining the nation, argue the authors, while it is coupled with visions of European success. The discus-sion proceeds in three sections that represent three particular Eurovision songs/case studies from the 1990s and the 2000s, which exemplify the complexities defining the issue of representation of subordinate groups: "Le dernier qui a parlé," sung by the French-Tunisian Amina Annabi (France, 1991) that was an early example of incorporating non-Western musical styles into a Eurovision song; "Words for Love," performed for Israel by Lior Narkis, a *mizrakhi* singer (2003); and third, the German entry for 1999, by the Turkish-German group Sürpriz, titled "Reise nach Jerusalem," a multilingual song apparently depicting a multicultural Germany. All the three examples stand as paradigms of the multimodal musical negotiation of difference, articulated either in gender, class, ethnicity, nationality, or religion, which is variously perceived and interpreted by different audiences. They exemplify the politics of difference performed in the dancing of the nations between the national and the transnational in the New Europe's ESC.

The aim of the present collection of essays stands beyond contributing to Eurovision scholarship—even though this is a growing and lively field.[59] This book certainly hopes to inspire novel ways of listening to, watching, experiencing, and reflecting upon the ESC. But it is also intended as a con-tribution to popular music studies. As a field which has a long romance with subcultural authenticity, it has not been comfortable operating with kitsch and trivia such as the ESC. And it has not usually been comfortable dealing with anything outside an Anglo-Saxon and narrowly Western Eu-ropean frame of reference. There is a challenge to methods and categories here, suggesting that popular music studies, committed as it is to a broad engagement with social and cultural theory, would do well to deepen its conversation with ethnomusicology and the cultural study of music.

Ethnomusicology and the cultural study of music is not just a matter of supplying "context." Rather than simply framing popular music phenom-ena like the ESC in the context of historical and political processes, the present book suggests their understanding as history and politics *them-selves*. To that extent, the timing of the present study should be taken into account. This is a book that among others questions the idea of "Europe" and "the nation" through and in music, at a time when the fragmented European self appears more and more cracked, if not shattered, than ever before. The book is coming at a historical moment when most of the world experiences Europeanness and the European project with embar-rassment, confusion, discomfort, even with fear and indignation, perhaps encapsulating an unprecedented quest for changing Europe.

EPILOGUE: BAKU—REFLECTIONS OF THE DAY AFTER

> My house is demolished
> I'm homeless
> No roof over my head
> Is Eurovision what I need now?
>
> Cameras are all over the place
> Someone is watching us
> Here is the message to them:
> Saint middle finger
> (from the song "Vermişel" by the
> Azerbaijani group Bulistan)[60]

Jamal Ali, the musician and lyricist of "Vermişel," was arrested and tortured by the police in a protest rally against human rights violations that took place in Baku a few weeks before the 2012 ESC final, where he was invited to participate as a musician.[61] The focus of the global media eye on the Azerbaijani capital because of the ESC inspired the organization of several antigovernment demonstrations that saw it as a chance to raise awareness over the state's repressive politics to the outside world. So far, protesters and journalists who had opposed Aliyev's rule were imprisoned, intimidated, threatened, and tortured, even murdered.[62] Paradoxically, Eurovision became both the target of the activists and the reason for expressing their resistance against the suppressive Azerbaijani state.[63] As Jamal Ali argued, "I was freed from the jail after ten days because of Eurovision. If there was no Eurovision, I would have been in jail for two years or even five years."[64] Interestingly, next to local political groups, such as the initiative "Sing for Democracy," and global organizations such as Amnesty International, the Human Rights Watch, and the Reporters Without Borders, the attack against Aliyev's rule was also joined by the German foreign minister, Guido Westerwelle.[65] Westerwelle issued a confidential report criticizing the suppression of freedom of expression and Azerbaijan's poor civil rights record. Even more, he stressed that the ESC creates "a critical public forum in order to . . . promote *our* democratic values."[66] In reaction, the Azerbaijani embassy in Berlin accused Germany "of a smear campaign" orchestrated by the German media and "certain circles in Germany."[67] Despite the growing media attention over Azerbaijan's totalitarian policy, Ingrid Delterne, the head of the European Broadcasting Union, stressed that "if we politicize the ESC . . . the ESC would be dead. It is an event that builds bridges." Why this is not considered a political action, as EBU insists, remains unclear. If the ESC, according to Delterne, "is an integrating event, not an exclusionary one," then perhaps EBU's reluctance to admit its involvement in European cultural politics becomes more and more problematic.[68] Instead, the EBU likes to present itself as an agent of universal humanitarian values—primarily thought of as European values—such as freedom, democracy, and "plurality of opinions."

Nonetheless, "freedom" also became the motto of the group of hackers who attacked the Azerbaijani official Eurovision websites a few days before the contest. "Cyberwarriors for Freedom" demanded that President Aliyev should prohibit a "gay parade" alleged to take place in Baku and cancel the event.[69] All the while, Iran withdrew its ambassador from Baku to protest against the hosting of the mega-event and the alleged planning of a "gay parade," which were thought to constitute an insult to the sanctities of Islam.[70] The diplomatic episode caused apropos the ESC further intensified the controversy between the secularist Azeri state and the fundamentalist Iranian authorities, embedding the turbulent geopolitical power games in the organization of a musical contest.[71] At the same time, "freedom" became the shibboleth of the universalist ballad-anthem "Toast to Freedom" composed for Amnesty International's campaign for the release of political prisoners in Azerbaijan.[72]

> Here's our toast to freedom
> To human rights and dignity
> Love, respect and forgiveness
> United in the dream for victory

Once more, the ESC became the arena for the performance of local and translocal geopolitics and of diverse, if not conflicting, conceptualizations of "freedom" and "democracy." First and foremost, there is the enduring struggle for freedom by the Azeri *homo sacer*, supported by several groups fighting for the promotion of democracy against the cruel biopolitics of an authoritarian state.[73] This pressing need for freedom of expression and for justice and the suffering Azeri oppositional voices were accommodated by neoliberal notions of "freedom" and "democracy" articulated by the German governmental authorities and EBU officials acquiring new meanings. Westerwelle's and Delterne's understandings of "democratic values" could perhaps become more comprehensible in the context of the urgent call of the German chancellor, Angela Merkel, for "more Europe, not less," or for "euphoria, forever 'till the end of time" (to recall the 2012 Swedish winning song "Euphoria"). It is also the promise of freedom associated with the vision of European belonging, of the Europe of "liberties," of "law" and "transparency" shaped in the threatening shadow of the European project's imminent failure as the current "debt crisis" is continually deepening. Such notions of "freedom" and "democracy," which have been instrumental in the shaping of the "new Europe," are contrasted by the notion of "religious freedom" according to the laws of the *sharia* that the Iranian state was urged to protect. And there is the "freedom" of the homophobic message uploaded by the activist hackers which seems to be closer to a belief, for which "the West" is seen as a menace.

Although Azerbaijan, for the EBU, is a state that abuses human rights, the suggested solution for such problems was to offer adequate "journalistic training" and "workshops led by us showing how one can increase the plurality of opinions in programming."[74] Sure, democracy in the country has a long way to go. Yet why is it primarily Europe's mission to bring it there? And what kind of democracy is Europe dreaming for the Azeri people? Is this the democracy that activists and protesters in the country have been fighting for? Ironically, according to ESC's democratic values, as argued by Delterne, it would be unfair to deny Azerbaijan the right to host the competition—despite acknowledging its nondemocratic nature. After all, the ESC, a contest of inclusion, provides a brilliant opportunity to allow space for "more Europe" much needed, supposedly, both for the country and the region, while safeguarding the empire within. Besides, it is only music, again, not politics. The EBU is happy to lead the way with a spectacular musical fiesta, which is estimated to have been the most expensive organization in its history—without an Armenian song, though, and despite the fact that in 2009 the Azeri state television distorted the TV signal at the time of the Armenian ESC entry's live broadcast and that people who voted for Armenia as a way to protest against censorship politics were accused of "security threat" and were interrogated by the Ministry of National Security. Nonetheless, Europe, the self-acclaimed guardian of democracy, ought, according to a certain logic, to promote its humanistic values in the country. The same way it accommodated Iberian dictatorships in the past, Europe embraces the authoritarian regime within its own empire of songs. This moral responsibility apparently motivated the German foreign minister to overtly make manifest his democratic sensitivities and to officially adopt a protective discourse supporting the oppressed of the Eurasian dictatorship. His humanitarian sensitivities were also shared by Loreen, the 2012 ESC winner, who met the human rights defenders in Baku expressing her compassion for the suffering Azeri people. Most of the global media, whatever their motivations, felt the same.

Yet alarmingly, democracy and civil rights are threatened in the heart of Europe too, as evident, for instance, by the growing representation of far-right parties in European parliaments at the beginning of the twenty-first century. EU itself becomes more and more alert over issues of "European heritage," "identity," its "external borders," "security," and the flows of migration from elsewhere in the world. Against such a perplexed background of cultural politics and toxic power games, the future of the suppressed people of the country when the ESC curtains fall remains uncertain. Or, as Jamal Ali's lyrics put it, "is Eurovision what I need now?" A few days before the final, Jamal fled to Germany, to save his life. In the end, there is perhaps something very disconcerting about the wish expressed by Anke Engelke, the ESC's spokesperson for Germany: "Good luck on your journey, Azerbaijan, Europe is watching you."[75]

ACKNOWLEDGMENTS

I would like to thank my colleagues at the Department of Social Anthropology at the University of Thessaly in Greece, especially the members of the organizational committee who initially embraced the idea for the conference "Singing Europe: Spectacle and Politics of the Eurovision Song Contest" in 2008 and supported the various stages of the organization: Sofia Handaka, Mitsos Bilalis, Penelope Papailias, and Ritsa Deltsou. Also, the then head of the Social Anthropology Department, Riki van Boeschoten, for overall encouraging the organizational project. Many thanks to Franco Fabbri, the author of the foreword, for his patience and warm acceptance of the proposal to introduce the present volume. I am deeply grateful to Martin Stokes and Philip Bohlman, who participated as keynote speakers to the conference and proposed the publication of a collection of essays based on the conference theme. As series editors they have generously provided precious guidance, intellectual inspiration, and support throughout the various phases of the publication, from the invitations to the contributing authors to the final stages of submitting the book manuscript. Many thanks to Phil Bohlman for encouraging my aspirations during my short field trips to Belgrade in 2008 and Dusseldorf in 2011. I am particularly indebted to Martin Stokes, who read an earlier version of the introduction and my chapter, providing constructive feedback on writing and editing the final draft. I owe him many refinements, improvements, and above all the inspiration and stimulation required for developing and completing the final manuscript. Many, many thanks to all the contributing authors for their excellent cooperation, patience, and commitment to the project. Finally I would like to thank the editorial staff at Scarecrow Press for making this book happen.

NOTES

1. Žižek here discusses Alain Badiou's ideas on "la passion du reel" (Alain Badiou, *Le Siècle*, Seuil: 2005).

2. Small suggests a theory of "musicking" as a framework for understanding music as a human activity and musical performance as a process of human relations where musical meaning is produced.

3. Butler in *Bodies That Matter* (New York: Routledge, 1993) discusses the iterated performances of subjectivity available in the media as the products of specific regimes of seeing.

4. *Te Deum* was composed between 1688 and 1698. Fornäs notices that *Te Deum*, together with the anthems appropriated by UEFA and EBU, cover the most influential European traditions, "though less relevant for the eastern and northern parts of the regions" (Fornäs 2012, 188).

5. See Kirkegaard in the present volume.

6. See Bohlman and Rehding in the present volume.

7. On the multimodal mediatic experience of ESC see Bohlman and Polychronakis in the present volume.

8. See Bohlman in the present volume.

9. For the making of the European music canon see Bergeron and Bohlman 1992.

10. For Huyssen, (*ibid.*), the belief in the Great Divide is still dominant in the academy today. Following Huyssen, we may trace its impact in the field of music studies, the demarcation of the "popular," for instance, in the naming of academic journals that specialize in the "popular" or in the naming of research groups of special interest and academic positions that legitimize "popular music studies" as a subdiscipline. For a critical approach of the field of popular music studies and the conceptualization of "popular music" see Fabbri 2010.

11. It is important to bear in mind that Huyssen is writing in the middle of the 1980s.

12. Interestingly, Malena Ernman has exhibited a cross-genres mobility, having also performed jazz, cabaret, and French *chansons*.

13. See Tragaki 2005.

14. Plastino refers to the ongoing resentment of the Sanremo Festival as "bad" music by Italian intellectual circles. The Sanremo Festival generated a heated debate over the value of Italian music and Italian cultural identity (see Plastino in the present volume).

15. Kirkegaard refers to the Danish radical cultural movement, a leftist initiative that disapproved of the mass-mediated pop music of the 1950s and 1960s. As a result, the 1965 Danish ESC entry was styled according to the elitist aspirations for "good taste" in popular song which was thought to be both educative for the masses and representative of the Danish nation. The failure of the entry resulted in the withdrawal of Denmark from the contest for the next ten years and the emergence of fervent debates over the character of popular song (see Kirkegaard in the present volume). Plastino also mentions the organization of a Sanremo counterfestival by Italian leftist circles driven by an ideology of songs being media of public awareness (see Plastino in the present volume). Björnberg notices the ambition of enhancing the quality of the entries in the Swedish ESC preliminaries over the period 1963–1966 and mentions the organization of alternative song festivals in Sweden (see Björnberg in the present volume; also Strand in the present volume).

16. It is noteworthy that this discourse resonates with the Kantian ideas on the autonomy of art.

17. For the European politics and the notion of cultural heritage in the Greek case see Deltsou 2002.

18. See ESC Rules 2011, 1.2.2./g. Accessed February 5, 2012. http://www.eurovision.tv/upload/press-downloads/2011/ESC_2011_Rules.pdf. Bohlman and Rehding mention the withdrawal of the Georgian entry "We Don't Wanna Put In" by EBU that implied an opposition to the then Russian Prime Minister Vladimir Putin.

19. See Lampropoulos in the present volume for the reluctant politicization of the Eurobodies by ESC fans.

20. See Teixeira and Stokes in the present volume for the marginalization of the Portuguese entries in the official ESC narrative.

21. Kirkegaard in the present volume provides a critical discussion on the notion of the "Nordic brotherhood."

22. The perception of the Sanremo Festival, the archetype for the ESC, as a fraud, for instance, is persistent in the cinematic and literature representations of the festival in Italy. Following Plastino, it stands as a metaphor of the mechanisms of corruption troubling the Italian political scene. See Plastino in the present volume.

23. See also Björnberg 2007. Kirkegaard also notices "the so-called 'ethnic turn' of the competition, which is mildly reproached, sometimes ridiculed, and generally perceived as a problem," while she describes the "return to ethnicity" trend in the ESC entries (see Kirkegaard in the present volume).

24. Fabbri defines genre as a set of music events regulated by conventions accepted by a community and formulates a semiotic/cognitive theory that serves the examination of the diachronic processes of the "birth," change, and "death" of genre (see Fabbri 2012).

25. See Fabbri for a semiotic and cognitive approach on the perception of genres (2007).

26. See particularly the chapters by Kirkegaard, Langlois, Strand, and Tragaki in the present volume.

27. See, for instance, the profiling of Malena Ernman at the Eurovision.tv website: "The mezzo-soprano from Sandviken—north Sweden—comfortably goes from the high culture opera houses of Vienna and Paris to comedy sketches at award shows without regard to the reactions from the sometimes-conservative world of opera." Ernman herself also commented on the place of the opera genre in the ESC: "I think we have worked very hard within the opera world to become a part of the popular music scene, but we can't!!! Only the audience can make opera popular music. Hopefully *La Voix* can play a small part in making that happen." ("About Malena Ernman." Accessed April 24, 2012. http://www.eurovision.tv/page/history/year/participant-profile/?song=24717). *La Voix* gained only the twenty-first place, although the Swedish expectations were high (see Björnberg in the present volume). For Kirkegaard, Ernman's case illustrates the fact that "sometime neighbours are conspicuously *not* voting for a song" (see Kirkegaard in the present volume).

28. Williams described the "structure of feeling" as "the distilled residue of the organization of the lived experience of a community over and above the institutional and ideological organization of the society" (Williams 1977).

29. See the detailed discussion on representations of the subaltern—the racial, the ethnic, the sexual—in the ESC by Bohlman and Rehding in the present volume; Solomon for a discussion of the production of Turkish identity, neo-Ottomanism, and orientalism; Strand on the celebration of capitalist/cosmopolitan spatial difference performed in the 2005 Swedish entry "Las Vegas."

30. For examples of representations of "otherness" in ESC see, for instance, the German entry in 1999 "Reise nach Jerusalem," performed by the Turkish-German band Sürpriz (in Turkish, German, and English lyrics); the queer performance of the transsexual singer Dana International representing Israel in 1998; the transformation of hip-hop to a national song style in the Ukrainian entry in 2005 "Razom nas Bahato" by the band Greenjolly, which became the unofficial anthem of the Orange Revolution; the U.K. entry for 2008 ("Even If") performed by Andy Abraham, a black singer and runner-up of the TV talent show *The X Factor*; also, the 2005 U.K. entry song that incorporated "oriental-styled" violin passages, percussions, and rhythmic patterns and was performed by Javine Hylton, an R&B singer (of black and white origin), who also appeared in a TV talent show; the 2003 Turkish entry, which capitalized upon the stereotype of the sensual "oriental" body (with Sertab Erener in "Every Way That I Can," see Solomon, in the present volume); the song "A Luta é Alegria" ("The Struggle Is Joy") by the band "Homens da Luta" representing Portugal in 2011 that became the anthem for the street protests against the austerity measures in Lisbon.

31. See, for instance, Langlois for an analysis of the changing poetics of Irishness, Strand and Björnberg on shifting representations of Swedishness, Kirkegaard for a critical approach of the notion of Nordic solidarity—all in the present volume.

32. Solomon explores the winning Sertab's 2003 entry "from the margins of Europe" in the background of the contested discourses of modernization-without-westernization and modernization-as-westernization regarding the ongoing production of Turkish identity both for internal and external consumption.

33. Interestingly, Björnberg refers to press critics who claimed that the Azerbaijani victory "in reality should be regarded as a Swedish triumph," since it "involved Swedish songwriters, Swedish background singers, a Swedish choreographer and a Swedish stylist" (see Björnberg in the present volume). To that extent, the victory of the periphery is considered as a by-product of the professionalism that defines the Swedish nation's know-how of the pop music production. Following Björnberg, such critiques of the Azerbaijani triumph imply the superiority of the older ESC participants, while undermining the potential of the periphery to stand by itself.

34. For a focused discussion on the Eurocity see Bohlman and Polychronakis in the present volume.

35. The construction of the Crystal Hall is part of a construction boom that aims at Baku's image-making as a rich postcapitalist metropolis with an Islamic cultural heritage. The city's so-called "historical centre" has been refurbished and gentrified as a tourist attraction; it has been partly declared as UNESCO's cultural heritage site. At the same time, it has been reported that 40 percent of the country's

population lives below the poverty line. See "Powerful Pipes and Pipelines: Can Eurovision Burnish Azerbaijan's Image?" *Spiegel Online International*, May 15, 2011. Accessed February 12, 2012. http://www.spiegel.de/international/zeitgeist/0,1518,762622,00.html; Esslemont, Tom, 2010. "Struggle for Central Asian Energy Riches," *BBC World News*, June 2. Accessed February 12, 2012. http://www.bbc.co.uk/news/10156909.

36. See "In Baku, Eurovision Supervisor Talks of Human Rights, Hopes for Event." *Radio Free Europe*, January 27, 2012. Accessed February 13, 2012. http://www.rferl.org/content/azerbaijan_eurovision_2012/24465301.html.

37. See Delterne's interview at the BBC 1 program *Panorama* entitled "Eurovision's Dirty Secret" broadcast on Monday 21.5.2012 (20:30 BST). I would like to thank Martin Stokes for bringing this to my attention.

38. Solomon in the present volume explores the winning Turkish 2003 entry in the background of the contested discourses of modernization-without-westernization and modernization-as-westernization regarding the ongoing production of Turkish identity both for internal and external consumption.

39. See Simon Storvik-Green. "Winner's Press Conference: We Want to Bring Europe Together," May 15, 2011. Accessed February 13, 2012. http://www.eurovision.tv/page/news?id=36503&_t=winners_press_conference_we_want_to_bring_europe_together.

40. The yearlong conflict over Nagorno-Karabakh region between Azerbaijan and Armenia and its possible effects have been a source of anxiety for the ESC organizers. There were also worries about the local reception of the gay fans' public display of affection and whether a gay pride will be welcomed in Baku.

41. See, for instance, the report by *BBC News*, March 3, 2012. Accessed May 13, 2012. http://www.bbc.co.uk/news/world-europe-17292360.

42. There are numerous reports by the global media, most of them available online. Teixeira and Stokes also question the European democratic traditions and their futures apropos the discussion of the Portuguese 1974 ESC entry and its political meanings. See Teixeira and Stokes in the present volume.

43. Azerbaijani state has repeatedly been reported by Human Rights Watch and Amnesty International. See the report by Human Rights Watch. http://www.hrw.org/news/2012/02/29/azerbaijan-homeowners-evicted-city-beautification. Accessed May 17, 2012. Also, the media briefing of Amnesty International. http://www.amnesty.org/en/library/asset/EUR55/001/2012/en/50e1c30b-e162-4c43-b34f-d23c90f7f185/eur550012012en.pdf. Accessed February 15, 2012.

44. Teixeira and Stokes bring to our attention the accommodation of the Iberian dictatorships by Western European democracies and the ESC in their chapter in the present volume, in order to trouble the "rather self-satisfied assumption of Western Europe's civilizing mission."

45. When asked about the meaning of the song lyrics Rambo Amadeus replied: "The E.U. and Euro are in some kind of neurotic situation. So I wanted to help. I do not have a cure. It is just a diagnosis. 'Euro Neuro' is a diagnostic song with therapeutic side effects." See "Rambo Amadeus Interview," April 3, 2012. Accessed April 23, 2012. http://wiwibloggs.com/2012/04/03/rambo-amadeus interview-montenegros-esc-star-talks-euro-neuro/16028/. The song did not manage to enter the final. For a critical discussion of the 2012 ESC see the blog entry

posted on June 12, 2012, by Philip V. Bohlman at the Oxford University Press blog entitled "Europe in Spite of Itself." Accessed June 13, 2012. http://blog.oup .com/2012/06/europe-in-spite-of-itself.

46. Loreen made the statement at the day she won the Swedish preliminaries. See "Loreen Wins Melodifestivalen 2012 with "Euphoria." March 10, 2012. Accessed March 12, 2012. http://wiwibloggs.com/2012/03/10/loreen-wins melodifestivalen-2012-with-euphoria/15133/.

47. Abélès resembled the European Parliament with a Tower of Babel in *La Vie Quotidiene au Parliament Europèen* (Paris: Hachette, 1992).

48. According to her profiling, Anggun has been awarded the title of Chevalier des Arts et Lettres by the French Ministry of Culture. She has been a global ambassador for the United Nations and has been involved in various humanitarian projects. See "La chanteuse Anggun choisie pour représenter la France à Eurovision." *Le Parisien*, November 29, 2011. Accessed February 15, 2012. http://www .leparisien.fr/flash-actualite-culture/la-chanteuse-anggun-choisie-pour.

49. See, for instance, the report by *The Guardian*. http://www.guardian.co.uk/ tv-and-radio/video/2012/may/27/eurovision-sweden-loreen-euphoria-video. Accessed May 28, 2012.

50. For Gledhill, "neoliberalism is . . . the ideology of the period in which capitalism deepened to embrace the production of social life itself, seeking to commoditize the most intimate of human relations and the production of identity and personhood" (Gledhill 2004, 340).

51. For Yuriy Syrotyuk, a member of the ultranationalist Svoboda Party, "Gaitana is not an organic representative of the Ukrainian culture. . . . As we want to be accepted to the European Union, it could be our opportunity to show the Europeans that we are also a European nation. We need to show our originality . . . [Gaitana] will provoke an association of Ukraine as a country of a different continent." Gaitana, however, proudly declared that "all my achievements both in music and in sport are devoted to my beloved motherland—Ukraine!" See "Gaitana Controversy Turns Eurovision into Platform for Identity," March 6, 2012. Accessed March 7, 2012. http://wiwibloggs.com/2012/03/06/gaitana-controvers y-turns-eurovision-into-platform-for-identity-and-race/14908/.

52. Following Lampropoulos, by participating in the ESC they are rendered to sanctified Eurobodies (see Lampropoulos in the present volume). As Bohlman puts it, "their lives become trapped in the temporality of the Eurovision song" (see Bohlman in the present volume).

53. See MacDonald 2000.

54. See EBU's announcement at the EBU website, December 7, 2007. Accessed February 10, 2012. http://www.ebu.ch/en/union/news/2007/tcm_6-55998.php. There is the "far East" region, where the show "Our Sound: the Asia-Pacific Song Contest" is licensed and the "Our Sound: the Arab Song Contest" for the Maghreb countries. Although they have been licensed, neither of them has yet taken place.

55. Such as Australia, Brazil, Canada, Chile, China, Egypt, India, Japan, Jordan, Mexico, New Zealand, the Philippines, South Korea, Taiwan, Thailand, and Uruguay.

56. See Bohlman and Polychronakis in the present volume.

57. To that extend, EU's political character oscillates between what the current president of the European Commission José Manuel Baroso described as "the first non-imperial empire" and Jacques Delors's famous definition as "an unidentified political object." See "Non-Imperial Empire," *Brussels Journal*, July 11, 2007. Accessed February 14, 2012. http://www.brusselsjournal.com/node/2244.

58. From the lyrics of the 2012 Azerbaijani entry "When the Music Dies" by Sabina Babayeva.

59. There are both scholarly and journalistic accounts on the ESC. See, for instance, Gambaccini 1998; Feddersen 2002; Kennedy O'Connor 2005; Rykoff and Tobin 2007; Spence 2012. The approach suggested in this book takes as its point of departure the writings of Philip V. Bohlman and his pioneering ethnomusicological study of the ESC phenomenon (see Bohlman 2004; 2011).

60. The song is accessible at http://www.youtube.com/watch?v=naylKpnn Cyo. Accessed on June 1, 2012.

61. See, for instance, http://www.freemuse.org/sw47686.asp. Accessed June 2, 2012.

62. See the BBC 1 program *Panorama* (op.cit.).

63. This is hardly the first time that the global media attention on the ESC has been used as a platform for activist politics. Teixeira and Stokes in the present volume describe an activist incident that took place on stage during the 1964 ESC held in Copenhagen, when a member of the Danish "Group 61" occupied the stage expressing his opposition to Franco's regime. See also Kirkegaard in the present volume.

64. See the report by *BBC News*, May 8, 2012. Accessed May 12, 2012. http://www.bbc.co.uk/news/world-europe-17997685.

65. More information about the "Sing for Democracy" campaign can be found at http://singfordemocracy.org/en/about-campaign/our-mission. Accessed June 3, 2012.

66. My emphasis. See "Protest Songs: Berlin Sees Eurovision as Forum for Civil Rights." *Spiegel Online International*, March 14, 2012. Accessed June 3, 2012, http://www.spiegel.de/international/europe/westerwelle-says-song-contest-should-be-forum-for-promoting-civil-rights-a-821261.html.

67. See, for instance, the report by *Spiegel Online International*, May 2, 2012. Accessed June 3, 2012. http://www.spiegel.de/international/world/azerbaijan-accuses-germany-of-media-smear-campaign-a-830962.html.

68. See Delterne's interview at *Spiegel Online International*, May 10, 2012. http://www.spiegel.de/international/europe/organizer-defends-decision-to-host-eurovision-song-contest-in-baku-a-832456.html. Accessed June 3, 2012. Also, Delterne's interview at BBC1 programme *Panorama* (op. cit.).

69. See, for instance, the *Reuters* news agency report at http://www.reuters .com/article/2012/05/17/us-azerbaijan-eurovision-hacker-idUSBRE84G0YP 20120517. Accessed June 4, 2012.

70. See, for instance, the report of the event by *The Guardian* newspaper at http://www.guardian.co.uk/world/2012/may/22/iran-ambassador-baku-euro vision-row. Accessed June 4, 2012.

71. Azerbaijan is strategically located between Russia on the north and Iran on the south and has supported the U.S. military operations in Afghanistan. It is the

main oil provider for Israel that recently described the Azerbaijani state as "an icon of progress and modernity" and has been granted access, together with its allies, to air bases in the country. For the United States it has been considered as a key player in securing global energy supply and a more reliable partner against Iran's nuclear program and "the fight against terrorism."

72. The song was purposefully released on World Press Freedom Day (May 3, 2012). See the official website for the song: http://toasttofreedom.org/the-song/. Accessed June 3, 2012.

73. For the notion of "homo sacer" see Giorgio Agamben, *Homo Sacer: Sovereign Power and Bare Life* (Stanford University Press, 1998).

74. Ingrid Delterne in her interview for *Spiegel Online International* (op. cit.).

75. The video with Engelke's commentary is available at http://www.youtube.com/watch?v=w1Jaa_HWcLI. Accessed June 7, 2012.

REFERENCES

Abélès, Marc. 2000. "Virtual Europe." In *An Anthropology of the European Union. Building, Imagining and Experiencing New Europe,* edited by Irène Bellier and Thomas Wilson, 31–52. Oxford: Berg.

———. 2004. "Identity and Borders. An Anthropological Approach to EU Institutions." *Twenty-First Century Papers: On-Line Working Papers from the Center for 21st Century Studies,* University of Wisconsin, Milwaukee, 4 (December). Accessed April 12, 2012. http://www4.uwm.edu/c21/pdfs/workingpapers/abeles.pdf.

———. 2010. *The Politics of Survival.* Translated by Julie Kleinman. USA: Duke University Press.

Abélès, Marc, and Irène Bellier. 1996. "La Commission Européenne: Du Compromis Culturel à la Culture Politique du Compromise." *Revue Française de Science Politique* 46(3): 431–55.

Bergeron, Katherine, and Philip V. Bohlman, eds. 1992. *Disciplining Music. Musicology and Its Canons.* Chicago: University of Chicago Press.

Bhabha, Homi. 1994. *The Location of Culture.* New York: Routledge.

Björnberg, Alf. 2007. "Return to Ethnicity: the Cultural Significance of Musical Change in the Eurovision Song Contest." In *A Song for Europe. Popular Music and Politics in the Eurovision Song Contest,* edited by Ivan Raykoff and Robert D. Tobin, 13–23. Aldershot: Ashgate.

Bohlman, V. Philip. 2004. *The Music of European Nationalism. Cultural Identity and Modern History.* California, Santa Barbara: ABC-CLIO.

———. 2011. *Focus: Music, Nationalism and the Making of the New Europe.* New York and London: Routledge.

Borneman, John, and Nick Fowler. 1997. "Europeanization." *Annual Review of Anthropology* 26: 487–514.

Bourdieu, Pierre. 1984. *Distinction: A Social Critique of the Judgment of Taste.* Cambridge, Mass.: Harvard University Press.

Crary, Jonathan. 1999. *Suspensions of Perception: Attention, Spectacle and Modern Culture.* Cambridge, Mass.: MIT Press.

Deltsou, Eleftheria. 2002. "Η 'Πολιτισμική Κληρονομιά' στο Παρόν και στο Μέλλον: Αντιλήψεις και Πρακτικές ενός Εθνικού Παρελθόντος και ενός Ευρωπαϊκού Μέλλοντος." In Το Παρόν του Παρελθόντος: Ιστορία, Λαογραφία και Κοινωνική Ανθρωπολογία, 209–231. Athens: Εταιρεία Σπουδών Νεοελληνικού Πολιτισμού και Γενικής Παιδείας.

Eco, Umberto. 1986. *Travels in Hyperreality.* Translated by William Weaver. San Diego, New York, London: Harcourt Brace.

Fabbri, Franco. 2007. "Browsing Music Spaces. Categories and the Musical Mind." In *Critical Essays in Popular Musicology,* edited by Alan Moore, 49–62. Aldershot: Ashgate.

———. 2010. "What Is Popular Music? And What Isn't? An Assessment after 30 Years of Popular Music Studies." *Musiikki* 2: 72–92.

———. 2012. "How Genres Are Born, Change, Die: Conventions, Communities and Diachronic Processes." In *Critical Musicological Reflections,* edited by Stan Hawkins, 179–91. Aldershot: Ashgate.

Feddersen, Jan. 2002. *Ein Lied kann eine Brücke sein: Die deutsche und internationale Geschichte des Grand Prix Eurovision.* Hamburg: Hoffmann und Campe.

Fornäs, Johan. 2012. *Signifying Europe.* Chicago: Intellect.

Gambaccini et al. 1998. *The Complete Eurovision Song Contest Companion.* London: Pavillion Books Limited.

Gledhill, John. 2004. "Neoliberalism." In *A Companion to the Anthropology of Politics,* edited by David Nugent and Joan Vincent, 332–48. Oxford: Blackwell Publishing.

Grillo, D. Ralph. 2003. "Cultural Essentialism and Cultural Anxiety." *Anthropological Theory* 3(2): 157–73.

Hall, Stuart. 1990. "Cultural Identity and Diaspora." In *Identity: Community, Culture, Difference,* edited by Jonathan Rutherford, 222–37. London: Lawrence and Wishart.

Holmes, Douglas. 2000. *Integral Europe. Fast Capitalism, Multiculturalism, Neofascism.* New Jersey: Princeton University Press.

Holt, Fabian. 2007. *Genre in Popular Music.* Chicago: The University of Chicago Press.

Huyssen, Andreas. 1986. *After the Great Divide. Modernism, Mass Culture, Postmodernism.* Bloomington: Indiana University Press.

Kennedy O'Connor, John. 2005. *The Eurovision Song Contest, 50 Years: The Official History.* London: Carlton Books.

MacDonald, Maryon. 2000. "Anthropology, Accountability and the European Commission." In *Audit Cultures: Anthropological Studies in Accountability, Ethics and the Academy,* edited by Marilyn Strathern, 106–132. London and New York: Routledge.

Mattéi, Jean-Francois. 2007. *Le Regard Vide. Essai Sur L' Epouisement de la Culture Européenne.* Paris: Flammarion.

Raykoff, Ivan, and Robert Deam Tobin, eds. 2007. *A Song for Europe: Popular Music and Politics in the Eurovision Song Contest.* Aldershot: Ashgate. (Ashgate Popular and Folk Music Series).

Shore, Cris. 1997. "Governing Europe: European Union Audiovisual Policy and the Politics of Identity." In *Anthropology of Policy: Critical Perspectives on Gov-*

ernance and Power, edited by Chris Shore and Susan Wright, 165–92. London: Routledge.

———. 2000. *Building Europe: The Cultural Politics of European Integration.* London: Routledge.

Small, Christopher. 1998. *Musicking: The Meanings of Performing and Listening.* Middletown: Wesleyan University Press.

Solomon, Thomas. 2007. "Articulating the Historical Moment. Turkey, Europe and Eurovision 2003." In *A Song for Europe. Popular Music and Politics in the Eurovision Song Contest,* edited by Ivan Raykoff and Robert D. Tobin, 135–46. Aldershot: Ashgate.

Spence, Ewan. 2012. *Eurovision: Beyond the Sequins.* London: Guardian Books.

Stolcke, Verena. 1995. "Talking Culture. New Boundaries, New Rhetorics of Exclusion in Europe." *Current Anthropology,* 36(1): 1–24.

Tragaki, Dafni. 2005. "'Humanizing the Masses': Enlightened Intellectuals and Music of the People." In *The Mediterranean in Music. Critical Perspectives, Common Concerns, Cultural Differences,* edited by David Cooper and Kevin Dawe, 49–75. Lanham, Md.: Scarecrow Press.

Williams, Raymond. 1977. *Marxism and Literature.* Oxford: Oxford University Press.

Žižek, Slavoj. 2002. *Welcome to the Desert of the Real.* New York: Verso Press.

———. 2010. "A Permanent Economic Emergency." *New Left Review* 64 (July–August): 85–95.

Chapter 1

Tempus Edax Rerum
Time and the Making of the Eurovision Song

Philip V. Bohlman

AVANT PROPOS — THE POSTCARD'S GROOVE

Dear Dafni, I'm here at the Eurovision, and everything's fantastic. Once upon a time, there was a fairy tale about a singer. The streets of the Eurovision city are full of people and of street musicians from everywhere. The great monuments of the past are unbelievable, but there's so much to do now that the future is here. I just can't believe what a musical people lives in this country. Wish you could be here, Phil.

Preceding every Eurovision song and punctuating the entire spectacle of the Eurovision Song Contest itself is a half-minute slot in which audience members and viewers at home or on the street alike watch the televised performance of a "postcard." Prepared by the host nation's broadcasting service, the postcard welcomes visitors as foreigners about to be embraced by the host country, its people, and, above all, its music. Postcards may be literal—in 2008, Serbia projected text on the broadcasting screens, in the language of the next competitor, closing the postcard segment by placing a stamp in the upper right-hand corner of the screen—or postcards may appear as another narrative genre or form—in 2002 Estonia broadcast traditional fairy tales, with Estonians looking either timeless or timely, while in 2009 Russia opted for rapidly unfolding cyberscenes that kept audiences guessing who the next performer would be. In 2011, the host country, Germany, promoted an image of multiculturalism, portraying the everyday worlds lived by "new Germans" (and the occasional tourist) from the country whose entry was about to perform. With the same narrative directness of a postal form that relies on brief messages and stereotypical, exaggerated, and falsified images, the Eurovision postcard connects the local to the global, and it provides crucial connection in the performative and performance networks that unfold as the Eurovision show itself.

The postcard is an act of enunciation that musically transforms the worlds that converge at the Eurovision Song Contest into the world of the Eurovision song. An enunciation already posted, that is, already sent to the audience from previous time and place, the postcard reinforces the liveness of the performance of the ESC song in time, evoking an alternating temporal rhythm between a postcard's past and the performance's present. Concentrating time and space, the postcard possesses the attributes of a popular-song cover, engaging the spectator at precisely the moment stage crews rush onto the stage to remove the sets from one performance and to replace them with those of the next. The ways in which the postcard musically covers time presage the ways in which the Eurovision song compresses time: Each postcard in the course of the evening inscribes its local-global mix in precisely the same amount of time—thirty-six seconds at Kyiv in 2005, thirty-three seconds at Belgrade in 2008—giving way to the Eurovision song, which, too, always transpires in the same amount of time, three minutes. The postcard is the bridge, from Europe with all its differences, political, ideological, and cultural, to the Europe celebrated for its potential sameness. The postcard recalibrates the temporal otherness as a utopian selfness, wherein Europeans sing of themselves as others, the hermeneutic inversion of the real and the imaginary (see Ricoeur 1992). Signed and signified, delivered and deliberate, the postcard is the musical portal into the temporal groove of Eurovision time.

THE CHRONOTOPE OF THE EUROVISION SONG

> Manchmal lief die Zeit mir durch die Hände,
> Manchmal wollt' sie einfach nicht vergeh'n.
> Doch die Zeit heilt viele Wunden.
> Und in manchen schweren Stunden
> Träumte ich, die Zeit zurück zu dreh'n, denn . . .
>
> Sometimes, time slips through my fingers,
> Sometimes, it just can't pass fast enough.
> Still, time heals many wounds.
> And in many difficult moments
> I dreamt I could turn back the clock, for . . .
> *Refrain*
> Zeit, Zeit, wo bleibt nur die Zeit?
> Zeit, Zeit, wann ist es so weit?
> Wer weiß, was noch passiert,
> Wer weiß, wohin der Wind mich führt.

Sag', wo bist Du?
Zeit, Zeit, was kommt in dieser Zeit
Noch auf mich zu?
Refrain
    Time, time, where does time stand still?
    Time, time, when have we reached that point?
    Who knows what's going to happen,
    Who knows where the wind will lead me.
    Tell me, where are you?
    Time, time, what lies before me
    In this time?

—Bernd Meinunger and Bianca Schomburg: "Zeit" /
"Time" (Eurovision entry for Germany 1997)

The very fact of this book attests to the sea change through which study of the Eurovision Song Contest has passed in recent years (see especially Raykoff and Tobin 2007, but also Bohlman 2007 and Maurey 2009). As the Eurovision has been de-exoticized, as research has shifted from the margins toward shared disciplinary turf, it has been customary at times to circumvent the questions about the music itself, separating the political and historical from the sound of song. As discourse about the Eurovision Song Contest becomes more public, for example, in 2009 with the extensive coverage of the controversy between Georgia and Russia, the meaning of music assumes a position of only secondary importance, or even unimportance. Whereas the Eurovision's spectacle wins greater visibility, the sound of Eurovision songs as banal, repetitive, bad, or entirely American resonates with the anachronism of saying "the Eurovision is not *really* about music." How often is the word "silly" used by those who wish to trivialize the music or simply deny music meaning? Indeed, the word "silly" appears all-too-frequently in some recent scholarship, hoping to stimulate interest in the Eurovision Song Contest *in spite of* the word "song" at its center. It was symptomatic of such dismissal of the music when, on the day of the Grand Finale, May 14, 2011, the *New York Times* gave substantial coverage to the Eurovision for the first time ever, but entitled its two-page analysis "Uniting a Continent through Wacky Song" (Ewing 2011).

In this chapter I return to the questions and criticisms of the music itself and examine the reasons to take them seriously, even if they were not meant to be serious when posed. I do so by addressing one of the most distinctive attributes of music, the fact that it takes place in time. In the making of the Eurovision song, I wish to claim, this attribute of music is particularly distinctive and powerful. It is, moreover, the intersection of the distinctive and the powerful that Ovid's Latin aphorism in my title embodies: Time, the Devourer of All Things. My consideration of time will have many dimensions, but I want to state from the outset that these dimensions often fall into two broad categories, sometimes dialectically, sometimes not. First of all, I draw upon Mikhail Bakhtin's notion of chronotope, in which cultural fields and human action take place at the intersection of time (χϱόνος) and place (τόπος) (see especially Bakhtin 1981). Second, I consider musical time in rather more structural terms: time as generated internally—musical time—and externally—the temporal context. In both of these categories, which I do not mean to be mutually exclusive, time can be abstract or naturally situated. Temporality comes to be both culturally and historically embedded in the music. It is crucial to the construction of a "good song" no less than it is exposed in the deconstruction of a bad song.

The parallel implications for the Eurovision song are that its dimensions cluster around two phenomenological conditions: object and subject. Debates about whether meaning is immanent in the object or whether it accrues only to the subject run through the history of aesthetics (Bowie 2007: 5). Objective and subjective meaning differ according to the ways in which language, particularly from the Late Enlightenment to the present, through dual paths of analytic and continental philosophy, understand the ways in which linguistic structure and meaning are temporally linked. For Johann Gottfried Herder and Immanuel Kant meaning emerged through sensation, *Empfindung*, which however was determined through human agency. Friedrich Schelling, G. W. F. Hegel, and Friedrich Schleiermacher, in the early nineteenth century, enhanced the debate by asserting that meaning was a necessary, indeed, central attribute in aesthetics. Schelling, for example, asserted that there was an archetypal (*urbildlich*) rhythm in nature, which was temporally consonant with the universe (Bowie 2007: 7). Jürgen Habermas and Andrew Bowie, in recent years, have called for a return to the interpretation of musical texts as phenomena in a lived-in world (Habermas 1991; Bowie 2007).

My turn toward the Eurovision song in this chapter follows from this persistent concern for meaning in the history of aesthetics. Song—as object and subject—is crucial in these questions about the nature of meaning for several specific reasons, all of which are fundamentally temporal. It is a crucial unit that generates performance, the text of ritual, and collectivity of common culture. Song is mobile, even portable, and it therefore circulates in numerous cultural contexts and in the listening culture. Song lends itself to mediation—recordings, videos, covers, parodies. Song is the medium of cultural translation. Song provides a unit that can be transported relatively unencumbered across borders. Structurally, song lends itself efficiently to repetition, as parts and as a whole. It is hardly surprising that one of the most widely used names for the ESC, indeed, throughout Southeastern Europe, is simply the "Eurosong" (see also Bohlman, forthcoming).

Clearly, one of my methodological goals lies in reestablishing the validity of analytical hermeneutics to the study of the Eurovision Song Contest.

My hermeneutic agents, nonetheless, have shifted, and they necessarily encompass, among others: the singer-songwriter; the performers; song producers and recording engineers; those who experience as listeners and auditors; the mediators who resituate song in society because of its mobility; the agents of historicism, the *griots,* so to speak, who inscribe European history through processes such as revival.

The chronotopes of the Eurovision song form around six different types of temporality, which appear schematically below and in figure 1.1. The six types of temporality, significantly, are not isolated, nor do they circulate only in paired constellations, rather they interact to produce the temporality of the Eurovision Song Contest, which I represent with figure 1.2.

1. Musical time—form, structure, genre
2. Historical time—narrative, culture
3. Ritual time/mediated time
4. Cyclical time
5. Performative/embodied time
6. Monumental time/epic time

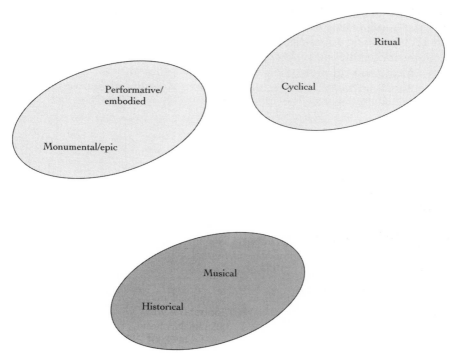

Figure 1.1.   Chronotopes of Eurovision Song Temporality.

The six categories also form three sets of pairs, each of them representing the contrasting relation of object and subject, thus containing not only multiple ontologies of music, but multiple phenomena for the expression of meaning in the Eurovision Song Contest. I turn to each of these categories in the course of this chapter, but before doing so, I should like to embark on a brief excursus, in which I reflect on the structure and meaning of national song, because it is, I believe, national song that lies at the heart of how the Eurovision song contributes to the narration of the European nation and of Europe itself (for theories of narrative genre and the representation of the nation cf. Bhabha 1990; and Berger, Eriksonas, and Mycock 2008).

ON THE MAKING OF NATIONAL SONG

The Eurovision song arises from the styles, forms, and genres of national song, and it contains nationalist functions, be these overt or subdued. I should like to turn briefly to nationalist song to examine just how, historically considered, music can and, in Europe, does move from the non-representational to the highly representational. In so doing, I consciously draw the Eurovision song into a larger context of nationalism and music, thereby refusing to essentialize the Eurovision song as a phenomenon unique and exotic unto itself.

I turn in two different theoretical directions for the concepts of song fragment that have the potential to cohere as national and nationalist

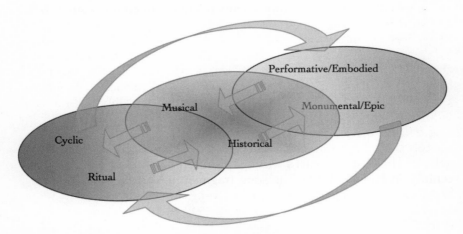

Figure 1.2.   Temporality of the Eurovision Song.

song. The first of these has been most convincingly articulated by Partha Chatterjee, in his *Nation and Its Fragments* (1993) and elsewhere (e.g., Chatterjee 1986). Song, to extend Chatterjee's examinations of Bengali and Indian nationalism for our purposes, not only belongs to the "inner domain" of the nation, but it accounts for differences in the spiritual and ideological practices that constitute that inner domain from within. The inner domain forms at the conjunction of the mythical and the proto-historical, hence contrasting with the temporality of the historical and its response to encounter beyond or at the borders of the nation. Song is not one kind of fragment, rather many. More to the point, different functions accrue to song over time, thus, within the multilayered history of a nation as it resists externally imposed forms of nationalism, for example, those from the colonial history of India that are Chatterjee's concern.

I also bring a theoretical approach from historical musicology and ethnomusicology to my consideration of fragments and the nation (e.g., Constantine and Porter 2003). It is possible to look at national and nationalist song as the products of fragmentation and as processes of combining and recombining fragments to create wholes that, unlike musical works themselves, are fragile and malleable (for a distinction of "national" and "nationalist music," see Bohlman 2011: 58–84 and 85–117). In the historiography of music and nationalism, attention to the functions of fragments begins in the eighteenth century but congeals theoretically in the second half of the century in the early writings of Johann Gottfried Herder, notably in his early aesthetic writings from the 1760s and 1770s, the Kritische *Wälder* (Herder 1769) and *Von deutscher Art und Kunst* (Herder 1773), which themselves at times deliberately assumed the form of fragments. Herder's engagement with the fabricated Ossian songs, called by their collector/author James Macpherson, "Fragments of Ancient Poetry" (Macpherson 1760), was published as "Extracts from "Correspondence about Ossian and the Songs of Ancient People" (in Herder 1773) and became a seminal essay in the historiography of musical nationalism. Critical for its historical function, the fragment of song embodies both the whole and the part, and it is hardly surprising that this dialectic of "das Ganze" [the whole] and "das Einzelne" [the part] was foundational for the role song played in nineteenth-century nationalist thought (cf. Schlegel 1797 [1956]; cf. Novalis's writings also from the turn of the nineteenth century in Novalis 1984). The song fragment already contains identity, and it can proffer identity as it conjoins other fragments to forge national and nationalist song (cf. Friedrich Hölderlin's litany, "Eines zu sein mit Allem" [to be at one with all], that runs through the opening chapters of *Hyperion*; Hölderlin 1999: 484). Identifying a song type to which he refers as "national popular music," Alf Björnberg connects the nineteenth-century nation to the present and beyond:

> Throughout the history of popular music, national popular-music styles have been functioning as free-floating signifiers, liable to extensive appropriation and re-interpretation in contexts alien to those of their origins. (Björnberg 2007: 15)

The relation of part to whole is one of agency. The fragments of song *constitute* the nation. Without them, the nation is empty and ultimately inchoate. Song is therefore critical to the making of the nation, no less so than the nation is crucial to the identity of song.

MUSICAL TIME—FORM, STRUCTURE, GENRE

Time is of the essence in the determination and manipulation of Eurovision song form, structure, and genre. Everything must fit within three minutes, and songwriters, performers, and studio producers, year after year, display an uncanny capacity to make them fit. The three-minute framework concentrates the many dimensions of melodic repetition, at once giving birth to the song itself and presaging its inevitable death, a contradiction in popular music that Richard Middleton describes as follows:

> Repetition extinguishes the original, and extinction (replication, fading, displacement, doubling) on one level is the condition for renewal on another. (Middleton 2006: 137)

The struggle for life and death in the three minutes of the Eurovision song conjoins the objective and subjective dimensions of song itself. Will those three minutes situate the song in one or several genealogies, with formal and structural repetitions acting as musical genetic material? Or will it accelerate the slide toward inevitable death, the sameness that standard and banal Eurovision criticism so often—and so repetitively—disdains? With my focus on time in this chapter, I should like to move toward answering these questions by suggesting that the formal constraints and internal repetition in Eurovision song can be, and often is, the source of creativity. That creativity resides, moreover, in the ways tightly formalized songs allow for difference, indeed, difference that does not so much disrupt repetition as confirm its potential.

Just how the songwriter and performer use the three minutes available to them depends on song form and genre. Dominating the forms historically used for Eurovision songs, not surprisingly, is popular-song form, with its three or four phrases juxtaposing an original section (A) with a contrasting section (B), before a return to the original A section, usually altered in such a way that the song quickly reaches its conclusion. This basic formal structure provides a template for many genres, of course, but it serves the diversity of genre particularly well. It fits popular-song form, such as the standard Tin Pan Alley style of thirty-two bars, with a Middle Eight bridge. It heightens the contrastive role of verse-refrain forms no less than the call-and-response in gospel, jazz, and Afro-Caribbean standards. It equally serves the blues and many other African American genres. Older genres in the history of Eurovision song, for example, French *chanson* and German *Schlager,* may adopt this basic formal structure, and new genres, notably *sevdalinka* in many Balkan Eurovision songs or *qaṣda* from styles reflecting Arab and Islamic influences, incorporate its formal principles to lay claim to European song-style kinship. Arguably, this has been the case even with the increase of heavy-metal entries in the years since Lordi's "Hard Rock Hallelujah," which won the Grand Prix in 2006.

I should like to turn first to two of many ways in which the middle section—the bridge in more common structural terms—becomes a site of difference. As a section of difference, the middle section shifts temporal registers to become the site of politics. If we examine style history in the Eurovision, for example, we quickly realize that hip-hop has not enjoyed enormous success. The global spread of hip-hop and its extensive localization notwithstanding, hip-hop is strikingly rare in the Eurovision, appearing somewhat more often, but still tentatively, in the past decade. Paradoxically, perhaps, the most dramatic—and even successful—moments of hip-hop appear in the bridges of Eurovision songs, where its sudden and temporally limited presence of rarely more than fifteen seconds becomes uncanny. This is clearly the case with the 2005 Ukrainian entry, Greenjolly's "Razom nas bahato" [Together We Are Many], which shifts musical styles from socialist *Kampflieder,* both East European and in the style of Chilean resistance songs from the Allende period, to African American urban protest.

> We won't stand this—no! Revolution is on!
> 'Cuz lies be the weapon of mass destruction!
> All together we're one! All together we're strong!
> God be my witness we've waited too long!
>
> *Bridge*
> Fal'sifikaciyam—ni! mahinaciyam—ni!
> Ponyatiyam—ni! Ni brehni!

Virimo—Tak! Mozhemo—Tak!
Znayu peremozhemo—Tak! Tak!

Chorus
Razom nas bahato—nas ne podolaty!

What you wanna say to your daughters and sons?
You know the battle is not over till the battle is won!
Truth be the weapon! We ain't scared of the guns!
We stay undefeated, 'cuz together we're one!

Bridge
My—vzhe razom! My—nazavzhdy!
My Ukrainy don'ki i syny!
Zaraz yak nikoly godi chekaty!

Chorus
Razom nas bahato—nas ne podolaty!

—"Razom nas bahato, Nas Ne Podolaty!"/"Together We Are
Many, We Cannot Be Defeated," Greenjolly—Ukrainian Entry in
the 2005 Eurovision Song Contest (Kiev, Ukraine)

The bridge is also the site at which religion, particularly as a marker of
European otherness, can enter a Eurovision song. Religion finds its way
into the Eurovision more often than not in oblique ways, for example,
as gospel-influenced styles. As a sign of identity, religion should suggest unity rather than announce difference. Accordingly, it may not be
surprising that against the backdrop of a spreading Islamist ecumene in
southeastern Europe, Muslim and Islamist themes have been relatively
rare, even since 2000 and the remarkable success of East European entries.
When the presence of Islam in Europe does announce itself, it does so in
the Middle Eight, say, as in the 2003 French entry, Louisa's "Monts et mer-
veilles" in which the singer shifts from a *chanson* to riffing on *layālī* over a
darbukka in the bridge. The question is whether religious difference serves
in such instances as a "hidden" or "public transcript" (see Scott 1990). The
time of difference in the bridge—usually beginning at ca. 1:45 into the
song and concluding at ca. 2:10—opens a place for difference in the song,
at once asserting and complicating its Europeanness (see Bohlman 2009
for further analysis of the place of Islam in the Eurovision Song Contest).

HISTORICAL TIME—NARRATIVE AND POLITICS

No one would reasonably dispute the Eurovision Song Contest is both
the product and agent of history and historiography. It is virtually im-

possible to refer to a song, singer, or nation without locating them in time and associating them with historical moments. "Waterloo" was ABBA's 1974 entry. "Diva" was Israel's last winning song, in 1998, still prior to the Second Intifada (see Maurey 2009). "Riva" was Yugoslavia's first and last winning song, sung as it was in 1989 on the eve of the fall of the communist government and the subsequent division of Yugoslavia. Dima Bilan's "Believe" provided Russia with its first victorious Eurovision song three months before it invaded Georgia in August 2008.

Even before the 2005 celebration of the Eurovision's first half-century, it had become customary to attribute a historical *longue durée* to the Eurovision, namely its inception as a response to the Cold War and its extension into the twenty-first century as a response to the reunification of and transition following the Cold War. In commentary on the meaning and identity of the Eurovision song we always turn to history, the songs and competitions that clearly, as Thomas Solomon notes, "articulate the historical moment" (Solomon 2007). In the beginning, it was Soviet tanks in Hungary. Since the turn of our own century, it has been EU membership for Turkey, the Orange Revolution in Ukraine, Kosovo's separation from Serbia, and the renewed shift of power from Eastern Europe to Russia. The moment in which chapters are gathered for this volume could not be more historically pregnant for the Eurovision Song Contest.

The inseparability of historical time from the Eurovision remains notable for the extent to which, in opposition, the denial of history still forms a trope for the critics of the Eurovision. Songs such as Germany's winning entry in 1982, "Ein bißchen Frieden" [A Little Bit of Peace], are treated as the exception rather than the rule. More common is the polite indulgence toward songs such as Finland's 2011 ecoballad, "Da Da Dam." In 2005, Greenjolly's "Razom nas bahato" is played as historically naïve against Wig Wam's glam metal "In My Dreams" the same year. Glam metal, in the year of the Orange Revolution, scored much higher than hip-hop. Are these, we might ask, really cases of an absence of history? Can we really imagine that a Eurovision song might be ahistorical, even when trying to be so?

I do not pose such questions rhetorically, because I contend that historical time manifests itself in many ways, and among those ways are some that we might consider the denial of history. History within and without the music is a sign of ownership, hence, a claim of agency. Whose history and what historical moment does any given entry wish to transform into performative spectacle? We have increasingly realized since 2000 that the historical claims on European unity might potentially be outweighed by those on disunity, or at least some kind of political control of the checks and balances in the European Union.

Historical time, too, asserts itself in the Eurovision song itself, specifically, that is, in the forms and narratives of "style history." Arguing against the ahistorical "mainstream style" that Eurovision critics bemoan, Alf Björnberg points out that the number of musical styles employed by Eurovision songwriters has sharply increased, especially since 1989, and taken an "ethnic turn" since 2000 (Björnberg 2007: 13). It is not simply a question that Celtic styles were favored in the 1990s or African American styles after 2000, giving way to Carpathian and Balkan ethnic styles in 2004, and to Norwegian folklike music in 2009. The question becomes, rather, that Eurovision song style displays itself as multicultural, hybrid, and contradictory. The historical moments for hip-hop and metal may be fading, but their importance to Eurovision songs for the past half-decade has been to articulate counterhistorical moments of their own, opening rather than closing the temporal space between object and subject, and further transforming the Eurovision song into a narrative for historical time.

RITUAL TIME/MEDIATED TIME

The moment we approach the Eurovision Song Contest as participants— be it as fans, collectors of Eurovision songs, ethnographers, or champions of a given nation's cause—at that moment, we enter a ritual world. What may appear at first glance a loose, even random, community quickly acquires the attributes of *communitas*. What may seem to outsiders as a move from the periphery becomes in the ritual world of the Eurovision a passage through liminality, with all its concomitant rites of passage (cf. Turner 1969).

Eurovision ritual time unfolds locally in counterpoint with the EBU technoculture rituals that unfold transnationally, and the communities that calibrate their lives with it make selective use of Eurovision song practices to draw their communities together. Entry into local ritual is, we also recognize, not easy, even when we are otherwise actively engaged with the Eurovision. Obtaining tickets, booking hotel rooms, and gaining access to the Grand Prix itself can be virtually impossible if one does not belong to one of the fan clubs or have affiliations to one of the more transnational organizations that also serve as keepers of ritual practice. Even gaining access to so-called "press kits," or promotional DVDs and CDs, depends on access to ritual organizations. This has surely been the case for me and my daughter, Andrea Bohlman, outsiders as Americans and scholars, whose entry into Eurovision ritual time in 2008, for example, was through the Serbian Academy of Sciences—I received tickets in exchange for a series of lectures in Belgrade—perhaps the most marginal of marginal ritual groups (see also A. Bohlman and Polychronakis in this volume).

The rites that constitute Eurovision ritual time differ from one another, radically at times, as we might expect from local practices. The most publicly visible ritual communities are surely those that maintain websites on the Internet. Eurovision websites respond to complex group and individual desires, and they play a particularly important role in tracking the passage of time through ritual moments. Online websites may be large and pan-European (e.g., http://www.escnation.com/) or national and intimate (e.g., http://www.allkindsofeverything.ie/ [Ireland] or http://www.kolumbus.fi/jarpen/ [Finland]). It is through the websites, for example, that regional and national ritual spectacles form a network. They provide the portal through which we see how the Greek, German, or Andorran entry will be chosen, and when. Virtual communities congeal around ritual communities, which in turn engender imagined communities. The subjectivity of ritual process, in this way, extends even to the objective product of the Eurovision song (Björnberg 2007: 16).

The Eurovision Song Contest itself is the product of highly ritualized spectacle (see, especially, Björnberg 1992). The restrictions placed on song length, the number of performers on the stage, the relation between singers and dancers, and the ways in which any given performative rite of passage depends on specific production techniques, all these depend on ritual time. The postcards between songs, the interviews with performers in the liminal space, and the countdown that limits the period of time in which it is possible to vote with one's mobile phone, all these depend on the constraints of ritual time, which however is precisely controlled and extensively mediated.

The chronotopes of local ritual groups and ritual spectacle also render the borders of ritual specialists and observers permeable. Reception and spectatorship assume the trappings of ritual practice. In Israel, for example, where I first began watching the Eurovision in the early 1980s, when I was researching my Ph.D. dissertation in Jerusalem, spectators gathered in homes in ways that resemble other kinds of intimate musical practice following *motzeh shabbat,* the end of the Sabbath. So empty were the streets in a country that took the Eurovision extremely seriously that more than a few Israelis compared it to the exit from the public sphere into the private that characterizes *Yom Kippur,* the Day of Atonement. The Eurovision communities I knew in the Israel of the 1980s, nonetheless, have changed dramatically, yielding to new and different kinds of communities, such as the intimate experiences described by Dafna Lemish in the past decade (Lemish 2007). How different were the ritual practices in the United Kingdom, where pubs organized special Eurovision evenings against the vocal counterpoint of ritual specialist, Terry Wogan, announcing the contest for the BBC for decades prior to his retirement in 2008?

CYCLICAL TIME

If ritual time and ritual practice are local, they are by no means isolated. The local subjectivities that they foster, instead, are powerfully connected to the cyclical chronotope of what I should like to call the "Eurovision Year." Please permit me to be clear that my choice of cyclical time unfolding during the course of the year was deliberate, and I mean thereby to evoke sacred metaphors, as we would, for example, in a liturgical year. The chronotopes of the Eurovision Year contain many of the attributes of a liturgical year, with its markers of sacred journey, pilgrimage, saint adoration, birth, death, and revival. The recitation of the Qur'an and the Torah in Islam and Judaism, for example, unfold in the course of an annual cycle, and particular texts within the annual cycle become the liturgical framework for smaller cycles, say, for pilgrimages large and small. The temporality of cycles, both metaphysically and soteriologically, proffer the Eurovision an almost transcendent sacredness, reflecting life and that which follows.

Though it may seem that the recalibration of the secular as the sacred comes precariously close to slipping into a sermon about the Eurovision as religion and religious practice, in fact, I am trying to avoid doing just that. On one hand, I am interested in the ways in which the sacred both do and do not emerge in the Eurovision song. The prevalence of songs with sacred-sounding titles—for example, Milk and Honey's "Hallelujah" and Lordi's "Hard Rock Hallelujah," or most recently Marija Šerifović's "Prayer" and Dima Bilan's "Believe"—may well be more ironic than representative. That irony itself may be worn on the sleeves of performers as parody, as in the infamous Eurovision episode of the television program about the fictional Irish priest, "Father Ted" (viewable at http://www.you tube.com/watch?v=jzYzVMcgWhg). Religion is, instead, I believe, local and personal, as in the cases of Israel, Armenia, and Bosnia-Herzegovina. Religion also obtains in the subtexts to the ways in which the Eurovision Song Contest reflects the politics of Christianity that shape so many chapters of European history, not least one of the most powerful underlying assumptions about distinctions between West and East during the Cold War.

On the other hand the sacredness of cycles carries over into the subjectivities of identity, life, and renewal. The sacredness of Eurovision cycles, for example in the birth and renewal of song styles, opens a fissure between Europe as sacred and Europe as secular. That fissure draws our attention to the very nature of Europeanness in the Eurovision song. In particular, I believe it is possible that the functions of musical revival—of musical style and identity—are enhanced by the chronotope of cyclicity. The question about song style, then, is not about borrowing or appropriating, or simply pandering to an atavistic and exhausted popular-music mainstream. Rather, the revival of song styles renews the life of the Eurovision from within. The formation of liturgy in the course of cyclical time may well be all about repetition, but it is in this crucial sense that Richard Middleton, returning to Freud himself, reminds us "that when we repeat psychic material it is as a defense" (Middleton 2006: 139). To return to the stylistic shrines of the past and to revive them undermines the very eschatology of which so many Eurovision musicians are accused. The cyclical time of the Eurovision does not simply sustain the life of the Eurovision song. It restores its life as a defense against the pervasive anxiety of European modernity: that European history itself will end.

PERFORMATIVE/EMBODIED TIME

Because of its soteriological affirmation of life through revival the Eurovision song is highly personal and performative. Accordingly, the Eurovision song bears witness to a chronotope we can call embodied time. Again, we recognize the qualities of embodiment embedded in various areas of product and process. Thematically, the concern for embodied time recurs repeatedly in the large number of songs devoted, on one level, to the physical nature of life. The word "life" is in a remarkably large number of Eurovision song titles. In embodied form, it is love that couples life and death, also yielding the frequent appearance of *Liebestod*, "love-death," as a theme of embodiment.

Embodied time provides a process that transforms the Eurovision song from object to subject. This transformation occurs, for example, through the growing interpretation of the song with dance and narrative/dramatic choreography. During the course of the annual Eurovision cycle, therefore, the identity of a song changes as it becomes increasingly embodied. Physical identity may even change through performance, be it the revelation of the singer's body upon the removal of clothing or even the increasingly complex expression of gender and sexuality, from Dana International to Marija Šerifović.

The embodiment of time in the Eurovision song also functions reflexively, or perhaps even as a kind of negative dialectic. I refer here to the singers and songwriters who fall victim to the very songs they create and perform. Their lives become trapped in the temporality of the Eurovision song. This embodiment-as-entrapment accrues to the lives of the "Mr. Eurovisions," the best-known of which, of course, is Ireland's Johnny Logan. Similarly, the German singer-songwriter, Ralph Siegel, has himself become a creation of the Eurovision Song Contest, at the very least, of the songs he has created over a Eurovision career—a lifetime—of three and a half decades (Hindrichs 2007; Feddersen 2002).

In his study of the lives of Eurovision contestants who received *nul points*, Tim Moore pursues an even darker side to the inability to free oneself from the embodiment of the Eurovision song (Moore 2006). Expecting singers such as Jahn Teigen and Finn Kalvik to move on beyond the ignominy of Eurovision failure, Moore discovered instead that both Norwegians continued to cling to the process of recovering from loss, that is, from Eurovision death. In a different way, there are singers such as Malta's Chiara who return to represent their nation again and again, hoping, as Chiara did for the third time in 2009, that their moment truly to live in Eurovision stardom has arrived. To the *Liebestod* of the Eurovision song accrues an extraordinarily complex transcendence.

MONUMENTAL TIME/EPIC TIME

In order to calibrate the life of a nation and give it meaning in the larger process of making Europe modern, particularly as modernity is a simulacrum for the uncertain unity of the future, Eurovision songs enact memory work. They commemorate the two chronotopes of my final category: monumental time and epic time. The two are conjoined by the ways in which music musters memory to connect the past to the future (see, e.g., Rehding 2009). Again, questions of repetition, revival, and soteriology come into play. The music of a nation represents its struggle for survival.

Because of its temporality music possesses an extraordinary capacity to contribute to the temporal dimensions of the memory work that monuments make possible, generating what Michael Herzfeld calls "monumental time" (Herzfeld 1991). When public performance and spectacle share a monument's space, they calibrate monumental time by drawing those experiencing music closer to the historical moment being memorialized. We enter the monumental time that allows the history of the nation to become fluid, or "transient" in the theoretical formulation Rudy Koshar uses to explain the endurance of German monuments (Koshar 1998). Music also intersects with the other arts to narrate mythical national past, shaping the processes necessary for what Stefan Gerner calls the "retrospective invention of the nation through art" (Gerner 1998). One might even go so far as to suggest that music participates in the invention of the nation most effectively when it achieves monumental status (cf. the various ways in which monumental works of art shape the national myths of Europe in Flacke 1998). Is it, we then ask, the nation of an imagined past or an invented future that we witness in the conscious architecture of monuments that fill Eurovision postcards and in the promotional videos that disseminate Eurovision songs?

The monuments of monumental time can and do become the fragments of national song when the border into epic time is crossed. In epic time song becomes the vehicle of the national *longue durée*. I turn to the genre "epic" here quite deliberately, for the metaphorical power it conveys. A national epic grows from the meaningful objects an epic poet or singer or collector can retrieve from the past. The epic song is forever changing, forever expanding in its temporality into a more distant past and a future yet to be realized. Ownership and authenticity, the national phoneme and episteme—all these are thrown into question as new hemistiches and stiches affix themselves through the hermeneutic agency of performers and audiences alike (see, e.g., Beissinger, Tylus, and Wofford 1999; Bohlman and Petković 2012).

Eurovision songs, too, accrue to this process of creating a Europe constituted of many parts. They, too, are parts—individual songs—whose meaning extends to the more expansive epic of nation-building and modernity. They may succeed or fail, but in either case they afford musical meaning to national meaning. The meaning of the German *schlager* or the Italian San Remo song is no less in the Eurovision histories of these two nations because of the cosmopolitan qualities of the genres themselves. The same can be said of the fragmentary hybrids formed from the styles of African Americans, the Celtic fringe, or the Ottoman Ecumene. The meanings that such fragments encompass are inseparable from the epic of Europe.

Epic time conjoins with real time in each Eurovision song as it creates a space of listening between one annual contest and the next. That juxtaposition is one of disjuncture, of historical crisis no less than of musical reality. The aural experience of the Eurovision song does not close the disjuncture, for songs form at this disjuncture, and many others in the making of modern Eurovision, drawing us into the very time and place of disjuncture. By listening to Eurovision songs, by experiencing their timeliness and temporality within and outside the music, in their objective and subjective meanings, we realize how the song bears witness to Europe at the most critical moments of its narration through history (for the historicist construction of epic history for the Eurovision cf. Gambaccini et al. 1999; Kennedy O'Connor 2005).

À LA *RECHERCHE DU TEMPS PERDU*—THE RETURN OF THE EUROVISION SONG

Eurovision 2009 was a one-horse race from the start. . . .

The Norwegian entry received more points and won by the largest margin in the 54-year history of the Eurovision Song Contest. . . .

Alexander Rybak's "Fairytale" was a mixture of folk tunes, fiddling, bubble-gum pop, and an Eastern European sound. . . .

Norway's victory and Iceland's strong showing dispel the belief that countries in the West of Europe could no longer win the Eurovision. . . .

Of course, it didn't hurt that Alexander Rybak was born in Belarus.

—Response and commentary immediately following Eurovision 2009,
May 16, 2009, BBC World Service

The luminaries will be looking for well-written songs and may not take kindly to over-the-top performances masking vacuous vocals. Welcome to the new world of Eurovision.

—Michael Osborn, "Battle of the Eurovision Ballads" (2009b)

May 17, 2009, an ethnographic moment as epilogue. On the morning after the fifty-fourth Eurovision Song Contest in Moscow, the most politically fraught ESC spectacle of the past two decades, an uncanny unanimity marks the still-inchoate moment opening a new chapter in the reception history of the Eurovision ("Norway Voted Eurovision Winners" 2009): with a single voice there was agreement that the best song won. Opinions may have differed about how Alexander Rybak's "Fairytale," which he wrote and performed, as singer and fiddler, captured the Grand Prix, but there was no disagreement about its achievement in the Finals: It stood out as the best song in a field of entries that was itself one of the strongest ever, as Michael Osborn expressed the sympathy of many, "with virtually all countries sending songs they feel have more credibility" (Osborn 2009b).

Just as the return of the Eurovision song marked a turning point in Eurovision history, it also rerouted the geographic shift to Eastern Europe that had come to dominate a concomitant shift in public anxiety about the Eurovision in Western Europe (see Bohlman 2004). The migration of the Eurovision to Eastern Europe—and beyond to the new Eurovision regions of the Eastern Mediterranean and the Black Sea—was mobilized more by the drama and choreography on the stage than by song. The anxiety became increasingly palpable in the rise of Russia on the heels of Dima Bilan's Timbaland-produced "Believe" and on the eve of Moscow's 30-million-dollar production of Eurovision 2009 during the week of May 12–16. What would be left of the Eurovision—what would be left of Europe—if song was lost to the power to produce and put on the best show?

There is little doubt in the Eurovision imaginary that the Eurovision song has returned from one region in Europe to another. The "new beginning" and the "new world of Eurovision" (Osborn 2009b) are in the West, the "Far West" of Europe for commentaries that seek to pair the second-place Icelandic entry with Norway. Accounts of Alexander Rybak's birth in Belarus, his presumably fluent Russian, and an Eastern European "sound" perhaps also present in the winning song form the counterpoint of a new chronotope. Whether or not one really senses an Eastern European sound in "Fairytale," which pairs Rybak's Norwegian fiddling with the formal devices of a folk ballad, may be less important than the seeming need to translate Norwegian localness to European globalness. "Simplicity," Rybak is claimed to have stated, "is the formula for Eurovision glory" (Galpin 2009). In 2010, the formula for victory would shift once again through the flirtatiously innocent voice of a German teenager, Lena, who would bring victory to one of the "Big Five" competitors for the first time in the twenty-first century. Azerbaijan's victory in 2011, nonetheless, provided evidence that the relocation to the East was far from over.

In 2009, however, the singularity of the Eurovision song asserted itself in the proliferation of form, style, and genre. Folk and ethnic song appeared in styles both adorned and unadorned by the popular-music styles predominant in the first decade of the twenty-first century, from techno to heavy metal to a noticeable turn toward country. Narrative genres, particularly ballad in both its folk and popular meanings, were mustered to blur the boundaries between story and history. France's Patricia Kaas unequivocally reminded Eurovision audiences of the historical debt to *chanson*. Cabaret, too, assumed multiple forms, evocatively transforming Moscow's massive stage into an intimate space for song. Classical song, whether the pop-opera style of Sweden's "La Voix" or buoyed by the chamber-music ensembles backing the Slovenian and Estonian entries, had a firm presence in Moscow. The space of song was possible only because of the return of Eurovision's original agency, that of the songwriter, the creator of song.

Once again, song is serious business. After a decade of entries that left the United Kingdom at or near the final places in the Finals, the United Kingdom turned to Andrew Lloyd Webber and Jade Ewen for a song that would bring the United Kingdom back to Eurovision fortunes, leading commentators to call Lloyd Webber a "Eurovision savior" (Osborn 2009a). Lloyd Webber's touch for song pushed the United Kingdom to fifth place, and a similar London West End sound worked even more effectively for Iceland's Johanna, who returned home with a second-place finish. Athletic dance acts were hardly absent, but they scored surprisingly poorly in comparison to the solo acts, the singer alone on the stage, vocally liberated from sexy choreography, and pyrotechnics. The singer's voice was the site of a different intimacy, realized by song.

The new world of Eurovision is temporally bounded, traversed not just by the return of the Eurovision song, but also by the return to the past and the search for lost time. As Moscow and the European Broadcasting Union strove to expand the spatial boundaries of the show, many singers consciously and convincingly reined in the temporal boundaries, claiming for Europe and the Eurovision a new presence for the past. Symbolically, even the winner of the 2009 Grand Prix, Alexander Rybak, turned to the past with his opening line: "Years ago, when I was younger." To the Eurovision song, at once ephemeral and transitory, conforming to an unyielding allotment of three minutes, accrues the vast reach of the *longue durée*, Eurovision's history poised at the threshold of Europe's future.

REFERENCES

Bakhtin, M. M. 1981. *The Dialogic Imagination: Four Essays by M. M. Bakhtin.* Edited by Michael Holquist. Translated by Caryl Emerson and Michael Holquist. Austin: University of Texas Press.

Beissinger, Margaret, Jane Tylus, and Susanne Wofford, eds. 1999. *Epic Traditions in the Contemporary World: The Poetics of Community.* Berkeley: University of California Press.

Berger, Stefan, Linas Eriksonas, and Andrew Mycock, eds. 2008. *Narrating the Nation: Representations in History, Media and the Arts.* Oxford and New York: Berghahn.

Bhabha, Homi, ed. 1990. *Nation and Narration.* London and New York: Routledge.

Björnberg, Alf. 1992. "Musical Spectacle as Ritual: The Eurovision Song Contest." In *1789–1989: Musique, Histoire, Démocratie,* vol. 2, edited by Antoine Hennion, 373–82. Paris: Editions de la Maison des Sciences de l'Homme.

———. 2007. "Return to Ethnicity: The Cultural Significance of Musical Change in the Eurovision Song Contest." In *A Song for Europe,* edited by Ivan Raykoff and Robert D. Tobin, 13–23.

Bohlman, Philip V. 2004. "Popular Music on the Stage of a United Europe—Southeastern Europe in the 'Eurovision Song Contest.'" In *Vereintes Europa—Vereinte Musik? Vielfalt und soziale Dimensionen in Mittel- und Südosteuropa,* edited by Bruno B. Reuer, 27–45. Berlin: Weidler Verlag.

———. 2007. "The Politics of Power, Pleasure, and Prayer in the Eurovision Song Contest." *Musicology/Musicologia* 7: 39–67.

———. 2009. "*Ex Oriente Lux:* Islam and the Eurovision Song Contest." In *Antropologia della Musica nelle Culture Mediterranee: Interpetatione, Performance, Identitá,* edited by Philip V. Bohlman and Marcello Sorce Keller, 171–80. Bologna: CLUEB.

———. 2011. *Focus: Music, Nationalism, and the Making of the New Europe.* New York: Routledge. (Focus on World Music Series).

———. Forthcoming. "Eurovision Song." In *Encyclopedia of Popular Music of the World: European Genres,* edited by Paolo Prado. London and New York: Continuum Books.

———, and Nada Petković, eds. 2012. *Balkan Epic: Song, History, Modernity.* Lanham, Md.: Scarecrow Press. (Europea: Ethnomusicologies and Modernities, 11)

Bowie, Andrew. 2007. *Music, Philosophy, and Modernity.* Cambridge: Cambridge University Press. (Modern European Philosophy)

Chatterjee, Partha. 1986. *Nationalist Thought and the Colonial World: A Derivative Discourse?* London: Zed Books.

———. 1993. *The Nation and Its Fragments: Colonial and Postcolonial Histories.* Princeton: Princeton University Press. (Princeton Studies in Culture/Power/History)

Constantine, Mary-Ann, and Gerald Porter. 2003. *Fragments and Meaning in Traditional Song: From the Blues to the Baltic.* London: The British Academy.

Ewing, Jack. 2011. "Uniting a Continent through Wacky Song." *New York Times.* May 14: C1 and C5.

Feddersen, Jan. 2002. "Ein Gespräch mit Ralph Siegel." In idem, *Ein Lied kann eine Brücke sein: Die deutsche und internationale Geschichte des Grand Prix Eurovision,* 280. Hamburg: Hoffmann and Campe.

Flacke, Monika, ed. 1998. *Mythen der Nationen: Ein europäisches Panorama.* Munich and Berlin: Koehler and Amelang.

Gadamer, Hans-Georg. 1986. *Hermeneutik: Wahrheit und Methode.* Tübingen: J. C. B. Mohr.

Galpin, Richard. 2009. "Norwegians Celebrate in Moscow." *BBC News* (online), May 17. Accessed May 17, 2009. http://news.bbc.co.uk/2/hi/entertainment/8054281.stm.

Gambaccini, Paul, et al. 1999. *The Complete Eurovision Song Contest Companion.* Foreword by Terry Wogan. London: Pavilion.

Gerner, Stefan. 1998. "Retrovision: Die rückblickende Erfindung der Nationen durch die Kunst." In *Mythen der Nationen: Ein europäisches Panorama,* edited by Monika Flacke, 33–52. Munich and Berlin: Koehler and Amelang.

Habermas, Jürgen. 1991. *Texte und Kontexte.* Frankfurt am Main: Suhrkamp.

Herder, Johann Gottfried. 1769. *Kritische Wälder, oder Betrachtungen über die Wissenschaft und Kunst des Schönen.* Vols. 1–3. Riga: Johann Hartknoch.

———. 1773. *Von deutscher Art und Kunst: Einige fliegende Blätter.* Hamburg: Bode.

———. 1778/1779. *"Stimmen der Völker in Liedern"* and *Volkslieder.* 2 vols. Leipzig: Weygandsche Buchhandlung.

Herzfeld, Michael. 1991. *A Place in History: Social and Monumental Time in a Cretan Town.* Princeton, N.J.: Princeton University Press.

Hindrichs, Thorsten. 2007. "Chasing the 'Magic Formula' for Success: Ralph Siegel and the Grand Prix Eurovision de la Chanson." In Raykoff and Tobin, *A Song for Europe,* 49–59.

Hölderlin, Friedrich. 1999. *Die Gedichte: Sämtliche Gedichte und Hyperion.* Edited by Jochen Schmidt. Frankfurt am Main: Insel Verlag.

Kant, Immanuel. 1968. *Kritik der Urteilskraft.* Complete works: 10. Frankfurt am Main: Suhrkamp.

Kennedy O'Connor, John. 2005. *The Eurovision Song Contest, 50 Years: The Official History.* London: Carlton Books.

Koshar, Rudy. 1998. *Germany's Transient Pasts: Preservation and National Memory in the Twentieth Century.* Chapel Hill: University of North Carolina Press.

Lemish, Dafna. 2007. "Gay Brotherhood: Israeli Gay Men and the Eurovision Song Contest." In *A Song for Europe,* edited by Raykoff and Tobin, 123–34.

Macpherson, James, ed. 1760. *Fragments of Ancient Poetry, Collected in the Highlands of Scotland and Translated from the Galic or Erse Language.* 1st and 2nd printings. Edinburgh: G. Hamilton and J. Balfor.

Maurey, Yossi. 2009. "Dana International and the Politics of Nostalgia." *Popular Music* 28(1): 85–103.

Middleton, Richard. 2006. *Voicing the Popular: On the Subjects of Popular Music.* New York: Routledge.

Moore, Tim. 2006. *Nul Points*. London: Jonathan Cape.

"Norway Voted Eurovision Winners." 2009. *BBC News* (online), May 17. Accessed May 17, 2009. http://news.bbc.co.uk/2/hi/entertainment/8052636.stm.

Novalis [Friedrich von Hardenberg]. 1984. *Fragmente und Studien, Die Christenheit oder Europa*. Stuttgart: Reclam.

Osborn, Michael. 2009a. "Lloyd Webber: Eurovision Saviour?." *BBC News* (online), February 3. Accessed February 3. http://news.bbc.uk/2/hi/entertainment/7864830.stm.

———. 2009b. "Battle of the Eurovision Ballads." *BBC News* (online), May 12. Accessed May 17, 2009. http://news.bbc.co.uk/2/hi/entertainment/8002018.stm.

Raykoff, Ivan, and Robert Deam Tobin, eds. 2007. *A Song for Europe: Popular Music and Politics in the Eurovision Song Contest*. Aldershot: Ashgate. (Ashgate Popular and Folk Music Series)

Rehding, Alexander. 2009. *Music and Monumentality: Commemoration and Wonderment in Nineteenth-Century Germany*. New York: Oxford University Press.

Ricoeur, Paul. 1992. *Oneself as Another*. Trans. by Kathleen Blamey. Chicago: University of Chicago Press.

Schlegel, Carl Wilhelm Friedrich von. 1956. *Kritische Schriften*. Ed. by Wolfdietrich Rasch. Munich: C. Hanser.

Schleiermacher, F. D. E. 1842. *Vorlesungen über die Ästhetik*. Berlin: Reimer.

Scott, James C. 1990. *Domination and the Arts of Resistance: Hidden Transcripts*. New Haven, Conn.: Yale University Press.

Solomon, Thomas. 2007. "Articulating the Historical Moment: Turkey, Europe, and Eurovision 2003." In *A Song for Europe*, edited by Raykoff and Tobin, 135–45.

Turner, Victor W. 1969. *The Ritual Process: Structure and Anti-Structure*. Chicago: Aldine.

Wolther, Irving. 2006. *'Kampf der Kulturen'—der Eurovision Song Contest als Mittel national-kultureller Repräsentation*. Würzburg: Königshausen und Neumann.

WEBSITES CITED

http://www.escnation.com/ (accessed May 2009).
http://www.allkindsofeverything.ie/ (accessed May 2009).
http://www.kolumbus.fi/jarpen/ (accessed May 2009).
http://www.youtube.com/watch?v=jzYzVMcgWhg (accessed May 2009).

Chapter 2

Eurovision Everywhere
A Kaleidoscopic Vision of the Grand Prix

ANDREA F. BOHLMAN
AND IOANNIS POLYCHRONAKIS

A colorful minimalist sketch, displayed as if refracted through a kaleidoscope, advertised the 2007 Eurovision Song Contest on buses and billboards in Helsinki, official and unofficial websites, and on commercially available DVD booklets.[1] This pink, yellow, blue, and green prismatic design captured several elements that the Finnish production developers envisioned for the contest. The clean, repetitive pattern against a white background echoed Scandinavian design aesthetics as well as the expansive winter landscapes of the north. Capturing the projection of a kaleidoscope, the designers framed the dynamic journey that the Helsinki production hoped the spectacle would present: the transformation of "true into fantasy." Traditionally, the contest's annual "local art theme" serves to visually represent the slogan in addition to presenting the national host through abstraction.[2] The Finnish catchphrase, "True Fantasy," described the victory of the death-metal, arockalypse-heralding band Lordi. The brightly colored palette of the design captured Finnish exhilaration upon their first Eurovision victory.[3] Its designers explained that the kaleidoscopic stylization of the theme aspired to "take Eurovision everywhere in Helsinki."[4]

LOOKING THROUGH THE KALEIDOSCOPE

Helsinki's kaleidoscope suggests a useful metaphor for understanding the annual production of the Eurovision Song Contest. Turning a kaleidoscope catalyzes change through a simple movement. Looking through the kaleidoscope, simple elements combine to create an intricate artistic

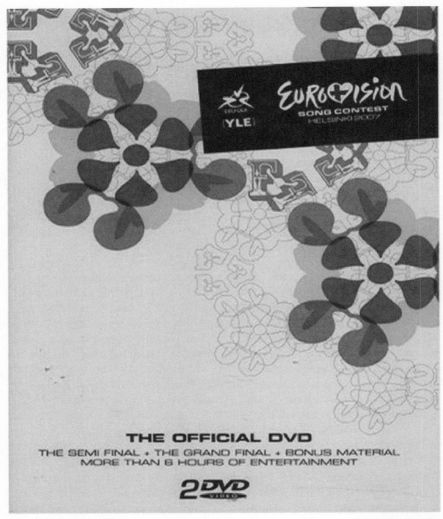

Figure 2.1. The Kaleidoscopic pattern of the 2007 Eurovision art theme, created by local company Dog Design, as it appeared on the official DVD. Reproduced with permision from the European Broadcasting Union.

balance, one that the subjective viewer can imagine to represent infinite worlds. The images conjured by this device are primarily colorful.[5] It refracts light around and through discrete particles, each with a pigment and shape that, one initially believes, boldly distinguish it from the whole of which it is a part. With each turn, the viewer follows individual particles as they tumble and travel. But, they also observes the "slide show" of kaleidoscopic images constructed through the shifting relations of particles. Over time, the differences between particles emerge as a continuity in construction, though difference and transformative potential never disappear. Through repeated refraction, disjuncture becomes continuity in the kaleidoscope—but the "spectrum" never coalesces—so the potential for change remains forever infinite. How is Eurovision cast through a metaphorical kaleidoscope? The instrument evokes the polymorphous and multilayered meaning of Eurovision as an annual phenomenon. The event's spectacle, too, performs the kaleidoscope's colors and wonders anew with each iteration. As every year lapses, renewed refractions through a rotating kaleidoscope reframe the competition's customs and trends. Eurovision acquires meaning again and again through novel perceptions.

But Eurovision's places also refract the competition kaleidoscopically. For Eurovision's Europe is a complex nexus of existing and imagined places, real and virtual platforms. The intersections of these geographies shift with the annual relocation of the contest's urban host and the constant renewal of musicians and producers. As these elements anchor the televised performances, Eurovision's yearly destination, the Eurocity, assembles European spectators, mass-mediated musics, and live voices at an intersection where identities are invested and interests are contested. This multimedia and multimodal function of the competition refracts transformative musical moments kaleidoscopically across Europe. The interplay between the live festival and the televised event represents one more way in which the contest resists the apparent binary opposition between local host and international broadcast or representative voice and singing nation.[6]

Situating the song contest at home in the Eurocity, the Internet, the press, and European television networks, we explore a kaleidoscopic array of meanings for the competition in this article. In considering the synchronic and diachronic geographies of the contest, we destabilize the broadcast event as a stable and bounded production, arguing for the critical contributions of Eurovision as live experience. We ground our theoretical reflections on Eurovision "everywhere," to follow the lead of the Finnish designers, in the local marketing hub of the European Broadcasting Union, the Eurocity, and the dispersed media networks of the press and Web-based fan culture. At the same time, three ethnographic moments—three rotations of the kaleidoscope—refract fieldwork at the 2008 contest in Belgrade, capturing the vital culture of Eurovision in its streets, Eurocity, and arena.

The present article is a product of collaborative fieldwork over the week leading up to the 2008 ESC in Belgrade, Serbia, the culmination of our shared Eurovision experiences from 2005 onward. As fieldworkers,

we traveled from Cambridge, United States, and Oxford, United Kingdom, respectively, to the Serbian capital, where we experienced an ethnographic snapshot of the competition. In this city, we met to experience
the competition together and on site. Sharing the 2008 competition with
each other, as well as numerous Eurovision scholars, many of whom are
contributors to this volume, proved tremendously personal, memorable,
and provocative—even multicolored. For although this was the first time
we had parallel involvement in the dress rehearsals, streets of the city,
and conversations with fans, it was hardly the first consonant competition
for our relationship as friends/fans and colleagues/scholars. Since 2006,
when we were both students at Royal Holloway, University of London,
Eurovision has brought us together through a flurry of e-mails analyzing songs, phone calls critiquing various acts' odds, and parties to screen
preview videos. In short, our collaborative fieldwork extends beyond the
singular competition that we both attended: it defines our relationship
to the competition. It is fieldwork that fundamentally challenges the perception of the competition as a fixed, consistent spectacle. It refracts *our*
visions of Eurovision, whether watched from a dank student accommodation basement in Egham, Surrey; in a crowded London pub with loyal
Eurovision fans; from the seats of OGAE Greece (the Greek branch of a
huge international fan club, the *Organisation Générale des Amateurs de l' Eurovision*, or simply OGAE) live at the event in Moscow; projected onto the
wall at a viewing party in Cambridge, Massachusetts; or huddled around
a television in Helsinki's press center. The live and mediated versions of
the competition do not merely coexist; they also supplement and exert influence upon each other. The very nature of the competition enables and
depends on the relationship between live and mediated, community and
home. Who is at home with Eurovision? Let's look at Belgrade.

ROTATING THE KALEIDOSCOPE I: "BELGRADE CALLING!"

Eurovision's ardent fans and harsh critics define the public discourse
around the competition. In fact, sometimes distinguishing between the
two constituencies presents quite a challenge. In Belgrade, we befriended
two university students thrilled to generously host us, fascinated by our
interest in their country, and excited about the recent Serbian ESC entries:
2007 winner Marija Šerifović and 2008 selection Jelena Tomašević. Many
claimed to be occasional followers of the competition, but they emphasized that this year it was important to watch, since they were hosts. Nevertheless, our own fervent, colorful critique of the competition—which
ranged from laughing at lack of resonance of the 2008 Greek entrant's
high-pitched voice ("Sounds like she just inhaled helium!") to excite-

ment over Denmark's charm ("Yes, the song clicks and he is cute. No, he will not win.")—contrasted with our friends'. They provided a rather measured response to the music of the night, particularly in the sociopolitical context through which we discussed the competition twenty-four hours after its conclusion, sitting at a quiet restaurant on the Danube and humming Euro-tunes. As Eurovision fans and scholars—in this moment a boundary between these identities could not exist—we remained more "at home" in the song contest's culture than our hosts.

We asked one Serbian friend, an artist, to respond to a queer reading of Marija Šerifović's opening act, in which she staged her own wedding to a female back-up dancer, complete with celebratory bouquet toss and white gown. Our friend quickly disregarded such significations and explained the singer's gestures within a critique of Šerifović's anti-EU politics, which she saw as a trace of anticosmopolitanism.[7] In other words, she ignored Šerifović's on-stage narrative in order to focus our attention upon what Šerifović's dismissal of the economic possibility joining the European Union would bring the nation. Reading Šerifović's performance of gender, our friend was reminded of the "traditionally clumsy and inelegant behavior" that she claimed "rural"—that is, noncosmopolitan—Serbian women usually have.[8] The young Serbian student was so committed to a pro-European discourse in the weeks following the early May national elections that her central critical lens could not be that of the long history of gender politics within Eurovision.[9] Another Serbian friend who had hosted a tour of Belgrade for us earlier that day told us that she felt totally unimpressed at the victorious and elaborate 2008 Russian act, fronted by heartthrob Dima Bilan. Whether or not our skeptical friends represent the local Serbian perspective, their disinterest in the celebrated music of that year's competition provided a notable counterpoint to the roaring fans in the arena, as we shall show. A Eurovision ethnography attuned to a broad range of local reactions would possibly confirm what we sensed as a variously ambivalent response to the 2008 Eurovision spectacle amongst our informants, local Serbian students.

The nature of our ethnographic engagement in the Eurovision Song Contest responds to the changing profile of this televised competition in the twenty-first century. Indeed, new, broader conceptions of the very location of the "field" parallel the expansion of Eurovision enabled by new media technologies.[10] For ethnographers, fieldwork can occur "everywhere," at home, abroad, or on the Internet. Likewise, the live webcasts of the song competition, online communities, and precirculation of national selections and preselections extend the music and spectacle of Eurovision by complementing the prereleased albums, televised broadcasts, and press tours by national entries that have long built up the single-week extravaganza. As scholars, our ethnographic engagement in the event follows the many modalities of the Eurovision Song Contest. We have studied it on site, on television, and through virtual spectatorship and social networking, reveling in the kaleidoscopic display of the competition's ontologies that results from the inherent contradictions and continuities in such a long-term engagement.

FOCUSING ON THE EUROCITY

Eurovision takes place in the space marketed to its fans as the "Eurocity." Each year the Eurocity manifests itself differently in the host city: there might be on-street vendors in the city's commercial district, outdoor performances in urban parks, discounts to draw tourists to museums, and more. Examining its spaces begs the question: what makes a Eurovision host city? Here we put the term—Eurocity—on the map as one of the central places from which the competition's identity emerges. Its name suggests its definition: the portable commercial and media world that acts as a "city." Traditional discourse on urban spaces outlines cities as bursting with novelty, foreign influences, and, pejoratively, corruption.[11] More recent scholarship, however, has avoided such value judgments and interpreted urban spaces as crossroads for people with different backgrounds and mentalities, allowing hubs' shifting social divisions and instabilities to define a transmutable culture.[12] A cosmopolitan environment, the Eurocity is partially served by this definition: for only select fans return year after year and, as we have already suggested, local inhabitants have unpredictable and complex attitudes toward the competition.

The city's prefix, "Euro-" draws attention to its complex relationship to geography. Neither national nor European capital on a political level, this designation suggests the Eurovision Song Contest's host a kind of temporary cultural capital of Europe, and encompasses fleeting cultural and political attributes, which rise from the unpredictable relationships between the contest and its revolving door of hosting nations.[13] "Euro-" references *Euro*vision, branding the city in name as well as through posters, sounds, and merchandise on the streets of host cities. "Euro-" also recalls the geopolitical tensions that, while officially excluded in the contest's musical discourse, are undeniably a part of the spectacle's identity from its cold-war origins, as the counterpart to *Inter*vision contests.[14] "Eurocity," too, is a result of the increased branding of the competition, as already referenced in the ever-present marketing tool that was the Finnish kaleidoscopic design.

The location of the Eurocity changes each year. The "City"—a Eurovision arcade that most often fills the host city's tourist center—exists for the weeks leading up to the competition and then disappears. The "City" is filled with billboards that signify the competition's theme and colors. Temporary street vendors set up shop and cultural organizations stage small events. Eurovision stars past and present give concerts. In Belgrade's Eurocity, for example, posters advertising the 2004 winner from Ukraine, Ruslana, in concert were plastered on top of national election posters. In Kiev in 2005, banks, hotels, and the city council advertised with the contest's theme colors—electric blue and green—and the color of the recent revolution, orange. The contrasting ways in which Eurovision marked the municipal buildings of the two Eastern European capitals shows the delicate boundaries between the commercial gain promised to hosting cities and the temporary transmogrification of everyday spaces that the contest brings.

Eurocity is the contest's yearly destination, usually the capital city or a big city of the previous year's winning country that is granted the responsibility and honor of hosting the singing spectacle in the following year. Although the Eurocity is a fixed place, it exists only after travelers' arrival at the competition. Fans, musicians, and journalists constitute the city as much as souvenir shops, pedestrian zones, and fashion shows. People have crossed physical and metaphorical borders and boundaries to meet at the host city, where the organizers would have them celebrate in mosaic, *New European*, harmony. Figuratively, the journey to the Eurocity transcends the many physical localities that collect over the course of the annual changes of address. The congregation and, more importantly, the competition, broadly conceived, amongst people from across Eurovision's Europe create an atmosphere of friendly reciprocity and cajoling appropriation in which individuals trumpet their country's music and blast that of their new, Eurovision friends. Every year conversations at the fan clubs across Europe, the Euro-club, and in the arena routinely reveal difference and sameness, surprise and stereotype, singularity and multiplicity among Europeans vying for a win.[15] The distinct character of the "Eurocity" emerges through the dynamic relationship between two spaces: the venue of the competition, where music and flags are ever-present, and the temporary crowd attractions in public spaces of the city. While the arena fosters fan rivalry in a space devoted to producing and merchandising the contest, image—both local and that of the Eurovision franchise—is less easily controlled on city streets.

ROTATING THE KALEIDOSCOPE II: BELGRADE'S EUROCITY THROUGH THE LENS

Back on the banks of the Sava and Danube Rivers in Belgrade the contradicting stances toward Eurovision were more audible in official discourse than not. The Kosovo Independence Movement in February 2008 and Serbia's parliamentary elections in early May set the local political tone. One result of the tensions was that the singing extravaganza failed to keep the whole of the Eurocity spellbound. Serbs campaigning for membership in the European Union conceived of Eurovision as an opportunity for the country to take a major step toward a new economic market.[16] Others did not wish to relate to the event at all, considering it yet another foreign intrusion.

Despite such discrepancies on a local level, the official Serbian organizers promoted a fresh image of the country at the "confluence" of Europe's rivers. The stage literally mapped the intersection of the Sava and the Danube, recalling the Balkans' history as a cultural crossroads, even suggesting that Serbia might constitute a "New" Central Europe. The formal events during the contest revealed the effort invested in creating a positive image for the city. On Saturday, May 24, 2008, the night of the ESC Grand Final, during a live link to the happenings in front of the Belgrade City Hall, a local TV presenter proudly announced: "Tonight Belgrade is the capital of the world; the capital of joy and happiness. We are all hosts. We are all participants [. . .] Belgrade invited the whole of Europe to our party [. . .] [in] the city where being alone is simply not an option!"[17]

Later that evening the basketball superstar Vlade Divać spoke in a similarly triumphant tone before initiating the contest's voting procedure: "It's my pleasure to be here. Thank you, Belgrade. Thank you, Serbia. We are part of Europe. It's nice to see Europe in the same place." Traces of the Kosovo War lay barely beneath the surface of the public and ceremonial discourse. Sandra Šuša, the Serbian executive producer of the 2008 ESC, alluded more directly to this turmoil when speaking to international journalists during the official EBU press conference on May 21, 2008: "In spite of turbulent times . . . by hosting the ESC we . . . succeeded in presenting our country and people in the best possible way. . . . Thank you for all your professional and wonderful coverage during those ESC days. Your support is of immeasurable value to Radio Television Serbia (RTS), Belgrade, and Serbia, . . . for giving Serbia the opportunity to shine."[18]

Euro-fans were constantly reminded of the violent action taken against Serbia by NATO in the 1990s, as bombed governmental buildings remained looming over McDonald's in the capital. The city's reality added new layers to Serbia's self-representation. The 2008 entry, "Oro," became more than a traditional Serbian dance, a sorrowful love song and a standard Balkan Eurovision ballad. It was a musically concealed farewell to Kosovo, to be presented and applauded on the international stage of Eurovision.[19] Against the blue, red, and white bands of light on the stage, the singers sang on the banks of the same rivers upon which the city is perched.

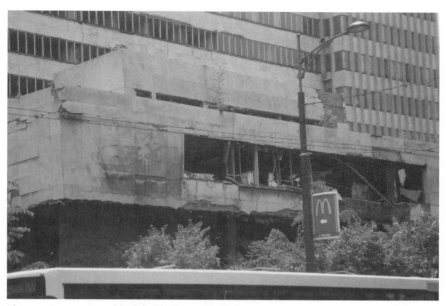

Figure 2.2.   McDonald's label in front of a building bombarded by NATO in the 1990s, as it appeared in central Belgrade in 2008. Photograph courtesy of Alexandros Liapis, vice-president of OGAE Greece (2011–2012) and secretary to the Administrative Board of OGAE International (2011–2013).

"HELLO, EUROPE!":
PROJECTING EUROVISION KALEIDOSCOPICALLY

Media structure Eurovision and are instrumental to its performances. Media make possible the many modes of Eurovision experience explored in this chapter. Organized by the European Broadcasting Union, this televised competition has, from its very beginnings, relied on media technology for the escalation of its spectacle. The collaboration between each year's hosting country and the EBU's production team creates a unified event out of diverse musical acts. The spectacle relies on tropes to establish continuities from one year to the next. For example, recently the presenters have expressed their gratitude for "a fantastic show" to last year's host in the latter's native language.

The presenters of the event host Eurovision's live broadcast, welcoming the television and live audiences to the competition and its annual location. The emcees' refrain, "Hello Europe!", promulgates television's ability to assert an imagined Europe, effectively shared amongst all participants and viewers across existing geographical, political, and cultural borders. Other aspects of the production, from images of national flags,

which cue the acts for audience members, to the intensely calculated cam-
erawork by the production team, contribute to the televised intimacy of
the event connecting viewers across Europe. During the lengthy parade of
singing nations, camera crews' concerted action captures dynamic dance
moves panoramically or emotional close-ups at the climax of ballads. The
short visual clips that introduce each act, known as "postcards," often
connect a local tradition either from the host nation or from the nation
of the upcoming act to the larger artistic vision and motto of that year's
contest.

Since 2000, the EBU has reserved reasonably priced tickets for members
of official Eurovision fan clubs in the first rows. Their spirited flag waving
renders the live transmission of the show all the more colorful and vibrant.
And since 1998, when the excitement of live audiences started getting
ever more visible on camera, fans' reactions in the arena have become an
integral part of the annual event's TV production. National broadcasters
contribute to Europe's televised diversity with their own commentators
and national announcers' delivery of voting results, refracting the musical
evening even further with their own production concepts.[20] At the BBC,
for instance, Sir Terry Wogan's wry commentary was inextricable from
the British perception of Eurovision during his tenure (1971–2008).

Eurovision's mediation extends beyond the camera's projection of a
live act from the main stage to Europe's living rooms. News and recording media facilitate the build-up to the competition and extend its life
for weeks after it has happened. That is to say, newspapers, television
programs, and radio broadcasts relate the drama of the national selection
processes and offer fans an opportunity to hear songs and get to know
contestants.[21] After the competition, the same television programs that
interviewed national acts in the precontest hype host the new celebrity of
the contest, contributing to the celebration of their victory. Record companies release and circulate the hit single across Europe.

Over the last ten years, the Internet has increasingly given rise to multimodal experiences of the competition. Fans download and discuss mp3
files of upcoming Eurovision entries in anticipation of the competition,
imagining staged choreography and predicting the success and failure
of individual entrants. The global character of video-sharing websites,
such as YouTube, increases the emphasis on the audiovisually mediated
engagement in Eurovision performances, while simultaneously extend-
ing the potential to invite viewers to the competition from around the
world.[22] Along these same lines, the live competition is no longer merely
broadcast across the EBU countries; the webcast is *live* everywhere.

Digital technologies from the CD to the Internet transform the locations
of fan discourse, complementing local or national fan clubs, as well as
engaging with the reactions of casual observers. Online fan communities

continue to trade in musical material, analyze the makeup of Eurovision songs, and predict the year's winners and losers.[23] Eurovision-devoted blogs zealously, and sometimes even obsessively, detail the competition's history, showing off their memorabilia collections and in-depth knowledge of Eurovision trivia and gossip.[24] Though the Internet has irreversibly extended the channels through which the Eurovision Song Contest is mediated, this increased presence of virtual communication is not disconnected from the live experience of the competition. On the contrary, friends and family gather to watch the webcasts together, especially in those parts of the world where the EBU's television signal cannot be received. For example, Andrea Bohlman viewed the 2009 Moscow competition at a party in Massachusetts, while Ioannis Polychronakis traveled to the Russian Eurocity and attended as a member of the press, as discussed below. At the same time, blogging fans from across the globe meet at the Euro-club every year, screaming and singing with glee along with classic Eurovision songs, while online clubs buy tickets in bulk and meet with each other in Eurovision costume at the performance venue.[25]

ROTATING THE KALEIDOSCOPE III:
LIVING THE COMPETITION

Standing inside the Beogradska Arena, the crowd awaited the trumpet refrain, Charpentier's *Te Deum,* which signals the beginning of every year's competition. We were among them, enveloped in the electric atmosphere of anticipation. The fanfare announced that the competition was on-air, and the spectacle of Eurovision 2008 unfolded in real time. The trumpets heralded this beginning for Europe, but even for those of us witnessing the contest's crescendo in Belgrade, it marked a ritual transition from anticipation to realization. Eurovision fans in Belgrade witnessed live performances of this year's contestants on the streets of Belgrade's old city and in the dress rehearsals within the New Belgrade's basketball stadium. From the previous evening's dress rehearsal to the 2008 Final, the crowd was transformed. The local audience that had filled the seats to cheer on the Serbian intermission acts, the Balkan entries, and the reigning champion's performance was replaced by a sea of Eurovision aficionados and novices from across Europe. Fans in costume supporting Sweden's Charlotte Perelli sat clad in yellow and blue to watch their twenty-fifth competition, while a nearby couple clung to the free flags dispensed in the concourse of the arena, braced for their first live Eurovision.

As soon as the televised broadcast started, the constant sea of flags across the floor of the stadium acquired an incredible momentum. This was projected back to stage and onto the diverse national acts, effectively turning Eurovision's "electric circuit" on. Simultaneously, flag wavers constantly vied for the camera's attention and the eyes of Europe on the other side of the lens. Through TV cameras Eurovision's "electric power" was subsequently relayed outside of the arena, where fans celebrated the realization of Eurovision in clubs and at parties in the privacy of their own home. In Belgrade, too, the anticipation climaxed as the Charpentier jingle cadenced, giving way to an instrumental arrangement of the chorus from Marija Šerifović's 2007 winning entry, "Molitva," which introduced the 2008 Eurovision sub-logo. As the melody soared out of an amplified violin and a synthesizer added pulsating chords, abstracted rivers in the form of two streams of red and blue paint crashed into one another to create a treble clef and announce the theme, "Confluence of Sound."

Moments later, in an intensely hushed moment, the production team had dimmed all but one intense spotlight. It was the final caesura before the first music on the stage of the arena. From our seats stage right, we followed the beacon's trajectory to the solitary figure hunched at the front of the stage. This time, no fanfare cued the Eurovision queen to plead into her microphone. Just as she stood alone at the front of the stage, her voice traveled alone into the hall. Marija Šerifović sang the refrain of her winning song, "Molitva." Huddled at the front of the stage, she piously held her microphone only briefly between her hands, before turning outward. Her voice was confident. Alone, she called out, repeatedly, her prayer.

The live experience of Eurovision cuts across television monitors, the stage, the arena, the press center, Europe's living rooms, and transpires before the eyes of the viewer everywhere. Thus, the present analysis departs from descriptions that draw upon the video footage now available on DVD and moves beyond them, in an attempt to capture our own enlivening of the Eurovision and our postevent reflections on the ESC press center.[26] The heavy-handed approach to journalists in ex-communist political systems, like that in the former Yugoslavia, had given way to the dexterous manipulation of fan-journalists in postmodern Serbia's Eurovision Press Centre.[27] But this was by no means a Serbian-specific characteristic of our Eurovision experience. The expansion of the contest since 2000 entailed a growing number of accredited journalists covering Eurovision. Fans that actually *were* journalists or managed to get a last-minute professional affiliation with a local newspaper or radio station rushed to take advantage of the many press passes on offer. The EBU needed all these fan-journalists to promote the contest, ideally in a way that would comply with its carefully constructed profile as prime-time "pure" entertainment. Significant effort was extended to maintain this policy at all Eurovision press conferences and, therefore, any questions about the political aspects of the contest or the infamous "bloc voting" were adroitly deflected. For example, at the press conference following Dima Bilan's victory in Belgrade on Sunday, May 25, 2008, Ioannis Polychronakis was prevented from further asking the winner to give more details on his experience of politics at the ESC.[28]

SCRAMBLING EUROVISION'S POLITICS? THE RUSSIAN EUROVISION

The 2009 Eurovision was held in a country still in postsocialist transition amidst a cataclysmic global financial crisis. As a result, the always-fraught identity politics of the competition were larger than life in Moscow. In the wake of the conflict with Georgia in August 2008, Russia's Soviet past continued to dictate European attitudes toward the former superpower. Ioannis Polychronaki's informants in the Eurocity observed contemporary Russian domination in the country's 2008 successes at the European Football Championship and, of course, Eurovision itself.[29] As travelers to the Russian capital in 2009 they experienced both the contest's festivities and the distance local citizens seemed to keep from them, interpreting this as a remnant of "socialist behavior." In on-site discussions about their experience of the Moscow Eurovision, fans narrated Russia's recent history the way they witnessed and perceived it there and then, emphasizing that the formerly-called "Mother Russia" still seemed to be suffering from what she had initiated herself, "the socialism that actually existed," as one fan put it. However, along with the outright clash with Georgia and the tensions with Ukraine over the gas supply in early 2009, many fans were convinced about the "reawakening of the Russian bear."

It was against the canvas of such emotional and political preconceptions that visitors evaluated the Moscow Contest and the Russian capital's Eurocity. Within crowds of Euro-fans one could hear effusive comments with nationalist foundations, alternately articulated as positive and negative value judgments: "Russia is the best country!", "The Moscow Euro-Club is disastrous! They hardly play any Eurovision music there," "They have organized the best Eurovision ever!", "The Russians are simply showing off before the media, but they haven't even built a decent Press Center!". The debate over the organization of the Moscow Eurovision never ceased.

Each rotation of a kaleidoscope allows a new perspective on the same colors. Likewise, elements of the Eurovision experience remain, albeit in new shapes and forms, every year. For fervent ESC fans, usually members of the OGAE or other Eurovision-related fan groups,[30] a roster of criteria for evaluating the Eurovision spectacle represent the core values of the competition. One such controversial criterion is the political discourse surrounding the contest, addressed so frequently in ESC scholarship. Fans usually interpret geopolitics and the so-called "bloc voting," as threats to the uncontested rapture presented on stage. In preparation for Moscow, the war between Russia and Georgia in August 2008 jangled the nerves of ESC aficionados, since the Baltic States had initially considered boycotting the 2009 Eurovision in support of Georgia's cause in August 2008.[31] A few months later, politics were boiled down to a dispute over the lyrics of the Georgian entry, inevitably resulting in its withdrawal. The EBU considered their entry, "We Don't Wanna Put In," an attack on the Russian prime minister Vladimir Putin.[32] The governing organization asserted the song was overtly political and therefore violated "the no-political-references rule."[33] Georgia's subsequent withdrawal sidestepped the organization's official request for rewritten lyrics or threat of disqualification.

On the other hand Russia's 2009 entry, while compliant with the EBU regulations, emerged as controversial and political through layers of interpretation by fans, journalists, and TV viewers across Eurovision's Europe. Having lost the Ukrainian National Final, singer Anastasia Prikhodko received a last-minute invitation to the Russian selection process with the same song, eventually winning and flying the Russian flag to Eurovision amidst allegations about rigged voting in both the Ukrainian and Russian national finals. At the Moscow Eurovision Prikhodko sang "Mamo" in Russian and Ukrainian, narrating the story of a daughter who sorrowfully regretted to have ignored her mother's admonitions, as she fell into the trap of a man who eventually betrayed her love.[34]

Television audiences in the United States and journalists at the arena in Moscow interpreted the pleading evocation of the mother, "Mamo," as a call to Mother Russia, rejecting the possibility of hearing this story as an unproblematic collaboration of Russo-Ukrainian voices.[35] Such a reading of the performance was supported by a poignant video projection of the singer's face that was technically aged through digital manipulation, reminding one of socialist-realist artwork that now flashed upon the Eurovision stage. On a prominent Russian blog, *Siberian Light*, journalist Andy Young predicted that this year's host entry would "delight conspiracy theorists and bloggers everywhere."[36] Another journalist, Tony Halpin, criticized Russia's entry more directly and in the context of its national politics: "[Prikhodko's] victory came weeks after the "gas war" between Russia and Ukraine, when Moscow turned off supplies to its former Soviet neighbor in a payment dispute. If organizers of the contest hoped that it would send a message of fraternal love between the two Slavic states, they were mistaken."[37]

Eurovision fans, a great many of whom are gay, were well aware of the political connotations regarding the National Finals in Ukraine and Russia. However, they seemed to consider politics completely separate from their judgment of the Russian entry, since they felt astounded by song's imposing stage presentation. The gradually aging face of the "singer/ daughter" that was projected onstage was frequently perceived as an allusion to "motherly" wisdom, gained at the cost of lost youth. Queer fan readings, however, framed this staged "realization" in terms of the coming-out process.

Just as on the banks of the Danube our local hosts' political readings of Šerifović had contradicted gendered interpretations of her opening act, various interpretations amongst Eurovision viewers in Moscow were at odds with each other. Each year millions of viewers tune in to the fast-paced juxtaposition of three-minute musical acts, and each of their opinions potentially accrues different meaning to the contest. The constellation of interpretations is fundamental to the panoramic spectacle that the Eurovision entails.

LOOKING AHEAD

Philip V. Bohlman claims that Eurovision's winners capture their historical moment when they capture Europe's attention.[38] In 2009, amidst the greatest global financial crisis in eighty years, a young man appeared on Moscow's Eurovision stage and sang about a love story. Facing the fans in the arena and looking straight into the camera's close-up, Alexander Rybak managed to connect so convincingly with his audiences that he seemed to be intimately speaking to everyone watching. His musical "Fairytale" offered an exuberant escape from the financial crisis by trading on intimacy, as his heartfelt story and enchanting performance kept people spellbound and lightened up their frustrations. The television broadcast's sweeping perspective from the balcony of the hall brought its audiences closer to the world of his music and charisma as it zoomed upon his face. The music of a solo violin punctuated the crowd's cheers on TV with a fiddling tune that used droning double-stops and abrupt triple-stops to create a beat for this one-man "simple" and effective intro. The rustic dance in common time had the crowd clapping along before the drum set and guitar began their folksy accompaniment. Rybak drew us into the web of his love story, his winking and grinning charming us into his world. Watching and hearing the winning entry, it was easy to get carried away from the pressure of financial unpredictability and move into an imagined reality, as simple and comfortable as Alexander's sung story.

Rybak spread his arms out and proclaimed, "I'm in love with a fairy tale," and many fans imagined themselves to be on stage with him, wherever they watched the competition. Literally reaching out to all people who voted for his glorious victory and beyond, Rybak captured his historical moment, when Eurovision seemed to be everywhere.[39]

NOTES

1. See, for example, a report on the graphic designers' rationale for this particular local art theme for the Helsinki Eurovision: Klier, Markus. 2006. "The Idea of a Kaleidoscope; True Fantasy: What We Can Expect," November 28. Accessed September 25, 2009. http://escfans.esctoday.com/news/read/6852. See also the graphic designers' website: Dog Design, "Eurovision Song Contest 2007." Accessed October 23, 2011. http://www.dogdesign.fi/ilmeet/ilmeet_1.swf.

2. Previously, each contest had a newly designed logo. In 2004 the European Broadcasting Union revealed a generic logo for the Eurovision Song Contest to be accompanied by a local logo capturing the specific theme of each running of the contest. See "ESC Brand Guidelines," *Eurovision Song Contest Media Handbook* 2009, 15. Accessed September 24, 2009. http://www.eurovision.tv/upload/brand/ESC_GUIDELINES_FIN08.pdf.

3. For a discussion of the significance of Finland's Eurovision failure and success see Pajala 2007.

4. http://www.viisukuppila.fi/euroviisut/eurovision-song-contest/true-fantasy-more-details.html. Accessed September 24, 2009. See Mills, Keith. 2007. "Eurovision 2007 Branding." Accessed October 21, 2011. http://www.keithm.utvinternet.ie/Helsinki2007commercial.htm; Nyman, Pirkko. 2007. "Helsinki Prepares for the Biggest Ever Eurovision Song Contest," *The Newsletter of the Tourist and Convention Bureau*, Winter–Spring, 1–2. Accessed October 21, 2011. http://www.visithelsinki.fi/loader.aspx?id=ee603670-e9e2-4ff8-8e34-6dac30827385.

5. The *Oxford English Dictionary* also emphasizes the significance of change and color for the kaleidoscope in its two-part definition: "a. 'An optical instrument, consisting of from two to four reflecting surfaces placed in a tube, at one end of which is a small compartment containing pieces of coloured glass: on looking through the tube, numerous reflections of these are seen, producing brightly-coloured symmetrical figures, which may be constantly altered by rotation of the instrument'. b. 'A constantly changing group of bright colours or coloured objects; anything which exhibits a succession of shifting phases.'" In *Oxford English Dictionary*, second edition, 1989; online version March 2012. Accessed May 10, 2012. http://www.oed.com/view/Entry/102387.

6. For further discussion of the fraught relationship between pan-European success and national goals, see the article by Andrea Bohlman and Alexander Rehding in this volume.

7. Her analysis was echoed in the Serbian press: "Early [in 2008] Šerifović backed the presidential campaign of Tomislav Nikolić, the candidate of the far-

Eurovision Everywhere: A Kaleidoscopic Vision of the Grand Prix   73

right Serbian Radical Party. The Radicals advocate freezing the process of closer integration with the EU, if it means giving up Kosovo, and party leader Vojislav Seselj is on trial before The Hague war crimes tribunal." (Jovanović, Igor. 2008. "Serbia: Save the Last Dance for Us." *Transitions Online*, May 30. Accessed June 27, 2011. http://groups.yahoo.com/group/decani2/message/34690).

8. A number of prejudices may have lurked behind this statement, for example, the assumption that Serbians campaigning against the European Union are less cosmopolitan or a subliminal response to Šerifović's Romani heritage. The characterizations "clumsy" and "inelegant" signaled a pressure point in our conversation and blocked further analysis of Šerifović's performance.

9. A gay Belgian couple traveling to the competition for the first time, for example, wasted no time in analyzing Šerifović as the most recent in a series of gay icons with celebrated performances at the competition. The opportunity for performers to challenge gender norms on the Eurovision stage as well as the significance of the competition for gay communities in Europe has attracted significant scholarly attention. See Lemish 2004; Feddersen 2002; Raykoff 2007; Heller 2007; Lemish 2007; [AQ2] also the special issue dedicated to Eurovision of the *SQS: Journal of Queer Studies in Finland*, 2007.

10. The revisions to two standard handbooks for ethnomusicologists in the field increasingly emphasize the ethnographic potential at home and the richness of music-making online and musical communities in cyberspace. See Nettl 2008, 184–96; Barz and Cooley 2008, 189–204; Wood 2008.

11. Risto Pekka Pennanen critically refers to such discourse surrounding urban culture in the context of scrutinizing popular music perceptions in Greece in the first half of the twentieth century (see Pennanen 1999, 11).

12. See, for example, Tragaki 2007, 148–55.

13. The Eurocity is, of course, not to be confused with the designation of the "European Capital of Culture," initiated and enacted by the European Union.

14. In the twenty-first century, Eurovision has critically provided a space for the negotiation of the "New Europe" through music. Through performance, countries geographically outside of Europe, such as Israel and Armenia or Azerbaijan, negotiate their relationship to it. Postsocialist transition influences Eastern European discourse on the Eurovision stage (see Bohlman 2004, 7; 16–21, 332–47).

15. The Euro-club is the party venue, where all fans, journalists, and Eurovision entrants gather every night and dance to Eurovision music.

16. See also: Divine, Peter. 2008. "There Are Only Positives at Belgrade's Eurovision Song Contest!" *Manchester Evening News*, June 19. Accessed September 25, 2009. http://blogs.manchestereveningnews.co.uk/eurovision/2008/06/there_are_only_positives_at_be.html.

17. Transcribed verbatim from the EBU's official DVD of the *Eurovision Song Contest 2008; The Official DVD* (EMI, CMC Entertainment A/S 2169979).

18. Transcribed verbatim from the official EBU press conference on May 21, 2008; see also "Eurovision Fever Hits Serbia Despite Political Turmoil," *Deutsche Welle Online*, May 20, 2008. Accessed September 25, 2009. http://www.dw-world.de/dw/article/0,,3346654,00.html.

19. Although the lyrics ("Don't rub salt on my wound, I have no more tears") recall a lover's goodbye, the later reference to Vidovdan, a religious holiday in

Serbia celebrating St. Vitus, alludes to the recent turmoil in Kosovo. The Serbian entry was received with standing ovation in the arena, whereas the performers on stage responded to this enthusiasm with a sober, modest, yet proud look on their faces. Both their emotional response and the reference to Vidovdan in the lyrics potentially indicate Serbian national sensibilities implicit in the 2008 home entry.

20. Announcers lend irony to this recitation, highlighting its significance for the competition's pageantry. For example, the 2008 Swedish announcer pretended to be drunk and jokingly allocated "douze points" to his home country, correcting it a moment later.

21. In recent years, National Finals are broadcast online across the globe and are followed by lengthy build-up info and after-show reviews on Eurovision-related fanzines. Any discrepancies, problems, or even lawsuits regarding the procedure of any National Final are widely discussed by fans online, the virtual Eurovision community. Russia's and Ukraine's National Finals in 2009 were particularly a case in point, since local politics and fierce antagonism were intensely debated.

22. In 2009 Eurovision had its own channel on YouTube, a profile on Facebook, and a Twitter account. YouTube promoted the competition on its homepage during the week leading up to the finals and even redesigned its logo to advertise the competition's Web presence.

23. *ESC Today* serves as the principal unofficial news site, organizing information about national selections, hosting fan forums and polls, and posting interviews (http://www.esctoday.com/). Other sites function more like fan communities (see http://schlagerblog.blogspot.com/; http://www.escnation.com/).

24. Fans invest in catalogs that capture the competition's global musical significance, such as multilingual covers of Eurovision entries, memorabilia, souvenirs, promotional materials, and the like; see for example http://eurocovers.blogspot .com/. Alternatively, fans may aim at making as much music digitally available as possible (see, e.g., http://www.eurovisionsongs.net/index.htm).

25. Eurovision costumes can be anything from simple feather boas to whole costumes in the colors of national flags, to memorable accessories of Eurovision entrants' dresses, such as the silver-coiled star Ukrainian Verka Serduchka famously wore as a hat at the 2007 Eurovision. Euro-fans imitate and/or reproduce such costumes and accessories, in order to experience the Eurovision's party atmosphere not only in a very vivid and tactile way, but most importantly to declare and perform in public their own perceptions and appropriations of Eurovision's polysemous and multilayered meanings.

26. Our notion of "enlivening" the Eurovision is based on Judith Okely's notion of fieldwork as a "total" experience, which is much more than "a cerebral exercise" and requires from music ethnographers to immerse into music cultures they study by activating all of their intellectual and emotional capacities, physical energy, and intuitive sense. See Okely 2008; also Tragaki 2007, 166. For elaboration upon the act of writing about fieldwork as a "meta-performance" that comes after the ethnographic experience, see Kisliuk 1997, 33.

27. The fact that the EBU's Svante Stockselius, executive supervisor of the Junior and Senior Eurovision Song Contest (from 2003 to 2010), and his assistants

kept addressing ESC journalists by saying "hey guys" was just one way to mitigate the effect of some very strictly demarcated lines between different professional roles in the press center and the consequent power relations between the
EBU and ESC journalists.

28. Ioannis Polychronakis was able to access the press center, participate
in press conferences as a journalist, and, concurrently, conduct fieldwork as a
doctoral researcher, due to his affiliation with the Greek newspaper *Cosmos tou
Ependytē*. Without this affiliation, he would have only been accredited as a fan and
he would have been unable to attend press conferences and ask questions. According to the EBU rules, doctoral students writing about Eurovision can only be
assigned fan accreditation. See the EBU's accreditation conditions 2011. Accessed
July 6, 2011. http://www.eurovision.tv/page/press/accreditation.

29. Both this paragraph and the next one summarize and selectively quote the
opinions Euro-fans shared with Ioannis Polychronakis in interviews and informal
discussions during his fieldwork at the Moscow Eurovision, May 2–17, 2009.

30. According to the official Eurovision website, "[OGAE] fan-clubs are not officially connected to the European Broadcasting Union and are private initiatives
by passionate Eurovision Song Contest fans." (Accessed August 24, 2009. http://
www.eurovision.tv/page/fan-zone/fanclubs.)

31. See for example: DELFI. 2008. "Lithuania. LRT Thinks about Withdrawing from Eurovision 2009." August 22. Accessed August 25, 2009. http://www
.oikotimes.com/v2/index.php?file=articles&id=3962; Floras, Stella. 2009. "Svante
to Estonia: Eurovision Is a Non Political Event," August 25. Accessed August 25,
2009. http://www.esctoday.com/news/read/12223.

32. Bakker, Sietse. 2009. "Georgian Song Lyrics Do Not Comply with Rules."
March 10. Accessed August 25, 2009. http://www.eurovision.tv/page/news
?id=1993.

33. "No lyrics, speeches, gestures of a political or similar nature shall be permitted during the ESC," Section 4, No. 9, *Rules for the Eurovision Song Contest 2009*,
p. 5.

34. "Out of the shadows once again, my enemy, my love / Inevitable is my destiny, no matter how much you're prepared / . . . / Mama, you've been telling me
not to desire / . . . / I will throw away my dream and crush it on the floor" (translation provided by a website dedicated to lyrics from all Eurovision songs, www
.diggiloo.net; Accessed August 25, 2009. http://www.diggiloo.net/?2009ru).

35. For more on Prikhodko's participation in both the Ukrainian and Russian
National Finals, as well as the controversy which her entries sparked, see Ma-
toshko, Alexandra. 2009. "Eurovision 2009 Ukrainian Finals." *Kyiv Post*, March 4.
Accessed August 25, 2009. http://www.kyivpost.com/guide/sevendays/music/
36732; see also, "Svetlana Loboda to Represent Ukraine at Eurovision 2009,"
Kyiv Post, March 8, 2009. Accessed August 25, 2009. http://www.kyivpost.com/
guide/guidenews/36980.

36. Young, Andy. 2009. "Russian Eurovision: Mamo Song Creates Controversy," March 10. Accessed August 24, 2009. http://www.siberianlight.net/
mamo-russian-eurovision/.

37. Halpin, Tony. 2009. "Eurovision Vote-Rigging Row as Ukrainian Wins Contest to Represent Russia." *The Times*, March 10. Accessed August 25, 2009. http://

entertainment.timesonline.co.uk/tol/arts_and_entertainment/music/article
5875152.ece.

38. Bohlman 2004, 9.

39. Rybak's victory was by all accounts a landslide: with sixteen countries allotting him "douze points," the majestic maximum, he received an unprecedented record number of points: 387 in total. This was not a surprise, though, for ESC audiences, fans, journalists, bookies, and betting agencies, who all considered him a "hot favorite" even prior to his official selection at the Norwegian National Finals.

REFERENCES

Barz, Gregory F., and Timothy J. Cooley, eds. 2008. *Shadows in the Field: New Perspectives for Fieldwork in Ethnomusicology*. 2nd ed. New York: Oxford University Press.

Bohlman, Philip V. 2004. *The Music of European Nationalism: Cultural Identity and Modern History*. Santa Barbara, Calif.: ABC-CLIO.

Eurovision Song Contest Media Handbook. 2009. Moscow: EBU.

Feddersen, Jan. 2002. *Ein Lied kann eine Brücke sein: Die deutsche und international Geschichte der Grand Prix Eurovision*. Hamburg: Hoffmann und Campe.

Heller, Dana. 2007. "'Russian Body and Soul.': t.A.T.u. performs in Eurovision 2003." In *A Song for Europe: Popular Music and Politics in the Eurovision Song Contest*, edited by Ivan Raykoff and Robert Deam Tobin, 111–21. Aldershot: Ashgate.

Kisliuk, Michelle. 1997. "(Un)doing Fieldwork: Sharing Songs, Sharing Lives." In *Shadows in the Field: New Perspectives for Fieldwork in Ethnomusicology*, 23–44. Oxford and New York: Oxford University Press.

———. 2007. "Gay Brotherhood: Israeli Gay Men and the Eurovision Song Contest." In A Song For Europe. Popular Music and Politics in the Eurovision Song Contest, edited by Ivan Raykoff and Robert D. Tobin, 123–34. Aldershot: Ashgate.

Lemish, Dafna. 2004. "My Kind of Campfire: The Eurovision Song Contest and Israeli Homosexuals." *Popular Communication* 2(1): 41–63.

Nettl, Bruno. 2008. *The Study of Ethnomusicology: Thirty-One Issues and Concepts*. 2nd ed. Urbana: University of Illinois Press.

Okely, Judith. 2008. "Knowing without Notes." In *Knowing How to Know: Fieldwork and the Ethnographic Present*, edited by N. Halstead, E. Hirsch, and J. Okely, 55–74. New York; Oxford: Berghahn.

Raykoff, Ivan. 2007. "Camping on the Borders of Europe." In *A Song for Europe: Popular Music and Politics in the Eurovision Song Contest*, edited by Ivan Raykoff and Robert Deam Tobin, 1–12. Aldershot: Ashgate.

Raykoff, Ivan, and Robert Deam Tobin, eds. 2007. *A Song for Europe: Popular Music and Politics in the Eurovision Song Contest*. Aldershot: Ashgate.

Pajala, Mari. 2007. "Finland, Zero Points: Nationality, Failure and Shame in the Finnish Media." In *A Song for Europe: Popular Music and Politics in the Eurovision Song Contest*, 71–82. Aldershot: Ashgate.

Pennanen, Risto Pekka. 1999. *Westernisation and Modernisation in Greek Popular Music.* Tampere: University of Tampere.

Tragaki, Dafni. 2007. *Rebetiko Worlds: Ethnomusicology and Ethnography in the City.* Newcastle: Cambridge Scholars Publishing.

Tuhkanen, Mikko, and Annamari Vänskä, eds. 2007. "Queer Eurovision." Special issue of *SQS: Journal of Queer Studies in Finland,* 2. Accessed May 4, 2012. http://www.helsinki.fi/jarj/sqs/sqs2_07/sqs_contents2_07.html.

Wood, Abigail. 2008. "E-Fieldwork: A Paradigm for the Twenty-First Century?" In *The New (Ethno)musicologies,* edited by Henry Stobart, 170–87. Lanham, Md.: Scarecrow Press.

Chapter 3

The Nordic Brotherhoods

*Eurovision as a Platform for
Partnership and Competition*

ANNEMETTE KIRKEGAARD

INTRODUCTION

The Nordic Countries[1] have been part of Eurovision almost from the beginning in 1956.[2] Due to the historical relations, which as a result of internal domination and numerous wars in the region are both friendly and hostile, and the particular importance of a relatively common language area, negotiations around national, regional, and European identities and cultural exchange are abundant. In this chapter I will examine whether the Nordic countries can be seen as a specific area within the ESC and how that relation appears in selected incidents in the now almost fifty-five-year-long history of Eurovision in the Nordic countries.

RESEARCH QUESTIONS

I take three general assumptions as points of departure for the discussion, which—the contested relations notwithstanding—dominates the Nordic discourse over the ESC:

1. Solidarity: The Nordic countries often support each other in the competition by casting top votes for each other, and this is understood as a positive thing. At the same time, the so-called buddy voting is regarded as a kind of foul play and looked down upon.
2. Unity: It is often claimed that a certain Nordic sound is audible, representing a unity in style, culture, and music which is attributed to the songs and the traditions regarded as unique to the Nordic

countries. In the sounded unity of the nations of the North, language plays an important role as a mutually understandable means of communication.

3. Seclusion/exclusion: The Nordic countries in various ways have troubled relations to the European project, and their role in the ESC is deeply, positively as well as negatively affected by the relation between home and away.

Based on empirical observation, I will discuss how concepts like partnership, brotherhood, and nationalism interact with the format, structure, and means of communication of the competition.

My analysis will focus on two TV programs which in recent time seem to have enhanced the discourse over Nordic unity in the ESC and which have perhaps strengthened public awareness of national issues in relation to the politics and cultures of the new Europe. One is the "Before ESC" programs in which a jury of representatives of the five Nordic countries present and discuss the entries from all participating countries.[3] In the programs the dialogue, at one and the same time, supports neighbors and enhances the stereotyping of the others. This is especially the case in relation to the so-called ethnic turn of the competition, which is mildly reproached, sometimes ridiculed, and generally perceived as a problem. It is my argument that the jury, through their visualizing and sounding of a Nordic unity, influence televoters significantly. The other event which will be subject to my reflections here is the "Congratulations—Eurovision at 50" production which took place in Copenhagen in 2005. The event celebrated the fifty years of Eurovision history and nominating the best-ever ESC song. The winner was Abba's "Waterloo," and its victory in 1974 and in 2005 brings out significant aspects of Nordic attitudes to the ESC. On a broader level I find the two shows to be showcases for the negotiations over national and regional affinities and as such important platforms for exposing the dilemmas of the Eurovision from a Nordic perspective.

WHAT IS THE ESC?

When the European Broadcasting Union in 1956 started the tradition of transmitting the shows as live programs, it came about as a political reaction to the conflicts which dominated the European postwar situation, and the show consciously used music as a means of uniting the nations. Singers were to "represent a participating nation with a new original song" (Raykoff and Tobin 2007, xvii). Initially only a handful of countries competed, but since the modest start, the number of nations has grown steadily. Not least the breakdown of the Berlin Wall in 1989 and the expansion of the European Union have increased the aspirations of newcomers to join the event. Even though many TV programs might carry similar ambitions, for instance the Olympic Games ceremonies and various versions of transnational charity shows, no other event has the special element of intended competitiveness in original songs and compositions and "potentially dense cultural meanings." (Björnberg 2007, 15) And no other invokes the nation in quite the same way. But as it is not only intended for competing but also for sharing, the ESC is one of the clearest examples of a staging of an imagined community (Anderson 1991, 6). Song and music give the event a special quality of oneness—both in the general assumption of what music can do as an assumed universal language and in relation to the oneness created by the ability of television to address a massive audience to a shared event. McLuhan's "global village" is a suitable metaphor for the 'togetherness' of the final competition which presently draws around one hundred and fifty million viewers. But it is also at the same time evident for all, I think, that the community is indeed contested and almost paradoxical in its mix of competition and brotherhood of song. Therefore, following Anderson, a conflict between nationality and inclusion in the transnational community of Europe is acted out in the special role of song—the unisonality, "the echoed physical realization of the imagined communities" (Anderson 1991, 145). With the inclusion of the televotes and most recently the sms (text message) votes this debate has been further invigorated.

In Denmark the ESC, locally called Melodi Grand Prix, is the oldest still-active TV concept in the history of the Danish Broadcasting Company (DR). Through its relation to the entertainment section of the company it is not—and probably never was—generally considered a very serious program with an important agenda and as such it differs greatly from sports and in particular football. ESC is "music, beautiful voices and a perfect performance" (Tøpholm 2009, 3). In other words, ESC in the Nordic countries was and perhaps still is "just for fun."

However, the ESC is an old institution and it has a complicated history. Accordingly there is no single explanation of the phenomenon, and even if the general idea of bridging contested spaces through evocation of imagined communities remains the official agenda, changes have been great: technologically in the development of music videos, mobile phones, and the Internet, and musically in the heated and continued discourse over high/low culture and insider/outsider perspectives. Research, however, exposes stereotypes, generalizations, and errors in the narratives of the event. As records, footage, and tapes have not always been kept, much unfortunately is lost.[4]

DENMARK IN THE EUROVISION

Denmark joined the ESC in 1957 with the entry "Skibet skal sejle nat" (The Ship Will Depart Tonight) sung by Birthe Wilke and Gustav Winkler. The song had been selected among six others, and the two singers performed all the songs for competition in the local show. As performance then as now was important, small cabaret shows were created for all six songs (Tøpholm 2009, 10). Chosen by a professional jury, the selected song was at great odds with international bookmakers. At the final, however, a scandal broke out as the singers on stage finished the performance with a kiss. The shot of the kiss lasted much longer than expected, and according to Danish interpretation it cost the expected victory. The incident testifies to the importance of the spectacle and has since been understood as a marker of the then all-important distinction between the North and the South, as it was believed that sexual morals in predominantly Catholic countries caused the turmoil. The relation of the North of Europe to the South has culturally as well as socially been complicated. Not only the religious difference of Catholicism-versus-Protestantism has been significant, but imagined stereotyping of sensuality and morals has also flourished. The musical evidence of this continued stereotyping can be found, for instance, in the reluctant and skeptical embracing of the emotional ESC ballads of the South by the viewers of the North. The North/South distinction and its musical dilemmas have since given way to a new frontier: that between the East and the West.

Despite the disappointment, Denmark continued as a devoted participant in the competition—gradually joined by other Nordic countries—and in 1963 the coveted victory was brought home to Denmark as Grethe and Jørgen Ingemann won with the jazz waltz "Dansevise" (Dance ballad). "Dansevise" has often been regarded as a sophisticated and slightly elitist entry, as it was influenced both by French *chanson* and jazz through the contribution of guitarist Jørgen Ingemann, who accompanied his wife on a semiacoustic guitar. As already customary, the winning nation hosted next year's final, which took place in the amusement garden Tivoli. The show thus promoted one of the major tourist sights of Copenhagen featuring the Tivoli Boy Band complete with bearskin hats, but significantly also the first, and perhaps only, openly political demonstration in direct ESC broadcast, to which I shall return.[5]

The Danish entry of 1964 did not do very well in the final, and a conflict over the cultural policy of the DR was building. The artists who had participated in the first decade of the ESC all came from the segment of the popular music scene which is tied to the Danish language pop chart, "Dansk Top" (*Schlager*). A powerful agent, who according to performers "ruled the event ruthlessly," (Tøpholm 2009, 16) was lyricist and TV host

Sejr Volmer Sørensen, who advocated the idea of "pure entertainment" and who was shortly to become one of the targets of the attacks by the left wing.

Volmer Sørensen's opponents were primarily the critical cultural elite, which drew on the thoughts of cultural radicalism (*Kulturradikalismen*)—a unique Danish movement which was formed in the 1930s and had architects, painters, and composers as acting spokespersons for the cause. It was a left-wing initiative headed by architect and world famous lamp creator Poul Henningsen (PH) and several composers, and the movement was critical to the European *schlager* music scene and preferred jazz and African American musics—not least because of its imagined relaxed relation to sexuality and body.[6] Again, perhaps, a hint at why the prudery south was broadly disrespected. More than anything, however, the movement disapproved of the mass-mediated pop music of the 1950s and 1960s. The performance of the musical *Teenagerlove* by Ernst Bruun Olsen, text, and Finn Savery, music, at the Royal Theatre in Copenhagen in 1963 was one long elegy over the damaging effect of popular music culture and its alienation of the masses.

PH stands as an important figure in the clashes on and over popular culture in Denmark. A convinced communist, he had challenged the establishment and its cultural agenda several times in the past. His "Denmark movie" in 1935 had been banned, as its jazz soundtrack did not fit in with the musical expectations of national representation, but significantly his songs in the extremely popular cabaret tradition (*revy*) had during the Second World War gained respect and popularity (Hammerich 1993). His ideas about using popular culture for education have been extremely influential in Denmark and were to a certain extent the basis of the shift of agenda which was to take over in the DR with the new director, Niels Jørgen Kaiser. Kaiser was strongly influenced by PH's thoughts on "serious fun" which meant that entertainment should be edifying for the masses and not just empty pastime (Hammerich 1993). This point of view was in sharp conflict with the policies of Volmer Sørensen—and also with the ideology of the ESC.

In an attempt to please the cultural elite the Danish ESC of 1965 was changed drastically. The intention was that only good composers—that is, professionals who knew how to make proper music as opposed to flippant amateurs—should create the Danish entry. Calls were sent to composers within classical and jazz music circles, and a jury selected the winner on the basis of professional qualities. The song chosen was "For din skyld" (For Your Sake) with music by Professor Jørgen Jersild of the Royal Danish Music Conservatory and lyrics by PH. The authorship of the lyrics and the music was not "revealed" until after the win. The effort to make ESC apply to good taste nevertheless failed, and in 1966 Denmark withdrew from the competition for a period of ten years. The show simply did not meet with the dogma of "serious fun" and the state-financed monopoly TV station DR under the rule of Kaiser found that the quality of previous entries, and in particular the style of the popular *Schlager* strongly associated with Volmer Sørensen, were not wanted to externally represent Danish culture, and more so even unwanted as internal custodians of the popular versions of the development of Danish song.[7] As such the divide between "strictly mainstream" and elitist aspirations is conspicuous in the ESC also from a Danish point of view (Björnberg 2007, 14).

The decision to withdraw caused riots among ESC fans, who since have baptized the period "The Dark Years," and it resulted in heated debates in which the one side accused the other of upholding a cultural hegemony based on elitist taste. During the years of Denmark's absence two important things happened in the European arena; first, a referendum to join the EEC took place in 1972, making Denmark a full member of the Union, and second, the victory of neighboring Sweden with ABBA's "Waterloo" in Brighton in 1974 caused a small revolution in the world of ESC. As a result, both Europe and the ESC moved closer together, and former pop and rock journalist of DR, Jørgen de Mylius, fought to get Denmark back into the ESC. The reentry took place in 1978 and introduced a much broader segment of Danish musicians and artists to the competition, such as rock stars Kim Larsen and Sanne Salomonsen. This turn of strategy—even if still discredited by the hard-core left wingers—drew a much larger attention and audience to the ESC.

It has been argued by ESC commentators and critics that for audiences in Denmark the victory of ABBA in 1974 had far greater impact than the European project.[8] On the other hand, political ideas have always played a significant role in the event, and also Nordic relations must be examined in relation to the politics of music.

POLITICS AND THE ESC

"Politics have absolutely nothing to do in Eurovision."

—Hilda Heick[9]

Despite the above common statement, politics and ESC have always been close. The initial idea of bridging a separated Europe was a political move, and recent incidents following the enlargement of Europe have openly been termed political. In between, songs like Italy's 1990 "Insieme 1992" and the antiwar song "Ein biβchen Frieden" from 1982 were clear examples of outspoken political meaning in the ESC. Politics, however, do not only concern lyrics; also the event in itself and its enormous number of viewers afford possibilities of usurping the show and making use of its platform for political messages. An early and interesting example from the Danish archives can highlight the discourse. At the 1964 Eurovision Final, which following the victory of "Dansevise" in 1963 was held in Copenhagen March 21st, the program was interrupted by a political activist climbing the stage with a banner encouraging the boycott of the dictatorships in Spain and Portugal (Tøpholm 2009, 25; de Mylius 2001, 53; O'Connor 2005, 24). A demonstration and several bomb threats had been announced due to Portugal's recent inclusion in the ESC, and the banner significantly read "Boycott Franco and Salazar." The intruder was immediately overpowered and ushered from the stage, but the incident bears witness to an early awareness of the unique platform provided by modern media. The newspaper *BT* on the day of the event read:

> Three or four members of "Group 61" have gotten hold of tickets to the concert hall tonight on the balcony.[10] They will (hidden) bring one or more banners with inscription against Franco and the hope to get these in front of the cameras, *so that they can be seen of the approximately 100 million who are expected to see the Grand Prix*." [my italics] (*BT*, March 21, 1964)

The incident appears as an early forecast of the classic use of direct TV for political agitation as in the Olympic finals in 1968 and lots of later actions. But sometimes even the mere choice of a certain performer or performance can be interpreted as a political statement, as for instance seen in the inclusion of gay culture and drag shows. Fundamentally, reflections over the relation between culture, nation, and song expose significant dilemmas to the negotiations over politics in the ESC.

NATIONALISM AND IMAGINED COMMUNITIES IN MUSIC

Bohlman argues that "music actually participates in the formation of nationalism," and he relates its role to the thoughts of Johan Gottfried Herder, who in 1778 with *Stimmen der Völker in Liedern* exposed the idea that song is of the people, that it is communal, has no author, and belongs to everybody (Bohlman 2004, 35). The process of making song a special representative coincided with political moves to make the nation-states gain importance and to prepare the birth of modern democracy. In Denmark thinker and clergyman N. F. S. Grundtvig cleverly proposed that popular song with historical and epic themes should assist in the edifying process, which would lead to the education of citizens with the right to vote and take responsibility in the nation-building project. Music in other words became national when popular music of the *folk* was merged with the ideas of art music (Weisethaunet 2011). Accordingly, national music was always a construct or, as Hobsbawm and Ranger's seminal book stated, invented (1983, 12).

The fundamental and initiating idea of the ESC without doubt resembles similar ideological superstructures, but is significantly also tied to another set of basic rules; those of the popular music market, the dominance of the modern media, and the effect of communication technology on cognitive and social organization (McLuhan 1962, 29). In that way the ESC both in the Nordic sphere and internationally follows the contemporary insight formulated by Homi Bhabha, that nationalism is by nature ambivalent (Bhabha 1990, 2). It is in other words not only imagined, but it is actively narrated through the performance, and audiences accordingly will almost by definition react very differently to this narrative.

ON LANGUAGE

Benedict Anderson's concept of "unisonality/unisonance" (1991, 145) is based on the importance of language in nation-building. It is mirrored in the ESC, where language has played and still plays an important role, and where the relation between mother tongue and fatherland was always contested. Until 1999 the contest had strict rules that songs should be performed in the national languages. These rules which were believed, one must assume, to secure national identity have always been the target of skepticism and conflict, since countries with marginal languages with some right claimed that bigger languages drew more votes, as their lyrics were not only easier to understand, but also closer to mainstream popular music styles representing fashion and modernity. Prior to the final in 1963, Jørgen Ingemann even stated that Danish was a bad language for singing, by which he indicated stylistic and aesthetic as well as semantic problems.[11] In order to bridge the gap, translations of songs became the order of the day,[12] and today the most commonly used language in the ESC is English,[13] even if it is not (as some claim) the language of Europe yet.[14]

In the Nordic countries languages are still mutually understood, even if today this inter-Nordic communication is slightly disturbed by the orientation toward English as the common language.[15] The semantic closeness implies that very many words are alike and only differentiated by the pronunciation, which until 1999 meant that the Nordic entries were the immediately most understandable to the majority of TV viewers in the region.[16] However, despite the usual dogma that English language songs have greater chances of making it in the ESC, numerous examples to the contrary exist. Israel won twice in Hebrew, the Nordic countries have had victories in the national languages amazingly often, and in 2007

Maria Serifovic (Marija Šerifović), completely against any model of what should and could be successful in the ESC, became a very convincing winner with a song in Serbian, which was semantically unintelligible to most audiences (Bohlman 2007, 43). So perhaps "understanding the lyrics" is not that important after all. One reason could be that the amount of bad and almost unintelligible English after 2000 is so big that audiences prefer (and can hear the aesthetic difference of) people singing in their mother tongue, where it in fact means something and is not just a kind of vocalized nonsense.[17] While generalizations are dangerous, the staging of difference—a concept of almost paradoxical value as both unity and diversity are required from audiences as well as arrangers—has increasingly gained ground.

ESC AND DIFFERENCE

On the politics of difference Bohlman writes: "At the level of the national competitions, it has become increasingly clear that there are many different nations and many different Europes (and Eurovisions)" and that these are based on different historical, political, and geographical zones (Bohlman 2008, 3). Longtime participants in the ESC are—at least officially—as active in the enlargement of the competitions as are the newcomers, but they relate very differently to the growth of the event. There are conflicting ideas, and some people in the "old" countries, who support the event the most stubbornly, are simultaneously against the threatening new practices of the former Eastern European countries.[18] Also the relation to Muslim nations—notably Turkey's mix of stylistic and social markers (Solomon 2007, 137)—is contested. The Northern response is partly based on another interpretation of nationalism which predominantly finds its cultural expression in sticking to previous times, sometimes invoking conservatism and nostalgia. Skeptics and nationalists see the conspicuous display of differences as a threat to the identity of the event, and thus the Nordic reception is clearly split between a nostalgic, national popular culture and a superficial and eclectic kitsch, including so-called ethnic entries with dance as an integral part of the performance.

INTERMISSIONS

Nowhere is this tendency more conspicuous than in the intermission show generally regarded as either ultimate kitsch or nostalgic imagination of the past. The intermission shows, entertaining audiences live or at

the TV screens waiting for results, have increasingly become sites of great
attention and they have also—quite generally—been more successful in
producing commercial breakthroughs and creating attention to artists as
well as for styles than the competing songs. They further represent the
growing attention to the body and dance, which have in my view spilled
over into the performances of the competition proper.[19]

The shows fall, roughly speaking, into two overall categories which
are of interest to the present discussion: on the one hand they display
traditional, nostalgic, or even historical presentations of the nation and
its heritage. The success of the *Riverdance* show (Dublin 1994) was pre-
dated in 1986 when Norway presented a rather nationalist and nostalgic
intermission which showcased the beautiful city of Bergen and brought
attention to the young Sissel Kyrkjebø. Folk costumes, *harding* fele, viking
ships, fishing, and mountains all went into the production with Sissel giving the last song, the *Ulriken*, live from the Grieg Hall.[20] The emphasis on
authenticity and folk song idioms was overwhelming. It is also very clear
that the show, like the later promotion of *Riverdance*, served to promote
the city of Bergen as an attractive tourist site.[21]

The other major trend is that the countries showcase their technological and highly modern abilities and competences through popular music
production and famous stars. In Copenhagen 2001 the Nordic best-selling
artists Aqua supported by Danish Safri Duo delivered an up-tempo performance, and at the 2007 Helsinki ESC Finnish heavy rock cello stars
Apocalyptica, supported by a dreamlike cirque-moderne extravaganza,
reminded the viewers that heavy metal not only won the ESC, but is big in
Finland. In these intermissions generally the amateurism of the competing participants is confronted by the professionalism of the real artists, as
noted by several critics,[22] and aesthetic considerations are clearly governing the event.

The debate over difference and nationality is complex, and it is certainly of major importance to the event. But I will also risk the assumption
that "the good song," unpredictable as it fundamentally is, is the idol for
all. Leif Thorsson in his introduction to the Swedish book *Melodifestivalen*
claims that to him the music is what makes it all worthwhile, and significantly not the sports and nationalism of the event (Thorsson and Verhage
2006, 6). Likewise Maria Serifovic in the press conference following her
victory in 2007 held that through her entry, music had been made the
center of attention again.[23] But if "the good song" could tentatively be
regarded as more important than all the talk of nationalism, difference,
and promotion, a relevant question would of course be, what constitutes
a good ESC song and how it relates to the intentions and demands of the
event.

THE ESC SONG: GENRE AND TASTE—HIGH/LOW

Genres and Rules

Genres preferred in the ESC are difficult to pinpoint. It is, however, clear that the *chanson* of French origin as well as the big power ballads and hymnlike anthems often have been favored. Second, up-tempo danceable entries have done well. Of musical characteristics Björnberg mentions Aeolian tonality (Björnberg 1984), and I will add that step-by-step melodies, obligatory modulations, and catchy choruses seem to be preferred, all in the service of making the song easy to remember. These characteristics are on the other hand generally found also in popular musics outside the ESC arena.

Bohlman discusses the management of difference in dialogue with a set of "Eurovision Rules," and he proposes the music of ABBA as the "single most dominating style" (Bohlman 2007, 60). While a musical formula including a modulation and a verse and chorus structure (and the above-mentioned elements) is very often applied, on the other hand much more is at work in the entries and "rules" are seldom really agreed upon. Many major victories in the ESC have rather been instances of breaking such rules and have instead unpredictably won due to elements of newness. ABBA's win in 1974 sounded new and so too did "Ein bißchen Frieden," which resembled a Dylan or Hannes Wader protest song and was unfamiliar to the ESC in 1981. The psalm-like hymn "Love Shine a Light" from Katrina and the Waves in 1997 was equally unusual, as was the heavy-metal "Hard Rock Hallelujah" of Lordi in 2007. Accordingly, stylistic rules in fact only exist in the imagination of the people who try to create a winner—i.e., the makers—and seldom do they succeed in doing so.

Rather, I find that the negotiation with and the element of imitation of the popular and successful musics in the global sphere is all important. In the 2007 final in Helsinki, for instance, the Finnish entry was a clear imitation of the world-famous and hugely selling group Evanescence. The singer dressed in black with coal black hair in the romantic goth dressing style and the music were so very close to the style of Evanescence that it *could* have been them. Previously, imitations were seen as belated and old school. They appeared outdated and were disliked by youngsters. Today, imitation is so integrated in popular culture, and accordingly it is often the music of the youth which appears in the commercial clothing of the ESC. While the imitation today may bridge the generational gap, it might still be problematic. By "eating" the styles of the youth in a process despised by many artists, the music is domesticated for the arena of the ESC, and in this way the imitations contribute to the negotiation on the high/low discourse in popular music in that it disconnects the relations between audiences and the social and cultural settings.

"WORLD MUSIC" AND THE RETURN TO ETHNICITY

Björnberg (2007), Strand (2008), and Bohlman (2007) relate their discussions to a special kind of imitation in the ESC which is often a little derogatorily termed "ethnic," but which could also be classified under the equally vague term "world music." The concept is famed and critiqued for its take on difference and its attempt at bringing folk and traditional musics into commercial music production (Erlmann 1993; Feld 2000). The complexities surrounding difference and sameness in "world musics" are similar to the double strategy of being part of the unifying project and at the same time state national identity and local style, which governs the ESC. Musical styles, which could in this way be labeled "world" or "traditional" music, have been in the ESC through time. Several countries have brought folklore and non-European sounds to the ears of viewers: the Moroccan entry "Bitakat Hob" with Samira Ben Said in 1980 might be a special case, but also Turkey and Israel have participated for more than thirty years.[24] It should also be noticed that in 1991 the song "Le dernier qui a parlé," which in the final gained exactly the same number of points as did Carola with "Fångad av en stormvind," was not only sung by Algerian singer Amina, but composed by the Senegalese musician Wasis Diop. These examples are well in line with traditional "world music" categorizations, but it is another trend in the world music debate which interests me here; the so called "return to ethnicity." Björnberg sees 1995, when Norway's Secret Garden won with "Nocturne" and Danish singer Aud Wilken dressed up in folk gown came fifth with "Fra Mols til Skagen," as the year of so-called ethno techno—paraphrasing its title from Enigma's "Return to Innocence" of 1993. The style can also be related to the so-called new age trend in "world musics," using imagined rather than traditional sounds. The "return to ethnicity" tag semantically indicates a very strong element of nostalgia, which combined with fragments of folk music, is repeated in the dressing and performance, adding "other" values and "better" times to the narrative.

The "world music" market is at the moment undergoing a change, which might in fact be connected to the development in the ESC. Whereas "world music" initially signified a radical degree of otherness and for its first big successes drew on African or African American styles, it is increasingly focusing and selling products which encompass a new kind of otherness.[25] The trend represents the "homecoming" shift in "world musics" toward interest in the internal others (Bohlman 2004, 20), a trend for instance represented in the Swedish entry "När Vindarna Viskar mitt Namn" (When the Wind Is Whispering My Name) by Roger Pontare, whose "ethnorockish" song claiming indigenous peoples' right to land could also be seen as ultranationalist (Thorsson and Verhage 2006, 279). The new kind of otherness seen here makes it increasingly difficult to define the music and separate it from what is not "other." Of course it also gives away the immanent impossibility of the term, so brilliantly criticized by ethnomusicologists Feld and Erlmann, even if negotiations over nationalism in the ESC are deeply, albeit unconsciously, influenced by it.

The technological and digital developments, however, have afforded renewed importance to Erlmann's term flavor (Erlmann 1993; Feld 2000). The concept of fusion has changed and given way to a more radical notion of fission. Whereas fusion can be interpreted as a coming together of various musical elements to create a new (more or less) cohesive style, fission describes the process in which various elements might come together, but significantly do not merge. Rather they stand out as fragmentized musical parts which are *meant* to be experienced as complex. In other words, the listeners are *intended* to hear traditional, historical, modern as well as foreign flavors in the same song. Alexander Rybak's "Fairytale" can serve as an example, in which the traditional violin (*harding fele*) and the sampled sounds of contemporary popular music are working side by side.[26] In the process the objects are freed from their "homes" and in the ESC interpreted out of context and as "free-floating signifiers" (Björnberg 2007, 15).

I realize that claims to what should or could represent the "true" nature of the nation are of course highly contested, and that applications of "old" instruments, costumes, melodies, or dance rhythms in a blend of popular song are rather features which add to the construction of images and symbolic meaning. Most "ethnic" musics in the ESC are filled with superficial flavors or free floaters which nevertheless have preserved their ability to point to specific topoi and make references to place (Strand 2008). But while Strand and Björnberg stress that ESC is moving toward a world music ideology and that crossovers are taking over at the cost of more national forms, instead I wish to argue that there never was—as particularly seen in the Nordic area—a truly national form.

NATIONALISM, ESC, AND THE NORDIC COUNTRIES

Structure of Nordic Solidarity

It is often suggested that the Nordic countries form a kind of regional entity—culturally, politically, and perhaps even musically. The interrelatedness is supported through established institutions and structured communities within the Nordic countries which add cohesion, such as the Nordic Council and the Nordic Union (*Foreningen Norden*), but also by numerous cultural agencies within sports, entertainment, and broadcast (like for instance *Nordvision*). Despite contested power relations, a connected history including even a shared royal family contributes to the feeling of relatedness. The idea of a certain Nordic tone and the shared languages augment the cultural explanations for the assumption of unity. The idea dates from the middle of the nineteenth century, where composers borrowed or imitated from folk song and rural musics. The idea of a Nordic tone and its reliance on thinking the national in music has for long been questioned by music scholars (Weisethaunet 2007).

In daily discourse it is, however, still claimed that the Nordic countries have a special Nordic sound, which is allegedly favored. In the ESC the support and solidarity between the Nordic countries do not seem to be dependent on genre, as it apparently does not matter, whether the music is folk (Alexander Rybak, Norway, in 2009), sing-along (A Friend in London, Denmark, in 2011), or heavy metal (Lordi, Finland, in 2006). Listening to the styles of the songs from the Nordic area which have won or simply participated in the international finals, it is actually very difficult to pinpoint any particular sound. The difference between "Dansevise" (Denmark 1963) and "Hard Rock Hallelujah" (Finland 2006) are extreme, but also "Take Me to Your Heaven" (Sweden 1999) and "Fairytale" (Norway 2009) differ greatly musically. The observation contradicts the notion of any kind of musical essentialism of either quality or style and confirms previous findings. In other words, success does not depend on musical structures, but rather follows the "sign of the times" and is as such somewhat random.

Still relations to the discourses on nation are strong, and performers seen as knights of honor. The yearly celebrations and performances of the ESC bring about many emotions and take up a great deal of attention in the media as well as in public discourse. A recurrent theme is the honour of representing the country, but the discourse is often split between pride and disappointment. In 2009 the Danish competitor, Brinck, told *Berlingske Web-tv* "I am so happy to represent Denmark in the Final—so proud."[27] Also the Norwegian winner, Alexander Rybak, had similar comments and with Anderson one can wonder what it is that causes the want to "die for the nation" (Anderson 1991, 141).

In Finland, a country now firmly based in the Nordic section of ESC,[28] pride can easily and quickly be challenged by defeat, and Finnish newspapers then speak of "national shame and the melodrama of repeated disappointment" (Pajala 2007, 72). However, in defeat and losses the brotherhood of the Nordic countries occasionally comes to the moral rescue, and comfort can be found in the shared feeling of regionality.

Buddy Voting and Nordic Solidarity

An emotional dimension of the ESC is often related to the phenomenon of buddy or bloc voting in which neighboring countries uncritically vote for each other.[29] Pajala emphasizes that the defeats of Finland and other Western European countries are increasingly explained by the accusation of the Balkans in particular to vote for their neighbors and of trading votes, which is interpreted ultimately as a kind of corruption. According to Pajala, this accusation, however, is exaggerated and also unfair not least so because of the historically documented tendency to do the same in the Nordic countries. Nevertheless, papers and TV commentators also in Denmark keep up the image of the Balkans as the villains and openly use the phenomenon as an explanation of their contempt or disregard for the newcomers. In some ways this increasing discursive divide resembles the rhetoric used to describe the difference from the Southern European participants applied in the 1960s and 1970s.

In Björnberg's discussion of the Nordic countries as a periphery to Europe, he sees the isolated victories as a possible "symbolic revenge of the Margins" and thus gives an actively positive interpretation of the cohesiveness to which outsiders might of course be more critical (Björnberg 2007, 17). So it was at least in the first incidence of buddy voting reported. In 1963, when the votes for Denmark's "Dansevise" were cast, trouble appeared. During the reading of the votes from the international juries, the Swiss entry was in the lead for some time. When the representative of Norway was to read the results of the Norwegian jury, a technical problem occurred which caused his disconnection. The host went on to call the other juries, and when finally the Norwegians were redialed as the last, the points given to Denmark had changed from two to four, giving the victory to "Dansevise" at the expense of the Swiss song. It caused much attention and was seen as a biased and brotherhood-friendly action.[30]

But even if buddy voting seems to be a recurring practice in all camps, equally convincing examples can be given to the opposite fact that sometimes neighbors are conspicuously *not* voting for a song. Denmark's all-time ESC classic "Disco Tango" from 1979, composed by Tommy Seebach, was suspected to do very well in Israel, and according to the protagonist, the Israelis "loved" the song. At the actual voting, however, the suspected success did not occur partly because the participating Nordic "friends" did not support Denmark: zero from Finland and Norway and one single point from Sweden. All three countries gave their *douze points* to Israel's "Hallelujah"—apparently in another kind of political action—and

Denmark only came sixth. When in 1981 Seebach again represented Denmark in the ESC final in Dublin with "Krøller eller ej," he came in eleventh. He was again very disappointed and to the papers stated: "We will never have a Nordic song as winner. At least not before we, in the Nordic countries, begin helping each other out with points. That system exists in the central European countries. Why shouldn't we," asks Seebach.[31]

The practice of buddy voting has been deplored and demanded respectively, but of course audiences do not follow the recommendations of the experts and critics. The Danish equivalent to Terry Wogan, Jørgen de Mylius, has for years rhetorically and half-jokingly begged the Nordic juries to cast their votes for Denmark for the brotherhood reason, alas mostly in vain. In 1982 Björnberg argued that the phenomenon of buddy voting would terminate, but the development has gone in another direction, as he himself acknowledges. At the 2009 Moscow Final the pattern of voting for neighbors was again fully at work.[32]

Perhaps the new seriousness of the ESC, the emergent right-wing populist parties, and the political projects of new participants in the European project have also affected the feeling of community among the Nordic countries. The creation of Nordic boards, negotiating and evaluating the quality of the entries, might be understood as a way of confirming the reconstruction of national identities in music. In Denmark the Danish Folk's Party has increasingly focused on the definition of Danishness, and they have openly used culture as a means of both controlling and correcting new tendencies in Danish public culture. In February 2011, after A Friend in London qualified for the ESC Final in Düsseldorf, party member Kim Christiansen complained not only that the winning song was performed in English, but also that it was a slippery slope that composers were increasingly not Danes. "It is as if the ESC has evolved into an idolizing of bad musical taste, in which the countries compete to create the least national and sexless piece of music"[33] His plea further was that Denmark should lead by example and stick to Danish-produced songs with Danish lyrics. The discourse over nationality and culture in this way becomes a tool for both the se- and exclusion to which I shall return.

THE "BEFORE ESC" PROGRAMS

The Nordic countries have recently joined forces in an interesting new TV production in which five representatives from Norway, Denmark, Sweden, Finland, and Iceland respectively evaluate the entries from all participating countries.[34] The programs expand on the traditional video preview of national entries broadcasted to the EBU members, and the panelists are either former participants or media people who have followed the shows for a long time. As such the participants are the "connoisseurs" of the game, and not surprisingly a lot of stereotyping is going on. It is in my view very likely that these "authoritative" comments with their built-in prejudices might have significant influence on the viewers and the subsequent voting, and importantly, that they contribute to the idea of the Nordic as a united area. It further adds to the sense of regionality that the jury members stick to the local languages, Danish, Norwegian, and Swedish, as the Finnish member speaks Finnish-Swedish and the Icelandic Norwegian.[35] The languages are understandable in common discourse, even if with some difficulties for some people and accordingly subtitled. The dialogue nevertheless is exclusively designed for Nordic audiences.

The participants of "Before ESC" in 2007 were[36] Charlotte Perelli (Sweden), Thomas Lundin (Finland), Eirikur Hauksson (Ireland), Per Sundnes (Norway), and Adam Duvå Hall (Denmark).[37] The show was chaired by Christer Björkman, former participant in the ESC with "I morgon är en andan dag" from 1992. The panelists one after the other introduced a national winner, the official video was shown, and afterward comments and points from zero to five were given for the entries. These were placed on a large screen so that both the points for each song and the points given from the five countries were summed up at crossing angles. The nations, not the names of the panelists, were written on the board, and flags were decorating the podiums. Most songs were quickly dealt with, and sometimes in a slightly condescending way. The five Nordic entries, however, were given special attention as well as a much longer presentation with footage. After each video an additional panel of five commentators—here showbiz people—gave their evaluation on the chances of the songs, but no points.[38]

The panel did not always agree, and it was clear that very different musical tastes were confronting each other. Charlotte was a fan of pop music as was Thomas, whereas the Icelandic commentator, who at this particular ESC was also representing Iceland in Helsinki as an artist, was a true rock and heavy-metal fan. The Dane was a supporter of electronica, whereas the Norwegian was generally broad-minded. It was obvious that Thomas Lundin was constantly looking for authenticity in the sense that he wanted songs to be real, to matter to him, and to be true to their idea. The heavy rocker was openly biased and made a show out of flagging his preference for hard rock. Charlotte much the same but for another style, and the Dane and the Norwegian were sort of the odd ones out—a bit kinky and "funny guys," giving less predictable comments.

The focus points of nationality, ethnicity, stereotyping, and politics that I have already mentioned were lavishly touched upon in the discourse, and the panel was amazingly sharp in their attitudes. In commenting on the entry from Belarus, "Work Your Magic" presented by Koldun, all liked the song but were in various ways openly critical of the internal political conditions. Thomas deplored the amount of money spent on producing the video and ended by stating: "I like it. I hope it will get a second position, because I do not want to go to Minsk and support the last dictatorship of Europe." A similar strong and political stand was taken by Per in the comments of the very daring video from Poland ("Time to Party" presented by The Jet Set): "A very challenging music video—highly erotic—and *that* is clammy, when you begin to speculate on trafficking! Europe is not ready for this kind of porno chock."

The ethnophobia of some of the comments was clear and exposed in the simultaneous search for and rejection of ethnicity. At the presentation of the entry from Albania ("Hear My Plea" presented by Frederik Ndoci), a light pop song, Per surprisingly announced that "This is one of the reasons why you either hate or love the ESC. You cannot understand that this is from the same continent." Eirikur's comments address the question a little differently, but maybe just as critical, by pleading the artist to change to his own language for the Final, a demand never put to Scandinavians. "If anybody knows them—call and tell them to sing in their mother tongue." Adam openly ridiculed the entry: "He looks like Al Pacino—they need a marriage counselor—we only need that she starts a strip." And the whole business made Charlotte sick: "I am about to vomit. So bad." The ever-sober Thomas again called for authenticity: "He does not succeed in conveying any emotions—at least not to me . . . " and Per gave "one point for the moustache."

On the negotiation on gender the panel was much more at "home" and appreciative. The song that was discussed was the Danish entry "Drama Queen" with the drag performer Peter Andersen, aka DQ. Adam introduced the song. Already in preshow ads, determined to "defend the honour of DQ" (DR web), he recounted Peter's devotion to ESC, and some footage was shown. We saw preparations; we heard about the dresses and were told that his husband is the tailor of all the gowns. The little story in itself was a flagging of the Nordic take on homosexuality and an open description of the relation between the ESC and gay and lesbian culture. The video was run, and the additional Nordic panelists brought their comments, followed by the jurors in the program. Attitudes were mildly spoken biased. Charlotte was neutral, but a little homophobic and refered to the better performance of her compatriot Christer Lindarw. Thomas was more open on the gay question, but again he asked for authenticity and more drama, in this way indirectly criticizing the lack of that in this particular song. Per then stated, "Gender bending is an integral part of ESC, and the comparison with Christer Lindarw is completely wrong. *He* is beautiful and divine. But this is down to earth. Even I can become a drag, DQ gives to all men in Europe a chance of wearing women's clothes.

Five points." Generally, though, the panel was disgruntled with the song and performance; it was only average!

When the Serbian song, "Molitva," by Maria Serifovic was presented, the panel agreed that this was a good song. But the staging that was shown was criticized.[39] Adam: "I believe in this song—strong ballad—she is compelling—and wears a T-shirt with the Ramones!" And Eirikur: "It is the kind of ballad that I connect with the Balkans. Heavy, minor-tonality, serious, and she sings very well." Charlotte found that it worked well; ". . . she is a very good singer. But a little femininity would not harm. Had it been included, then the song would have been able to reach very far— but five points!"[40] Thomas: "It is one of the most beautiful songs ever in the ESC. It contains all that I love about ESC. It has a beautiful melody, a surprising arrangement, a good chorus—emotions—drama. The styling is not good. But you do not see that when you listen to the song—which I intend to do all summer." Here gender bending certainly mattered, but the discussion also introduced the importance of the good song and the extraordinary voice and performance. Only Per strongly disagreed: "Terrible staging—one point."

Throughout the programs the Nordic solidarity was valued high and the sense of unity permeated the talk. The tendency toward exclusion was overwhelmingly and surprisingly strong, and the stereotyping—at least from some of the panelists—outspoken. The discursive descriptions of the music were in relation to some of the songs amazingly essentialized and repeated the prejudices which are at work when music is treated as a flavor or a free floater. It must nevertheless be remembered that the panel favored the overall attitude of *not* being biased. They regarded themselves as musical and performative experts, and they took a lot of effort in explaining that their evaluation might not be shared by all viewers. Still, the "Before ESC" programs affect the positions of its audience, and it blurs the distinctions between "intended" objectivity and very personal and idiosyncratic interpretations. No doubt, "Before ESC" can be interpreted as a modern and highly efficient agency which aims at supporting and constructing Nordic cultural cohesion. And it certainly prepares the soils for potential buddy voting.

CONGRATULATIONS: THE WATERLOO OF POP[41]

In 2005 the EBU decided to celebrate the fiftieth anniversary of the ESC in a special performance. The show was initially scheduled for London, but as the Royal Albert Hall was not available, it was transferred to Copenhagen, possibly paying homage to the successful ESC final in 2001, the first so-called stadium/mega final, and for being the first host and initiator of the Children's *Melodi Grand Prix,* MGP.[42] The show, produced by EBU in cooperation with DR and Have P/R,[43] was a celebration of the history of ESC and titled "Congratulations—Eurovision at 50." It took place in Copenhagen October 22, 2005, and was hosted by Katrina Leskanich, the 1997 ESC winner of "Love Shine a Light," and Renars Kaupers from Latvia.[44]

The plan was to coin the best ESC song ever, and through a system of online voting, fourteen songs were chosen for the competition. In order to represent all decades in the event, songs were spaced into five-year sections. The chosen few included mostly winning songs like "Diva," "What's Another Year," "Ein Bischen Frieden," "Fly on the Wings of Love," and "Waterloo," but also "losers" like "Volare" and "Éres Tú," which nevertheless went on to become ESC-classics. "Waterloo" convincingly and expectedly won by 329 votes over "Volare"'s 267.[45] The competing songs were on the demand of EBU displayed on screen in the original TV takes accompanied by choreographies of live dancing.[46] A former ESC participant would prior to the screening introduce the competing song and pay tribute to its alleged uniqueness. This structure gave a possibility for not only the competing fourteen but in fact twenty-eight songs to be presented. It also, according to *Politiken* critic Anders Bodelsen, made the show long and rather boring.[47]

On stage in Copenhagen were Dana International, Carola, and Sertab Erener and the Spanish group Mocedades, who were so moved by the occasion that they were unable to voice "Éres Tú." Other heroes of the production like the first winner Lys Asia, the Olsen Brothers, Johnny Logan, and a short section of *Riverdance,* also appeared. Danish critic Mads Kastrup in his harsh critique of the event commented on *Riverdance,* that "The ESC has meant far more for the revival of Irish folk dance than for the development of European popular musics."[48] The show was broadcasted to thirty-one countries but significantly not to the United Kingdom, France, and Italy. Votes were given via sms (text messages) and telephone calls, and locally, it was estimated that 2,155,000 Danish viewers saw at least five minutes of "Congratulations."[49] DR staff estimated that the total number of spectators was between 50 and 100 million.[50]

Despite all the preparations and high expectations, the general reception was negative. TV viewers at home as well as audiences in Forum were disappointed and thought they did not get their money's worth. Ticket prices were between 500 and 900 DKR (equivalent to $100 to $180), and people felt that for that amount too little real action was had and too many videotapes. "We went to the bar to have a pint instead of glaring at this. Because it is not worth glaring at," one spectator told the press. He had looked forward to the show together with his wife.[51] Also the press disapproved of the choice of screening. Under the headlines "Video

Evening in Forum" and "Karaoke-Show" the efficiency of the production was praised, but Logan was quoted as saying, "I am sorry that it has developed into a karaoke show."[52]

The disappointment also hit the winning song, and it was critiqued that ABBA did not appear. Several rumors in the papers hinted that they did not want to come unless they had proof that they would win—or at least know the result. The arrangers suggested hiding them in a nearby hotel so that they could be brought to the arena, when the result was known.[53] The vox-pop had it that ABBA had become too greedy or too highbrow, and many were outright furious with their absence.[54] The expectation was linked to the idea that ESC had created ABBA, and that they should pay their respect to the event. But others found that ABBA saved the ESC, since they allegedly renewed the show and brought it closer to contemporary popular music. Both positions are mirrored in the comments on their absence in Forum and their victory as the all-time greatest ESC song. BT repeated: "The claim that ESC back then created ABBA is however wrong. Of course a group with Anni-Frid, Benny, Björn and Agnetha's talents would have been a success with or without the international ESC."[55] Kastrup, clearly a fan of ABBA, ends his criticism with the words "Let us thank Agnetha, Björn, Benny and Anni-Frid for the music. And not least for having done a 'millard million' times more for the ESC than the reverse. The latter now has bowed and thanked ABBA for dropping by. Why not? It was the only time in fifty years that a pop phenomenon of that class passed by."[56]

On a very general level the ABBA story is typical of the mythlike narratives which are so obvious in ESC. "Congratulations" was filled with media-based symbolic value, and referring to McLuhan's take on the intended homogenizing of experience in the *Global Village*, it is obvious that the quick conclusions dominate (McLuhan 1962, 154). But the narratives also connect to music more specifically: The relation of ABBA's music to Nordic folk tradition is complex and interesting; first their music was heard as quintessentially global pop disco, while later the success was explained particularly on the basis of the Nordic sound. Essentialist readings, as discussed above, are not operational in relation to the ESC, but only add superficially to the flavors of imagined nationality. The fact that ABBA won at "Congratulations" has raised accusations that placing the show in Copenhagen focused the competition so much on Scandinavia that Logan was cheated for the victory he felt he deserved as the most frequent winner. ABBA might have won at any circumstance, but what is more conspicuous is that all of the fourteen competing songs—with the exception Turkey's "Every Way That I Can" from 2003 were originating from the Western part of the party, so to speak. Buddy voting or neighbor camaraderie notwithstanding, a lot of skepticism toward new members of the ESC family was visible. In a vox pop in *Berlingske Tidende* October 23, 2005, statements on the best and the worst of ESC songs were brought. Danish and international songs mingled as the interviewees answered the question. Most supported the ABBA victory, but also mentioned the few Danish successes. One had it "the worst are the majority from Eastern Europe, with a few exceptions."[57] Even performers expressed such attitudes: "ESC has become so geographically and musically diverse that it no longer is about traditional, easy Western European rhythms. Lately it has turned into tribal dance with tailored amounts of undressed silicone" . . . "Let them have their gypsy party" suggests chorister and ESC veteran Kenny Lübke after this year's final in Kiev.[58]

Some Danish critics found the very proof of their attitude toward the ESC in the production of "Congratulations," hence the above-quoted wordplay on the Waterloo of pop. Mads Kastrup of *Berlingske Tidende* aired his all-time disrespect of the phenomenon by the statement that "It might be that intellectuals have committed [unfair] scholarly assaults on popular culture for years, but in relation to the ESC they have always been right. It is a terrible business"[59]

DISCUSSING REGIONALITY AND NORDIC RELATIONS

In this chaper I have presented selected bits and pieces of the ESC history from a regional perspective. The examples pose the question whether it can be concluded that the Nordic countries through exertion of solidarity constitute a unity which tends to exclude them from others. My answer will have to be both yes and no. It is undeniable that a certain kind of regional cohesion is present and that shared history, language, and a relatively frequent presence in each other's *locales* add to the feeling of community. It is also commonly held that the Nordic countries—and their peoples—feel an obligation to support their neighbors and as such the ESC is of significance, as it constantly examines the relations according to political, artistic, or emotional shifts.[60] The connectedness is emphasized in press coverage where both commentators and newspapers ask for and highlight the mutual bonds. On May 17, for instance, the NRK proudly brought the headline "Rybak is acclaimed by our neighbours," as the entry got twelve points from most Nordic countries.[61]

The tendency of buddy voting can perhaps be seen as the most convincing expression of solidarity amongst the countries. But going through the large material, it is just as clear that some songs, Nordic or not, just do not get very many votes. The 2009 Moscow ESC was remarkable in the sense that not only did all five Nordic entries make it to the final, but that Norway's Alexander Rybak was a very convincing winner with Iceland as an almost equally stable number two. Apparently, some would say, a good year for the North. But the Swedish operatic song flopped—perhaps for stylistic reasons—dramatically, the Danish appeared a little boring and did relatively badly, and the Finnish song ended last. In this case brotherhood as so often before did not help.

One thing that might both unite the countries and seclude them from the rest of Europe is the grand narrative and favorite slogan that "We are small," which has a particularly strong hold in Denmark but is also well known in the other Nordic countries. Previously I quoted Björnberg for likewise relating the Nordic countries to a marginalized position in the European community. This master narrative of smallness is closely tied to an emotional understanding of the North as partly outside or at least on the borders of Europe and to a conspicuous and more firm reluctance in relation to membership in the EU: Norway never joined, Denmark voted against the Maastricht Treaty in 1992 and maintained membership with exceptions, and neither Sweden nor Denmark have accepted the euro. With the upcoming of several right-wing political parties in the Northern part of Europe who all are strongly anti-EU, the imagination of the nation has been radicalized to also mean exclusion.

The Nordic countries, accordingly, are caught in a conflicting interplay between regionality and homogenization: The ESC as well as the EU celebrates and articulates the particularity of national identity and modes of life, while at the same time a kind of homogeneity is increasingly experienced by citizens. Accordingly the structure in itself creates a qualitative problem. A competition which is built on and celebrates the diversity and national particularities cannot easily decide or elect a universally best song. When criteria used are as diverse as I have described here, it is perhaps only the "system," that is, the formal rules, the shared behavior, and so on, which provides the shared ground for this vast imagined community. The ESC is a paradoxical event, and its development in the twenty-first century has increased the conflict; the more music is claimed to be representing the nation, the less the musical codes can be recognized as national. They are truly imagined and they are narrated in a self-perpetuating circuit.

In my discussion of the concepts of "world music" (Strand) and "return to ethnicity" (Björnberg) in the ESC, I described how the efforts to relate a musical sound to a particular place or national area have in popular culture taken the form of flavors or free floaters, which disembedded from their imagined point of origin, can be applied freely in musical crossovers. The insight also informs my interpretation of the so-called Nordic sound and the alleged musical unity. Nothing in the material I have exposed points to the conclusion that a certain Nordic tone can be substantiated.

Like composers of the nineteenth century also contemporary musicians and singers look to the outside—or to the global village—for inspiration and aesthetics and for the good songs. While I do not disagree on the importance and significance of the ESC, I find that the connection between nation and music is casual and somewhat arbitrary, and accordingly that the claim of a special Nordic musical sphere in the ESC is constructed and politically willed.

Finally, the case of ABBA in the ESC and "Congratulations" highlights the cultural complexity of a media event of this size, which even includes the insight that Björn and Benny do not want to be remembered for their ESC successes. It also represents the Nordic—and possibly other countries'—contemporary take on the ESC. Even if flippant hysteria over results, entries, victories, and defeat are celebrated even more ferociously at the beginning of the twenty-first century, the event has become hollow musically and culturally and has itself become a free floater. In this way the seminal aphorism of Marshall McLuhan that "the medium is the message" is also valid for the ESC. It is there, it is big, and it has an enormous attention while it lasts, but when it is over it is as good as forgotten, just like most winning songs—except, of course, the Waterloo.

NOTES

1. The Nordic countries include Sweden, Norway, Iceland, Finland, and Denmark and are not equivalent to Scandinavia, which is limited to Denmark, Norway, and Sweden. The Nordic countries also include contested nationalities of Greenland and the Faeroe Islands, which are structurally tied to Denmark, and the Sami people dispersed all over the northern parts of Norway, Sweden, and Finland.

2. Denmark 1957, Sweden 1958 with Alice Babs, Norway 1960, Finland 1961, but with Iceland only joining in 1986 for the Bergen Final in Norway.

3. In Danish "Før melodi grand prix."

4. In Denmark the DR had a policy of not preserving popular culture (shows, concerts, etc.) but only classical music. Many tapes were reused and the result is that only occasional cuts, often copied by technicians, survived. The ESC Final in Copenhagen in 1964, for instance, was not archived and as such is not available.

5. After several visits of Walt Disney to the amusement park in the 1950s, the Tivoli Gardens dating back to 1843 became the model for Disneyland.

6. In the Danish daily *Politiken* June 28, 1928, PH wrote an excited ode to Josephine Baker praising her naturalness and celebrating her values to "our civilisation." See Henningsen 1980, 60.

7. Song has for a long time (since N. F. S. Grundtvig) and especially during and after the Second World War been regarded as very closely related to the spirit of the nation—and as such open for contestation and conflict.

8. See, for instance, Kastrup, Mads. 2005. "Wåw, wåw, wåw, wåw Waterloo." *Berlingske Tidende*, October 24 (vol. 2): 5.

9. Hilda Heick is a Dansk Top singer and is married to Keld Heick, who made lyrics for Denmark in the ESC for decades. Jon Bøge Gehlert, "Hold politik uden for Melodi Grand Prix" (Keep Politics Out of ESC) *Kristeligt Dagblad*, May 14, 2009, Web edition. Accessed May 20, 2009.http://www.kristeligt-dagblad.dk/search ?keywords=Hilda+Heick&time=0&parentid=1&sort=datedesc.

10. The "Group 61" was a political youth group with origins in the antiatomic campaign. The group was anti-imperialistic, and members were loosely organized of young people from a variety of left-wing parties. They were openly socialist in their attitudes, antimilitaristic, and they organized actions and demonstrations against racist South Africa, the Vietnam War, and the rule of Franco in Spain. See Jacobsen, Rasmus. "Gruppe 61." Accessed June 4, 2010. http://www.leksikon .org/art.php?n=3255.

11. *Aktuelt* March 23, 1963, quoted in de Mylius 2001, 53.

12. The practice was commonly used in European popular song between 1930 and 1970. See Smith-Sivertsen (2007).

13. See a discussion on the retreat of the French language in Le Guern (2000).

14. The conflicts over integration and the continued buildup of political and administrative structures are precisely concerned with this question, as seen in the use of the European Parliament of a large (and very expensive) group of translators.

15. Since Finnish is not included in the inter-Scandinavian language, but belongs to a totally different family of languages, conferences and meetings in the Nordic countries are increasingly performed in English.

16. Nevertheless, a practice developed in the 1980s in which local winners during the encore both nationally and internationally changed to English, in order to allegedly reach a larger audience.

17. In the Nordic pre-ESC jury, which I will discuss later, a returning plea from the jurors is that the singers should rather use their own language.

18. On Terry Wogan's attitude see Bohlman 2007, 40.

19. The relation to the body is increasingly interesting in the staging and interpretation of the ESC. Here I will just mention that Ruslana's Wild Dances, Sertab's orientalist belly dancing and Alexander Rybak's male dancers, all brought dancing much closer to the competitive part of the event, in my view inspired by the intermission acts.

20. The performance is available at www.youtube.com. Accessed May 27, 2011. http://www.youtube.com/watch?v=1q5juUsRM2Q.

21. The importance of winning the ESC is today of great commercial interest for the tourism industry. I will not comment further on this fact here, only acknowledge its crucial interplay with the organization of EBU and national/independent TV stations.

22. On the entry of Ronan Keating in "Congratulations" see Kastrup, Mads. 2005. "Wåw, wåw, wåw, wåw, Waterloo." *Berlingske Tidende*, October 24, section 5.

23. *Eurovision Song Contest Helsinki 2007, DVD*, extra material, interviews. 2007 CMC Entertainment A/S 1003594.

24. The explanation for these kinds of participation in the ESC is simply that the EBU covers a larger geographical area than the continent of Europe, and that for-

mer colonial powers—notably France and the Netherlands—include immigrant culture also in their representation.

25. The review sections in the magazine *Songlines* presently comment on twice as many European as African albums.

26. The same procedure is used in other world music performances, for instance in the highly hybrid but still traditional opening concert, The Great Nordic Night, of the 2009 Womex in Copenhagen. See Kirkegaard (2011, 25).

27. Line Scheibel Mitchell and Christina Pedersen. 'Træt MGP-Brinck: Jeg er rigtig glad' (Tired ESC-Brinck: I am very happy). *Berlingske Tidende*, Web edition, May 15, 2009, http://www.berlingske.dk/article/20090515/kultur/90515065/.

28. The Finnish connection is further complicated by a unique language, the closeness to the Soviet bloc, and the occasional participation in the Eastern equivalent to the ESC, the Intervision. In 1980 Marion Rung won this competition with the song "Hyvästi yö."

29. Björnberg (2007) uses "buddy," while Le Guern (2000) prefers "bloc" voting.

30. This obviously happened before the jurors were excluded from knowing the votes of other countries, see Tøpholm (2009, 21).

31. *Aktuelt.* Monday, April 6, 1981. Quoted in de Mylius 2001, 93.

32. For exact numbers see the ESC website, www.eurovision.tv.

33. Pernille Holbøll "Så Syng Dog Dansk" ("Sing it in Danish!"), *Ekstra Bladet*, February 27, 2011. Accessed May 31, 2011. http://ekstrabladet.dk/nyheder/article1510261.ece.

34. It could be seen as a follow-up of the Nordic cooperation under the "Nordvision" in the 1960s, in which live performances of the top three of each Nordic country were presented. It was staged in Helsinki, Finland, and the elitist 1965 Danish entry "For Your Sake" was only made public to the Danish audiences through this program.

35. Eirikur lives in Norway but has represented Iceland at the 1986 premiere with "Gletnirbankir" and in 2007 with "Valentine Lost."

36. "Før Melodi Grand Prix" parts 1, 2, 3, and 4, airplay 12. April 12, 23:45, April 19, 23:20, April 26, 22:25 and May 3, 00:30 all on DR1, 2007. All four programs are produced by SVT in cooperation with YLE, RUV, NRK, and DR.

37. Perelli is singer and former winner of the ESC in 1999 with "Take Me to Your Heaven." Thomas Lundin is also a performer, Eurikur commentator, and heavy-metal singer, and Hall and Sundnes are both radio journalists.

38. In 2007 this group was Sigga Beinteinsdóttir (Iceland), Christer Lindarw (S), Ami Asplund (F), Martin Brygman (DK), and Jahn Teigen (N).

39. It was very different from what was done in Helsinki and had clowns and dancers.

40. It is of course a peculiar/ironic remark since Maria is openly lesbian and later devoted her victory to the cause of respect for homosexuality.

41. The headline in the Daily *Ekstra Bladet*. Simmel, Rene, and Anne Højgaard. "Poppens Waterloo" (The Waterloo of Pop). October 23, 2005, 1, section 22.

42. This show deserves special attention and further research. Originating in the Nordic countries as MGP, the idea spread to other European areas and was

named Junior Eurovision Song Contest. At the moment, however, the Nordic countries have withdrawn from the all-European competition, because they disapprove of the too "grown-up" and sexualized presentations accepted in middle European countries.

43. The firm Have P/R again is interesting in this relation since the owner Christian Have participated for Denmark in the ESC Final in 1978 (the first year after the break) with the song "Boom Boom" by boy band Mabel.

44. Most of the following has been observed either through the actual seeing of the show on October 22, 2005 (and copy) or through "fieldwork" on the www.you tube.com platform and in the newspaper archives in Royal Library in Copenhagen.

45. See the songs at "Winners, 'Congratulations' Copenhagen" at http://www .youtube.com/watch?v=-668mxQwpKQ and a detailed description of the production at http://dic.academic.ru/dic.nsf/enwiki/1717540.

46. According to the head of entertainment in DR, see Therkeldsen, Søren. "Jubilæumsshow floppede" (Jubilee Show Flopped). *Berlingske Tidende,* October 24, 2005, section 1, 4.

47. Bodelsen, Anders. 2005. "Musikalsk tidsrejse" (Musical Journey through Time). *Politiken,* October 24, section 2, 16.

48. Kastrup, Mads. "Wåw, wåw, wåw, wåw Waterloo" *Berlingske Tidende,* October 24, 2005. section 2, 5.

49. Anon. "Noter: Kultur" (Notes: Culture). *JyllandsPosten,* October 25, 2005, 13.

50. Pedersen, Christina. "Jubilæumsshow var en fuser" (Jubilee Show Became a Flop). *BT.* October 24, 2005, section 1, 4.

51. Pedersen, Christina. "Jubilæumsshow var en fuser" (Jubilee Show Became a Flop). *BT.* October 24, 2005, section 1, 4.

52. Mortensen, Anne Højgaard, and Rene Simmel. "Video-aften i Forum" (Video Evening in Forum). *Ekstra Bladet* 23. October 2005, section 1, 22.

53. Eriksen, Jam, and Don Panas. "ABBA ville kende resultatet" (ABBA Wanted to Know the Result). *BT.* 29 October 2005, section 1, 18.

54. Lundsteen, Jakob. "Ynkeligt afbud" (Pathetic Cancellation). *BT.* October 30, 2005, section 1, 44.

55. Jungersen, Steffen, and Bertel H. Jensen. "ABBA blev de Andres Waterloo" (ABBA Became the Waterloo of the Others). *BT.* October 23, 2005, section 1, 29.

56. Kastrup, Mads. "Wåw, wåw, wåw, wåw Waterloo." *Berlingske Tidende.* October 24, 2005, section 2, 5.

57. Anon. "Debat: Den bedste og den værste Grand Prix-sang" (Debating the Best and the Worst ESC Song). *Berlingske Tidende,* October 23, 2005, Berlinske.dk.

58. Anon. "Debat: Den bedste og den værste Grand Prix-sang" (Debating the Best and the Worst ESC Song). *Berlingske Tidende,* October 23, 2005, Berlinske.dk.

59. Kastrup, Mads. "Wåw, wåw, wåw, wåw Waterloo." *Berlingske Tidende.* October 24, 2005, section 2, 5.

60. This is somewhat similar to the feeling during sport events—generally all like it when Nordic competitors do well.

61. NRKnet TV, accessed May 17, 2009 (no longer accessable).

REFERENCES

Anderson, Benedict. 1991. *Imagined Communities*. New York: Verso.

Bhabha, Homi K. 1990. "Introduction: Narrating the Nation." In *Nation and Narration*, edited by Homi K. Bhabha, 1–7. London: Routledge.

Björnberg, Alf. 2007. "Return to Ethnicity." In *A Song for Europe—Popular Music and Politics in the Eurovision Song Contest*, edited by Ivan Raykoff and Robert D. Tobin, 13–23. Aldershot: Ashgate Popular and Folk Music Series.

———. 1984. "On Aeolian Harmony in Contemporary Popular Music." Lecture presented at a research seminar, Department of Musicology, University of Gothenberg. Accessed April 30, 2010. http://www.tagg.org/others/bjbgeol.html.

Bohlman, Philip V. 2004. *The Music of European Nationalism: Cultural Identity and Modern History*. Santa Barbara: ABC Clio.

———. 2007. "The Politics of Power, Pleasure, and Prayer in the Eurovision Song Contest," *Musicology* 7: 39–76.

———. 2008. "On Track to the Grand Prix—the National Eurovision as National History." Paper presented for the NHIST Carpathian Workshop. Romania, August.

Erlmann, Veit. 1993. "The Politics and Aesthetics of Transnational Musics." *The World of Music* 35(2): 3–15.

Feld, Steven. 2000. "A Sweet Lullaby for World Music." *Public Culture* 12(1): 145–71.

Guern, Philippe Le. 2000. "From National Pride to Global Kitsch: The Eurovision Song Contest." *Web Journal of French Media Studies* 3(1), October. Accessed June 10, 2010. http://wjfms.ncl.ac.uk/leguWJ.htm.

Hammerich, Paul. 1993. *Lysmageren: En krønike om Poul Henningsen*, Copenhagen: Gyldendal.

Henningsen, Poul. 1980. *Sandheden er altid revolutionær, Tekster 1918–1967* ["The Truth Is Always Revolutionary"], edited by Olav Harsløf. Copenhagen: Hans Reitzels Forlag.

———. 1953. *Alvorlig sjov*. Copenhagen: Stig Vendelkærs Forlag.

Hobsbawn, Eric, and Terrence Ranger, eds. 1983. *The Invention of Tradition*. Cambridge: Cambridge University Press.

Kirkegaard, Annemette. 2011."Spillet mellem det lokale og det globale—Hvilke udfordringer stiller det til musikforskning 2011?" *Svensk Tidskrift För Musikforskning*, 93: 11–31.

McLuhan, Marshall. 1962. *The Gutenberg Galaxy: The Making of Typographic Man*. Toronto: University of Toronto Press.

Mylius, Jørgen de. 2001. *Det danske Melodi Grand Prix 1957–2000*. Copenhagen: DR Multimedie.

O'Connor, John Kennedy. 2005. *Eurovision Song Contest—50 År med Melodi Grand Prix*. Copenhagen: Carlton Books Ltd., DR og Turbine Forlaget.

Pajala, Mari. 2007. "Finland, Zero Points: Nationality, Failure, and Shame in the Finnish Media." In *A Song for Europe: Popular Music and Politics in the Eurovision Song Contest*, edited by Ivan Raykoff and Robert D. Tobin, 71–82. Aldershot: Ashgate Popular and Folk Music Series.

Raykoff, Ivan, and Robert D. Tobin, eds. 2007. *A Song for Europe: Popular Music and Politics in the Eurovision Song Contest.* Aldershot: Ashgate Popular and Folk Music Series.

Smith-Sivertsen, Henrik. 2007. *Kylling med soft ice og pølser: Populærmusikalske versioneringspraksisser i forbindelse med danske versioner af udenlandske sange i perioden 1945–2007.* Ph.D. dissertation, University of Copenhagen.

Solomon, Thomas. 2007. "Articulating the Historical Moment: Turkey, Europe, and Eurovision 2003." In *A Song for Europe: Popular Music and Politics in the Eurovision Song Contest,* edited by Ivan Raykoff and Robert D. Tobin, 135–45. Aldershot: Ashgate Popular and Folk Music Series.

Strand, Karin. 2008. "Performing Affiliation: Chronotopes at Work." Paper presented at the conference "Singing Europe. Spectacle and Politics in the Eurovision Song Contest," Volos, Greece, February 29–March 2.

Thorsson, Leif, and Martin Verhage. 2006. *Melodifestivalen genom tiderna. De svenska uttagningarna och de internationella finalerna.* 2nd edition. Stockholm: Premium Publishing.

Tøpholm, Ole. 2009. *De største øjeblikke: dansk melodi grand prix,* Copenhagen: DRs Forlag.

Weisethaunet, Hans. 2007. "Historiography and Complexities: Why is Music 'National'?" *Popular Music History,* 2(2):169–99.

———. "Music and National Identity in Norway." 2011. In *Music and Identity in Norway and Beyond: Essays Commemorating Edvard Grieg the Humanist,* edited by Thomas Solomon, 41–85. Bergen: Fagbokforlaget.

Chapter 4

The Big Match

Literature, Cinema, and the Sanremo Festival Deception

GOFFREDO PLASTINO

INTRODUCTION: MUSIC IN ITALY IS OVER

The 2009 Sanremo Festival is drawing to a close. The winner is Marco Carta: a young singer who first appeared last year on *Amici* ("Friends"), an American-style reality show similar to *American Idol* or *Operación Triunfo*. Marco Carta's victory this year had been predicted by many. While watching Carta's onscreen performance, broadcasted in Eurovision from Sanremo's Teatro Ariston,[1] I am also reading comments posted in real time on their blog by Ernesto Assante and Gino Castaldo, music critics for the newspaper *La Repubblica*.[2]

Castaldo writes: "Well, as was expected, Carta wins . . . It's been a sure thing for quite a while . . . A really bad sign for our country's musical taste." In about twenty minutes the post receives about one hundred and twenty comments. Many agree that Carta's victory was old news, since the voting system used (through sms text messaging) is the same one that had let the young singer triumph on *Amici*:

"It's been common knowledge for several days."
"Carta's victory is a stinking shame."
"Carta had been predicted to win for weeks . . . no surprise."

Amici is broadcasted by Mediaset, the TV network owned by the family of Italian prime minister Silvio Berlusconi, and is presented by talk and talent show host and author Maria De Filippi, who on this very concluding night of the Sanremo Festival was invited by the well-known host and author, and this year's Sanremo artistic director, Paolo Bonolis, to award the prizes with him. His invitation to Maria De Filippi and his adoption of *televoto* (televoting) are widely seen as an improper interference by Mediaset in the organization of the festival, an unholy collusion between Sanremo, RAI (Italian Radio and Television), which sponsors the festival, and the prime minister's TV network:

> "what a disgrace! . . . Berlusconi has even bought Sanremo. It's really over."
> "Just look at who governs this country."
> "An all-Mafia finale."
> "A complete shame . . . it makes you puke."
> "Disgusting."
> "Yuk!"
> "I'm speechless!"
> "Maybe it's what we deserve."

The general tone, however, is of disenchantment caused by the realization that the Sanremo Festival doesn't reflect the richness of Italian popular music:

> "A minute of silence for Italian music."
> "Up with music, down with Sanremo!"
> "What's the future of music?"
> "Mediocrity has won the prize."
> "Thank goodness, it has nothing to do with music!"
> "This kind of outcome is disgusting. It's a trick played on young people who love good music, on everyone who studies in conservatories, and on anyone except the masses of ignorant people who only know how to press their cellphone keys to vote for a kid who doesn't have a voice."
> "It's the same old story, all the worst music Italy has to offer summed up in five evenings."
> "Music in Italy is over."

CHEAT AND LOATHING IN SANREMO

The above comments during the final night of Sanremo 2009 are just a small sample of the overwhelmingly negative reactions to the festival that appeared in the Italian press, social networks, and online media. To me, who's been following the festival at least since the 1970s, reading and listening to these angry reactions to it, its songs, what it represents, its organization, and the tricks and manipulations that appear to have been used to make this or that singer win, this is all in all a pleasant, intimate, and shared habit.

Sanremo annual festival is held in February, but in fact it begins in December or November and ends in March, sometimes in April, a long period of time when this kind of discussion seems to be all over—on TV and in the magazines and newspapers. One of the festival's most famous hosts, Pippo Baudo, has actually maintained that Sanremo is the veritable national celebration that produces a yearlong discussion (Lomartire 2012, 289). Sanremo is everywhere, and just about everywhere the festival is a lot more than its songs: it's a public and heated debate on the value of Italian popular music and how and by whom it ought to be judged in a competition, and about which rules should apply. Sanremo is an event larger than the festival. It is also an aspiring literary genre. Gigi Vesigna's recent *Vox populi. Voci di sessant'anni della nostra vita* ("Vox Populi: The Voices of Sixty Years of Our Lives," 2010), for example, despite the impressive title, is a memoir of his personal recollections about events, discussions, and gossip *around* the festival in the last sixty years (and see also, in the same perspective, Gennaccari and Maffei 2008). Paolo Jachia and Francesco Paracchini's *Nonostante Sanremo. 1958–2008: Arte e canzone al Festival* ("Despite Sanremo. 1958–2008: Art and Song at the Sanremo Festival," 2009) affirms that some good songs have been actually performed in Sanremo *despite* Sanremo, that is, despite the festival's notorious promotion of bad taste.

Year after year, millions gather round their television sets to watch a festival of songs they know in advance they won't mostly enjoy and then to comment on any available media about how much they hate the songs, or that the whole festival is a musical fraud and deception. Why? In this essay I will look at this issue from an eccentric perspective: I will consider how the Sanremo deception theme has been accepted, employed, expressed, and further reinforced in contemporary Italian literature and cinema. I will not focus on how "the sound of music [is] captured in literature" about Sanremo, nor do I wish to evaluate how "theories in musicology and in literary criticism might apply across the borders" (Cohen and Street 2005, 163), using Sanremo as a case study. I'm more interested, rather, to see how Italian contemporary literature has advanced the perception of Sanremo as a fraud[3] (a perception that, as the reader will see later on, has even influenced me in my career as a musician) at a level different from the festival's representations in discussions or reports on TV, radio, popular press, political press, and online;[4] Italian cinema in this essay is used as a starting point and as a comparative element. Histories and analysis of the Sanremo Festival— *the* festival, in Italy,[5] and arguably the template for many music and song competitions elsewhere, including the Eurovision Song Contest— are already available (Borgna 1985: 124–37; Borgna 1986; Fabbri 2005; Fabbri 2008: 83–87; Anselmi 2009; Anselmi 2010; Prato 2010: 262–68; Facci et al. 2011; Lomartire 2012; and more specifically Agostini 2007): so I can continue my own narrative *in medias res*.

Goffredo Plastino

PAY TO PLAY

To show how the Sanremo deception theme has been depicted in Italian popular and mass culture first I'd like to talk about an Italian 1960s movie musical: *Sanremo, la grande sfida* ("Sanremo, the Big Match"). Directed by Piero Vivarelli and released in 1960,[6] it is generally considered by Italian film critics a mere pretext to showcase recent performances at the 1960 Tenth Sanremo Festival. In fact, many of the performers at that festival act in the movie: Domenico Modugno, Mina, Tony Dallara, Sergio Bruni (see Gennaccari and Maffei 2008, 40–44).[7]

The story line is simple. Two big-shot music publishers arrive at Sanremo determined to secure top prizes for their own company's songs and artists. They try above all to get their hands on the greatest possible number of tickets of admission to the *Salone delle feste*, the theater of the Sanremo Casino, hoping these will translate into favorable votes. As the film progresses, the struggle between the rival publishers intensifies, but instead of harming his adversary each ends up damaging himself: they actually turn down an offer of a hundred valuable admission tickets, in the mistaken belief that they are counterfeit. In the end both publishers are defeated when a song and a performer represented by a third publisher carries off the prize. The plot is strictly based on the rules of the 1960 festival. In that year 189 out of 389 jurors were in the audience, randomly selected by a roulette machine that picked numbers stamped on the casino admission tickets; those holding a ticket whose number matched one of the ones picked by lottery automatically were becoming jurors, able therefore to determine the success of a song or performer (Anselmi 2009, 115; 114–22).

Before considering in more detail the repeated underscoring of the theme of fraud, I also want to point out the Fascist overtones of some of the terms used to describe the illegal machinations of the festival. At the beginning of the movie the voiceover commentary affirms:

> The fifty million inhabitants of our *bel paese* ("beautiful country") in days of old land of saints, poets, and navigators, and now of *musichieri* (musicians) subdivides into two great categories: 25 million Italians today either compose or aspire to compose songs and the other 25 million sing or aspire to sing them. So it's no wonder that Sanremo, cradle of Italian song as well as pearl of the Riviera, is our authentic moral capital.

The description of Italy as a "land of saints, poets, and navigators" vividly recalls Mussolini's description of the Italians as a "a people of poets, artists, heroes, saints, navigators, and travelers" from his speech, much celebrated during the Fascist dictatorship, delivered on October 26, 1935, on the eve of the invasion of Abyssinia (Ethiopia). The addition to

Figure 4.1a. Italian movie poster for *Sanremo, la grande sfida* (1960).

Figure 4.1b.   Yugoslavian movie poster for *Sanremo, la grande sfida* (1960).

Mussolini's list of musicians and music lovers (including fans of music on film) suggests a continuity between Fascist propaganda and the musical organization of the festival. There are repeated references in the film to the Fascist ideology of the Sanremo's producers: for example, behind the desk belonging to one of the music publishers is a clearly visible sign: "Silence, the enemy is listening," a ubiquitous World War II Fascist slogan.

The film's principal theme, however, is the stratagems and machinations of the music publishers and their henchmen. The perverse necessity of illegality is underlined with such cynical phrases as "No ticket, no vote, and no votes, no prizes," and with the emphasis on the subordination of the music (songs, singers, and performances) to the subversion of the rules of competition: "It's a contest, right? So who cares about violins, songs, singers, or quartets. A contest is like a battlefield, you win it with strategy." When one of the music publishers seeks the professional advice of a lawyer to help him win, it is a lawyer who specializes in "traps, schemes, and musical crimes." Even the secondary characters observe that "it's all bribery. They're all obsessed here with payola." When the two music publishers' scheme to control the admission tickets to the casino, and thus indirectly the mechanism for voting, appears to be successful the voiceover comments, "In roulette, he who pays, loses, at the festival, he who pays, wins." And when their schemes go awry, a character observes: "Why bother organizing a festival, if they can't get the winning fix right?"

Italian film critics place *Sanremo, the Big Match* in the genre *musicarelli* (movie musicals, or, more precisely, movies built around a sequence of pop songs, or on a famous singer's performances); the *Dizionario dei film Morandini*, a "bible" for Italian film fans and scholars, awards it just one star, observing that it "satirizes the fauna that congregates around the most famous Italian song festival." Admittedly, the plot is feeble and the acting unremarkable, yet in evaluating this film we should go beyond cinema aesthetic standards. In spite of its consoling ending the movie ironically asserts that what unites producers, contestants, and spectators is their consciousness of corruption, the suspension of its rules during the actual festival and in its film representation.

There are two other, important although seemingly "light" elements in this film. The first is the centrality of television not only to the festival but also as an element that unites Italy by broadcasting the event, which exists only as mediated by television, a "show" or spectacle par excellence. In the words of the voiceover: "The TV cameras are ready to fill Italian hearts with delight. At this hour the streets of the peninsula are deserted, everyone is holding his breath, the festival is about to begin."[8] The other recurring theme is the reiteration of complaints over the decline in quality of Italian songs. The film's voiceover is a counterpoint to its images, a kind of *vox populi*: "The Italian song . . . no one ever thinks about renewing it." In one scene, unrelated to the story line, five bored journalists are shown seated around a table talking among themselves as the performances in the casino are going on:

> "How disgusting, how disgusting!"
> "Why, didn't you like the songs?"
> "Certainly not. We intellectuals think songs should be bridges toward the future."
> "No, no, no, no . . . Haven't you read [incomprehensible]? You're young, but if you had, you'd have known that songs should go back to something basic, something new. There should be criticisms, yes, but of a moral nature, but . . . "
> "You mean, like in the cinema, we should hope for a return to silence!"
> "A silent song . . . "

The harshness of this little vignette arises from the fact that the criticism originates from inside the workings of the festival itself. To declare its uselessness and to bewail the unreality and lack of connection of its songs to the genuine Italian music scene means to be part of the festival propaganda already. The scene constitutes an internal opposition that counterbalances the festival's official ideology and system of rules, but only apparently criticizing it.

IN THE BLUE

Just two years before Vivarelli's cinematic depiction in his film, Domenico Modugno and Franco Migliacci's "Nel blu dipinto di blu," known worldwide also as "Volare," was performed by Modugno at the 1958 Sanremo competition (achieving first place), and later the same year at the Eurofestival (achieving third place). The possibility that trickery was involved even in the festival's greatest success ever is suggested in writer and poet Nico Orengo's novel *La curva del latte* ("The Milk Bend," 2002).

"Nel blu dipinto di blu" is one of the most famously successful Italian pop songs, and its arrangement and Modugno's vocal performance marked a real change in Italian popular music in the fifties (Borgna 1985, 141–44). Modugno and Migliacci have given varying accounts about the origins of the lyrics: the inspiration for the refrain could have been Modugno's sight of his wife seen against the blue sky through the window of their Roman flat; or Migliacci's observation of Marc Chagall's painting *Le coq rouge*, or one of his nightmares; or a walk in Rome city center by both (Borgna 1985, 141).

Orengo's *La curva del latte* depicts the daily life of the Riviera village of Latte in 1957. (Latte is a real place: a hamlet in Ventimiglia, near the French border.) In the novel the village and its inhabitants appear suspended in a state of grace: the great Italian economic boom had not yet arrived, the war was far enough in the past to have been partly forgotten, but a different modernity is on the brink of arrival, brought by the first televisions, Fiat automobiles, and foreign pop songs whose success appears to herald a new and positive collective engagement with popular music.

> Jolanda was hanging out the sheets in the sunlight. Old Lucia was rocking Matteo. Dolores was shelling peas.
> "I like Elvis Presley singing 'Jailhouse Rock.'"
> "I like Buddy Holly's 'Peggy Sue.'"
> "And 'Blueberry Hill' by Fats Domino."
> "What about Pat Boone, 'April Love'?"
> "'Diana' by Paul Anka?"
> "'Banana Boat' by Harry Belafonte."
> "'Keep A-Knockin' by Little Richard."
> Both women laughed.
> "Our lives are a song," Jolanda said. (Orengo 2002, 121)

On the eve of great social, cultural, environmental, and economic changes, an obscure person in Latte is working anonymously to transform Italian popular music, composing a song whose words and music are immediately pleasing to listeners. Orengo imagines a Sicilian schoolteacher, Puglisi, who, smitten with the view of the Ligurian Sea outside his window, composes a song virtually identical to the well-known "Volare":

> "It's a song dedicated to this serene, magical place that has been so welcoming to me. Dedicated to this sea that for me, who am from Sicily, is equally beautiful and redolent of perfume. You see, ever since I've come here, I wake up with the sea in my eyes, and I fall asleep with the sea in my heart. So, little by little, this song was born. . . . I'm no singer, and besides, I would need an accordion, or a piano, or even a guitar, but I can tell you how it goes: 'I think that a dream like this can never return, / I was painting my face and my hands all blue. / Then suddenly, I was transformed, / and I began swimming in an infinite sea. / Swimming, oh, oh! / Singing, oh, oh!'"
> Red in the face, Puglisi told us that that was the beginning of the song. Dolores, Jolanda, and Lucia applauded.
> "Bravo!"
> "It's so poetic! Congratulations!"
> "Beautiful! So original!"
> Puglisi moistened his lips with his little glass of *passito* (a wine) and Jolanda asked:
> "What are you going to call it?"
> "I hadn't thought about that. Maybe 'Into the Blue.'"

"What about 'Nuotare' (to swim)?" asked Dolores.

"I like the idea of swimming in an infinite sea. It sounds so liberating," said Jolanda. (Orengo, 2002: 82–83)

In the book, the songs of Sanremo are a part of everyday life; everyone knows and sings them. Participation in the contest is quite easy and open to everybody. The schoolteacher, Puglisi, composes for himself, but someone suggests that he should send in his new song to Sanremo, where he could, in the opinion of his audience in Latte, be very successful.

The music was unusual, joyous, full of life, the refrain drew you in. You immediately wanted to sing it. . . .

"It's lovely and fresh, it makes you want to sing along, to dance to it, it will make your fortune."

Jolanda and Dolores clapped their hands.

"More, more, again."

The two girls made the teacher sing it three times. Applauding again and again.

Puglisi had risen from his stool and bowed, visibly moved, as though on a stage.

"What will you call it when you present it to the commission at Sanremo?" . . .

"I don't know. I thought maybe 'In the Sea, Painted Blue.'"

"Maybe it's a little long. Or maybe, 'In the Blue Painted Blue' would work."

Jolanda broke in: "I think whatever the title, they're going to call it 'Nuotare, oh, oh.'"

Dolores . . . said: "The melody is really new, it's sort of like American music, like Elvis or [Little] Richard, but it's Italian music." (Orengo 2002, 202)

The novel ends with the schoolteacher Puglisi sending the words and music of his song to the Sanremo Festival Committee. We are in an imaginary 1957, in Latte, in Liguria: in 1958 "Nel blu dipinto di blu" won first prize at the festival. Through the character of Puglisi and his spontaneous songwriting, Orengo constructs an alternate version of the creation of Modugno and Migliacci's hit song, and by doing so, gently invokes the usual theme of Sanremo fraud: of a different reality behind the success or failure of its songs, embedded in its very organization.

BLACK SANREMO

There is actually a type of crime fiction set during the Sanremo Festival, which depict it as enveloped in an atmosphere of danger, with fraud and trickery leading to murder. In Antonio Incorvaia and Carmelo Perrone's online murder mystery *E dimmi che non vuoi morire: Un thriller sanremese* ("And Tell Me You Don't Want to Die: A Sanremo Thriller," 2005) a serial killer throws the town into a panic a few days before the end of the 2005 festival, with seven murders based on lyrics of songs performed at Sanremo nineteen years earlier. For example: "Senza un briciolo di testa" ("Going Off My Head") sung by Marcella Bella at Sanremo in 1986, corresponds to the decapitation of a girl named Marcella. The solution of the mystery is counterintuitive (as so often in this kind of fiction) and the main moral of the novel is that an obsession with songs produces violence: the festival is not a wholesome event.

Daniele G. Genova's *Hanno ucciso Lucio Dalla* ("Lucio Dalla has been killed," 2006) is another interesting example of how music, the Sanremo Festival, and murder in Italian contemporary crime novels are now linked. In the novel, the 2008 festival promoters decide to refurbish its reputation, tarnished by a series of scandals in previous years, by entrusting its artistic direction to the well-known Italian *cantautore* (singer-songwriter) Lucio Dalla. But Dalla unexpectedly disappears a few days after arriving at Sanremo, and police investigators find evidence of a crime in the villa where he had been staying: traces of blood and a bullet lodged in the wall. It's not clear if Dalla has been kidnapped for ransom, or has been killed and his body disposed of after accidentally witnessing a crime. Libero Corti, a private detective who happens to be working on another case, becomes involved against his will. The novel's plot is not always clear, but mysterious intrigues of local mafia members play a role. In the end, Lucio Dalla turns up alive and well and the festival takes place as usual with great success, although during the final evening a murder is committed right in the Teatro Ariston, an event that has been foreshadowed during the narrative. As in the previous book, the case serves as a framework for a cultural criticism of the Sanremo system, which Genova sees as deeply dishonest and as having little to do with the merit of actual songs. The book features numerous cynical comments by Libero Corti and his friends disparaging Sanremo and its values, which they characterize as a screen, a seemingly acceptable front of a corrupt organization, behind which the real political and economic power unfold:

> In the modern festival, the singers, songs, musicians, and conductors were completely secondary. No one really cared for the beauty of Italian music, or the art of television broadcasting. The golden age of national pride was over. Now there was only the business of the world-wide broadcasting industry. Millions of television watchers ready to spend fortunes on the Internet, downloading bestselling recordings. Or buying vast quantities of merchandise gadgets and T-shirts made in China with the logos of the sponsors at inflated prices. That was all that counted. The festival in fact was just an

excuse for advertising and other manoeuvres, political or not. Virtually all its
internal elements could be easily interchanged, or, if necessary, eliminated.
(Genova 2006, 170)

The festival is even more strongly linked to violent crime in Filippo
Ferrari's online novel *Nero Sanremo* (*Black Sanremo*) (Ferrari 2008). In this
story the well-known singer Adriano Celentano contacts a member of
the festival staff, who tells him about a prearranged plot organized by
the famous Sanremo presenter, Pippo Baudo, to choose the winner of the
contest:

> "Baudo is the head of a shadow cabinet in the music world, one that has its
> own highly organized secret structure, its own intelligence and personal mi-
> litia, with virtually absolute power over who records, who gets to sing and
> who is forgotten. Over life and death."
> "I know Pippo Baudo, I've been working with him almost a year. He's
> strange sometimes and even a monomaniac, but he's no mafia music boss."
> "No, you don't really know him. I'm the head, along with Caterina Caselli
> of the Independent Resistance. But we're losing. We're not strong enough to
> withstand him. And after this Sanremo he'll be unstoppable. He's going to
> murder an artist to create a new Tenco case. . . . He'll manipulate the fake
> suicide and show his infinite compassion to the public and his power to his
> adversaries. After that no one will be able to stop him." (Ferrari 2008, 8)

The reference is to a historical event: the death of the noted singer-songwriter Luigi Tenco, who committed suicide during the 1967 contest. According to the most widely circulated interpretation by historians, Tenco
killed himself in disappointment over the elimination of his song. Over
the years the event and the subsequent contradictory inquest findings
were widely discussed by writers and journalists, some of whom came to
believe Tenco had really been murdered (see Guarneri and Ragone 2011).
Even today on blogs and websites conspiracy theories abound.

Ferrari's allusion to Tenco's suicide, however glancing, brings to the
mind of the Italian reader the controversies over the circumstances of his
death, and frames Sanremo as a place of obscure plots and of death, real
and symbolic, of the Italian song and of music in general. The novel's plot
thus acquires an aura of reality, since if murder occurred there once it
could happen again. The novel's message is that the festival's illegalities
cannot be modified or stopped, and fictional Adriano Celentano's attempt
to thwart the powerful presenter and with him the fatal machinery of
Sanremo is doomed to fail. After several textbook murders, for example,
Baudo decapitates a Mossad agent who is assisting Celentano—the presenter, on the evening of the final broadcast, turns to the spectators in the
Teatro Ariston and the television audiences:

Pippo Baudo enters, walking in measured steps to center stage, looks toward the spectators, and lowers his eyes with composure. The rhythm is perfect. "Dear friends," he says, "there has been a terrible tragedy at the Sanremo Festival. In such a moment words fail. Gianluca Grignani has been found dead in his room. He has committed suicide. He was an artist of extraordinary talent and great humanity and our deepest sympathies go to his family, his friends, and those who loved him."

I stand motionless in the center of the room watching Baudo triumph. . . . Besides myself there are 24 million other Italian television viewers. The biggest audience in the festival's history. (Ferrari 2008, 23)

ARRIVAL AT THE FESTIVAL

In contrast, Carmine Abate's recent novel, *Gli anni veloci* (*The fast years*, 2008), depicts Sanremo apparently as a place of positive opportunities. Like other novels by this writer, *Gli anni veloci* is set in a Southern Italian town in Calabria during the 1970s. Abate describes a group of Calabrian teenagers experiencing, in a remote suburban context, their time and their social space as defined by the popular music they listen to and perform. One character in the book is a singer-songwriter who rises to stardom out of provincial obscurity. The character is based on Rino Gaetano, a real singer-songwriter well known in Italy in those years. Abate in fact narrates how the real Gaetano, who had already issued three albums, is persuaded by his label to appear at the 1978 Sanremo Festival, a venue he had considered too commercial for his radical material. Gaetano performs at the Teatro Ariston "Gianna," a quite surreal song, which unexpectedly achieves third place and quickly becomes a huge success (the single selling more than 600,000 copies).[9] Abate reworks these events and represents Sanremo as the indispensable starting point for a pop singer who wants to be successful in Italy:

Mario would have gone through fire for his friend [Gaetano]. He was crazy about his iconoclastic and ironic, popular and refined musicianship. Most of all he liked how Rino's songs evoked the colors, tastes, smells, annoyances and frustrations of his homeland, and he foresaw a brilliant future for him. That evening, in fact, in introducing him to a small audience, he was euphoric, his words filled with pride and affection:

"Here, for you, is the greatest singer-songwriter we have today in Italy, even if few people are aware of it yet: Rino Gaetano. So far he has only cut one record, but give him a few years and see if I'm not right. My mother made me realize it, she may not know much about music but she's a bit of a psychic: 'this boy is going to make it, he has fire in his eyes, he's smart, and he sings from the heart, you'll be hearing him at the Sanremo festival.'" (Abate 2008, 68)

Abate stresses Gaetano's ambivalence about Sanremo, through the comments of his friends who have known him since he began performing and who are eager for him not to lose the opportunity of reaching larger audiences:

> In those days Rino was more anxious than usual. He had agreed to participate at Sanremo, among other things performing a song chosen by his producer, whom he didn't really trust anymore, and his friends were continually reminding him that this decision could be suicidal for a singer as outrageous and artistically refined as himself.
>
> "Bullshit," Anna counter commented scornfully. "What does that mean? It's not as though Rino were responsible for all the whining melodies drowning the stage at Sanremo every year. . . . In my opinion, what Rino needs is a showcase that will make him popular." (Abate 2008, 182)

In Abate's novel Sanremo represents a critical moment in a career inexorably headed for success. The 1970s setting reinforces this viewpoint, through the opposition between the Sanremo system's negative features and the positive, informal music making of Gaetano and his friends. In a way Gaetano is incapable of avoiding the festival; he needs it. But neither can he bend the logic of commercialism to his artistic sensibility. It matters little that this is what actually happened to Gaetano in real life: in Abate's on the whole gentle and rather circumspect narration, the backdrop of Sanremo is still a musically negative and potentially dangerous event.

GOFFREDO PLASTINO VS. SANREMO TRICKERY

Over many years, I have read a great deal about deception at Sanremo: in the press, in novels, and on the web. Maybe I myself was once involved in Sanremo intrigues, or at least this is what I actually believed many years ago. For I, too, performed onstage at the Teatro Ariston—virtually during the days of the festival. Let me explain.

From 1985 to 1990 I and a few of my friends belonged to a group produced by the well-known Neapolitan rock and pop singer, and guitar player, Pino Daniele. Those were the years when "world music" first became big on the international recording market: Paul Simon's *Graceland* was released in 1986; the label "world music" was supposedly "invented" during a 1987 meeting in the United Kingdom, and 1989 saw the release of Peter Gabriel's *Passion*. I (with my degree in ethnomusicology and a background mostly in folk revival music and jazz) was performing with a percussion player with a jazz background and a singer with previous pop music experience and a conservatory degree in piano. We were collaborating on a rather vaguely defined project. Today probably our repertoire would be called "world music" Italian style, with real or imaginary "Mediterranean" influences and some space for improvisation. But we were not aware of that.

After a few months of taped performances, Pino had decided to issue our record through his new record label, CGD. At the end of the studio production, the sound of our "band" had notably altered: we had definitely become, without knowing quite how, a "world pop" band. Our passage to a new phase of our group activity became official when we appeared as the opening act at Pino's 1989 concert at the Partito Comunista Italiano (Italian Communist Party) Festa dell'Unità in Florence, where we played before 25,000 people—the biggest audience I have ever had.

Our album was scheduled for release in early 1990; it was going to include a song composed by Pino, with him on guitar. According to Pino, having us performing his song live at the Sanremo Festival, with orchestral accompaniment, would be perfect publicity for the album and for us. Pino's idea was quickly realized, in fact, by the beginning of 1990. After having chosen a keyboard, an electric guitar, and an electric bass player among our friends, we were in a studio ready to learn our new orchestra parts. But in the middle of our rehearsal there was a call from Pino telling us that we weren't going to appear at the festival after all, and that we were being replaced by a girl band, Lipstick, whose album like ours was being issued by CGD. That phone call stopped our rehearsals.

In 1990 the Sanremo Festival was organized for the second time by Adriano Aragozzini, who decided to hold it in a 14,000-square-meter shed outside Sanremo, instead of in the historic Teatro Ariston, its traditional venue. The change provoked negative reactions from the city's inhabitants and merchants, who saw the festival (and part of its economy) relocated for no good reason. It was the first appearance at the festival by Pooh, one of Italy's most famous pop bands on stage and on tour since 1965 (Gennaccari and Maffei 2008, 190–95). Lipstick's Sanremo song and subsequent albums were produced by Pooh (see Anselmi 2009, 394–402). I don't remember exactly how Pino explained the reasons for our exclusion, but we were sure that somehow Pooh, who were among the CGD's most important artists, had succeeded in negotiating Lipstick's presence by making it a condition of their appearance at the festival. Whatever the case, because the Teatro Ariston was standing vacant, Aragozzini decided to create there a mirror festival: Sanremo International, a kind of big opening before the main event. He intended this show to be primarily televised—no live performances, just playback—a vehicle for non-Italian musicians: but we were asked to perform there to compensate for our absence at the festival.

My recollections of those hectic days are fragmentary. My bouzouki was stolen at Rome's Termini railroad station, so at Sanremo International

I ended up playing a really bad Chinese violin that couldn't hold a tune, an instrument found in one of the theater store rooms: but we were in playback. I remember that there was a lot of money: our tour manager gave me 500,000 lire (about 250 euros) for a one-kilometer taxi ride, and I remember thinking the taxi fares at Sanremo really expensive (I gave her the change at the restaurant). I remember a state of general excitement on the part of everyone connected with the festival, which I thought of as typically "Sanremo-ese." I remember the exaggerated friendliness of the reporters and announcers, of everyone who spoke to us (after all were being produced by Pino Daniele), these conversations, brief but very polite, invariably ending with the phrase: "Now, don't forget to say hello to Pino for me." I remember being stared at intensely by Sinead O'Connor (whose big hit that year was "Nothing Compares 2 U"), and how Adam Ant was incensed after his stage performance, because he felt his director had done a bad job of framing him. I also remember that nobody paid attention to what was happening on stage, but only watched the performances on the TV monitors. During the makeup session a girl asked me: "Are you Nick Kamen?" and was disappointed when I answered that I was not. In fact, I was left with my makeup half-finished when the real Nick Kamen sat down right beside me and was quickly surrounded by many admiring makeup women, while I was left totally forgotten to contemplate from close range what it means to be a real pop star.

We eventually did perform onstage at the Teatro Ariston and, in a few months, both we and Lipstick were entirely forgotten by the few people who had noticed our music. In less than a year our band broke up. I had decided that I lacked the *physique du rôle* to be a pop musician and that ethnomusicology was a lot more interesting. Pooh won Sanremo 1990 with their song "Uomini soli."[10]

SANREMO COLLATERAL

The Sanremo Festival becomes a respectable topic of contemporary Italian literature with the publication of the Alessandro Zaccuri's novel *Infinita notte* ("Endless night," 2009), published in Mondadori's prestigious "Scrittori italiani e stranieri" series. The caution with which the festival is elevated to this position is revealed in Zaccuri's brief note at the end of the book, where the writer virtually apologizes for dealing with such "compromised and compromising material," recalling that during the 1960s the filmmaker (and count) Luchino Visconti, the director of *The Leopard*, would invite prominent Italian intellectuals to Sanremo listening parties at his home, and that some declined because of the "insupportable mediocrity" of the festival's "horse race" (Zaccuri 2009, 272). Zaccuri had previously written a short narrative text, "Sanremo Collateral," describing the event as usual:

> In Sanremo, during the days of the festival, not things but people are eaten. Here careers are decided and power relations established. The bloodiest battles take place at the foot of the pyramid, and for newcomers this year when things go wrong, it's one count and you're out. That's it. *Kaputt*—it's all over. That's why early in the morning (around ten, which is early indeed, since here no one who is anyone dines before two in the morning) producers, publicists, press, and their ilk are glued to their cellphones, "Listen, she's good, I guarantee it, she'll make it, not like that other one." In play there are a newspaper interview, a shot on a picture spread, a miniscule television spot. The journalists know how to wield a power not really theirs but on loan from a fantasy world that from moment to moment has to be mediated, recaptured, and adjusted. (Zaccuri 2005, 95)

In *Infinita notte* Raffaele Maria Ferri is a writer catapulted to fame by the success of his latest novel and taken on by the producers of the imaginary 2010 Sanremo Festival as an author. Ferri's perspective is a bit blurry—he just happens on Sanremo by chance, while his wife stays home reading Baudrillard, Žižek, and Nancy (see Zaccuri 2009: 120)—and allows Zaccuri to simultaneously describe the festival from within and from outside. Each brief chapter is prefixed by a line or title of a Sanremo song of years gone by. The reader is introduced to the workings of press conferences, talk show interviews, and meetings. The introduction in the plot of Gabo, a young rapper who challenges the festival by performing on street corners, complicates the picture. We discover that he is the son of a powerful RAI executive who happens to be in attendance at Sanremo. Gabo had also submitted a song that had previously been rejected, but is nevertheless invited to participate with a new song, "Infinita notte." His onstage performance at the Teatro Ariston makes Gabo a star and the festival the television event of the year, demonstrating that the system sooner or later co-opts even its musical opponents, and that all challenges to it are internal or arise out of it opportunistically.

The biggest difference between Zaccuri's novel and the others is his greater attention to descriptive detail and ability to cast light on the mechanisms and behind-the-scenes aspects of the live show and broadcast. The singers appear under their real names, and the televised commentaries about the participants are familiar to Italian readers. But in *Infinita notte* (the title has an obvious double meaning), as in the other novels discussed here, Sanremo is more than it appears, a means of media publicity but mostly a dangerous way to arrive at a cultural consensus, that, ultimately, is political. Obviously, "The festival is a metaphor" (Zaccuri 2009, 192).

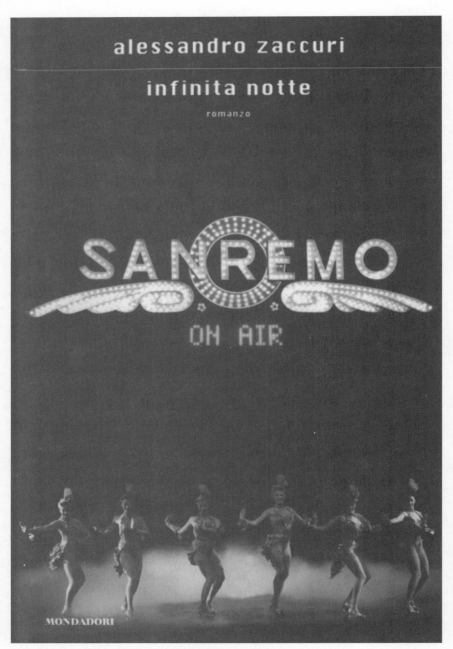

Figure 4.2.   Cover of Alessandro Zaccuri's *Infinita notte* (2009).

SAINT NOTHING

A notably different take is that of Aldo Busi, doubtless one of the best contemporary Italian writers. In two books Busi turns from the event, its songs, and their related controversies to what he considers its real relationship to questions of Italian identity. This shift in critical perspective allows Busi to avoid ritual discussions about the festival and to present an original point of view.

In *Altri abusi* ("Uses and Abuses," 1991), Busi employs the narrative stratagem of a journalistic report to be written by the character "Aldo Busi." The narrative shows a progressive distancing of the semifictional "Busi" from the Teatro Ariston, where he has gone to watch the festival and write about it. On the first evening he leaves the audience and stands out in the hallway. From there he goes to the atrium and then to the press room: "I spent almost the whole first and last evening away from the audience, waiting for it to end." He spends the second night of the show in Rapallo, about 170 kilometers from Sanremo. On the third he travels even farther away. While all of Italy is converging on or is already in Sanremo (really and virtually), Busi uses scenes of conscious flight in which distance becomes part of the narrative to express his brief and scathing criticisms:

> Is it really so hard to understand that when there's no respect for the Italian language you can install state terrorism, albeit disguised as a confection?
> I'll never understand why anyone thinks Sanremo is important, except, politically, as a way to tame the docile public to the yoke of rhetoric and bad faith, to the thought Mafia's message of "let's all love each other, but love me the most."
> The festival must be seen on *tivù* (tv), not live, because it's dead. (Busi 1991, 312–15)

Busi's views are even more radical in the latest edition of *Sentire le donne* ("Feeling Women," 2008), where he considers the festival from a perspective that, compared to the usual critical discourses, is destabilizing. The Sanremo chapter of the book is entitled "Cronache da San Niente" ("Chronicles from Saint Nothing").[11] In these pages "Busi" continues his nonparticipation, ignoring pressroom protocols in asking questions and then going away to observe the festival from time to time from afar.

> The music is over as soon as it begins: tomorrow the opening of the Festival of Italian Song is closed, and since I who had just arrived have already seen it all, I officially report that never has this most significant Non-Event better fulfilled its promises: Non-News, Non-Presenters, Non-Audience,

Non-Songs, and therefore, I hope, an absolutely Non-Listening television audience. (Busi 2008, 335)

Miraculous billionaire decay of the Non-Event and its Political Prayer that from San Niente ("Saint Nothing") nothing will continue to come neither for our citizens nor for our country. (Busi 2008, 337)

Where there is no sense of the need to consider the value of individual letters to give meaning to individual words, the architectural devastation of Liguria, to say nothing of the entire Italian coastline, will be endless, never to be reclaimed, and everything will be consumed, instantly incinerated, sacrificed to the Great Moloch of the Ephemeral Festival, the Festival of Italian Nothingness dozing before a domestic appliance where everything persists and through which nothing flows. (Busi 2008, 337)

By creating a reporter who refuses to follow the boring and repetitive rules of journalism and abandons Sanremo and its songs to their predestined fate, Busi overturns the usual references to festival chicanery to affirm the fraudulence of the entire event, not only in regard to music but to Italy.[12] He evades the festival's system, which foresees and even promotes a kind of cynicism toward the singers and the songs. He uses his analytical skills as a writer to shows that Sanremo is both a cheat and also a perfect metaphor in sound for the most widespread kind of Italian behavior, for the Italian who avoids all civic and national responsibility and whose time is spent "dozing before their household appliances," or in petty and ultimately irrelevant role-playing games.

SONGS THAT THEY LIKE TO HATE

On February 15, 1969, Pier Paolo Pasolini publishes a short essay in the weekly newspaper *Il Tempo* called "Sanremo: povere idiozie" ("Sanremo: Poor Stupid Things"):

The Sanremo festival has begun and ended. The city streets were deserted as Italians gathered round their television sets. The Sanremo festival and its jingles are something irremediably corrupting to a society. (Pasolini 1999, 1183–84)

Pasolini goes on to mention the organization by the Partito Comunista Italiano and other Left political organizations of a *Controfestival* at Sanremo, in which, among others, Dario Fo (1997 Nobel Prize in Literature) and the actress and writer Franca Rame took part. At the Counterfestival Fo declared that "Songs have the right to exist only when they perform a cultural function, when they serve to raise men's consciousness and make them aware that there is a world of exploiters and exploited" (see Facci et al. 2011, 169). Pasolini observes that:

> It is not generally known that by now all sixty million Italians . . . would like to watch the spectacle at Sanremo live and in person. . . . All of them: workers, students, rich, poor, industrialists, day laborers. The few thousand unfortunates that stop their ears and cover their eyes before this mad bestiality inhabit a ghetto, where they look at each other, appalled and hopeless. (Pasolini 1999, 1184)

There is nothing outside of Sanremo, therefore, except the opposition of a few unfortunate diehards, who however are afraid to protest against the festival for fear of the consequent unpopularity and therefore, according to Pasolini, are like "the innocent, 'integrated' singers and their 'audiences.'" In looking over the excerpts assembled above, as well as the various Internet discussions, things don't appear to have changed much in the way Sanremo is represented in Italy since Pasolini's days. The entrenched pattern of fandom vs. vilification appears to frame all approaches and reactions from year to year. In many ways the festival is a great example of bad music (Frith 2004), the kind of music that some people love to hate because it is cheesy, dumb, and politically and culturally dangerous, noxious to serious musical appreciation or career—for Pasolini yet more an evidence of Italy's transformation into a neocapitalist country; for Busi, the perfect soundtrack for the Italian middle class, and for Italy *tout court*. It is a quite old pattern, declined almost always according to the same Adornian, highbrow rules of disgust: Sanremo is the epicenter of Italian (musical) conventionality (Straniero 1964, 88–89).

In conclusion, one of Simon Frith's classifications of angry reactions to a (supposedly bad) musical performance (Frith 2004, 30–31) can be useful here: the anger experienced when "other people are enjoying something that is not *worthy of enjoyment*." What are they enjoying? A possible answer can be found reconsidering Vivarelli's film *Sanremo, la grande sfida* in the light of Ferruccio Rossi-Landi's 1978 work on ideology, and more specifically following his analysis of ideology as social practice, that is the strategies through which ideology must be consumed individually and collectively (Rossi-Landi 2005, 91–121). In Vivarelli's film the transgression of the festival rules is at the center of the events depicted. The film shows the enjoyment that the festival provides not (only) through its songs but mostly through the unveiling of its "other" rules as the story unrolls. Whoever sees the film or attends the festival, then as now, realizes that its overt rules are not sufficient and have to be somehow "completed" by a hidden code. (This has also been my feeling whenever I've been involved in the festival in some way.) The contrast between the official rules and the hidden rules, and the indeterminacy in the competition between songs and singers determines the festival audience's enjoyment and the angry reactions to it.[13]

If we accept this viewpoint, Sanremo appears then as an ideological/musical apparatus whose internal "hidden" mechanism can be seen in operation while listening to its music. It is a musical game that mirrors bigger and more dangerous games; the Italian carnival play in which legal and shared rules are transgressed through songs.

OUTRO: IF THE FESTIVAL DIES OUT

The 2010 edition of the Sanremo Festival is almost over. The winner is Valerio Scanu, a young pop singer who almost a year ago appeared on *Amici* ("Friends"), an American-style reality show similar to *American Idol* or *Operación Triunfo*. Valerio Scanu's victory was widely predicted. While I watch the final images transmitted in Eurovision from the Teatro Ariston, I'm also reading comments posted in real time on Ernesto Assante's and Gino Castaldo's blog.[14]

Some assert that Scanu's victory is once again not news, since the new voting system is the same that the previous year permitted the victory of Marco Carta (also an *Amici* participant):

"Guys . . . words fail me . . . but what can you expect from folks who last year awarded the prize to Marco Carta?? People who for years have elected a *psiconano* . . . "

Amici is broadcasted by Mediaset, the network owned by the family of Silvio Berlusconi (nicknamed *psiconano*, the "psycho-dwarf"), and is presented by Maria De Filippi, whose husband, Maurizio Costanzo, is arguably the most famous and powerful talk show host and author in Italy, and who on this final evening of the contest is just invited onto the stage of the Teatro Ariston. The invitation extended to Maurizio Costanzo, mentor and power behind Maria De Filippi, as well the adoption of the *televoto* are interpreted as a further interference in the festival on the part of Mediaset, and as evidence of the unholy collusion between Sanremo, its sponsor, RAI, and the prime minister's media conglomerate.

"People, Mediaset is prepared to spend millions to publicize and increase audience numbers for *Amici*, what do you expect?"
"All these votes were purchased by Mediaset."
"How disgusting, sold to Mediaset!"
"De Filippi wins again, the mafia doesn't let go."
"Maria De Filippi two, music nil."
"Rightwing crap has triumphed."

There is widespread disenchantment and even despair, based on the conviction that the festival in no way reflects either the diversity and richness of Italian popular music or the complexity of the country:

"Italy is on the road to irreversible decline, in music as in everything else."
"The mediocrity of the Italian people!!!"
"It's shameful, an insult to music. Throw the bums out!"
"What we are witnessing is the mirror of a country, and I'm ashamed of Italy."
"We've touched bottom. Italy is a country of crap."
"We are celebrating the funeral of music."
"Why are we astonished? I repeat, this country is dead."
"If the festival dies out maybe music will revive."

POSTSCRIPTUM: BREAKING NEWS

ACTRESS HAILED FOR REJECTING SILVIO BERLUSCONI'S ADVANCES

An actress who refused an alleged invitation to sleep with Silvio Berlusconi in exchange for being given the chance to host the country's most prestigious music festival found herself being hailed as a heroine by Italians.

By Nick Squires, Rome
6:47PM BST 16 Sep 2011

Manuela Arcuri was praised for standing up to the prime minister's alleged offer, with tongue-in-cheek demands for her to be declared a saint or to replace Mr. Berlusconi as premier.

Her repeated refusals of the proposal emerged from telephone conversations that were recorded as part of an investigation into allegations that more than thirty models and starlets were recruited to attend the prime minister's private parties. . . .

"To know that she didn't give herself to that dwarf is priceless," one Italian wrote, while others called for her to be made the presenter of the Sanremo festival for life.[15]

NOTES

1. The performance is available on YouTube: http://www.youtube.com/watch?v=D9DdZ8TOPpI. (Accessed March 12, 2009.)

2. All the comments are quoted from the posts to http://sanremo-repubblica.blogautore.repubblica.it/2009/02/22. (Accessed February 22, 2009.)

3. In a perspective close to that proposed by Ana María Ochoa in her evaluation of Gabriel García Márquez's role in the canonization of *vallenato* as folk genre
(Ochoa 2005).

4. It is telling that in recent reviews and analysis of the role of music in Italian
literature Sanremo is almost totally absent: in Favaro (2002, 294–307) there are
passing references to Pier Paolo Pasolini's novel *Una vita violenta* (1959), in which
some characters sing successful songs performed at the 1957 Sanremo Festival
(see also Prato 2010, 269).

5. "The SF [Sanremo Festival] is the oldest and most important contest still in
existence dedicated to the Italian *canzone* (song). It began in 1951 and since then
has been held annually in the town of Sanremo, on the northwest coast of Italy. It
immediately became the bench-mark for all Italian popular music and today it is
widely accepted that no consideration whatsoever can be given to Italian popular
music from 1951 onwards without taking the SF into account. From the very beginning, it has been not only an important shop window for songs, but also one
of the great media events of the year, often broadcast outside of Italy" (Agostini
2007, 389).

6. Screenwriter as well as director, Vivarelli started his career in cinema with
movies on Italian pop music and singers. He has also been the author of the lyrics
of some Italian pop hits.

7. Some excerpts from the movie are available on www.youtube.com.

8. In a sequence from another 1960s Italian movie, partly set at the festival
(*Appuntamento in riviera*, directed by Mario Mattioli, with Tony Renis, Graziella
Granata, Santo Versace, Mina; Cineriz, 1962), some label owners and music
publishers observe the singers' performances in front of a TV. When somebody
arriving from the casino asks one of them: "Why don't you go there in the hall?
You can see them better," the answer is: "I don't care, I care of what eight million
people can see." At the 2010 festival a journalist has asked Toni Maiello, the winner of the young performers' group where his producer was; Maiello replied: "She
is at the hotel: she only watches the Sanremo performances on TV."

9. Rino Gaetano's performance of *Gianna* at Sanremo 1978 is available on
YouTube: http://www.youtube.com/watch?v=ScsxXxq-1IQ. (Accessed July 16,
2010.)

10. Their performance is available on YouTube: http://www.youtube.com/wa
tch?v=zowkUJPhkmo&feature=related. (Accessed January 10, 2010.)

11. Sanremo, or San Remo, takes its names from a Genoese Saint, San Romolo.
Busi therefore is also ironic about the origins of Sanremo.

12. Busi has also written and performed some pop songs (see Busi 1990; see
also http://www.youtube.com/watch?v=wXv4--GkjMc). It is not therefore the
Italian popular music scene *per se* which he criticizes in his writings, but the Sanremo system as a whole.

13. It must be noted that the Sanremo Festival has been and is not the only
event in which discussions about systems of legal/illegal rules are constantly
produced and elaborated. For the past a well-known example is the Festival della
canzone Napoletana, suspended in 1971 after some legal actions related to alleged
irregularities in the songs' selection process (Sciotti 2010, 214–15). Another good
example is the Strega Prize literary award, the most prestigious in Italy and the

one constantly criticized because of alleged irregularities in the selection's and award's procedures.

14. All the comments are quoted from the posts to http://sanremo-repubblica .blogautore.repubblica.it/. (Accessed February 21 and 22, 2010.)

15. From http://www.telegraph.co.uk/news/worldnews/silvio-berlusconi/ 8769238/Actress-hailed-for-rejecting-Silvio-Berlusconis-advances.html. (Accessed September 18, 2011.)

REFERENCES

Abate, Carmine. 2008. *Gli anni veloci*. Milan: Mondadori.

Agostini, Roberto. 2007. "The Italian Canzone and the Sanremo Festival: Change and Continuity in Italian Mainstream Pop of the 1960s." *Popular Music* 26(3): 389–408.

Anselmi, Eddy. 2009. *Festival di Sanremo. Almanacco illustrato della canzone Italiana*. Bologna: Panini.

———. 2010. *Sanremo 1951–2010. 60 anni di Festival della canzone italiana*. Bologna: Panini.

Borgna, Gianni. 1985. *Storia della canzone italiana*. Rome-Bari: Laterza.

———. 1986. *Le canzoni di Sanremo*. Rome-Bari: Laterza.

Busi, Aldo. 1990. *Pazza*. Milan: Bompiani (includes a cassette tape with songs performed by the author).

———. 1991. *Altri abusi. Viaggi, sonnambulismi e giri dell'oca*. Milan: Leonardo Editore (first edition: 1989).

———. 2008. *Sentire le donne*. Milan: Bompiani.

Cohen, Sara, and Street, John. 2005. "Introduction to 'Literature and Music' special issue." *Popular Music* 24(2): 163–64.

Fabbri, Franco. 2005. "Sanremo, il festival." In *L'ascolto tabù. Le musiche nello scontro globale*. Milan: il Saggiatore.

———. 2008. *Around the clock. Una breve storia della popular music*. Turin: Utet.

Facci, Serena, Matteo Piloni, and Paolo Soddu. 2011. *Il festival di Sanremo. Parole e suoni raccontano la nazione*. Rome: Carocci.

Favaro, Roberto. 2002. *La musica nel romanzo italiano del '900*. Lucca: Ricordi-LIM.

Ferrari, Filippo. 2008. *Nero Sanremo*. www.eleanorerigby.com. Accessed May 20, 2008.

Frith, Simon. 2004. "What Is Bad Music?" In *Bad Music: The Music We Love to Hate*, edited by Christopher Washburne and Maiken Derno, 15–36. New York and London: Routledge.

Gennaccari, Federico, and Maffei, Massimo. 2008. *Sanremo è Sanremo. I retroscena del Festival dal 1951 al 2007*. Rome: Armando Curcio Editore.

Genova, Daniele G. 2006. *Hanno ucciso Lucio Dalla*. Reggio Emilia: Aliberti.

Guarneri, Nicola, and Pasquale Ragone. 2011. *Luigi Tenco. Storia di un omicidio*. Chieti: Tabula Fati.

Incorvaia, Antonio, and Carmelo Perrone. 2005. *E dimmi che non vuoi morire. Un thriller sanremese*. Available at: www.bottomfioc.net. Accessed March 12, 2010.

Jachia, Paolo, and Francesco Paracchini. 2009. *Nonostante Sanremo. 1958–2008: Arte e canzone al Festival*. Rome: Coniglio Editore.
Lomartire, Carlo Maria. 2012. *Festival. L'Italia di Sanremo*. Milan: Mondadori.
Ochoa, Ana María. 2005. "García Márquez, Macondismo, and the Soundscapes of Vallenato." *Popular Music* 24(2): 207–22.
Orengo, Nico. 2002. *La curva del latte*. Turin: Einaudi.
Pasolini, Pier Paolo. 1999. *Saggi sulla politica e sulla società*. Edited by Walter Siti and Silvia De Laude. Milan: Mondadori.
Prato, Paolo. 2010. *La musica italiana. Una storia sociale dall'Unità a oggi*. Rome: Donzelli.
Rossi-Landi, Ferruccio. 2005. *Ideologia. Per l'interpretazione di un operare sociale e la ricostruzione di un concetto*. Rome: Meltemi.
Sciotti, Antonio. 2010. *Enciclopedia del Festival della canzone Napoletana 1952–1981*. Naples: Luca Torre.
Straniero, Michele L. 1964. "Antistoria d'Italia in canzonetta." In *Le canzoni della cattiva coscienza. La musica leggera in Italia*, edited by Michele L. Straniero, Sergio Liberovici, Emilio Jona and Giorgio De Maria, 29–106. Milan: Bompiani.
Vesigna, Gigi. 2010. *Vox populi. Voci di sessant'anni della nostra vita*. Milan: Excelsior 1881.
Zaccuri, Alessandro. 2005. "Sanremo Collateral." *Lo Straniero* 59: 94–96.
———. 2009. *Infinita notte*. Milan: Mondadori.

FILMOGRAPHY

Sanremo, la grande sfida. Directed by Piero Vivarelli. With Mario Carotenuto, Teddy Reno, Vania Ricordi, Gisella Sofio, and several singers at the 1960 Sanremo Festival (Mina, Adriano Celentano, Tony Dallara, Sergio Bruni, Domenico Modugno and others). Lux Film, 1960.

WEB RESOURCES

What follows is a list of websites containing information about the writers, directors, singers, musicians, bands, label owners, and presenters that are mentioned in the essay.

Pippo Baudo: http://it.wikipedia.org/wiki/Pippo_Baudo
Paolo Bonolis: http://it.wikipedia.org/wiki/Paolo_Bonolis
Aldo Busi: http://www.altriabusi.it
Marco Carta: http://www.marcocartaofficialsite.com
Caterina Caselli and the label Sugarmusic: http://it.wikipedia.org/wiki/Caterina_Caselli; http://www.sugarmusic.com
Adriano Celentano and his Clan: http://www.clancelentano.it
Maurizio Costanzo: http://it.wikipedia.org/wiki/Maurizio_Costanzo
Lucio Dalla: http://www.luciodalla.it

Pino Daniele: http://www.pinodaniele.com; http://en.wikipedia.org/wiki/ Pino_Daniele; http://it.wikipedia.org/wiki/Pino_Daniele

Maria De Filippi: http://www.mariadefilippi.mediaset.it

Rino Gaetano: http://www.rinogaetano.it; http://it.wikipedia.org/wiki/Rino_ Gaetano

Gianluigi Grignani: http://www.grignani.it

Domenico Modugno: http://www.domenicomodugno.it/pagine/Italiano.html

Nico Orengo: http://www.nicoorengo.it

I Pooh: http://www.pooh.it

Valerio Scanu: http://www.valerioscanu.com

Luigi Tenco: http://it.wikipedia.org/wiki/Luigi_Tenco; http://luigi-tenco.tripod .com/

Piero Vivarelli: http://it.wikipedia.org/wiki/Piero_Vivarelli

Chapter 5

Performing Affiliation
On Topos in the Swedish Preliminaries
KARIN STRAND

Where do songs happen? Where do they take place, according to their own logic as fictional, yet representative texts? What places are generated by the singing voice; expressed by the musical setting, the visual features, the words?[1]

There are of course many aspects of the spatial issue. As far as wider cultural meaning is concerned, the last decade has seen a growing scholarly interest in place within popular music research, a *spatial turn*, where relationships between music, space, and cultural identity are focused.[2] From a more general, practical point of view, a multitude of places are always evoked in a song performance. The most obvious ones are of course the actual space of the stage where the singer performs and the event in question takes place (whether a live performance, a recording studio, or a music video); the location of the audience and the mindscape of the individual listener.

There is also a more literal, explicit, and yet quite complex dimension of the song's place, namely the topos of the lyrical world, the fictive setting. This textual place is above, and potentially beyond actual context, but, consciously or not, always in dialogue with it.[3] The milieu of the lyrical world is a narrative prerequisite; an organizing principle, a bearer of certain qualities, moral points, and set of emotions. In the particular situation of performance in the Eurovision Song Contest there is a double scene, a show in the show. In a direct sense, the entries of course represent their countries and thereby reflect national affiliation; cultural belongings that sometimes are visualized by the (usually somewhat generalizing) "postcard" glimpses in the show.

In the lyrical world (and in the stage setting), other places are often evoked, in more or less elaborated ways. In this chapter, I discuss the use and workings of topoi in the context of the Swedish national preliminaries, "Melodifestivalen" (*The Melody Festival*), exemplified by a couple of songs from the mid-2000s. The reason to focus on songs in the Swedish *preliminaries* rather than the ESC is that they illustrate the ambition to appeal to a wider European audience in its greatest variety. In the end, of course, only one song each year turns out to be the entry for the international competition, but until the winner has been chosen (which has become an elaborate process in Sweden), they are all candidates.

"MELODIFESTIVALEN"—THE SWEDISH NATIONAL PRELIMINARIES

Over the years, the national contest in Sweden has experienced various fates. From time to time it has been harshly debated on ideological and aesthetical grounds. Especially in the 1970s, the commercial logic of the event and the apparent connection between public service television and the multinational record industry were criticized. Alternative song festivals were arranged, explicitly in opposition to Melodifestivalen, and songs were made, mocking the spectacle.[4] Partly as a result of these protests, Sweden did not take part in the ESC in 1976.

During the last decade, however, there has been a drastic change—a growing interest from the mass media and the public. In 2002, the broadcasting company Sveriges Television expanded the form of the national competition to include four qualifying contests and one "second chance" contest; all together, thirty-two songs/acts competing. For one month, these preliminaries are broadcast every week on Saturday prime time, until finally ten entries are selected for the national final.[5] Since 1999, the voting procedure is a combination of televoting and geographically based expert jury groups. In addition to the eleven Swedish jury groups, an international jury was introduced in 2009, supposed to reflect international tastes that might be missed by the domestic audience. The faith in international judgement has since then grown to the point that in 2011, all eleven jury groups were from European countries outside Sweden.

As far as lyrics are concerned, there was an important change of rules in 2002 when lyrics in any language were allowed in the national preliminaries as well (this had been an option in the international contest since 1999).[6] This linguistic release was simultaneously an acknowledgment of the tactics and the growing necessity to address wider when entering—and aspiring to success in—the European arena. Just to adapt, linguistically and stylistically, to some vague and mutable "ESC norm" is of course not enough to make a Eurovision hit. In order to stand out, to attract, and to gain votes the issue is also, to a certain degree, to express specificity.

NATIONAL SPECIFICITY—EUROPEAN BELONGING

Apart from the obvious necessity to appeal to the domestic audience, entries in the Eurovision Song Contest always have a double aim: to *represent* a particular nation and to *appeal* to a wider, European audience. It has never has been an official requirement that the songs should represent their countries by a music style indigenous to that country, but it has often been expected, not to say desirable (see Björnberg 2007, 19). Especially in the early days, cultural characteristics could be part of the show—it is quite significant that Alice Babs, Sweden's first delegate, wore a traditional costume in her performance in 1958.

Over the years, the act of presentation has become less and less obvious in terms of expressing a "Swedish style." Rather, as musicologist Alf Björnberg argues, there is a growing inherent tension within the ESC between homogenizing tendencies and expressions of a style culturally specific to each country (see Björnberg 2007, 19). On the one hand there is an increasing number of contemporary (youth) music styles, hybrid genres, cultural crossovers, and ESC versions of "europop." On the other hand there is also, as Björnberg remarks, an emergence since the 1990s of entries in an "ethnic" musical style, a (re)construction of national or ethnic identity in music (see Björnberg 2007, 21).

The flourishing of homogenizations, hybrids, and neotraditional musical genres seems to correspond with movements outside the competition as well as innovations within it. The geopolitical changes and the establishment of newly formed nations in Europe after 1989 have increased the number of participating countries in the ESC, countries with different musical traditions and preferences than those within the old West European hegemony. Regarding dynamics within the competition, the telephone voting that was introduced in the late 1990s has apparently intensified the ambition of the entries to "address widely," a quest for which the *multifying* (increasing the options for meaning) of a song's potential meanings is one, somewhat paradoxical, strategy.[7] What is at stake is of course to be understood by, and to appeal to, as many potential voters (individuals and taste communities) as possible.

From a Swedish point of view, the issue of "Swedishness" has itself become more complex by the increasing presence and awareness of ethnic diversity, creating a more multicultural society within Swedish domestic culture. The globalization of the popular music market in general of course also affects the competition and the character of entries.

INTERNATIONAL AMBITIONS OF TITLES

To state the obvious: songs in the Eurovision Song Contest are always vocal, which means they contain—and foreground—voices and words. The very choice of lyrical/sung language can be a significant statement of cultural identity and visions of affiliation.

Sweden has been fortunate to win the ESC five times, the first time back in 1974.[8] These successes have undoubtedly had a positive effect on the national self-esteem and expectations in the contest.[9] Nonetheless, Sweden belongs to the geographical and cultural periphery of Europe, and Swedish is a minority language in Europe. The fact that for many years, entries in the ESC had to be sung in (one of) the national language(s) has obviously been perceived as an obstacle or at least a limitation by Swedish songwriters. To overcome this, composers have used different strategies to make the songs as intelligible and attractive as possible for an international audience.

The most striking and revealing textual aspect is, of course, a song's title. Not only does the name of the song represent and market the song even before its performance—as printed in newspapers and presented on the TV screen, for example—but in varying degrees, the title also hints at the atmosphere and setting of the song as a whole.

The case of ABBA's "Waterloo" (1974) is a good example of the tactics and potential success of internationally working titles. The song used a concept that was frequently copied and used in varied ways by other Swedish songwriters in later years with titles and catchphrases that had transnational currency. Referring to European history, the very names of

Table 5.1. Some rough categories and examples of "international" titles in the Swedish national preliminaries before 1999.

Geographic commonplaces	Monte Carlo (1966), Waterloo (1974), Hollywood (1977), Rocky Mountain (1981), Piccadilly Circus (1985), Dover-Calais; Eldorado (1986), World Wide Web (1997)
Formulas, concepts	1+1=2 (1985), ABC (1986), 100% (1988)
Mythic characters, celebrities	Michelangelo (1975), Charlie Chaplin; Beatles (1977), Sankta Cecilia (1984)
Nonsense, onomatopoetics	Ding-Dong (1973), Hey-Hi-Ho (1982), Diggi-Loo Diggi-Ley (1984)
Personal names (women)	Nancy Nancy (1960), Lolo Lolita (1962), Jennie Jennie; Lady Antoinette (1975), Annie (1991), Eloise (1993)
Other	Rockin 'n' Reeling (1975), Åh Evergreens (1978), Fender-62 (1982), Rendez-vous (1984), We Are All the Winners (1993)

Waterloo and Napoleon are cultural *commonplaces*. In the case of "Waterloo," the commonplace happens to be geographical (and geopolitical). Other examples of title strategies with an obvious mission to appeal to and communicate with a European audience include referencing mythical and popular culture characters, using personal names, adding nonsense syllables, or employing catchy phrases in English or French.

PLACE MAKING SENSE

In terms of literary discourse, the mode of lyrics is rather more *dramatic* than *poetic*. Considering the performance, a communicative context is already inscribed at the text level. Most lyrics are written and thus narrated from a first-person point of view, and there are obvious parallels between a singer and an actor in the staging of a text.[10] To sing a song is, quite literally, to give voice to a perspective; to personify, embody a protagonist in a fictive situation. This *persona* is always located in a more or less accentuated milieu. With a concept borrowed from the linguistic vocabulary of *deixis* ("point of reference"), this experiencing (talking/singing) subject is the *origo*, the point of view from which the rest of the textual world is defined (described).[11] As with speech, acts of real-life pronouns ("I" and "you," for example) only get their meaning in relation to this voiced center. It is the same with locations in space and time which gain meaning through words such as "here" and "yesterday." These are examples of such deictic words whose denotational meaning requires contextual information.

A point of view, a position from which to make utterances, is thus a general precondition for the lyrical subject. As far as the lyrical milieu is concerned, it can be more or less thematically elaborated in songs. As a dominant motif, a topos, the place is a crucial prerequisite for contents and meaning, an organizing principle for moods and actions that sets the dramaturgic frame.

Topos is never timeless; the location has always a temporal determination or presupposition (if only "timelessness"). This entity of time and space is a meta-fictive category that Mikhail Bakhtin has described with the term chronotope (Bakhtin 1997, 14–15). According to Bakhtin, the chronotope, whether prototypical or individual, is always linked to somebody in a specific situation and is charged with emotions, ideology, and values. Those spatiotemporal relations are always gendered, as the feminist critic Lynne Pearce has argued, elaborating Bakhtin's gender-blind formal scheme (see Pearce 1998, 99).

Topos is more prominent in some lyrics than others, which I would characterize as "topical" (swe: *topiska*). There are whole genres that are structured around a certain topos, in which the musical setting as well may work to emphasize the sense of place that is expressed thematically. It seems as if such a generic use of topos occurred more often in older popular music idioms. Within the Swedish *schlager* from the interwar period, for example, popular subgenres like "mother songs" (with their notions of a rural childhood home longed for) and "Hawaii *Schlager*" (with their "exotic" settings) both had certain milieus at the core.[12] As we shall see, there still are remnants of such emotionally charged spatial formulas at work within popular music of our days.

In the ultrarepresentative context of the ESC, topoi potentially have important functions, whether about staging affiliations or simply enacting exciting fictive worlds. This double scene is of course not an isolated textual matter but a guiding principle for the design of performances in the contest in general—usually the costumes, the choreography, the scenery, and the musical arrangement all contribute to the setting of the song world as a whole.

Leaving topos in general, we are now turning to the lyrical worlds of the Swedish preliminaries for the ESC and take a closer look at two quite different, recurring, types of milieus—one "international" and one "national." These topoi will be exemplified by two significant songs from the period after 2002 (since it has been permitted to sing in any language), that is, since the lyrical narrative is just as much a linguistic as a thematic concern.

As is obvious by the very title, the pop song "Las Vegas"[13] (2005) takes place in the city of Las Vegas—a thrilling, cosmopolitan milieu known for its casinos, shows, and extravagant pleasures. In contrast, the ethno ballad "Här stannar jag kvar" ("Here I Will Remain")[14] (2004) praises the native home region as a place for belonging, tradition, and continuity. It should be said that neither of them did particularly well; it is true that "Las Vegas" won the Swedish preliminaries, but in the ESC it ended up at nineteenth place (out of twenty-four). "Här stannar jag kvar" was only eighth in the national final. Nevertheless, each expresses different versions of affiliation with place, aimed at a European audience.

ENTERING THE CASINO: "LAS VEGAS"

Over the years, topoi of the exotic, of cosmopolitan cities, and exciting "foreign" milieus have regularly been used in entries of Melodifestivalen.[15] Thematically, this group of "international" or "out there" topoi seems to be especially productive for (erotic) adventure, desire, risk-taking, and new possibilities.

Of all "foreign" places, the casino is probably the most emblematic in this sense; it is a milieu charged with dramatic contrasts, where possibilities and risks are maximized. It is an exemplary topos for the use of expressive symbols of the "lottery of life" where one has to expose oneself to the caprice of Fate (by putting one's trust in Fortuna); where success and disaster is only a throw of the dice away.[16] It's a world of its own, located outside the everyday society and notions of time and place, with its own laws and logics, kings and queens, "inhabitants" from all corners of the world, all only temporally there.

"Las Vegas" was performed by the singer Martin Stenmark. The act was inspired by rock 'n' roll aesthetics from the early 1960s, performed in a nice, mildly sexy manner. Stenmark himself wore a black, thin, leather-like outfit, the jacket open, exposing a tight white T-shirt. The four female dancers (entering the stage at the bridge "Dancing girls and cabarets . . . "), wore white low-cut sporty catsuits, their long hair hanging down. The singer and the dancers had white broad belts on their hips.

As far as musical arrangement is concerned, the song begins very simply with back beat finger snaps and a single piano playing a base ostinato. After the first verse, the musical arrangement grows, with brass sections as one of the most salient features.

Las Vegas

1. I've got a room here at the Mandalay Bay
I take a shower then I'm on my way
I bring a friend if someone picks a fight
Here in Las Vegas tonight

2. It's close to midnight when I hit the Strip
The maiden voyage of my Vegas trip
The night is young and everything's all right
Here in Las Vegas tonight

Dancing girls and cabarets
You can spend your money in a million ways
Let's have a ball
The winner takes it all

Chorus
In Las Vegas, in the neon lights
You'll be a star if you do it right
In Las Vegas, whoa-oh-oh
You'd better hold on tight
In Las Vegas, can't believe your eyes
Your luck can turn in a throw of a dice
In Las Vegas, whoa-oh

You'd better hold on tight
Here in Las Vegas tonight

3. I'm leaving with a million-dollar smile
The hotel manager can check my file
Fred the limo driver's asking polite,
"Leaving Las Vegas tonight?"

Dancing girls and cabarets
You can spend your money in a million ways
Let's have a ball
The winner takes it all

Chorus

We meet a persona positioned in Las Vegas, singing out the temporal
and spatial presence using deictic devices: "*Here* at the Mandalay Bay";
"*Here* in Las Vegas *tonight*." Thematically, his presence is only temporary,
though, which is made evident from the very beginning by the mentioning of the (hotel) room. The use of actual location names (Mandalay Bay;
the [Las Vegas] Strip) colors and anchors the sense of place in a "realistic"
setting. Details typical of (the popular image of) Las Vegas—cabarets,
dancing girls, million-dollar smiles, neon lights, and limousines—complete the picture.

As a motif and theme, the city of Las Vegas is itself a myth, a formula
invested with stereotypes of Western popular culture that we have come
to know through movies, literature, and song lyrics. It is a symbol for
hazard, glamour, pleasure, and extravagancy, and it also happens to be
one of the most emblematic popular images of the United States. The
fact that this song did so well in the Swedish national final but was a
real failure in Eurovision might actually mirror differences in attitudes
toward the United States. Sweden is presumably, at least when it comes
to consumption and popular culture, one of the most U.S.-friendly countries in Europe. The national expectations of this entry reveal a naïveté,
or at least a blind spot, regarding alternative opinions in other parts of
Europe.

Nevertheless, the song's ambition was obviously to enact international
qualities and to invite and appeal to an audience (and telephone voters)
outside of Sweden. The choice of English for the lyrical language, the
suggestive milieu of Las Vegas, and the performance as a whole stages
an image of the adventurous, of admission to a place "out there," both
on a manifest level and as an effect. Stylistically, the song is devoid of
"Swedish" national characteristics, but the very choice of topos, ironically, makes the song feel quite Swedish, after all.

STAYING AT HOME: "HÄR STANNAR JAG KVAR"

To turn from the glamorous and dramatic world of the casino to its op-posite, we are now entering the topos of the native home community. Now and then in Melodifestivalen songs turn up that adopt nostalgic themes and romanticism of the wilderness that depict a Nordic cultural specificity; of Home in a more or less literal sense. This mindscape can be expressed by the use of traditional instruments, by iconography or by costumes that connotes roots and tradition. Lyrically, the native home can be foregrounded as a main motif, or simply constitute a common, vaguely archaic timescape.[17]

As a main motif, songs that explicitly pay tribute to a native home district have been immensely popular in Sweden. From its prevalence in school songbook and chapbook repertoires in the late nineteenth cen-tury, the motif found its ways into the emerging *schlager* market in the early twentieth century, forming a virtual subgenre during the interwar period.[18] However rare today, songs are still written explicitly thematiz-ing fidelity, love, or longing for the (rural) home region. One example is the song "Här stannar jag kvar" ("Here I Will Remain"), performed in Melodifestivalen by the singer and co-composer Sandra Dahlberg in 2004.

The stage setting was made in ice blue colors, with smoke rolling low over the stage, creating an image of fog, of mystical nature. The blond, slender singer was dressed in a light blue costume (pants and top), with a bare belly; straps with feathers were hanging from the sleeves, a decora-tive detail with "primitive" or "native" connotations.

The song makes use of certain musical "folk" features or markers: there is a recorder playing in the introduction and the refrain, a mandola with a backbeat accompaniment, and the bass sitting on the tonic note, creating a drone effect. As an interlude later in the song, the singer attempts to *yoik*, a traditional Sami singing style. The harmony is modal, which is typical of folk pop of this kind. The melody formula and the modal cadence form, with its sense of "coming home," correspond to the textual message: the zeal to return, to stay, to stand on the forefathers' ground.

> Här stannar jag kvar
>
> 1. Rimfrost på fjällbjörksgren i månljusets Klimpfjäll
> Här är jag född och här ska jag dö
> Landskap i vinterskrud med snötyngda vidder
> Här står min fot på förfäders mark
>
> Du ska veta jag vänder hem
> innan morgonen gryr igen

Chorus
Vindarna vänder bort mot nya världar
Men jag lovar dig här stannar jag kvar
Forsarna strömmar fram dit andra färdar
Men jag lovar dig här stannar jag kvar

2. Vildmark med urtidsklang så långt ögat skådar
Här syns allt klart, jag stillnar till ro
Nattsömn med fjälluftslugn, så tryggt att få drömma
Sov så gott, vi ses snart igen

Du ska veta jag vänder hem
Innan morgonen gryr igen

Chorus

Helegoleja, Helegoleja [yoik]

Du ska veta jag vänder hem
Innan morgonen gryr igen

Chorus

Here I will remain[19]

1. Hoar frost on a branch of mountain-birch
on "Klimp," the moonlit mountain
Here I was born, and here I will die
Landscape in winter dress with snow-heavy plains
Here I stand on my forefathers' ground

Know that I will come home
Before morning dawns again

Chorus:
The winds blow towards new worlds
But I vow I will remain
The rapids stream to where others go
But I vow I will remain

2. Wilderness with primeval clang
As far as the eye can see
Here all is clear, I grow calm
To sleep in the calmness of mountain-air
How safe to dream
Sleep well, we will meet soon again

Know that I will come home
Before morning dawns again

Chorus:
The winds blow towards new worlds
But I vow I will remain
The cascades stream to where others go
But I vow I will remain

In this text, too, the deictic devices of presence are frequent (*här* står *min* fot; *här* syns allt klart [*here I* stand; *here* all is clear]). As compared to the temporary state in "Las Vegas," the presence in this song is actually life-long; as is declared already in the third line of the first verse: "Här är jag född, här ska jag dö" (Here I was born, and here I will die); a statement with the pathos of a national anthem.[20]

The place referred to, "Klimpfjäll," exists in reality: it's a mountain region in the northwest of Sweden, in southern Lapland. From interviews, marketing, and other metatexts surrounding the artist we know that this is the native home of the artist/songwriter herself. From within a Swedish cultural context, this bond between lyrics, artist, and place suggests a sense of authenticity. The native home region is more than a textual topos, it is a true home for the artist. The devotion, the emotions expressed, are (supposedly) "for real."

As in most lyrics with a similar motif, the pure and wild nature represents qualities like continuity, comfort, and, at the core, organic belonging. Depicted by features of the northern mountain milieu: rapids, snowy plains, mountain birch, and mountain air, this particular topos is a landscape unaffected by the changes and scars of modernity. In an outspoken contrast to mobility, as resembled here by the winds and the cascades that are constantly in motion, the protagonist has no wish to discover "new worlds." Rather, she solemnly makes the promise to stay on her forefathers' ground, implicating that remaining is not a passive state but an active choice.

A QUESTION OF TIME

The initial question of this chapter was where songs take place. One could add: *when* do they happen, what is their time? As has been touched upon, topoi are per definition chronotopes; the lyrical milieu always assumes a certain location in time: versions of the present, relations to the past, visions of possibilities ahead.

As mentioned above, both of the lyrics discussed go back to earlier topical traditions in Swedish popular music history. "Här stannar jag kvar," as we have seen, is a late successor of the nostalgic type of *schlager* that was preoccupied with the praising and sentimental longing for the childhood native home region in a significant and redeeming countryside. As far as gender relations are concerned, the protagonist yearning for home in those texts has almost exclusively been male (like the majority of the singers of the genre). The separation from the original place implies a socially and geographically mobile man; a person unbound but thus potentially alienated—a man of Modernity. The Home, on the other hand, the image of roots and tradition, has usually been gendered as feminine, embodied by a mother figure or a girlfriend left behind. In this late modern application of the topos, the female persona is a subject with a choice; wanting the native home region rather than symbolizing it. The topoi as such, whether described "from within" or at a distance, represent a particular cultural innocence, a circular rather than a linear notion of time, a "before." In Bakhtin's typology, this is the chronotope of the Idyll (Bakhtin 1997, 136–46).

The topos of "Las Vegas" is, in some respects, a variation of the exotic motifs prevalent in the *schlager* from the interwar period, sharing the romantic escapism and visions of adventure and fulfillment. Whereas, for example, the Hawaii *schlager* preferred the paradisiacal qualities of the exotic, states untouched by modern experience, the Las Vegas casino, by contrast, *is* the modern experience. Its preoccupation with chance, mobility, and social turmoil bear resemblances to the Bakhtinian chronotope of the Road (see Bakhtin 1997, 153–54).

But what significance do the topoi have today as aspects of entries within the particular context of Melodifestivalen, and aiming at the Eurovision Song Contest? It might be the case that affiliation in the golden age of globalization is no longer a simple matter of geographical, cultural, national space. The aesthetic tendency in the ESC toward homogenization, genre hybrids, and uses of ethnic styles as floating signifiers can be interpreted as a decreasing concern with the implicit *tension* between the national and the international as qualitative counterparts. What might be an issue, though, is a relation in time—how long have we traveled from our imagined past, how far have we come in the promised land of modernity? Where do we want to be?

The songs of course have no answers, but they do present us with various options; images of belonging that become comprehensible, singable, and performed through and by their topoi.

NOTES

1. This chapter is a slightly revised version of a paper presented at the conference *Singing Europe. Spectacle and Politics in the Eurovision Song Contest* in Volos, Greece, 2008.

2. See, for instance, Stokes 1997; Connell and Gibson 2003; Bennett et al., 2004.

3. There are sometimes confusions about what "text" really is in arguments about song lyrics, since there actually are several different representation forms. One clarifying distinction is, for example, that between *text* in a narrow sense (designating "words on paper," printed or transcripted), and *phonotext* (referring to the sung lyrics; words in performance). cf. Strand 2003: 71–72; Lindberg 1995, 14.

4. A significant character in this protest movement was Sillstryparn (alias Ulf Dagerby from the progressive rock group Nationalteatern) whose single record "Doin' the omoralisk schlagerfestival" was made in favor of the "Alternativ festival 75."

5. In 2009, there were eleven entries in the national final.

6. In Melodifestivalen 2002, half of the songs (sixteen out of thirty-two) were sung in Swedish; the other half used other languages (fourteen had titles and lyrics in English, one song had a Spanish title and text, and one had an English title and a Spanish-English text). In 2011, the number of songs with lyrics in Swedish has decreased to one-fourth of the entries.

7. My thanks to Karen Fricker, who used the term in her inspiring paper "The Eurovision Song Contest: Kitsch, Queer, or Otherwise?" presented at the conference *Singing Europe: Spectacle and Politics in the Eurovision Song Contest* organized by the University of Thessaly in Volos, Greece, 2008.

8. 1974: "Waterloo" (performed by ABBA); 1984: "Diggi-Loo Diggi-Ley" (performed by Herreys); 1991: "Fångad av en stormvind" (performed by Carola); 1999: "Take Me to Your Heaven" (performed by Charlotte Nilsson); 2012: "Euphoria" (performed by Loreen).

9. cf. the Finnish history in the ESC analyzed by Pajala 2007, 71–82.

10. cf. Frith 1998, 169–71.

11. See, for example, Jarvella and Klein 1982. For application of deixis in literature, see, for example, Berg 1995, 18–28.

12. For an extensive analysis of mother songs and other sentimental subgenres of the early *schlager*, see Strand 2003.

13. Songwriters: Niklas Edberger, Johan Fransson, Tim Larsson, Tobias Lundgren.

14. Songwriters: Sandra Dahlberg, Johan Becker.

15. See, for example, "Rocky Mountain" (1981); "Piccadilly Circus" (1985); "Dover-Calais" (1986); "Paradise" (2004).

16. Another topical "casino song" in the history of Melodifestivalen is "Monte Carlo" (1966).

17. See, for example, "Den vilda" (1996); "Silverland" (2006); "I lågornas sken" (2008).

18. Crooners like Sven-Olof Sandberg (1905–1974) and Bertil Boo (1914–1996) made careers out of nostalgic songs praising a mother figure and a childhood rural home. See further Strand 2003.

19. Trans. by Birgit Sawyer.

20. cf. the Swedish national anthem "Du gamla du fria" by Rickard Dybeck, the end line of the second verse: "Ja jag vill leva, jag vill dö i Norden." (Yes, I want to live, I want to die in the North.)

REFERENCES

Bakhtin, Mikhail. 1997. *Det dialogiska ordet*. Trans. Johan Öberg. Gråbo: Anthropos.
Bennett, Andy, et al. 2004. *Music, Space and Place: Popular Music and Cultural Identity*. Aldershot: Ashgate.
Berg, Mari-Ann. 1995. "A Metamorphic Complexity: Chronotopes, Deixis and Literary Meaning in Patrick White's *The Twyborn Affair*." *Liverpool Studies in Language and Discourse* 3: 18–28.
Björnberg, Alf. 2007. "Return to Ethnicity: The Cultural Significance of Musical Change in the Eurovision Song Contest." In *A Song for Europe. Popular Music and Politics in the Eurovision Song Contest*, edited by Ivan Raykoff and Robert Deam Tobin, 13–23. Aldershot: Ashgate.
Connell, John, and Gibson, Chris. 2003. *Sound Tracks: Popular Music, Identity and Place*. London: Routledge.
Frith, Simon. 1998. *Performing Rites. Evaluating Popular Music*. Oxford and New York: Oxford University Press.
Jarvella, Robert J., and Klein, Wolfgang, eds. 1982. *Speech, Place and Action: Studies in Deixis and Related Topics*. Chichester: Wiley.
Lindberg, Ulf. 1995. *Rockens text. Ord, musik och mening*. Stockholm: Symposion.
Pajala, Mari. 2007. "Finland, Zero Points: Nationality, Failure and Shame in the Finnish Media." In *A Song for Europe. Popular Music and Politics in the Eurovision Song Contest*, edited by Ivan Raykoff and Robert Deam Tobin, 71–82. Aldershot: Ashgate.
Pearce, Lynne. 1998. "Another Time, Another Place: The Chronotope of Romantic Love in Contemporary Feminist Fiction." In *Fatal Attractions: Re-scripting Romance in Contemporary Literature and Film*, edited by Lynne Pearce and Gina Wisker, 98–111. London: Pluto.
Stokes, Martin, ed. 1997. *Ethnicity, Identity and Music. The Musical Construction of Place*. Oxford: Berg.
Strand, Karin. 2003. *Känsliga bitar. Text- och kontextstudier i sentimental populärsång*. Skellefteå: Ord & visor förlag,. Diss.

WEBLINKS USED FOR DATA ON MELODIFESTIVALEN

http://svt.se/melodifestivalen
http://sv.wikipedia.org/wiki/Melodifestivalen
http://poplight.zitiz.se

Chapter 6

Delimiting the Eurobody

Historicity, Politicization, Queerness

APOSTOLOS LAMPROPOULOS

THE EUROBODY, BETWEEN
MATERIALITY AND FICTIONALIZATION

In 1965, France Gall won the Eurovision Song Contest (ESC) for Luxembourg with Serge Gainsbourg's song *Poupée de cire, poupée de son*. In
a moment of postmodern bliss, the doll evoked by the title declared:
"My records are a mirror where everyone can see me. I'm everywhere at
the same time, split into a thousand shouts."[1] These two verses bring to
the foreground ideas such as the malleability of a body made of sound
and wax, a dissident version of the mirror stage mingling with an act
of projection, and a sense of ubiquity combined with the dissonance of
polyvocality. Hence, they give rise to discussions about how a body can
be recited as a *corpus,*what kind of meanings it can receive, and to what
extent it is dissociable from its initial context (see Nancy 1994, 17–18).
Such issues of corporeality, fictionalization, and contextualization are the
very matter of this essay, and it is through them that I will be attempting
to shed some new light on the complex relation between the ESC, its history, and its politics.

In *Twilight Zones*, Bordo gives a lucid definition of materiality, saying
that the term signifies our finitude, that is to say our "inescapable physical locatedness in time and space, in history and culture, both of which
not only shape us [. . .], but also *limit* us" (Bordo 1997, 181–82; 185–86).
She then attaches materiality to corporeality, saying that their combination is "first and foremost concreteness and concrete (and limiting) location." In this approach, the notions of materiality and corporeality cannot
be separated from an idea of relative solidity, constraint, and rootedness

in a here-and-now. This is precisely the meaning of Eurobody in this essay: any specific moment in the history of the ESC, a tangible aspect of the event ensuring its exposability, an unquestionable specimen of its "truth,", and a link to surrounding realities. However, even this Eurobody could not avoid intermingling with fiction. In an excerpt from *Netocracy,* (see Nancy 1994, 30–31). Bard and Söderqvist summarize some significant points about the role and functionality of fictions in view of virtual realities:

> Fictions [. . .] come in all possible forms, from private hallucinations to scientific theories. [. . .] Our culture consists of a perpetual evaluation and combination of both seemingly promising fictions and already proven fictions. [. . .] In attempting to study and gain an impression of the world around us we have to learn to differentiate between our prejudices—simplified models that we use, not because they reflect empirical evidence but because they appeal to our own personal interests—and factual analyses and prognoses—necessary and intelligent simplified models of reality that make reality comprehensible to us, even if the results do not appeal to us or fit in with our cherished fictions. (Bard and Söderqvist 2002, 5)

Despite the essentialist undertones of their position, Bard and Söderqvist place special emphasis on the omnipresence of fictions, which cover a wide range of phenomena from the psychic life of individuals to the formation of epistemologies. They stress the fact that even if fictions are falsifiable, they also maintain their "fictionality" and at the same time claim an interpretive function. Given that they combine memory with imaginative prospection, fictions oscillate between an intentional construction, an involuntary reconstruction, and a hermeneutically oriented study of "reality." In the context of this multifarious relationship to reality, self-bound fictions merge with explanatory and occasionally oversimplifying ones. If fictions undermine the thickness of corporeality and open it up to continuous renegotiation, then corporeality is not only a successful metonym for materiality—as Bordo's statement would like it—but also a mischievous description and destabilization of fixed concepts. The unavoidable combination of body and fiction might make the compactness of the "out there" less obvious than what it might initially seem. It might also be useful for unveiling some features of the body's political technology (see Foulcault 1975, 26); in that sense, the Eurobody is not only a sample of ESC's being-in-the-world or being-a-world, but also the substratum or the alibi of its fictionalization.

The aim of this essay is to examine how corporeality is fictionalized in Eurovision narratives and, inversely, how specific Eurobodies incorporate some of the founding fictions of the contest. In what follows, I will be tackling issues such as the types of body-related fictions produced by the Eurovision phenomenon and their contribution to the establishment of the Eurovision community;[2] doing that, I will also propose some ways of understanding Eurovision fandom. Among the elements at stake in what Butler calls "reformulation of the materiality of the bodies," the most important for this essay is "the recasting of the matter of bodies as the effect of a dynamic of power, such that the matter of bodies will be indissociable from the regulatory norms that govern their materialization and the signification of these material effects" (Butler 1993, 2). In a word, the Eurobody interests me as the supposedly plain truth of Eurofictions.

I will briefly explain the concepts of "Eurovision community" and "Eurovision phenomenon," which I will be using regularly in the rest of this essay. For several years, coming out as an ESC fan was a considerably hard task. A recurrent pattern in many fans' narratives of that era is the annual family gatherings in front of the television and the subsequent negotiation of their secret passion for the ESC under these circumstances (see Singleton et al. 2007, 12–24). Finding information on the contest was not easy either, as one had to count on rare newspaper articles, amateur editions of local fan clubs, epigrammatic televized summaries, or private audio and video recordings of previous contests. Scarcity of news in the pre-Internet era along with a decline of general interest in the event had limited the dedicated Eurovision audience to small groups of fans and condemned them to a solitary archive fever, without nevertheless preventing them from experiencing "a cosmopolitan exploration and not a reproduction of habitual popular musical choices" as well as from forming dedicated audiences among which "national stereotyping [was] still present but playfully negotiated" (Georgiou 2008, 150; 153).

Things have changed significantly during the last decade. The contest itself was modernized with the abandonment of the orchestra which had proved to be incompatible with more contemporary music styles, and it became more accessible to its polymorphous international audience thanks to the abolition of the language rule and the introduction of televoting. More than a few websites devoted to the contest were created, the flood of news about the ever-growing pantheon of the 1,000-odd Eurovision artists became increasingly stronger, reliable history sections were put together, and reaction to all possible aspects of the event was made extremely convenient mainly through fans' comments to Web posts. Additionally, YouTube offered almost unlimited access to Eurovision-related material, such as stage performances, voting processes, national finals, rehearsals, and participants' interviews. This material is equally available for individual comments and online discussion among the fans. As a consequence, the younger fans' knowledge of older contests is often fragmentary, fortuitous, and largely influenced by comments on the Internet. To cut a long story short, the Eurovision community I refer to is not only the people involved in the contest—artists, technicians, European Broadcasting Union (EBU) officials, journalists, Eurovision tourists—but also the coming together of the heterogeneous crowd of fans in the broadest possible sense, that is individuals who follow the event, look for relevant information, and feel the need to express their views on it. So, this community is newly born, stemming from different and unpredictably distinct sociopolitical backgrounds, to a large extent Web-based and constantly open to new pioneers. Accordingly, what I term Eurovision phenomenon is not only the grand narrative from Lugano 1956 to Baku 2011 and beyond, but also the succession of the complex layers of what I conceive of as an idiosyncratic phenomenon: the annual building up of the competition, its aftereffects, the revisiting of its history, its mythologies and icons, its ticks and obsessions, its repercussions well beyond the hard core of the event, not to mention a number of broader issues—such as nationalism and Europeanness—that have been inextricably related to it from its very beginning.

The choice of the episodes on which I will be commenting is based on their relation to issues of corporeality. Most of them remain relatively unknown to the nonspecialized audience, while they seem to be intriguing for the Eurovision community. What will be analyzed are the fans' reactions to Eurovision narratives and myths (rather than the truth of the events itself), which were found on websites such as Esctoday.com (one of the most popular fan sites); Eurovision.tv (the official EBU site for the contest); Youtube.com; and Wikipedia.org. The reactions quoted or referred to in this essay are definitely not the only, and perhaps not even the most important ones available on the websites mentioned above and several others. It should be clear from the very beginning that I neither can nor will prove their significance with statistical arguments. My choice was to a certain extent conducted by my own theoretical interest in issues of corporeality and politics, but it was also fed by my own experience both as a follower of the event and a regular visitor of relevant websites. Keeping in mind that an analysis divergent from mine might be equally possible, I will be reading these reactions as indicative of some recognizable and recurring patterns in the numerous heterogeneous discourses articulated around the Eurovision phenomenon, and at the same time as an essential component of its overall diversity. Everything that follows is part of what one might call the "Eurovision mosaic" consisting of broadcasters' policies, artistic intentions, fans' habits, publics' reactions, and so on.

HOLY ICONS, REPUTABLE DRESSES,
AND THE WRITING OF EUROVISION HISTORY

The very first ESC took place in 1956. The seven participating countries submitted two songs each, no open voting took place, and only the winner—Lys Assia's Refrain for Switzerland[3]—was announced. The mythical character of this first contest and victory is further strengthened by the fact that the visual archive of the event was lost and only the recording of the winning performance's reprise has reached us. Lys Assia also sang the second Swiss entry in 1956 and she competed again in the 1957 and 1958 contests, but almost every single mention of her name on cyberspace leaves out her three nonwinning participations. Instead of that, she is permanently described as the *Grande Dame Eurovision*, hence as an icon unanimously deserving the audience's profound respect. Nonetheless, on at least three occasions reactions were mitigated, to say the least.

The first incident occurred in 2005, when the eighty-one-year-old Lys Assia gave an interview in which, besides talking about her golden years, she overtly expressed her desire to participate once more, exactly fifty years after her legendary victory.[4] The second incident happened in 2007, when Lys Assia eventually took part in the *Grand Prix der Volksmusik*.[5] Even though she was expected to easily win the trophy, she finished twelfth out of sixteen performers. Disappointed with the result, she bitterly declared: "Next year I'll take part in the ESC! We'll see, maybe I can get a few more points there." The third incident relates to the fact that Lys Assia has been the official guest of either the EBU or the local organizers for about ten years now, always representing the irreplaceable debut and proving the longevity of the contest. This was particularly noticeable in a press conference organized during the fortnight of the 2009 contest held in Moscow. The special guests were Lys Assia as the first winner and Dima Bilan as the most recent one, and the point of the interview was to celebrate both continuity and progress. The official coverage of the event underlined Lys Assia's statement that "she enjoyed the ESC back in her day," as well as her desire that "the song would be at the front, not the dancers, the loud sound." She also stated that she "would like to see the contest return to focus more on the singing tradition, singing a simple song."[6]

Most fans' reactions focused on the inappropriate perspective of Lys Assia's fifth participation: "Sigh, she's so old nobody even knows when she was born"; (*sic*) "I'm just disappointed that she gave herself away for such a cheap freak-show, singing in front of deaf [. . .] people"; "She is about to destroy her reputation and might end up as a person to be laughed about. Can someone prevent it from happening?" For some others, it was excellent news: "It would be great to have this kind of quality in Athens, fifty years after the historic start of Eurovision!" "The joke here is people who give Lys Assia no respect. (*sic*) The first lady of Eurovision, what a legend! Personally I think it would be a mistake for Lys to enter for 2006, but who am I to say that! " The same pattern of the return to the good old times, as well as of the need for pure songs of quality instead of noise and mess, is repeated in Lys Assia's statement. Such statements undoubtedly preserve her as an emblematic figure and an exemplary reminder of the glorious origins of the contest.

In my reading, disillusionment in the comments was partly due to the violent decontextualization of the *Grande Dame*'s previously young and vibrant body or, at least, to the questioning of the lively memory of that body, as well as to its sudden exposure to natural decline. On the other hand, anticipation of Lys Assia's comeback is based on that body's quasi-magical possibility to carry a specific there-and-then with it, while fans' speechlessness is justified by its exquisiteness and superiority. The constant exposure of the current Lys Assia body to the public sphere (either on cyberspace or in real-life situations) does not cancel its matchlessness, as long as she appears in circumstances which remain peripheral to the contest, does not remedy the amnesia to which her nonwinning participations are condemned, and does not attempt to duplicate the precious 1956 one.

The unique 1956 winning Lys Assia's corporeal self attains the status of a quasi-holy body, as it becomes a kind of essence capable of perpetuating what it stood for back then, while overwhelming the competence of today's fans to express their objections. This holy body is not simply concurrent with the genesis of the contest, but it is almost expelled from the realm either of the past or our era, hence it is timeless. In fact, it puts together a particular Eurovision ethics based on a *noli me tangere*, because this unique body is respected only as far as it is fixed, trapped in time, embalmed in the aura of the unrepeatable and mummified, thanks to the fans' protection to which it is involuntarily submitted. According to a fan's opinion, a nameless someone should prevent the holy body from refinding the track of time and a higher power should take it into custody in order to forbid its desecration. It could neither be consumed by the profane Eurovision fans who do not realize the importance of the matter and its historical depth, nor by the numerous non-Eurovision freaks hanging around. The impotent subject, Lys Assia, cannot let itself get older, and it definitely does not have the last word on its own destiny as a founding body.

Let me turn our attention to a case of almost accomplished disrespect. In 2006 the post-Olympic city of Athens would be hosting the contest and, in order to support the Netherlands, who since the late 1990s had suffered poor results, the Dutch national broadcaster announced its intention to organize a special event for the selection of its entry. The last Dutch representative, Glennis Grace, would carry an Olympic flame into the venue of the national final and a former participant's dress would be burnt. According to a speculation made by the Esctoday.com columnist, the project was most likely to make the "symbolic statement that the

Netherlands is leaving its history behind to make a new, fresh start."[7] The three candidate dresses for this redoubtable honor were those of Heddy Lester (1977),[8] Maribelle (1984),[9] and Alice May (1990).[10] In order to better understand the criteria of this selection, one could take a closer look at the case of Maribelle, who gained huge popularity among fans and, despite her modest joint thirteenth position, her performance was included in the official *50 Years of Eurovision* DVD containing the fifty winners and another fifty favorite entries. This was possible thanks both to Maribelle's performance and to her unforgettable romantic dress which earned a somewhat endearing "Barbara Dex" reception almost a decade before the appearance of Barbara Dex herself.[11]

As soon as this project was announced, many fans focused on the idea that this is an ultimately discourteous act vis-à-vis past achievements and in a sense they were willing to defend Dutch performers' integrity. Some of the comments read: "That's sacrilege! I hope it's not the real dress"; or, "If the dress burning means they want to forget all the brilliant Dutch songs from the past, I think only a miracle will ever see the Netherlands in a final again!" Some other fans see this as an asset to the Eurovision show, or as another proof of the Eurovision extreme: "Just when you thought pre-selections this year could not get any stranger. Imagine if the Dutch win Eurovision this year; former losers hold on to your dresses! " or, "This gives me an excellent idea. I am sure we would like to use a torch and a can of gasoline for some past participants in Eurovision"; or even, "This is so camp! It can only happen at Eurovision." Yet, some others adopt a more realistic attitude and recall the organizers back to order: "Come up with a decent song and stop complaining—your songs so far this year suck"; or, "Netherlands, shut up, put your energy into writing a good song instead of symbols."

What I see in these reactions is a certain concern about the basics of Eurovision history and the recognizable references of the Eurovision saga; a touch of nostalgia for the Eurovision classics and oldies; a tendency to see the minor event announced by the Dutch broadcaster as the extravagant supplement to the always already eccentric major event that is the ESC; the black humor or even the macabre dryness with which the application of the same method to less respected Eurobodies is recommended; and, finally, the scorn for moves with a metaphysical dimension, as well as the urge to move away from symbolic gestures and focus on professional work instead. These reactions to the Eurovision flame show can also be read as another attempt to protect the integrity of Eurovision moments (in this case a well-remembered performance) and, as a result, the consistency of the contest's *long durée*. Such a concern is not incompatible with the usual cruel critique against the ESC, as the frequent comments about its kitsch and lack of measure do not necessarily result in an effort to dismantle, standardize, and normalize it. The respect for disproportionate Eurobodies is supposed to save Eurovision as a fascinating or ludicrous object and at the same time to maintain it within the realm of the earthly, the regular, and the approachable.

To sum up, fans' reactions to Lys Assia's statements and to the Dutch broadcaster's project indicate that there is no haunting ESC past fans should get away from, no repulsively lingering Eurobodies, and probably no skeleton in the Euro-cupboard either. On the contrary, one should face them in their original shape, which is the only one to guarantee them a place in the ESC gallery; and if Eurobodies are the "there-and-thens" of the contest, their materiality neither should nor could be extended. Just as Lys Assia is not only identifiable but also praisable in her fayum portrait, Heddy Lester, Maribelle, and Alice May cannot disappear, not even for the good of their compatriots or the achievement of the national cause. In the all-embracing Eurovision mythology bodies had better rest in peace where they belong and, as Sekula commented on photographic portraiture, be part of "a system of representation capable of functioning both *honorifically* and *repressively*" (Sekula 1986, 6). If the Eurovision iconography presupposes a sanctifying procedure, envisioning the future of the ESC should by no means pester the truthfulness of those historical bodies turned into icons.

BULLETPROOF JACKETS, PEACE SONGS, AND THE RELUCTANT POLITICIZATION OF THE ESC

The fixed Eurobodies resemble a nonnegotiable basis for comments and discussion, which should not be altered if the "value system" of the ESC is to be sustained. But how does this protectionism vis-à-vis Eurobodies work when non-Eurovision elements (such as "raw" politics, violence, or even terrorism) attempt to intrude on Eurovision realities? The answer to this question presupposes a different type of reaction than the embarrassment provoked by what Coleman would call the "cultural disembeddedness" of the ESC, that is to say the intrusion of a foreign, non-Eurovision-related logic or attitude.[12] What needs to be explained is how the secluded Eurobodies are venerated and protected from a violent recontextualization. To this effect, I will comment on reactions to three Israeli entries.

Ilanit was the very first Israeli representative in 1973 and, dressed almost like a flower child, she sang "Ey Sham."[13] The ESC took place only seven months after the twentieth Summer Olympics held in Munich and only a few hundred miles from the site of the massacre,[14] in the city of Luxembourg. It is a widespread legend that, due to security reasons, Ilanit was wearing a bulletproof vest during her performance, and this possibility is mentioned in the history sections of several websites. A couple of years ago, Ilanit stated that the security was very tight, but she also added that "there was a story that I had a bulletproof vest under my dress for security but it was not true. It was just a story."[15] A similar legend circulates among Eurovision fans about the Israeli entry ten years later. In 1983 Ofra Haza sang "Chai" in the very city of Munich.[16] Memories of the massacre were still strong, it was the first contest after the 1982 war in Lebanon, and the audience was asked to remain seated while applauding due to fear of a terrorist attack. The pro-Israeli presence in the hall was remarkably loud, as were the boos every time Israel got low points and every time, especially toward the end of the show, Luxembourg, the eventual winner of the evening, got high ones. It is also believed that Ofra Haza's behavior was rather unexpected at least when it is compared to today's Eurovision manners: she was rumored to have refused any social activity, spent all her time in a hotel room, and showed up only for the rehearsals and the final evening. This information is persistently repeated around the Web and has created the conviction that the 1983 Israeli act was a particularly sensitive moment in the history of the contest. They also have nourished the suspicion, or even the belief, that Ofra Haza was another Israeli representative to sing under some kind of threat.[17]

I think that similar narratives reflect upon what the ESC had to go through back in those "wild times." Although fans are usually well informed about new developments and discoveries in the history of Eurovision and despite the official EBU and many fans' principle that one should not mix up Eurovision with politics, such legends tend to live on at the expense of historical accuracy. However, neither the fact that such myths are not as easily discredited as they are constituted, nor the will to verify whether Ilanit actually wore a bulletproof jacket seem to me of major importance. What I find significant is that such stories keep canceling the cruel intrusion of the profane world into the sacred space of the Eurovision temple. In some way, they keep helping the contest's spirit overcome the attacks of other worlds and survive in its autonomy. More generally, I see this as a claim for a light politicization of the contest: on the one hand, there is a thin layer of pragmatics that guarantees Eurovision's being-in-the world; on the other hand, the potentially vulnerable corporeality of the contest adds a minimum of realism to a continuing fiction and, at the same time, asserts the very existence of the show.

Parenthetically, I could mention that the step-by-step emergence of the two legends and the various references to them are constantly reinforced by the recurring astonishment about the very fact that Israel as a non-European country regularly participates in the ESC[18]—thus the idea that Israel is a country somehow aside[19]—and by the underlying assumption that Israel's participation is by definition more political than other countries', something largely due to its involvement in local conflicts and to its role on the international scene.

This postulation became very obvious in 2009, when Israel was represented by Noa and Mira Awad, a Jew-Arab duo who sang "There Must Be Another Way."[20] The choice of the performers, the lyrics of the song, and a staging that included fraternal touching and caressing were seen as clearly political statements. Not surprisingly, the wrap-up post of Eurovision.tv was entitled "Israel trying to find 'another way,'"[21] while before the contest, Esctoday.com focused on the particular interest that media even outside Europe showed for the Israeli entry.[22] Fans' reactions to those posts were more or less predictable, as they related to the meaning this entry had for the country it represented and for the European audience. Some of them read as follows: "The girls presented themselves very well. My wife [. . .] voted for it, [because] it was very moving. I think it was bland and a bit obvious on the politically correct side." Or, "my criticism is not about the song itself, nor the lyrics or performers. My criticism is aimed against the Israeli Broadcasting Authority (IBA) who chose this kind of duo on purpose to convey a non-written/spoken message about peace—'Look at us! Nothing is wrong here! If so, how come an Arab Israeli and a Jew Israeli can stand together side by side and sing about peace?' Ridiculous." Another comment approaches the matter in a more general way: "I criticize the performers as well for expressing themselves politically by their opinions about the song. In my opinion anyone can sing about peace, but politically promoting the ideas of peace behind the song is killing the song and is killing the contest. If you wanna sing—sing, don't preach and don't involve politics. If you want to express yourselves politically, ESC does not welcome you! Do it somewhere else! Let us all ESC fans welcome Eurovision music plain—as it is—no surrounding topics or background involving politics."

As I mentioned earlier, fans' reactions to historical and political issues often depend on information available on Eurovision-related sites. These reactions tend to adopt some basic—and often totally unsophisticated—patterns of understanding political issues, which ignore the broader contexts and privilege Eurovision-bound approaches. What is rather simplistically said a propos of the Middle East in terms of a bilateral Israeli-Arab conflict which goes on for years and will certainly remain unsolvable if people do not give the best of themselves, is more or less repeated about the situation in postwar Balkans, the relationships between ex-Soviet states, or the division of Cyprus. Other matters with considerable historical depth, such as whiteness and blackness in the ESC, are almost totally ignored in a way that makes one think that relevant issues are undeniably ignored (see Mulsaers 2007). Politically oriented comments are for the most part confined to the headlines of a stereotypical perception of history, and political reality, and automatically translated into a description, explanation, or prediction of Eurovision alliances. In other words, political issues tend to be seen in a bluntly Eurovision-oriented perspective and in a naïvely linear way. For example, if ex-Yugoslavian states exchange points regularly, this means that things in the region have improved quite fast and in the right way; and the fact that a Jew-Arab duet has appeared on stage is either a typical case of Israeli propaganda, or strong evidence that consensus is possible on an individual basis, thus it might give us a hint about how to proceed in the future.

Moreover, fans' reactions focus on the fact that the contest is politicized because of non-Eurovision meanings injected into it, that politicization is detrimental to its music-centeredness, and finally that the contest is not meant to be a site of political debate. This last point explains why the contest is thought to be misused each time the diffusion of disorienting messages is tolerated. Similar discourses echo what is regularly repeated both by EBU officials[23] and participating artists, who tend to describe the event in terms of music, spectacle, and entertainment as opposed to a multifaceted glocal forum. The same leitmotiv is repeated whenever voting patterns are discussed: regular exchange of votes between specific countries is thought to be politically, rather than culturally, motivated, but nevertheless avoidable if new voting systems aligned to the much-wanted depoliticization of the event are adopted.[24] In a nutshell, the implied conviction seems to be that politics is not only harmful to the essence of a—nevertheless international—event like the ESC, but also virtually separable from it.

THE LOUD POLITICS OF THE QUEER EUROBODY[25]

In 2000, after a fierce debate within Israel and despite the reaction of ultra-orthodox religious groups, the group PingPong, consisting of two male and two female performers who could hardly be distinguished for their singing skills, was chosen to represent the country in Stockholm with the song "Sa'me'akh."[26] The postcard introducing the song was filmed in Stockholm public library; it was a tribute to the well-known Israeli writer Amos Oz and figured his novel *A Panther in the Basement*, initially published in 1995, that was translated into Swedish under the title *Panter i källaren* the year before the contest. The choice of an author who has been a longtime supporter of the idea of a two-state solution in the Israeli-Palestinian conflict underlined, in quite an obvious way, the performance's straightforward political message. But let me focus on the entry itself. Even though Eurovision lyrics usually fail to gain the attention of commentators or fans, these ones quickly became notorious. The translation goes as follows:

> All day long I sit in the kibbutz
> In my hand a cigar and it feels a little sour
> All the time only depression and boredom
> If I don't come, it will end with a bang [. . .]
> All day long wars on television [. . .]
> Here comes the Sunday depression
> I want, I want a cucumber [. . .]
> And now I have a new boyfriend from Damascus
> When I'm sad, he sends me a red rose [. . .]
> I want to do it with him the whole day long.

Bohlman describes this song as one of "national entries that flaunt their own abnegation of a more serious nationalist voice," because it does not "espouse an apolitical ennui, but rather draws the listener's attention to the very danger that it signals" (Bohlman 2001, 291). The neo-hippie peace-and-love pattern of the lyrics was repeated on stage: during the first minute of the song the two boys of the group approached each other and kissed instantly, some seconds later one of them ironically repeated a military salute, and just before the end of the performance the group started waving Israeli and Syrian flags in a clearly celebratory way. The IBA had initially backed the controversial decision of the selection committee that wanted to keep track of the highly sexualized and successful Dana International's entry in 1998.[27] Neither the provocative lyrics nor the more or less open gayness of the group prevented a state television station from selecting it.[28] In fact, the IBA withdrew its support only after one of the last rehearsals, when waving Syrian flags first became part of the act. It was only at that point that the chairman of the IBA, declared that PingPong will "now have to pay its own way to the event which takes place tomorrow night in Stockholm [. . .]. They will compete there, but not on behalf of the IBA or the Israeli people. They are representing only themselves."[29] In my view, this declaration confirmed the ambiguous stance of a public instance systematically tolerating and even promoting sexual libertinage as an element to be staged and, at the same time, taking a much more conservative position as far as the manipulation of national symbols is concerned.

The fans' perspective is, however, quite different. Whenever this entry comes up, the reactions vary from recurrent references to the gay kiss as a political statement or an activist act to comments honoring the libertine Israeli body politics only two years after the triumph of Dana International and the presumed outing of the ESC. Comments also include connections between sexual freedom and pacifist political movements in the Middle East, remarks about the contest's establishing links of brotherhood between people, hence achieving its primary goal which was to bring European people closer to each other after the Second World War, as well as the hope that the spirit of the performance should be applied to real situations both in the Middle East and worldwide. Nevertheless, it remains to elucidate what differentiated the case of PingPong from other politicized entries. If a pacifistic statement coming from an Israeli entry is mistrustful, the factor that helped it come across the Eurovision fan community so well needs to be explained. The difference might reside in the role of the desiring body which is described by the song and freely expresses itself on a stage where no apartheids should be conceivable. Gayness might also have facilitated this contact between Eurovision and politics. But should then the Eurovision stage be conceived of as an open-plan boudoir? And to what extent is the previous scheme of suspicion vis-à-vis the political dimension of the contest renegotiated, loosened, or even suspended?

In order to sketch some answers to these questions, I will attempt a reading of two more Eurovision episodes.[30] The first one concerns the song which, according to Terry Wogan's memorable comment, "we have been waiting for since the beginning of the evening, or perhaps since the beginning of time."[31] In 1997 Paul Oskar sang "Minn hinsti dans" for Iceland, and the performance involved the main singer and four female dancers starting off as a *tableau vivant* set around a white leather couch, then on several occasions adopting sexually suggestive poses which were never seen on the Eurovision stage before. The entry ended up quite low on the scoreboard. However it became one of the fans' favorites, and on the relevant websites it is often mentioned that it had a remarkable appeal to the big public, for the simple reason it received almost all its points from the five countries that used televoting that year.[32] Fans' reactions have made explicit all kinds of traits and connotations of the performance: the mystical element of the rhythm, the flamboyant androgyny of the central figure, the hedonism implied by the excessive use of makeup, the hybrid glam-and-gothic character of the jewelry, the almost sadomasochistic connotations of the dancers' latex outfit, the ritual-like choreography which insisted on overexposing the figures while acting on stage, the atmosphere of a potential orgy à la *Eyes Wide Shut*, and finally the explicitness of an almost pansexual proclamation. In the context of Eurovision fandom, the above elements are most times considered to be not only memorable constituents but also major advantages of the performance which have not been fully appreciated by the unadventurous juries. One can also easily speculate that the aesthetics of "Minn Hinsti Dans"'s visualized fantasy has become emblematic mainly thanks to the cumulative use of recognizable gay insignia.

A different version of the gay imagery is included in another incident, almost every aspect of which has already been properly spelled out by fans and made its way to non-Eurovision forums.[33] During the second part of the 2006 contest held in Athens, the Dutch vote was presented by the openly gay TV persona, singer and comedian Paul de Leeuw. While almost always the announcement of the results includes nothing more than some greetings, congratulations on the quality of the show, and the famous "points," in this case things happened quite differently. A few seconds before De Leeuw appeared on screen, the female presenter Maria Menounos headed for the green room and left the male presenter Sakis Rouvas alone on stage. Paul de Leeuw began with an ambiguous "good evening" in Greek, which sounded like a *"kalisper(m)a"*; *sperma* meaning semen, the greeting was a cheesy gay pun shifting the tone from that of a routine Eurovision voting to a potentially dirty chat. De Leeuw then went on to say "you look like Will and Grace," the reference being of course to the cult American sitcom telling the story of a gay male and a straight female character who obviously corresponded to de Leeuw's perception of Rouvas and Menounos respectively. Instead of starting the announcement of the results with the expected "here we go" or "let's go," de Leeuw chose a naturally pronounced and fast "let's come"; immediately after that, he deviated from the rule not to pronounce points from one to seven and did a hurricane-like presentation, or, as it has been pointed out, a quickie. Just before the peak of the big points, he resumed the normal tempo of the presentation and asked Rouvas: "Are you ready, chaki, katsiki, chikaki?" Moving from "Saki" to "Chaki," de Leeuw brings Rouvas a little closer to *chico* (meaning "boy" in Spanish, therefore adding a little Latin flavor to his discourse and alluding to the stereotype of the Mediterranean stud represented in this case by the host), as well as to *katsiki* (which stands for "young male goat" in Greek, thus indirectly referring to satyrs, the goat-like mythological creatures that are remembered both as unprincipled and playful, and as timid and cowardly), not to mention the diminutive *–aki* which was added to the third appellation and rendered the little naughty boy even littler. De Leeuw went even further before the ten points, when he addressed Rouvas as "Chica, Chuca." In just two words, he described him as the female equivalent of the *chico* mentioned earlier (*chica* meaning "girl" in Spanish) and he almost placed him in *Chueca*, namely the gay village of Madrid. The combination of the *chaki, chika, chuca*, and *katsiki* elements oriented the dialogue toward both the fascination with geographically defined types of men and bestiality as the most extreme or spectacular version of sexuality. In other words, it was by combining the globally appreciated mediterraneanness and a touch of folklore that Rouvas was seen as a gay icon and safely replaced in his homeland.

But this episode did not end with that jokey mélange of origins and stereotypes. De Leeuw voluntarily gave his imaginary cell phone number to Rouvas (0031-6-2474443210 #1), correctly using the international code for calling the Netherlands and the digit 6 for reaching a cell phone in that country, whereas the "dial 1" component at the end of the number alluded to professional sex services and added to the "sluttishness" of de Leeuw's move. At his turn, Rouvas, the local, omitted the international code and gave a rather embarrassed response ("I bet it's 69-69-69"). In doing so, he chose what could be the beginning of a real cell phone number in Greece (the number 69) and also opted for a multiple innuendo: the repetitive mode of this imaginary number could imply de Leeuw's awkward manners and banal sense of humor, his tiring obsession with sex, gay mannerism, and perhaps a certain lack of variety in his repertoire. De Leeuw's counter answer replaced the discussion in its initial context: "No, no, no, I'm not *the* French guy" referred, according to some testimonies, to Rouvas's interview with a French journalist who assumed that Rouvas was gay and asked questions according to his presumptions. It is no need to mention that a gay-oriented interview of a closeted or straight media persona is the kind of news to be effectively propagated mainly within the gay community. In any case, with his last line de Leeuw reassumed the role of the progressive Nordic/Western/European gay individual who has come to terms with his sexuality, and placed Rouvas within the Southern/Oriental/Mediterranean sensual yet traditionalist space censoring him.

All in all, my close reading of reactions to and comments on the three episodes aimed to show that an important part of PingPong's entry, Paul Oskar's performance, and the De Leeuw episode were frequently read in a precise manner by a specific audience. According to what I analyzed in the first two sections, the Eurovision community often seems to avoid the renegotiation of Eurobodies as an act of disrespect for its historicity and to be relieved when the intrusion of harsh reality is avoided. In the third section, however, the same Eurovision community did not abstain from a pragmatic reading. On the occasion of three explicitly queer moments, a rich and explicit discourse vaguely referring to the ESC and clearly relative to issues of the "queer world" and, consequently, to body politics, was articulated. Varying from the interconnections of peace and gayness to a particular homo-aesthetics and from there to the trivia and the codes of the gay scene, queerness was legitimately present in the context of the ESC, thus considered as utterly harmless, if not reinforcing, to the integrity of the event.

FIXED HISTORY, MENACING POLITICS,
AND THE INHERENT QUEER

In the first part of the essay, I explored a number of ways in which Eurobodies are quasi-sanctified and attached to the idea that, in order to be
preserved, the ESC could even become a kind of audiovisual mausoleum.
References to Eurovision figures and events are in fact references to different versions of Euro-corporeality—that is to a specific here-and-now,
thus often accompanied by an implicit and impossible demand that the
Eurobodies are stabilized and the corpus or the Eurovision self-imaginary
is set. In the second part, I insisted on the Eurobodies' reluctant politicization. Placing special emphasis on the fans' repetitive quest for a
contest freed from politics, I showed how fans describe the Eurobodies
as instances both including and excluding, in very different ways and
intensities, the "out there." While the holy Eurobodies of the first section
enjoyed a soothing autonomy, the endangered Eurobodies of the second
one benefited from the safety that the Eurovision circuit offers them. To
my understanding, the almost lacerated body or the body-to-be-killed
are embraced to the extent that they are firmly located in the past, they
escaped the risk, and they can now serve as a proof or a reminder of the
ESC's aptitude to survival. In the first two parts of this essay, the fans'
reactions do not deny, reject, or altogether exclude the blatantly political
body, but they both see and ignore its political dimension; they can only
notice it and at the same time they put it aside as a by definition non-
Eurovisionesque element. In other words, even though it is clear that the
attempt to dehistoricize and depoliticize a non-dehistoricizable and non-
depoliticizable event like the ESC is bound to fail, it is also perceived as a
proof of loyalty to its supposed essence.

In the third part, I observed a selective tolerance toward politics, which
was especially obvious in the cases of queer Eurovision episodes and
testified for a different attitude of the Eurovision community vis-à-vis
corporeality, more open to non-Eurovision realities and more willing to
admit its unpreventable relation to politics. In this case, corporeality was
thoroughly analyzed by fans, explanations were given, and parallels were
made, always in the mode of spontaneous reactions but with a remarkable persistence. Queer Eurobodies were more exportable to reality than
those described in the first two sections, or at least more overtly in touch
with parallel public fictions and life practices.

I wanted my analysis to be a response to the usual disbelief vis-à-vis
the ESC, which has persuasively been summarized by Philip Bohlman:
"watching the May television extravaganza, one can only wonder how

such a spectacle of bread and circus could possibly signal political issues of any real significance," because "everything from national costume to national musical nuance is remade for television and transformed to sound more familiar than different" (Bohlman 2004, 289). Assuming that the leveling of differences and the management of oppositions between different tastes and traditions often leads to the choice of harmless songs, I tried to understand the counterpart of this leveling in fans' reactions and their insistence on the comforting depoliticization of the event. Talking about Eurobodies, I tried to figure out which edges of the Eurovision phenomenon were the ones to be smoothened.

Going through a number of Eurovision episodes, I noticed a fan's attitude toward history reducing it to the celebration or rejection of well-shaped and nonamendable snapshots, a durable suspicion against the invasiveness of politics as a permanent threat to Eurovision's uprightness, and the ease with which the queer finds its way to Eurovision discourses. A thread uniting fragmentary historicity, reluctant politicization, and abundant queerness is obviously needed here. If these three elements are projected onto corporeality as a there-and-then, it is important to understand what exactly is thought to have been *there*, in other words what stuff Eurovision is made of. Questioning the state of the Eurobody meant investigating into the Eurovision community's perception of what belongs to the event itself and what is potentially added to it. If the Eurobody is defined as a momentum and politics is excluded as hostile to the ESC, queerness can only be seen as a different kind of politics, a non-menacing politics, or even as a politics which is inherent to the Eurovision phenomenon. If the Eurovision community is surprisingly sensible to the idea of an immaculate contest, its tolerance to queerness can only be explained if the latter is attributed to the event itself, in other words if it is already there waiting to be discovered; in a way, this could be the most recent version of Eurovision's queer "common secret" (Tuhkanen 2007, 46). Queerness transgresses the boundaries separating the event from its fans, the show from its following, or the text from its receptions. An effort to explain the well-known idea that the ESC is a major gay event of our time should perhaps take into consideration the quasi-naturalization of queerness I described here. Seen as inherent to the ESC rather than as a value added to it, queerness remains a basic key to its understanding, maybe illegible for those indifferent to it but nonetheless captivating for those initiated to its codes. After all, where a good number of fans think that Eurovision history is written once for all and that Eurovision politics should be as skimmed as possible, queerness could be the materialistic shibboleth of the Eurovision community.

NOTES

1. The original French lyrics read as follows: "Mes disques sont un miroir, dans lequel chacun peut me voir / Je suis partout à la fois, brisée en mille éclats de voix."

2. It is needless to remind that similar body-related fictions also abound outside the ESC context; among the most obvious examples one could mention the "low culture" discourses associated with the blackness and the death of Michael Jackson, or the "high culture" ones related to the performances of body artists such as Stelarc or Orlan.

3. The music of the song was composed by Géo Voumard and the lyrics were written by Émile Gardaz.

4. See Bakker, Sietse. 2005. "A Wish to Come True: Lys Assia's Dream to Participate Once Again!" *ESCtoday.com* (August 18). Accessed June 16, 2011. http://www.esctoday.com/news/read/4882.

5. The *Grand Prix der Volksmusik* is the major German-language folk song contest uniting Germany, Austria, Switzerland, and the German-speaking part of Italy. Lys Assia performed the song "Sag mir wo wohnen die Engel" (Tell Me Where the Angels Live), accompanied by the eighteen-year-old Beatrice. See Holyer, Steve. 2007. " 'Maybe I Can Get a Few More Points in Belgrade': Lys Assia Disappointed by Folk Music Result." *ESCtoday.com* (August 29). Accessed June 16, 2011. http://www.esctoday.com/news/read/9146.

6. See Glenn, Web. 2009. "EBU Press Conference: Two Legends Attend." *Eurovision.tv* (May 14). Accessed June 16, 2011. http://www.eurovision.tv/page/news?id=2586.

7. See Bakker, Sietse. "National Songfestival 2006: Olympic Flame and Dress to Burn in Dutch Final." *ESCtoday.com* (March 7). Accessed June 16, 2011. http://www.esctoday.com/news/read/5723.

8. Heddy Lester sang "De Mallemolen" (The Merry-Go-Round), music by Frank Affolter and lyrics by Wim Hogenkamp.

9. Maribelle sang "Ik hou van jou" (I'm in Love With You), music and lyrics by Peter van Asten and Richard Debois.

10. This dress was the same as that of her stage partner Karen Wood of the group Maywood. Maywood sang "Ik wil alles met je delen" (I Want to Share Everything With You), music and lyrics by Alice May.

11. Barbara Dex represented Belgium in the 1993 ESC with the song "Iemand als jij" (Someone Like You), music by Marc Vliegen and lyrics by Tobana, to come twenty-fifth and last. The performance is mostly remembered because of the self-made dress worn by the singer; it was due to this dress that an annual prize for worst costume called "The Barbara Dex Award" was introduced. In a similar sense, comments about Maribelle's dress are abundant every time her performance appears either on Eurovision-related sites or on Youtube.

12. According to Coleman, "Public embarrassment is a response to feelings of cultural disembeddedness: people's sense that they are witnessing the lifting out of cultural expression from its local context and its enforced rearticulation in terms designed to be comprehended by an amorphous global market." In addi-

tion to that, "Eurovision songs can be accused of such performative contradiction by assuming to communicate transculturally, but in an unmistakably national tone." See Stephen Coleman: "Why Is the Eurovision Song Contest Ridiculous? Exploring a Spectacle of Embarrassment, Irony and Identity," *Popular Communication* 6(3) (2008): 131–32.

13. The title of the song means "somewhere" (music by Nurit Hirsch and lyrics by Ehud Manor).

14. The eighteenth ESC took place on April 7, 1973, while the Munich summer Olympics were held from August 26 to September 11, 1972.

15. See Klier, Marcus. 2007. "No Bulletproof Vest in '73: Another Eurovision Myth Is Debunked." *ESCtoday.com* (May 20). Acessed June 16, 2011. http://www.esctoday.com/news/read/8749.

16. The title of the song means "Alive" (music by Avi Toledano, lyrics by Ehud Manor); one of the verses clearly states that "the nation of Israel is alive."

17. See Shinefield, Mordechai. 2008. "What Eurovision Teaches Us About Israel." *Jewcy* (June 10), Accessed June 16, 2011. http://www.jewcy.com/arts-and-culture/what_eurovision_teaches_us_about_israel.

18. As opposed, for example, to Turkey's orientalism which very rarely comes up in online discussions, whereas it remains a hot topic in the political arena. On the interconnections between "postmodern orientalism" and the ESC (see 2007, 151–54; n. 16); Gumpert also, the chapter by Solomon in the present volume.

19. Israel's geographical eccentricity as far as Europe is concerned is, in my opinion, different from what Björnberg means when he talks about "a symbolic 'revenge of the margins,' an opportunity for culturally peripheral nations to come out on top of those nations normally playing the principal parts in the dissemination of popular culture." Both in cultural terms (Jewishness, Judeo-Christian culture) and in political ones (the establishment of the state of Israel, the Israeli-Palestinian conflict, Israel's relations with the United States, and so on), Israel has been much less "peripheral" than other countries participating in the ESC both before and after its expansion to the East (see Björnberg 2007, 17: 16–19).

20. The song was composed and penned by Noa, Mira Awad, and Gil Dor, and was performed in Hebrew, Arab, and English. Much attention was paid to the fact that Arab was heard on the Eurovision stage for the second time in history, twenty-nine years after Morocco's one and only participation in 1980.

21. Eurovision.tv is the official website of the ESC. See Siim, Jarmo. 2009. "Wrap-Up: Israel Trying to Find 'Another Way.'" *Eurovision.tv* (June 11). Accessed June 16, 2011. http://www.eurovision.tv/page/news?id=3093&_t=Wrap-up%3A+Israel+trying+to+find+%27another+way%27.

22. See Hondal, Victor. 2009. "Oshida to Design Costumes. Israel: World Media Focus on Noa & Mira." *ESCtoday.com* (April 15). Accessed June 16, 2011. http://www.esctoday.com/news/read/13723.

23. cf. for example the statement made by Svante Stockselius, executive EBU coordinator, during a press conference in the 2009 contest in Moscow.

24. Let us not forget that "the live TV-voting allows countries to declare their sympathy with, disinterest in, or disapproval of each other. This competition can be understood as a playful version of war" (see Rehberg 2007, 62).

25. Throughout this section, I understand "queer" both as a term summarizing lesbian, gay, bisexual, and transgender, and as an overall defamiliarizing and questioning process (see Sullivan 2003, 37–56).

26. The title of the song means "Happy" (music and lyrics by Guy Asif, Ronen Ben-Tal, and Roy Arad).

27. This is, of course, not common practice for many broadcasters around Europe that tend to opt for "safer" performances. The example of Finnish television is analyzed by Pajala in (see Pajala 2007).

28. On Israel's liberal sexual politics as it is expressed through the ESC see Tobin 2007 31–35; 33; also Solomon 2003, 149–65. On the repercussions of Dana International's victory see Lemish 2007, 131–33.

29. See Goldenberg, Suzanne. 2000. "Outraged Israel Disowns Daring Eurovision Entry." *Guardian.co.uk* (May 12). Accessed June 16, 2011. http://www.guardian.co.uk/world/2000/may/12/israel.

30. In my analysis, I will not try to figure out whether the three Eurovision episodes analyzed in this section belong to "commodity" or to "dissociative camp," but I have reasons to suspect that fans' reactions to them emerge owe a lot to their ambiguity. About this useful distinction see Rehberg and Tuhkanen 2007, 47–50, 50–57.

31. Terry Wogan's comment was also referring to the fact that the song appeared on stage twenty-fifth and last. The title of the song means "My Final Dance" (music by Páll Óskar Hjálmtýsson and Trausti Haraldsson, lyrics by Páll Óskar Hjálmtýsson).

32. 1997 was the year when televoting was introduced. It was originally used by five countries (United Kingdom, Sweden, Austria, Switzerland, and Germany). For more information see "Eurovision Song Contest 1997," ESCtoday.com, http://www.esctoday.com/annual/1997/participants.php (June 16, 2011).

33. Among many other references to this particular episode see "Paul de Leeuw," Wikipedia.org, http://en.wikipedia.org/wiki/Paul_de_leeuw. Accessed June 16, 2011.

REFERENCES

Printed Sources

Bard, Alexander, and Jan Söderqvist. 2002. *Netocracy: The New Power Elite and Life after Capitalism*. London: Reuters.

Björnberg, Alf. 2007. "Return to Ethnicity: The Cultural Significance of Musical Change in the Eurovision Song Contest." In *A Song for Europe: Popular Music and Politics in the Eurovision Song Contest*, edited by Ivan Raykoff and Robert Deam Tobin, 13–23. Aldershot: Ashgate.

Bohlman, Philip V. 2004. *The Music of European Nationalism: Cultural Identity and Modern History*. Santa Barbara: ABC-CLIO.

Bordo, Susan. 1997. *Twilight Zones: The Hidden Life of Cultural Images from Plato to O.J.* Berkeley, Los Angeles, London: University of California Press.

Butler, Judith. 1993. *Bodies That Matter: On the Discursive Limits of "Sex."* New York, London: Routledge.

Coleman, Stephen. 2008. "Why is the Eurovision Song Contest Ridiculous? Exploring a Spectacle of Embarrassment, Irony and Identity," *Popular Communication* 6(3): 127–40.

Foucault, Michel. 1979. *Discipline and Punish: The Birth of the Prison* [1975], translated by A. Sheridan. New York: Second Vintage Books.

Georgiou, Myria. 2008. "'In the End, Germany Will Always Resort to Hot Pants': Watching Europe Singing, Constructing the Stereotype," *Popular Communication* 6(3): 141–54.

Gumpert, Matthew. 2007. " 'Every Way That I Can': Auto-Orientalism at Eurovision 2003." In *A Song for Europe: Popular Music and Politics in the Eurovision Song Contest*, edited by Ivan Raykoff and Robert Deam Tobin, 147–57. Aldershot: Ashgate.

Lemish, Dafna. 2007. "Gay Brotherhood: Israeli Gay Men and the Eurovision Song Contest." In *A Song for Europe: Popular Music and Politics in the Eurovision Song Contest*, edited by Ivan Raykoff and Robert Deam Tobin, 123–34. Aldershot: Ashgate.

Mutsaers, Lutgard. 2007. "Fernando, Filippo and Milly: Bringing Blackness to the Eurovision Stage." In *A Song for Europe: Popular Music and Politics in the Eurovision Song Contest*, edited by Ivan Raykoff and Robert Deam Tobin, 61–70. Aldershot: Ashgate.

Nancy, Jean-Luc. 1994. "Corpus," transl. by C. Sartiliot. In *Thinking Bodies*, edited by Juliet Flower MacCannell and Laura Zakarin, 17–31. Stanford, Calif.: Stanford California Press.

Pajala, Mari. 2007. "Closeting Eurovision: Heteronormativity in the Finnish National Television." In "Queer Eurovision," edited by Mikko Tuhkanen and Annamari Vänskä. *SQS: Journal of Queer Studies in Finland* 2(2): 25–42.

Raykoff, Ivan, and Robert Deam Tobin, eds. 2007. *A Song for Europe: Popular Music and Politics in the Eurovision Song Contest*. Aldershot: Ashgate.

Rehberg, Peter, and Mikko Tuhkanen. 2007. "Danzing Time: Dissociative Camp and European Synchrony." In "Queer Eurovision," edited by Mikko Tuhkanen and Annamari Vänskä. *SQS: Journal of Queer Studies in Finland* 2(2): 43–59.

Rehberg, Peter. 2007. "Winning Failure: Queer Nationality at the Eurovision Song Contest." In "Queer Eurovision," edited by Mikko Tuhkanen and Annamari Vänskä. *SQS: Journal of Queer Studies in Finland* 2(2): 60–65.

Sekula, Allan. 1986. "The Body and the Archive." *October* 39: 3–64.

Singleton, Brian, Karen Fricker, and Elena Moreo. 2007. "Performing the Queer Network: Fans and Families at the Eurovision Song Contest." In "Queer Eurovision," edited by Mikko Tuhkanen and Annamari Vänskä. *SQS: Journal of Queer Studies in Finland* 2(2): 12–24.

Solomon, Alisa. 2003. "Viva la Diva Citizenship: Post-Zionism and Gay Rights." In *Queer Theory and the Jewish Question*, edited by David Boyarin, Daniel Itzkovitz, and Ann Pellegrini, 149–65. New York: Columbia University Press.

Sullivan, Nikki. 2003. *A Critical Introduction to Queer Theory*. Edinburgh: Edinburgh University Press.

Tobin, Robert Team. 2007. "Eurovision at 50: Post-Wall and Post-Stonewall." In *A Song for Europe: Popular Music and Politics in the Eurovision Song Contest*, edited by Ivan Raykoff and Robert Deam Tobin, 25–35. Aldershot: Ashgate.

Tuhkanen, Mikko. 2007. "Introduction: Queer Eurovision, Post-Closet." In "Queer Eurovision," edited by Mikko Tuhkanen and Annamari Vänskä. *SQS: Journal of Queer Studies in Finland* 2(2): 8–11.

Chapter 7

The Oriental Body on the European Stage

Producing Turkish Cultural Identity on the Margins of Europe

THOMAS SOLOMON

"'Göbek dansı Avrupa'yı fethetti'"—"'Her belly dance conquered Europe.'" So read the headline above one of the several articles that formed the Turkish newspaper *Radikal*'s print and online coverage the day after Turkish singer Sertab Erener won the Eurovision Song Contest (ESC) in May 2003.[1] But the story under the headline reported not so much on the result of the contest itself, but on how the U.K.-based news agency Reuters had reported on it in a wire story widely picked up, with similar headlines, by other European news outlets. The point of the article—in particular its quoting of Reuters's use of the term *belly dance* (in literal translation as *göbek dansı*, not a term actually used much in Turkish) to characterize Sertab's performance—was thus to show how Turkey's performance was received, interpreted, and commented on elsewhere in Europe.[2] In the coming days after the contest, other Turkish newspapers ran similar stories under titles such as *Hürriyet*'s "Dış Basın Ne Dedi" ("What the Foreign Press Said"),[3] again picking up on references in European media to belly dancing in Sertab's performance. This near-obsession in the Turkish press with how Sertab's and Turkey's victory in the ESC was represented in other European countries reflects a long-standing concern in Turkey with Turkey's image in Europe.

Even before the contest date arrived, the way in which Turkey was to be represented in the 2003 ESC was publicly much debated during the process of choosing Turkey's eventual song entry. Should Turkey's song be sung in English or Turkish? Is it appropriate that the musical style of the song, and visual style of the accompanying clip and live performance at the contest itself, draw on orientalist stylistic tropes that would help Turkey stand out from the crowd? Or should Turkey's entry in the contest try to be as European as possible? And what, indeed, does it mean to be "European," and how can "Europeanness" be represented? These debates were about much more than just how to market Turkey in Europe shortly after the turn of the millennium. They form part of an ongoing discussion about Turkish cultural identity going back at least to the founding days of the modern Turkish republic after the First World War, if not to even an earlier cycle of reforms during the late Ottoman period.

In this chapter I explore some aspects of the internal cultural politics that surrounded Turkey's 2003 participation in the ESC. I focus in particular on the controversy surrounding orientalist imagery in the song's promotional video clip, other promotional materials, and the live stage performance during the contest itself. The local discussions in Turkey about orientalism in Sertab's ESC performance, and in the various media texts surrounding the performance itself, show how seriously many in Turkey regard the ESC as a vehicle for Turkey's self-representation on the wider European stage. Turkey's participation in the ESC in 2003 was thus an important moment in the ongoing production of Turkish cultural identity, both for export and for internal consumption.

In a well-known discussion of cultural identity, Stuart Hall has argued that "perhaps instead of thinking of identity as an already accomplished fact, which . . . cultural practices then represent, we should think, instead, of identity as a 'production,' which is never complete, always in process, and always constituted within, not outside, representation" (Hall 1990, 222). The debates in Turkey surrounding its participation in the ESC in 2003 suggest that Turks are keenly aware of how representation constitutes identity and have taken very seriously the representational potential that the ESC has for producing Turkish cultural identity in the European context.

My concern here is not with the politics of Turkey's accession to the European Union (from the European side, largely a politics of economic exclusion, racism, and Islamophobia), but with the ways in which events in the cultural arena are interpreted and play out in Turkey in relation to that politics. Turkey's complex relationship with Europe is an important backdrop for much cultural production in Turkey, especially cultural production meant for export. Many regard those who work in cultural production such as popular music as bearing the responsibility to represent Turkey in particular ways that are thought to help advance Turkey's ambitions to join Europe. Anthropologist Yael Navaro-Yashin discusses what she refers to as the "culture of representation" in Turkey:

> The term "image" (in Turkish, *imaj*, as in the French pronunciation) entered public discourse with the influence of the culture of commercials . . . The advertising industry in Turkey succeeded, in the 1980s, in transforming

the notion of the image of Turkey (in relation to the West, of course) into a popular concern. . . . So much emphasis has been discursively loaded onto the notion of Turkey's image vis-à-vis the West, that it has turned out to be the matter at stake in every public and publicized issue in Turkey. (Navaro-Yashin 2002, 220–21; n. 14)

Navaro-Yashin perhaps overstates the point, but such a concern with the "image of Turkey" in Europe clearly framed the internal debates surrounding Turkey's participation in the ESC in 2003 (and has in other years as well). But to understand the terms of the debate, and what was at stake in these representations, it is necessary first to review the competing imaginations of Turkish cultural identity. Two "master narratives" have recently dominated public discourse in this regard: the westward-looking Kemalist secular nationalism of the "founding fathers" of the republic, and the more recently emergent attempt to reclaim Turkey's Islamic Ottoman heritage.

FROM OTTOMAN TO TURK: INVENTING MODERN TURKISH CULTURAL IDENTITY

Since the Republic of Turkey was founded in 1923 out of the remains of the Ottoman Empire, Turks have been taught that their country is part of the West—that it is fundamentally a European country. Mustafa Kemal, later Atatürk, the father of the modern Turkish republic, introduced a wide program of political and cultural reforms designed to sever Turkey from its multiethnic, Islamic, imperial Ottoman past and create a secular, monoethnic nation-state of Turks modeled on and oriented toward those of Western Europe.

This political and cultural modernization project and the ideology behind it—generally referred to as Kemalism—were comprehensively designed and implemented from the top down to reorient Turkey toward the West (see Lewis 1968, 256–79; Poulton 1997, 87–129; Göle 1996, 57–82). For example, in 1928 a new Latin alphabet for writing Turkish was introduced, replacing the Perso-Arabic script used to write Ottoman Turkish. Reforms of the language itself included attempts to purge it of elements from Persian and Arabic and replace them with forms adapted from rural vernacular Turkish or from contemporary or historical Central Asian Turkic languages, or even with wholly new invented forms thought to be consistent with those of ancient Turkish.[4] Other top-down reforms in the cultural arena include legislated dress reforms such as the "Hat Law" of 1925, which banned the fez and mandated the use of European-style brimmed hats for men (see Göle 1996, 60–61; Lewis 1968, 267–70). This reform had implications for religion as well, since the

brimless fez facilitated the prayer posture of bending forward in sup-
plication until the forehead touches the ground, which the brimmed hat
does not allow. Musical reforms promoted an attempt at a synthesis of
Anatolian folk music and European polyphonic compositional practice.[5]
Whereas the Ottoman emperor had also claimed to be caliph of the Muslim world, Atatürk abolished the caliphate, declared the new republic a
secular state, and introduced other reforms designed to move religion
from the public to the private sphere. The seat of government was moved
from Istanbul, historical capital of the Ottoman Empire, to the formerly
obscure Anatolian town of Ankara, where heritage was reimagined in
terms of continuity with pre-Islamic Anatolian civilizations such as that
of the Hittites. The flip side of this modernization project is that for everything new introduced, something old, connecting republican Turkey
to its Ottoman past, was consequently devalued and officially, at least,
repressed. For example, deprived of official sponsorship after its teaching
institutions and performance contexts were closed down, and banned for
a period from broadcast on the state radio monopoly, the classical music
of the Ottoman courts essentially went "underground," becoming the
preserve of aficionados (see Stokes 1996).

GENDERING THE MODERN[6]

Women, and particularly women's bodies, were especially privileged as
the site where the new political, social, and cultural policies were to be
embodied and performed. Turkish sociologist Nilüfer Göle argues that
"in the Turkish case, the project of modernization equates the nation's
progress with the emancipation of women" (Göle 1997, 86). A number
of Turkish feminist scholars have discussed how the place and role of
women in society were crucial to the modernization plan implemented
during the early Republican era.[7] In contrast to the Ottoman "society of
men," in the Kemalist program women were now to take an active place
in the public sphere. Specific political reforms included abandoning the
Islamic *sharia* law of the Ottoman Empire and replacing it in 1926 with a
new civil code (modeled closely on the Swiss code) which among other
things meant outlawing polygamy and giving equal rights of divorce to
both men and women; and giving women the right to vote and stand for
national office in 1934. Women were (in theory, at least) to have equal
access to education and participation in the professions, and a general
principle of male-female equality was to govern social life.[8]

Besides the structural changes introduced through legislation, there
was also to be corresponding change in the symbolic realm—in ways of
thought, manners, and everyday behavior such as style of dress. While

the veil was not specifically outlawed, women were strongly encouraged to discard it and adopt Western clothing, and the new dress code for women was institutionalized through a network of girls' institutes throughout the country (see Navaro-Yashin 2002, 26). As Göle explains, "the aim of the Atatürk reformation may be said to have been the abolition of the *harem*, both as fact and symbol" (Göle 1993, 20). Women were thus to (be) move(d) symbolically from the harem into the public sphere. The new public roles envisioned for women also represented a symbolic counterattack against prevailing European orientalist views of the backwardness of the Ottoman Empire. Anthropologist Alev Çınar argues that:

> because European perceptions of the Ottoman were heavily conditioned by Orientalist conceptualizations of Islam represented by images of veiled women and women behind harem walls, what better means could the new secularist Turkish state find to distance itself from the Ottoman than by projecting images of women "emancipated" from the confines of the harem having a vivid presence in the public sphere wearing Western clothing? Indeed, women's emancipated and modernized visibility in the public sphere proved to be an excellent means through which the new state displayed its difference from and triumph against its Ottoman-Islamic predecessor. (Çınar 2005, 60)

"The woman question" remains a touchstone issue until this day. Contemporary secularists continue to differentiate themselves from contemporary Islamists on the basis of gender norms,[9] with Islamist women's veiling practices, and the corresponding commodification and politicization of the veil, being the most recent arena where these debates are being played out.[10]

"THE RETURN OF THE REPRESSED": NEO-OTTOMANISM AND ITS DISCONTENTS

The Republican Peoples Party (*Cumhuriyet Halk Partisi*, CHP), the party of Atatürk, pushed through these and other reforms during the early years of the republic and largely consolidated the new cultural regime through a virtual monopoly on political power until 1950, when in the first truly multiparty elections since the new state's founding, a party more tolerant of invocations of Turkey's Ottoman heritage came to power. After an unstable period of several decades characterized by alternations between elected governments and military coups, the center-right administration of president Turgut Özal in the mid-1980s was a watershed, introducing political stability and combining neoliberal economic policies with cultural populism while embracing the Ottoman legacy, setting the stage for the development of what is now widely referred to as "neo-Ottomanism" (*yeni Osmanlılık*), which anthropologist Jenny White usefully defines as "a widespread nostalgia for things Ottoman" (White 2002, 30).[11] This recovery of an imagined Ottoman heritage quickly expanded to fill the areas of cultural life perceived to have been left vacant by the failure of Kemalism to provide people with a sense of cultural identity to adequately replace what it so dramatically had attempted to cut them off from.[12] At the popular level, this recovery of things Ottoman has been manifested in growing interest in heritage arts like Ottoman calligraphy (in Perso-Arabic letters) and *ebru* (marbled paper), these two also being frequently found in combination. In the musical realm it can be seen in revivals of the classical music of the Ottoman courts, the commercialization as nostalgia and "pop-ization" (complete with celebrity singers and slickly produced MTV-style music videos) of the Turkish art song genre *Türk Sanat Müziği*,[13] and the formation of ensembles performing, in full Ottoman costume and on authentic instruments, re-creations of the *mehter* music of the Ottoman Janissary band. Other related developments include the renewed interest in "Ottoman" cuisine in Istanbul since the 1990s[14] and the wave of new fantasy and drama films since 2000 set in Ottoman times.[15] In terms of everyday leisure practices, neo-Ottomanism can be discerned in the explosive growth in popularity since the 1990s of cafés for smoking (using sweet-scented tobacco) the *nargile* (hookah or waterpipe, see Bowman 2009). Turkish anthropologist Öykü Potuoğlu-Cook particularly associates the revival of belly dancing in Istanbul during the 1990s with what she, emphasizing consumption practices, prefers to call "neo-Ottomania" (Potuoğlu-Cook 2006a, 634).

In the sense that it is perceived as a reaffirmation of traditional Turkish culture that had been denied by the Kemalist project, neo-Ottomanism has been characterized by various authors as "the return of the repressed."[16] It has also become the cultural idiom of choice of a new class of Muslim capitalists and "Muslim democrat" politicians who continue the pattern, begun in the Özal era of the 1980s, of "Ottomanist revivalism combined with a version of laissez-faire Westernism" (Navaro-Yashin 2002, 124). When thus politicized, neo-Ottomanism becomes a set of discourses and practices for imagining and performing a specifically Turkish kind of "alternative modernity," in contrast with the modernization-as-westernization paradigm of Kemalism.

While many commentators associate neo-Ottomanism with the revitalization of Islamic movements in Turkey since the 1980s,[17] Potuoğlu-Cook argues that the discourses and consumption practices of neo-Ottomanism actually cut across Islamist and secularist circles (Potuoğlu-Cook 2006a, 634). Ironically, but perhaps not surprisingly, the vocabulary and aesthetics of European orientalist representations provide a ready-made well of representations and practices—from hookah smoking to belly dancing—that neo-Ottomanism, in its various manifestations, has drawn on. Potuoğlu-Cook thus characterizes "neo-Ottomania" as "a classed and gendered self-Orientalism particular to the post-1980s Turkish free-market modernity" (Potuoğlu-Cook 2006a, 638).[18]

The above outline of positionings in regard to what contemporary Turkish cultural identity could or should be—the Europe-oriented legacy of modernization-as-westernization of Kemalism, and the more recently emergent neo-Ottomanism which imagines the possibility of modernization-without-westernization—provides a background for understanding the debates surrounding Turkey's participation in the ESC in 2003. Given Turkey's preoccupation with its relation to Europe, it is no surprise that the ESC stage is considered an important arena for staging Turkish identity for consumption by a European audience.

TURKEY IN EUROVISION 2003

In Turkey, the state-run Turkish Radio and Television (TRT) oversees the country's participation in the ESC. For the 2003 contest, the process to select Turkey's entry started in mid-2002, when TRT decided that instead of having the usual televised Turkish national final to select both the artist and the song, TRT would internally choose the artist, and let the artist create and record three songs for TRT to choose one from. This is a procedure Turkey and other nations have sometimes used in the past, in contrast to the more familiar procedure of each country having a televised national final where the country's representative in the contest is chosen either by popular telephone vote or by a jury of experts. After Turkish pop stars Tarkan and Candan Erçetin reportedly declined TRT's invitation to represent Turkey at the contest, TRT asked its third choice, the well-known Turkish pop singer Sertab Erener.

Sertab has been on the Turkish pop scene since the late 1980s. After finishing classical training as a coloratura soprano in the state conservatory in Istanbul, she became a backup singer for Turkey's famous pop singer Sezen Aksu. She participated (unsuccessfully) in the Turkish ESC national finals in 1989 and 1990, and struck out on her own with her first album *Sakin Ol* in 1992. Several successful albums and a string of hit singles and video clips followed through the 1990s into the early 2000s. Of the three commissioned songs Sertab recorded, TRT eventually chose "Every Way That I Can," an up-tempo pop number—with some Turkish stylings[19]—about a woman's attempts to get an estranged lover to take her back. When TRT announced the English language song and plans for promotional strategies, a veritable storm of debate erupted, with politicians, journalists, and pop music performers all weighing in with their opinions. The controversy centered largely on two issues: Sertab's insistence on singing in English for the contest performance and per-ceived orientalist content in the video clip made to promote the song (see Solomon 2007, 136–37). As the contest date approached and the plans for Sertab's stage performance took shape, the issue of orientalism continued to gain attention as people learned that the live stage performance would include some of the same orientalist tropes as the video clip, in particular belly dancing.

These debates were consistently phrased in terms of issues of represen-tation—since Turkey's participation in the ESC symbolizes its participa-tion in and belonging to Europe itself, how should the song, accompa-nying media texts, and live performance at the contest itself represent Turkey to a European audience?

ORIENTALIST IMAGES: HAREM, *HAMMAM,* HOOKAH, AND BELLY DANCER

The trope of the harem—the hidden interior of the home, be it Ottoman palace or more humble abode, in which women are kept segregated from outside males—has long been a key figure in Western fantasies about the orient. Reina Lewis describes the harem as "that most fertile space of the Orientalist imagination" and notes that in the minds of the West, polygamy and concubinage have been inseparable from this domain of exoticized, hypereroticized women (Lewis 2004, 4; 100).[20] Lewis notes how, by the early twentieth century

> the West's image of the secluded, polygamous Oriental woman had accrued the layers of myth, rumour, and stereotype of a longstanding fascination. The vision of the harem as a sexualized realm of deviancy, cruelty and excess has animated some of the West's best known examples of dominant Orientalism from fine art, to operas, to novels and popular literature. For political thinkers, the (inevitably sexualized) tyrannies of Oriental despotism provided a foil to Europe's own image of just governance, be it monarchy or republic. (Lewis 2004, 96)

As a highly charged symbol of oriental exoticism and backwardness in the West, the harem has a particularly complex position in Turkey. For secular Kemalist proponents of modernization-as-westernization, it sym-bolizes all that Turkey left behind when the new republic was founded and supposedly broke with Ottoman traditions. For Islamists and other neo-Ottomanists, the harem is a historical fact, an undeniable part of the high civilization achieved by the Ottoman Empire, and nothing to be ashamed of. The presence in Turkey today of historical Ottoman sites that once were used as harems—particularly Ottoman palaces in Istanbul—continues to draw Western tourists to the country, making these sites an important economic resource, while also guaranteeing the continuation of Western fantasies about the harem into the future. So it is no surprise that, when the image of the harem began to figure prominently in the representations of Turkey at the ESC in 2003, controversy emerged.

The video clip made to promote Sertab's ESC song, widely shown on television in Turkey during the period surrounding the contest, was shot in two historical Ottoman settings: in a *hammam*, or Turkish bath (the famous Cağaloğlu Hammam in the Sultanahmet area of old Istanbul, built in 1741 by Sultan Mahmut I), and in the harem or former secluded women's quarters of historic Topkapı Palace in Istanbul. The concept of the clip, as explained by Sertab in a press conference held several weeks before the contest, is that Sertab plays a concubine (Turkish *cariye*) of the historical eighteenth-century Ottoman Sultan Abdülhamid I[21] who has fallen out of favor with the sultan and been banished from the harem.[22] Using this historical setting to dramatize the song's lyrics, she is pleading for the Sultan to take her back into the harem.[23] The clip incorporates a veritable catalog of gendered images straight out of orientalist paintings and postcards, including the Turkish bath and harem settings themselves, and women scantily clad in vaguely Middle Eastern–style clothing, smoking hookah water pipes, belly dancing, lying about on cushions, and caressing each other in ways suggestive of lesbianism among the women of the harem (figures 7.1–7.5). The plot device of Sertab being a concubine who has been thrown out of the harem allows her to do all her scenes in the clip alone. Whether deliberate or not, this allows Sertab to distance herself from the more blatantly sexist orientalist images populated by the women inside the harem, which seem designed to appeal to (male) orientalist fantasies about harems and what goes on inside them.

Discussion of the clip focused especially on the *hammam* (Turkish bath) and harem settings, since these were perceived to be among the most egregious stereotypes of Turkish culture. One story in the newspaper *Hürriyet*, titled "Strong Reaction to Clip with Turkish Bath," quoted unnamed "authorities" criticizing the clip saying that it presented Turkey in the wrong way.[24] One person was quoted as saying, "You can't argue about Sertab Erener's singing. But the clip she made for the song she will sing at the Eurovision contest is extremely oriental[ist]. If you present Turkey with this clip, European cartoonists will draw Turkish figures on a camel, wearing a fez, with a long thick mustache, and with a sword in

Figure 7.1. Image from the video clip for "Every Way That I Can": Belly dancer in the harem. © 2003 Sony Music Entertainment (Turkey). Used by permission.

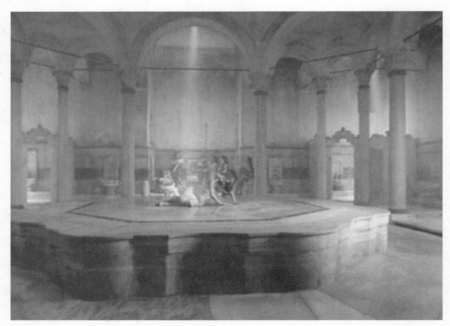

Figure 7.2. Image from the video clip for "Every Way That I Can": Hammam (Turkish bath) scene. © 2003 Sony Music Entertainment (Turkey). Used by permission.

Figure 7.3.   Image from the video clip for "Every Way That I Can": Harem girls smoking a hookah. © 2003 Sony Music Entertainment (Turkey). Used by permission.

Figure 7.4.   Image from the video clip for "Every Way That I Can": Harem girls in (homo-)erotic pose. © 2003 Sony Music Entertainment (Turkey). Used by permission.

Figure 7.5. Image from the video clip for "Every Way That I Can": Sertab in opulent palace setting. © 2003 Sony Music Entertainment (Turkey). Used by permission.

their hand, and you won't have the right to get angry about it."[25] An editorial titled "Damn Turkish Bath" in the same paper argued that "filming a clip with a Turkish bath is not right. We are presenting Turkey in the wrong way."[26] A story in the magazine section of *Star* newspaper titled "Sertab Would Disgrace Turkey" criticized the clip and Sertab personally in the strongest language, asking rhetorically "Are you going to present us to Europe with Turkish baths and concubines?"[27] The same article singled out in particular the way that "Especially the parts shot in the Turkish bath are full of exaggerated scenes evoking lesbian relationships in the harem during the Ottoman period and using drugs by smoking hookahs."[28] Sertab responded defending the clip, saying—somewhat disingenuously—that Turkish baths are in fact a part of Turkish culture, and that she thought the combination of a song with English lyrics and a clip with a Turkish bath would give Turkey an advantage.[29]

In a perhaps ironic development, the state-run TRT, which had itself commissioned the song and video clip in the first place, censored some scenes when broadcasting the clip. Cut from broadcast were the scenes with the harem women smoking hookahs—on the grounds that they could be interpreted as promoting drug use—and the scenes suggestive

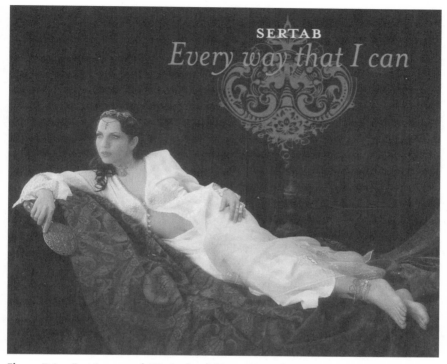

Figure 7.6.　Front cover of CD single of "Every Way That I Can." © 2003 Sony Music Entertainment (Turkey). Used by permission.

of lesbianism, in which the harem women are sensually caressing each other.

　The harem theme and orientalist imagery of the video clip also featured in the packaging of the CD single release of the song and a special compilation album including the ESC song and a number of Sertab's older Turkish-language songs from her previous albums, also sold throughout Europe to market the song and Sertab during the period surrounding the ESC in 2003.[30] Here Sertab herself assumed orientalist poses for the camera. In the photograph on the front cover of both the CD single (figure 7.6) and the compilation album (figure 7.7), Sertab reclines on an Ottoman *divan* (large couch without a back), a mirror in her right hand and bangles on her left hand, feet, and forehead, gazing off into the distance. The *divan* is draped with a deep-red textile with floral motifs, suggesting the opulence of an Ottoman palace. Sertab wears a gauze-thin, almost see-through white top and skirt. The top is fastened in just one place over her chest; below this point it flows open to each side, exposing her midriff. Sertab enacts here a pose found in countless nineteenth-century orientalist paintings and postcards—the *odalisque*, the (imagined) slave girl or concubine in the harem who has been chosen to spend the night with the Sultan, freshly bathed and finely, if minimally dressed, conventionally represented as reclining (often nude or partially nude) on a *divan* in an opulent setting and lying in wait for her Sultan to come for her. The French term *odalisque* is derived from the Turkish word *odalı*, which can literally be translated as "the one who has (responsibility for) the room," or more colloquially rendered as "chambermaid." Within the strictly regulated hierarchy of the Ottoman harem, historically the low-status *odalı* acted as servant to the senior women of the harem, and actually had no direct contact with the sultan. Nevertheless, the fictional image of the odalisque-as-concubine was a staple of nineteenth-century orientalist iconography, embodying European fantasies about the Ottoman harem in which the Sultan supposedly had his pick of any woman he happened to fancy. In his study of early twentieth-century photographic images on French colonial postcards from Algeria—which draw on the same iconography as continental orientalist painting—Malek Alloula evocatively describes the hypererotic attributes of the odalisque as a fantasy figure:

> Ideal figure above all others, the odalisque is the very symbol of the harem, its highest expression. She fills it with a presence that is at once mysterious and luminous. She is its hidden, yet available, core, always throbbing with restrained sensuality. (Alloula 1986, 74)

The use of exotic eroticism is further accentuated in another pose used on the back of the CD compilation, in which Sertab is stretched out on the same *divan*, this time nude from the waist up and viewed from behind as she turns her profile toward the viewer (figure 7.7), again mimicking countless orientalist paintings such as the French artist Jules Joseph Lefebvre's *Odalisque* from 1874. The photographs with Sertab's poses for these CD covers, along with other similar images from the same photo sessions, were also used in other promotional material. Many of these images of Sertab seem to mimic various orientalist paintings, including well-known works such as Pierre-Auguste Renoir's *Odalisque* (1870), Jean Auguste Dominique Ingres's *La Grande Odalisque* (1814), Eugène Delacroix's *Arab Woman Seated* (1832), and Jean-Joseph Benjamin-Constant's *Odalisque* (undated).[31] These highly eroticized images of Sertab, with their familiar iconography, thus played a significant role in marketing Sertab and Turkey's 2003 ESC song. In effect, the campaign to promote the song took orientalist iconography that historically originated in the countries of Western Europe and used it to market Turkey back to those same countries. Turkey, in the person of Sertab, was thus constructed as the exotic, erotic, feminized object presented to the gaze of an (implicitly male) European subject, waiting both to seduce and to be seduced.[32]

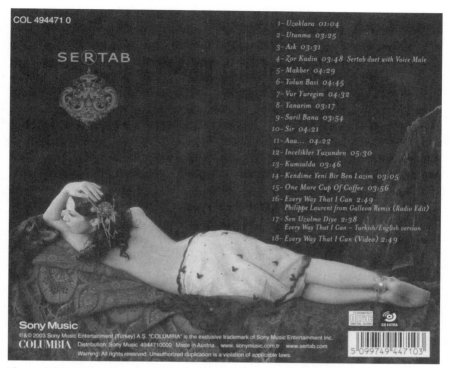

COL 494471 0

1- *Uzaklara 01:04*
2- *Utanma 03:25*
3- *Ask 03:31*
4- *Zor Kadin 03:48 Sertab duet with Voice Male*
5- *Makber 04:29*
6- *Yolun Basi 04:45*
7- *Vur Yuregim 04:32*
8- *Tanarim 03:17*
9- *Saril Bana 03:54*
10- *Sir 04:21*
11- *Aaa... 04:22*
12- *Incelikler Yuzunden 05:30*
13- *Kumsalda 03:46*
14- *Kendime Yeni Bir Ben Lazim 03:05*
15- *One More Cup Of Coffee 03:56*
16- *Every Way That I Can 2:49*
     Philippe Laurent from Galleon Remix (Radio Edit)
17- *Sen Uzulme Diye 2:38*
     Every Way That I Can - Turkish/English version
18- *Every Way That I Can (Video) 2:49*

Sony Music

®&© 2003 Sony Music Entertainment (Turkey) A.Ş. "COLUMBIA" is the exclusive trademark of Sony Music Entertainment Inc.
COLUMBIA Distribution: Sony Music 4944710000. Made in Austria. www. sonymusic.com.tr www.sertab.com
Warning: All rights reserved. Unauthorized duplication is a violation of applicable laws.

Figure 7.7.   Back cover of a CD anthology of Sertab Erener's songs marketed in Europe around the time of the 2003 ESC. © 2003 Sony Music Entertainment (Turkey). Used by permission.

Sertab's live performance of the song at the contest itself on May 24, 2003, in Riga (figures 7.8–7.10), while not as elaborately staged as the video clip discussed above, also drew heavily on orientalist tropes.[33] The choreography (by Turkish choreographer Candan Baş, performed by Sertab and a chorus of four female dancers—one Turkish and three German) did not actually consist entirely of belly dancing, but rather liberally borrowed various moves from the belly dance vocabulary and integrated them into what could be called a sort of "modernist pop" choreography, with some elements from jazz dance as well.[34] There were, however, a few moments in which classic belly dance moves and poses—shoulder shimmies, lateral and vertical hip accents, hip circles, undulating "snake arms"—came to the fore and were sustained for several seconds at a time. These moments were greeted with loud, enthusiastic cheers from the audience in the auditorium, clearly audible during the contest's broadcast.

The four female dancers/backing vocalists who accompanied Sertab wore low-slung, hip-hugging harem pants with slits up the sides of the legs and tight-fitting sports bra–type tops, evoking—but not entirely copying—belly dance costumes, while also enabling movements such as the high leg kicks derived from modern dance vocabulary. Sertab herself wore a floor-length billowing skirt, with several layers on her upper body. Outermost she wore a sort of bodice or loose-fitting corset to which four several-meter-long, wide strips of cloth were attached. At various points during the performance the four accompanying dancers took hold of these strips and extended them to their full lengths, literally pulling Sertab in four directions at once, or alternately wrapped them partially around themselves or around Sertab, enacting the themes of control and desire expressed in the song's lyrics. At the song's climax, the return of the chorus after the bridge, Sertab pulled off the bodice and attached cloth strips, revealing her midriff, partially covered in front by a gold flap of cloth hanging from her pink bikini top. Some of the "jazzy" elements in the choreography—including feline prowling on the stage, in which the four chorus dancers got down on their hands and knees and suggestively crawled forward toward the audience like a cat about to pounce—can also be read as having an erotic subtext. Potuoğlu-Cook has suggested that these elements bring "a contemporary sexual layer to the orientalist eroticism evoked by belly dance."[35]

Figure 7.8.   Sertab Erener's live performance at the ESC in Riga: Belly dancing. © 2003 LTV (Latvian Television). Used by permission.

Figure 7.9. Sertab Erener's live performance at the ESC in Riga: Feline prowling. ©
2003 LTV (Latvian Television). Used by permission.

Figure 7.10. Sertab Erener's live performance at the ESC in Riga: Final pose. © 2003
LTV (Latvian Television). Used by permission.

Sertab's performance in the ESC thus represented a kind of strategic essentialism, knowingly drawing on widely circulating stereotypes and deploying them to advantage by feeding them back to those who had originated them. The orientalist images were meant not so much for consumption in Turkey, but for distribution, promotion, and consumption outside Turkey—in Europe, where these images would, together with the musical Turkisms in the song itself, help Sertab and her song stand out from a crowded field of twenty-six entrants in the contest. Trading on, and taking advantage of, familiar orientalist tropes and Europe's fascination with an imagined, exotic Turkey was simply shrewd marketing. Inevitably, however, these representations created for export were also consumed in Turkey, and interpreted according to existing discourses and debates about Turkish cultural identity—the Kemalist modernization-as-westernization project, and the neo-Ottoman imaginative recovery of Turkey's prerepublican heritage. The visual vocabulary of orientalism used in the performance intersected with neo-Ottoman representations of Turkishness, just as it clashed with westward-looking conceptions of what Turkish cultural identity should be.

THE POLITICS OF BELLY DANCING IN TURKEY[36]

Besides the harem and *hammam* settings in the video clip for "Every Way That I Can," critical commentary in Turkey also focused on the use of belly dancing in both the video clip and in Sertab's live performance in Riga. Here as well, the issues involve gendered representations of the nation produced for consumption in Europe, with the added dimension that the focus is even more tightly on (Turkish) women's bodies.

Belly dance has been in Turkey "historically a morally and economically suspect profession" (Potuoğlu-Cook 2006a, 634).[37] Besides questions related to gender and orientalism, the issue of race and ethnicity also comes into play here, since "Historically, most if not all urban female belly dancers have come from Rom ["Gypsy"] backgrounds" (Potuoğlu-Cook 2006b, section 3).[38] Despite the low social status of belly dancers and the suspicion their art is regarded with, since the early 1990s Turkey, and the city of Istanbul in particular, have seen a revitalization of belly dance in "a time when the global fashionability of the dance form converged with local neo-Ottoman desires" (Potuoğlu-Cook 2006a, 643). Also contributing to this "upgrading of belly dancing as historic praxis" is the fact that it has become a significant source of revenue, as elite "oriental"-themed night clubs featuring belly dancers and catering to tourists from Europe and the Arab world, with entrance fees priced at over fifty dollars, become sites for Ottoman heritage tourism (Potuoğlu-Cook 2006a, 635).

Despite the economic benefits derived from the commodification of belly dancing, recent secular republican Turkish administrations have regarded it with suspicion, including (maybe even especially) when the intended audience is primarily non-Turkish tourists. Potuoğlu-Cook recounts how

> In April 2002, the center-Left Turkish government banned belly dance performance at "Turkish nights" for the non-Turkish clientele at southern [i.e. in and near the popular tourist destination of Antalya on Turkey's Mediterranean coast] holiday resorts. Officials claimed that as a dance of Arabic origin, belly dance misrepresents Turkish identity to Western tourists . . . The ban's secular nationalist tone, as in multiple other controversies over the dance form, evokes the constant struggle and deep contradiction between the past and present Orientalist and nationalist discourses: between the "dirty" yet essential revenue from the embodied Orientalism of belly dance shows and a Westernized self-image distinct from and superior to other, especially Arab, Orientals . . . [T]he Orientalism of belly dance performances continues to be an open sore in ongoing moral and nationalistic Turkish modernization projects. (Potuoğlu-Cook 2006a, 641–42)

Dance researchers Shay and Sellers-Young describe a similar controversy that emerged when Mustafa Turhan, director of the Turkish State Folk Dance Ensemble, added a highly orientalized choreography including belly dancing to that ensemble's usual repertoire of regional folk dances. While this move was apparently justified in neo-Ottomanist terms as being about recovering the Ottoman past, criticism of it characterized the new choreography as "appealing to the orientalist images of foreigners" such as Hollywood "Arabian Nights" films and "Kismet" musicals (Shay and Sellers-Young 2003, 28).

In her discussion of how Islamists and Muslim elites in Turkey have also "extensively commodified potent Ottoman symbols," Potuoğlu-Cook argues that Islamists have also rejected belly dancing, despite its (imagined) association with the Ottoman palace, because it conflicts with their emphasis on moral and religious discourses (Potuoğlu-Cook 2006a, 648–49). Professional belly dancers in Turkey are thus caught between secular and Islamist positions that both regard their work as a suspect profession: "[S]ecular nationalists shun them as bearers of ethnic [i.e. Roma]/cultural impurity and the Islamists morally condemn their suggestive public mobility and, hence, unredeemable immodesty" (Potuoğlu-Cook 2006b, section 9). Sertab's appropriation of belly dancing and incorporation of it into her ESC performance thus touched a raw nerve feeding into the articulation of race, gender, and class in the ongoing constitution of Turkish identity at the turn of the millennium.

THE IRONIES THAT COME WITH SUCCESS

Sertab's—and Turkey's—victory in the 2003 ESC was widely interpreted in Turkey as an indication that Turkey was finally being accepted as a European country by Europe itself. Sertab's success on the European stage effectively hushed her critics. Those who had earlier decried the use of orientalist tropes to represent Turkey to Europe had to admit that in the end the strategy had been successful, and perhaps worth it. After years of humiliating finishes at or near the bottom of the ESC rankings, Turkey's long-sought-after victory in the contest had to be considered a good thing. Many of Sertab's former critics thus did an abrupt about-face and began to argue that Turkey's ESC win was sure to help promote Turkey in its quest to fully join Europe. A number of politicians, who had previously in grandstanding style criticized Sertab's performance in the strongest terms, nearly stumbled over each other in the rush to publicly congratulate her after her unexpected win. Neo-Ottomanists, on the other hand, could hardly contain their glee, since Sertab had shown that one could successfully use Turkey's Ottoman heritage to represent Turkey to Europe. In that viewpoint, Sertab had in effect forced Europe to accept Turkey on its own terms, not Europe's. This argument, however, disingenuously overlooks the fact that, as noted above, Sertab was not necessarily representing Ottoman culture in an authentic, historically accurate way, but rather in the orientalist image created by Europe itself, and so was simply feeding back to Europe what it already expected.

An example of a neo-Ottomanist reading of Sertab's victory can be seen in an editorial by Ali Bulaç, regular columnist in the "pan-Ottomanist and Islamist" (Navaro-Yashin 2002, 124) newspaper *Zaman*, who offered what he specifically called a "different reading" ("başka bir okuması") of Sertab's ESC victory, putting a positive spin on her use of orientalist tropes.[39] Bulaç, a prominent Islamist intellectual, argued that Sertab's performance effectively reclaimed the image of the harem woman from European orientalists and liberated her: "Sertab Erener's first place in Eurovision actually represents the breaking of the historical chains of the 'traditional Muslim woman' in orientalist paintings, letting her spread her wings to fly to freedom."[40] In his view, then, the issue is not the content of the representation, but who is doing the representing—it is insulting when Europeans represent Turkey with orientalist imagery, but when a Turkish woman appropriates this imagery and engages in the same representational practice, it can be liberating.

The attention newly turned toward Turkey in the wake of the contest revealed, however, how orientalist stereotypes of Turkey remain entrenched in many quarters in Europe, and as these began to surface, they were also covered by the Turkish press. As Sertab's European career took off in the wake of her victory and she criss-crossed Europe for concert and promotional appearances, she encountered these stereotypes in the questions people asked her. Sertab recounted this in an interview with the newspaper *Hürriyet* given in Brussels in November 2003, six months after she won the contest. In terms ironically recalling the prophetic critical quote reproduced above about how European cartoonists would represent Turkey in the wake of the orientalist self-presentation in her video clip, Sertab complained that people were asking her "everything short of whether I have a flying carpet or not, and whether I have ever traveled by camel or not."[41] She added that she actually had met with questions like whether when she went back to Turkey, she wore a headscarf or not.[42] The tone of righteous indignation with which Sertab related all this (especially the question about the headscarf) suggests that for her, it should be self-evident to all, even to those from other countries without direct knowledge of Turkey, that she was a modern Turkish woman—conservatory trained as a classical singer of the Western operatic repertoire and living a modern, cosmopolitan lifestyle as a pop singer—would of course *not* wear a headscarf, the ultimate symbol of all that is *not* modern in the Kemalist ideology that made her very career and lifestyle possible. She said in the interview that she is representing the "civilized face of Turkey," and can see that in other countries Turkey is misunderstood and regarded simplistically.[43] In this and other published interviews she seems to never have acknowledged that her own complicity in the orientalist representation of Turkey in the ESC—by framing herself from the outset as a gendered orientalized subject—may well have contributed to this simplistic understanding of Turkey and what she considered to be ignorant questions based on old stereotypes.

CONCLUSION

In his recent discussion of what he calls the tendency toward "creative (re)construction of national or ethnic identity in music" in the ESC since the 1990s, Swedish musicologist Alf Björnberg notes that "inherent in the particular reception conditions of transnational broadcasting there is ample scope for misinterpretation of the cultural significance which any particular contest entry representing a 'foreign' country may possess in its original context" (Björnberg 2007, 21; 15). Most viewers of the 2003 ESC would certainly not have known about the internal debates in Turkey surrounding Sertab's performance, and may very likely have taken the performance at face value as an unambiguously authentic expression of "Turkish culture." The audible enthusiasm of the audience in Skonto Hall in Riga when Sertab and her dancers broke into belly dance moves

certainly suggests this. In her own analysis of the representational strategies Ukraine and the Balkan countries have recently used in the ESC,
Catherine Baker builds on Björnberg's argument in suggesting that the
very format of the contest creates pressures toward "representing the nation through simplified, well-known images," and that, from one critical
standpoint, participating countries on Europe's periphery are compelled
to play up to the expectations of "a foreign gaze which exoticizes difference" (Baker 2008, 173; 175). In the Turkish case explored here, the
internal debates in Turkey about how it should be represented in the ESC
suggest that the deployment of exoticized difference may not necessarily
be a matter of simply being compelled by external pressures, but rather
a strategic choice by musicians and producers (including the state-run
TRT, which commissioned and sanctioned the performance by allowing
it to go ahead despite the controversy). Sertab's deployment of orientalist
tropes to represent Turkey on the European stage also effectively blurred
the distinction Bohlman draws between Europe's "internal" and "external" others—others within Europe and those outside its borders—and
problematized a similar inner/outer duality within Turkey itself (Bohlman 2000, 189). From the perspective of Kemalist nationalism, Turkey's
internal "oriental other" (discursively constructed as originating externally in Arab lands) must be repressed, if Turkey is to take its rightful
place among European nations. But in the person of Sertab, the "oriental"
Turk, arguably historically the external other provoking the most powerful combination of fear and fantasy, dread and desire in Europe, took
pride of place on the quintessentially European stage of the ESC. While
Sertab's performance was directed to a European gaze, the result was also
the validation of neo-Ottomanist desires and fantasies at home in Turkey,
and a winning of space for imaginations of Turkish identity that embrace
its oriental, Ottoman heritage.

Kevin Robins has written about how the desire to show a "European"
face to Europe can cause tension when that means repressing or deny-
ing Turkey's history and cultural distinctiveness (Robins 1996). On the
other hand, much of what can be most easily marketed outside Turkey
as the country's unique history and culture lapses easily into old essentializing stereotypes. Strategies for culturally representing Turkey on the
European stage have to confront and deal with these issues in one way
or another. If one of the goals of the Kemalist secular nation-building
project had been to move women out of the harem and into the public
sphere, Sertab's performance, by putting herself symbolically back into
the harem, engaged in play with tropes that remain highly charged in a
Turkey very sensitive about its place in Europe, and about the power of
representation to affect how it is perceived in Europe.

NOTES

1. Anonymous, "'Göbek Dansı Avrupa'yı Fethetti'" ["'Her Belly Dance Conquered Europe'"]. *Radikal*, May 25, 2003. Accessed June 20, 2003. http://www.radikal.com.tr/veriler/2003/05/25/haber_76241.

2. The newspaper *Milliyet* ran a similar story. See Anonymous, "Reuters: Sertab Erener'in, Göbek Dansı Avrupalı'nın Gönlünü Fethetti" ["Reuters: Sertab Erener's Belly Dance Conquered the Hearts of Europeans"]. *Milliyet*, May 25, 2003. Accessed November 2, 2004. http://www.milliyet.com.tr/2003/05/25/son/sondun04.html.

3. Anonymous, "Dış Basın Ne Dedi" ["What the Foreign Press Said"]. *Hürriyet*, May 26, 2003, 4.

4. See Aydıngün and Aydıngün 2004; Aytürk 2004; Lewis 1999; Mardin 2002; Poulton 1997, 109–114; White 2002, 33–34.

5. See Stokes 1992 and 1996; Tekelioğlu 1996 and 2001; Yarar 2008.

6. My subheading here is taken from the title of an article by feminist Turkish social scientist Deniz Kandiyoti (Kandiyoti 1997).

7. See Arat 1997; Göle 1996, 63–80 and 1997; Kandiyoti 1987 and 1989; Tekeli 1986. I am not able to do justice in this necessarily short summary to the various feminist critiques of Kemalism. Suffice it to say that all of these authors point out in different ways the contradictions in or problems with the Kemalist program for women, such as (to give only one example) its privileging of upper-class urban women at the expense of rural women.

8. Another important feminist critique of Kemalism focuses especially on the educational reforms carried out in the early years of the new republic, in particular the divide between rhetoric and actual practice. This critique argues that, despite a sincere belief in the "equality of intellectual ability" of women and men and the rhetoric of equality in professional opportunities available to both sexes, the underlying ideology was actually based on "the Kemalist expectation that educating women would provide Turkey with better wives and mothers" (Childress 2008, 560; see also Arat 1999). The main contribution of women was thus actually to use their new education in their traditional roles in the home, particularly in the raising of future model citizens. On this point see also Gök 1995; Arat 1994.

9. See Göle 1996, 82; Navaro-Yashin 2002, 26–27.

10. See Çınar 2005, 59–98; Göle 1996; Navaro-Yashin 2002, 82–84, 94–112; Potuoğlu-Cook 2006a, 648–49; Poulton 1997, 195–96; White 1999 and 2002.

11. See also Bartu 1999 and 2001, 141; Göle 1993, 23 and 1997, 93, n. 10; Navaro-Yashin 2002, 124; Potuoğlu-Cook 2006a; Stokes 1996.

12. See Robins 1996; Stokes 1996; Keyder 1997.

13. See Stokes 1996; Klaser 2001.

14. See Karaosmanoglu 2009.

15. Prominent examples of this type of film, referred to in Turkish as *dönem filmi* ("period film"), include *Keloğlan Kara Prens'e Karşı* (2006), *Hacivat Karagöz Neden Öldürüldü* (2006), *Cenneti Beklerken* (2006), *Ulak* (2007), and *Son Osmanlı "Yandım Ali"* (2007).

16. See Göle 1993; Robins 1996; Robins and Aksoy 1995.

17. See for example Göle 1997, 93, n. 10; White 2002, 31; Bartu 2001, 141; Navaro-Yashin 2002, 92; Yavuz 2003, 235–36.

18. This necessarily brief discussion of neo-Ottomanism has focused on cultural aspects. For consideration of political dimensions of neo-Ottomanism, see Çolak 2006; Grigoriadis 2007; Fisher Onar 2009; Yavuz 1998.

19. For a brief discussion of the song's musical characteristics, see Solomon, 2007, 137.

20. For further discussions of orientalism from gendered and feminist perspectives, see Abu-Lughod 2001; Çelik 2002; Lewis 1996; Roberts 2002; Yeğenoğlu 1998.

21. Abdülhamid I lived 1717–74 and reigned as Ottoman sultan 1757–74.

22. The video clip for "Every Way That I Can" can be viewed on YouTube at http://www.youtube.com/watch?v=1P1pJ8OHMmE. Accessed on June 23, 2011.

23. See Ercan Öztürk and Feride Çıkıt, "Dil Değil, Duruş Önemli" ["The Performance, Not the Language, Is Important"]. Akşam, March 13, 2003. Accessed June 20, 2003. http://www.aksam.com.tr/arsiv/aksam/2003/03/13/magazin/magazin2.html; and Anonymous, "TRT Müdürü'nün İngilizce Gururu!" ["TRT Head's Pride in English!"]. Aygazete, March 12, 2003. Accessed June 20, 2003. http://www.aygazete.com/haber/habersonuc.asp?ID=6474.

24. Anonymous, "Hamamlı Klibe Büyük Tepki" ["Strong Reaction to Clip with Turkish Bath"]. *Hürriyet*, April 21, 2003. Accessed June 20, 2003. http://www.hurriyetim.com.tr/haber/0,,sid~6@nvid~257926,00.

25. "Sertab Erener'in şarkıcılığı tartışma kabul etmez. Ama Eurovision yarışmasında söyleyeceği şarkıya aşırı oryantal bir klip çekmiş. Eğer siz bu kliple Türkiye'yi tanıtırsanız, elin Avrupalı karikatüristi de Türk figürünü devenin üstünde, fesli, pala bıyıklı ve elinde de bir kılıçla çizer. Kızma hakkınız da olmaz" (quoted in *ibid.*). All translations from Turkish-language media reports in this paper are my own.

26. "…hamamlı klip çekmek doğru değilmiş. Türkiye'yi yanlış tanıtıyormuşuz"; Tolga Akyıldız, "Lanetli Hamam" ["Damn Turkish Bath"]. *Hürriyet*, April 26, 2003. Accessed February 25, 2004. http://arama.hurriyetim.com.tr/devam.asp?id=142773.

27. "Bizi Avrupa'ya hamamlar ve cariyelerle mi tanıtacaksınız?"; Anonymous, "Sertab Türkiye'yi Rezil Edecekti" ["Sertab Would Disgrace Turkey"]. *Star*, April 20, 2003. Accessed June 20, 2003. http://www.stargazete.com/index.asp?haberid=22227.

28. "… özellikle hamamda çekilen bölümler, Osmanlı döneminde haremde yaşanmış lezbiyen ilişkileri ve nargile yoluyla uyuşturucu kullanımını çağrıştıran abartılı sahnelerle doluydu" (*ibid.*).

29. "Türk kültüründe hamam zaten var. İngilizce şarkı ve hamamlı klip. Bence bu çok iyi bir avantaj"; quoted in Demirhan Hararlı, "Hamamlı Klip Avantaj" ["Clip with a Turkish Bath an Advantage"]. *Hürriyet*, April 23, 2003. Accessed June 20, 2003. http://www.hurriyetim.com.tr/haber/0,,sid~6@nvid~258808,00.asp.

30. I bought my copies of these CDs in the airport in Amsterdam around the time of the 2003 ESC; their availability there is perhaps an indication of how effective the marketing and distribution campaigns for Sertab in Europe were during

this period. Both of these CDs also include as a bonus CD-ROM track the video clip discussed above.

31. A high-quality image of Lefebvre's Odalisque can be viewed at http:// en.wikipedia.org/wiki/File:Odalisque.jpg (accessed June 23, 2011). A collection of images of more paintings in this genre can be found at http://www.orientalist -art.org.uk/odalisque.html (accessed June 23, 2011). For brief art-historical discussions of the iconography of the odalisque with numerous full-color reproductions of paintings as well, see Thornton 1994, 112–36; Tromans 2008. See also several of the paintings reproduced in the plates in Lewis 1996 and the photographic images from colonial postcards reproduced in Alloula 1986, 79; 82–83. For a contemporary example recycling this same imagery, see the drawing in the promotional flyer for "Sultana's," a small-scale Istanbul tourist entertainment venue featuring belly dancing, reproduced in Potuoğlu-Cook 2006a, 639.

32. In this regard, see also Gumpert's reading of the lyrics of Sertab's song, "Every Way That I Can," as an allegory of the relations of desire and rejection played out in Turkey's ongoing quest to join the EU (Gumpert 2007).

33. A video of Sertab's live performance at the 2003 ESC can be viewed at http://www.youtube.com/watch?v=m3i4S4E7h3I (accessed October 15, 2011).

34. My discussion here of the choreography in Sertab's live performance at ESC 2003 is indebted to anthropologist Öykü Potuoğlu-Cook, who watched a clip of the performance and sent me her analysis of the choreography in a private e-mail message on July 3, 2009.

35. Öykü Potuoğlu-Cook, personal communication July 3, 2009.

36. This section draws extensively on the work of Potuoğlu-Cook (2006a, 2006b, and 2008).

37. For a parallel case of the gender politics surrounding female performers (who often combine belly dancing with singing) in Egypt, see van Nieuwkerk 1995, 1998, and 2003; Lorius 1996; Arvizu 2004–2005.

38. For a discussion of the politics of representations of and by Roma musicians in Turkey see Seeman 2002 and 2006. For a more general overview of Roma musical culture in Turkey, see Duygulu 2006.

39. Ali Bulaç, "Sertab Erener Özgürlüğe Kanat Açtı" ["Sertab Erener Opened her Wings to Freedom"]. *Zaman*, May 28, 2003. Accessed May 13, 2009. http:// arsiv.zaman.com.tr/2003/05/28/yazarlar/alibulac.htm.

40. "Sertab Erener'in kazandığı Eurovision birinciliği özü itibarılya oryantalist resim tablolarındaki 'geleneksel Müslüman kadın'ın tarihsel zincirlerini kırıp özgürlüğe doğru kanatlamasıdır" (*ibid.*). The English translation here is my own; another English version of this newspaper column is Alic Bulaç, "Sertab Erener Taking Wings of Freedom." *Zaman* [English edition], May 28, 2003. Accessed July 9, 2003. http://www.zaman.com/default.php?kn=2643.

41. "Bir tek uçan halım olup olmadığını, develerle seyahat edip etmediğimi sormadıkları kaldı"; quoted in Zeynep Lüle, "Türkiye'de Başımı Örtüp Örtmediğimi Soruyorlar" ["They're Asking Me If I Wear a Headscarf in Turkey"]. *Hürriyet*, November 17, 2003: 17.

42. "Türkiye'ye dönünce başını kapatıp kapatmadığı [soruyorlar]" (quoted in *ibid.*).

43. "Türkiye'nin medeni yüzünü temsil ediyorum . . . Yurt dışında yanlış anlaşılmış ve tek yanlı bakılan Türkiye olduğunu görüyorum" (quoted in *ibid.*).

REFERENCES

Abu-Lughod, Lila. 2001. "*Orientalism* and Middle East Feminist Studies." *Feminist Studies* 27(1): 101–13.

Alloula, Malek. 1986. *The Colonial Harem*. Manchester: Manchester University Press.

Arat, Yeşim. 1997. "The Project of Modernity and Women in Turkey." In *Rethinking Modernity and National Identity in Turkey*, edited by Sibel Bozdoğan and Reşat Kasaba, 95–112. Seattle: University of Washington Press.

Arat, Zehra F. 1994. "Kemalism and Turkish Women." *Women and Poltitics* 14(4): 57–80.

———. 1999. "Educating the Daughters of the Republic." In *Deconstructing Images of "The Turkish Woman,"* edited by Zehra F. Arat, 157–80. New York: Palgrave.

Arvizu, Shannon. 2004–2005. "The Politics of Bellydancing in Cairo." *Arab Studies Journal* 12(2)–13(1): 159–87.

Aydıngün, Ayşegül, and İsmail Aydıngün. 2004. "The Role of Language in the Formation of Turkish National Identity and Turkishness." *Nationalism and Ethnic Politics* 10(3): 415–32.

Aytürk, İlker. 2004. "Turkish Linguists against the West: The Origins of Linguistic Nationalism in Atatürk's Turkey." *Middle Eastern Studies* 40(6): 1–25.

Baker, Catherine. 2008. "Wild Dances and Dying Wolves: Simulation, Essentialization, and National Identity at the Eurovision Song Contest." *Popular Communication* 6(3): 173–89.

Bartu, Ayfer. 1999. "Who Owns the Old Quarters?: Rewriting Histories in a Global Era." In *Istanbul between the Global and the Local*, edited by Çağlar Keyder, 31–45. London: Rowman & Littlefield.

———. 2001. "Rethinking Heritage Politics in a Global Context: A View from Istanbul." In *Hybrid Urbanism: On the Identity Discourse and the Built Environment*, edited by Nezar AlSayyad, 131–55. Westport, Conn.: Praeger.

Björnberg, Alf. 2007. "Return to Ethnicity: The Cultural Significance of Musical Change in the Eurovision Song Contest." In *A Song for Europe: Popular Music and Politics in the Eurovision Song Contest*, edited by Ivan Raykoff and Robert D. Tobin, 13–23. Aldershot: Ashgate.

Bohlman, Philip V. 2000. "Composing the Cantorate: Westernizing Europe's Other Within." In *Western Music and Its Others: Difference, Representation, and Appropriation in Music*, edited by Georgina Born and David Hesmondhalgh, 187–212. Berkeley: University of California Press.

Bowman, Jim. 2009. "Time to Smell the Sweet Smoke: Fantasy Themes and Rhetorical Vision in Nargile Café Cultures." *Journal of Popular Culture* 42(3): 442–57.

Çelik, Zeynep. 2002. "Speaking Back to Orientalist Discourse." In *Orientalism's Interlocutors: Painting, Architecture, Photography*, edited by Jill Beaulieu and Mary Roberts, 19–41. Durham: Duke University Press.

Childress, Faith J. 2008. "Creating the 'New Woman' in Early Republican Turkey: The Contributions of the American Collegiate Institute and the American College of Girls." *Middle Eastern Studies* 44(4): 553–69.

Çınar, Alev. 2005. *Modernity, Islam, and Secularism in Turkey: Bodies, Places, and Time*. Minneapolis: University of Minnesota Press.

Çolak, Yılmaz. 2006. "Ottomanism vs. Kemalism: Collective Memory and Cultural Pluralism in 1990s Turkey." *Middle Eastern Studies* 42(4): 587–602.

Duygulu, Melih. 2006. *Türkiye'de Çingene Müziği: Batı Grubu Romanlarında Müzik Kültürü* ["Gypsy Music in Turkey: Musical Culture of the Western Group of Roma"]. Istanbul: Pan Yayıncılık.

Fisher Onar, Nora. 2009. "Echoes of a Universalism Lost: Rival Representations of the Ottomans in Today's Turkey." *Middle Eastern Studies* 45(2): 229–41.

Gök, Fatma. 1995. "Women and Education in Turkey." In *Women in Modern Turkish Society: A Reader*, edited by Şirin Tekeli, 131–40. London: Zed Books Ltd.

Göle, Nilüfer. 1993. "Istanbul's Revenge." *Istanbul* (English edition) 1(1): 20–23.

———. 1996. *The Forbidden Modern: Civilization and Veiling*. Ann Arbor: University of Michigan Press.

———. 1997. "The Quest for the Islamic Self within the Context of Modernity." In *Rethinking Modernity and National Identity in Turkey*, edited by Sibel Bozdoğan and Reşat Kasaba, 81–94. Seattle: University of Washington Press.

Grigoriadis, Ioannis N. 2007. *"Türk or Türkiyeli*? The Reform of Turkey's Minority Legislation and the Rediscovery of Ottomanism." *Middle Eastern Studies* 43(3): 423–38.

Gumpert, Matthew. 2007. "'Everyway That I Can': Auto-Orientalism at Eurovision 2003." In *A Song for Europe: Popular Music and Politics in the Eurovision Song Contest*, edited by Ivan Raykoff and Robert Tobin, 147–57. Aldershot: Ashgate.

Hall, Stuart. 1990. "Cultural Identity and Diaspora." In *Identity: Community, Culture, Difference*, edited by Jonathan Rutherford, 222–37. London: Lawrence & Wishart.

Kandiyoti, Deniz. 1987. "Emancipated but Unliberated? Reflections on the Turkish Case." *Feminist Studies* 13(2): 317–38.

———. 1989. "Women and the Turkish State: Political Actors or Symbolic Pawns?" In *Woman–Nation–State*, edited by Nira Yuval-Davis and Floya Anthias, 126–49. Basingstoke: Macmillan.

———. 1997. "Gendering the Modern: On Missing Dimensions in the Study of Turkish Modernity." In *Rethinking Modernity and National Identity in Turkey*, edited by Sibel Bozdoğan and Reşat Kasaba, 113–32. Seattle: University of Washington Press.

Karaosmanoglu, Defne. 2009. "Eating the Past: Multiple Spaces, Multiple Times— Performing 'Ottomanness' in Istanbul." *International Journal of Cultural Studies* 12(4): 339–58.

Keyder, Çağlar. 1997. "Whither the Project of Modernity? Turkey in the 1990s." In *Rethinking Modernity and National Identity in Turkey*, edited by Sibel Bozdoğan and Reşat Kasaba, 37–51. Seattle: University of Washington Press.

Klaser, Rajna. 2001. "From an Imagined Paradise to an Imagined Nation: Interpreting Şarkı as a Cultural Play." Ph.D. diss., University of California, Berkeley.

Lewis, Bernard. 1968. *The Emergence of Modern Turkey*. 2nd edition. London: Oxford University Press.

Lewis, Geoffrey. 1999. *The Turkish Language Reform: A Catastrophic Success*. Oxford: Oxford University Press.

Lewis, Reina. 1996. *Gendering Orientalism: Race, Femininity and Representation*. London: Routledge.

———. 2004. *Rethinking Orientalism: Women, Travel and the Ottoman Harem*. London: I. B. Tauris.

Lorius, Cassandra. 1996. "'Oh Boy, You Salt of the Earth': Outwitting Patriarchy in *Raqs Baladi*." *Popular Music* 15(3): 285–98.

Mardin, Şerif. 2002. "Playing Games with Names." In *Fragments of Culture: The Everyday of Modern Turkey*, edited by Deniz Kandiyoti and Ayşe Saktanber, 115–27. London: I. B. Tauris.

Navaro-Yashin, Yael. 2002. *Faces of the State: Secularism and Public Life in Turkey*. Princeton: Princeton University Press.

Nieuwkerk, Karin van. 1995. *'A Trade Like Any Other': Female Singers and Dancers in Egypt*. Austin: University of Texas Press.

———. 1998. "'An Hour for God and an Hour for the Heart': Islam, Gender and Female Entertainment in Egypt." *Music and Anthropology* 3. Accessed March 25, 2009. http://levi.provincia.venezia.it/ma/index/number3/nieuwkerk/karin_0.htm.

———. 2003. "On Religion, Gender, and Performing: Female Performers and Repentance in Egypt." In *Music and Gender: Perspectives from the Mediterranean*, edited by Tullia Magrini, 267–86. Chicago: University of Chicago Press.

Potuoğlu-Cook, Öykü. 2006a. "Beyond the Glitter: Belly Dance and Neoliberal Gentrification in Istanbul." *Cultural Anthropology* 21(4): 633–60.

———. 2006b. "Sweat, Power, and Art: Situating Belly Dancers and Musicians in Contemporary Istanbul." *Music & Anthropology* 11. Accessed March 25, 2009. http://www.fondazionelevi.org/ma/index/number11/potuoglu/pot_0.htm.

———. 2008. "Night Shifts: Moral, Economic, and Cultural Politics of Turkish Belly Dance Across the *Fins-de-Siècle*." Ph.D. diss., Northwestern University.

Poulton, Hugh. 1997. *Top Hat, Grey Wolf and Crescent: Turkish Nationalism and the Turkish Republic*. London: Hurst & Company.

Roberts, Mary. 2002. "Contested Terrains: Women Orientalists and the Colonial Harem." In *Orientalism's Interlocutors: Painting, Architecture, Photography*, edited by Jill Beaulieu and Mary Roberts, 179–203. Durham: Duke University Press.

Robins, Kevin. 1996. "Interrupting Identities: Turkey/Europe." In *Questions of Cultural Identity*, edited by Stuart Hall and Paul du Gay, 61–86. London: Sage.

Robins, Kevin and Asu Aksoy. 1995. "Istanbul Rising: Returning the Repressed to Urban Culture." *European Urban and Regional Studies* 2(3): 223–35.

Seeman, Sonia Tamar. 2002. "'You're Roman!' Music and Identity in Turkish Roman Communities." Ph.D. diss., University of California, Los Angeles.

———. 2006. "Presenting 'Gypsy,' Re-Presenting Roman: Towards an Archeology of Aesthetic Production and Social Identity." *Music & Anthropology* 11. Accessed April 10, 2009. http://www.fondazionelevi.org/ma/index/number11/seeman/see_0.htm.

Shay, Anthony, and Barbara Sellers-Young. 2003. "Belly Dance: Orientalism—Exoticism—Self-Exoticism." *Dance Research Journal* 35(1): 13–37.

Solomon, Thomas. 2007. "Articulating the Historical Moment: Turkey, Europe, and Eurovision 2003." In *A Song for Europe: Popular Music and Politics in the Eurovision Song Contest*, edited by Ivan Raykoff and Robert Tobin, 135–45. Aldershot: Ashgate.

Stokes, Martin. 1992. *The Arabesk Debate: Music and Musicians in Modern Turkey.* Oxford: Clarendon Press.

———. 1996. "History, Memory and Nostalgia in Contemporary Turkish Musicology." *Music & Anthropology* 1. Accessed June 8, 2009. http://www.levi.provincia.venezia.it/ma/index/number1/stokes1/st1.htm.

Tekeli, Şirin. 1986. "Emergence of the Feminist Movement in Turkey." In *The New Women's Movement: Feminism and Political Power in Europe and the USA*, edited by Drude Dahlerup, 179–99. London: Sage.

Tekelioğlu, Orhan. 1996. "The Rise of a Spontaneous Synthesis: The Historical Background of Turkish Popular Music." *Middle Eastern Studies* 32(2): 194–215.

———. 2001. "Modernizing Reforms and Turkish Music in the 1930s." *Turkish Studies* 2(1): 93–108.

Thornton, Lynne. 1994. *Women as Portrayed in Orientalist Painting.* Paris: ACR Edition-PocheCouleur.

Tromans, Nicholas. 2008. "Harem and Home." In *The Lure of the East: British Orientalist Painting*, edited by Nicholas Tromans, 126–59. New Haven: Yale University Press.

White, Jenny B. 1999. "Islamic Chic." In *Istanbul Between the Global and the Local*, edited by Çağlar Keyder, 77–91. London: Rowman & Littlefield.

———. 2002. *Islamist Mobilization in Turkey: A Study in Vernacular Politics.* Seattle: University of Washington Press.

Yarar, Betül. 2008. "Politics of/and Popular Music: An Analysis of the History of Arabesk Music from the 1960s to the 1990s in Turkey." *Cultural Studies* 22(1): 35–79.

Yavuz, M. Hakan. 1998. "Turkish Identity and Foreign Policy in Flux: The Rise of Neo-Ottomanism." *Middle East Critique* 7(12): 19–41.

———. 2003. *Islamic Political Identity in Turkey.* Oxford: Oxford University Press.

Yeğenoğlu, Meyda. 1998. *Colonial Fantasies: Towards a Feminist Reading of Orientalism.* Cambridge: Cambridge University Press.

Chapter 8

Invincible Heroes

The Musical Construction of National and European Identities in Swedish Eurovision Song Contest Entries

Alf Björnberg

INTRODUCTION

Throughout the more than fifty years of Swedish participation in the Eurovision Song Contest, the notion of nationally specific popular-music styles has played an important part in the public discourse surrounding the contest. During this period, however, the characteristics of what has been perceived as specifically Swedish popular music have undergone fundamental changes. Swedishness in popular music has been defined in relation to different points of reference at different points of time—"Continental" European pop, British and U.S. pop/rock, and the "ethnic" pop of other European nations, as well as domestic "ethnic" music, both traditional and "reinvented." Also, Sweden's position in the global mediascape has changed, as the country has gradually turned from a net importer—in economic terms—to a significant net exporter of music, a process whose starting point is often located at Sweden's first ESC victory in 1974 with "Waterloo." The purpose of this chapter is to discuss changes in the musical characteristics of Swedish ESC entries and their cultural significance as representations of Swedishness in relation to variable "others." The context within which this discussion is carried out comprises the history of public-service media in Sweden, their relationships to the Swedish music industry, and the relationships of these two centers of musical-cultural power to musical changes within Swedish mainstream popular culture. In this discussion, both ESC entries, that is, winners in the Swedish preliminaries, and nonwinning entries in these preliminaries are taken into account; the degree of diversity among the latter is, of course, greater (if nothing else, for reasons of sheer quantity), but examples illustrating general tendencies have been chosen rather than isolated, if interesting, exceptions.

SOUNDING SWEDISH—TO WHOM?

Audiences and judges expect an Irish entry to sound Irish, though similar expectations do not extend to, say, Swedish entries. (Bohlman 2004, 7)

From a local, that is, Swedish perspective, Philip V. Bohlman's (as he suggests, rather arbitrary) choice of Sweden as an exemplary source of somewhat nonspecific musical representations of national identity provides food for much thought. The point of this statement seems to amount to Sweden being a typically modern Western European, and thus "nonethnic," nation, producing music which contains little that to listeners from other nations sounds recognizably Swedish, that is, there are few, if any, musical signifiers which denote or connote Swedishness to outsider listeners. As I have suggested in a previous context, this very lack of musical representations of cultural specificity may be part of the explanation for the international success of Swedish popular music in the last decades (see Björnberg 2007, 20–23). Still, to Swedish audiences, as well as broadcasting officials and music-industry representatives, each Swedish ESC entry "sounds Swedish" by virtue of the sheer fact of its being, precisely, a Swedish entry; that is, it constitutes in one way or another a proposal as to what might be desirable to present as Swedish music to the rest of the world. Thus, it involves—possibly even by negation—notions both of what is perceived as typically Swedish and of how this Swedishness is related to other possible national or transnational cultural identities, notions which change over time. The importance to Swedish audiences of the theme of "representing the nation" is indicated by the prominent part this theme plays in public discourse around the ESC throughout the history of Swedish participation in the event. In fact, Sweden, despite being one of the regular participants since the early days of the competition, belongs to the group of nations which "still show a fair amount of enthusiasm for the ESC" (Raykoff 2007, 7).

SWEDEN: A FAITHFUL ESC PARTICIPANT

The Swedish national public-service radio and television broadcaster, then called *Sveriges Radio* (SR), first entered the ESC in 1958. Since then, Sweden has participated in the contest continuously with the exception of three occasions, 1964, 1970, and 1976. In 1964, an artists' strike due to a conflict over fees for broadcast performances prevented the arranging of Swedish preliminaries. In 1970, Sweden, along with several other countries, withdrew as a direct consequence of the chaotic outcome of the 1969 ESC, with four entries sharing first place and no procedures at hand for the separation of these. Sweden's absence in 1976, however, had more specific reasons having to do with national cultural circumstances; it was the result of considerable domestic cultural-political pressure exerted on the broadcaster in a quite particular situation, to which I will return in greater detail below.

In 1958, no broadcast Swedish preliminaries were held; instead, the Swedish ESC entry was selected by way of an internal contest among the members of SKAP, the Swedish popular composers' and authors' association. Starting in 1959, however, each subsequent Swedish ESC entry has been selected by way of a nationally broadcast preliminary contest. Since 1967, the Swedish preliminaries have been presented under the designation Melodifestivalen ("The Melody Festival"; henceforth the MF), in order to distinguish it from the ESC finals. In addition to its nominal purpose of selecting an entry for an international contest, this event has played a quite important part in the national contexts of both Swedish media policy, as a showcase for public-service professionalism, and the actions of the Swedish popular-music industry, as a showcase for its products.

THE PIRATES AND CHANGES IN THE SWEDISH MEDIASCAPE

In the early 1960s, a major reorientation of the programming policy of the national public-service broadcaster occurred, as a direct result of the influence of commercial pirate-radio activities in the Swedish mediascape. Pirate radio had been present on the Swedish airwaves since 1958, but the inception in March 1961 of Radio Nord, the first pirate station whose transmissions covered the capital area, provoked a swift response from the public-service broadcaster, and in May 1961 the SR launched the twelve-hour-a-day light-music channel Melodiradion ("Melody Radio"; see Björnberg 2007). The pirates had proved chart-based popular-music shows to constitute a popular program format, and in October 1961 the popular-chart radio show *Tio i topp* ("The Top Ten"), based on listener voting, went on the air. In the course of 1962, increasing public criticism of the dominance of Anglophone songs on this chart induced the SR to launch, in October of that year, its counterpart *Svensktoppen* ("The Swedish Top"), which was restricted to songs with lyrics in Swedish. It deserves mentioning that this unexpected and rapid "democratization" of music broadcasting policies was also noticeable in the 1962 ESC preliminaries: for the first time in Sweden, audience voting was practiced in this context. Viewers submitted their votes by mail, some 200,000 votes were cast, and the results were presented in a separate transmission one week after the broadcast of the competing songs.

Svensktoppen provided an important forum for the Swedish popular-music industry, and patterns of synergy between this chart-show and the Swedish ESC preliminaries were clearly discernible from the mid-1960s onward. At the time, the designation *svensktopp* was also used as a genre concept, and to a large extent, the distinction between *svensktopp* ("adult mainstream music") and what in Sweden was called "pop" ("youth music") was drawn along lines of language: Swedish vs. English song lyrics. In stylistic terms, *svensktopp* was a fairly heterogeneous genre, comprising songs in older popular styles, such as nineteenth-century broadsheet ballads or interwar Austro-German *Schlager*, as well as songs representing more recent styles. While parts of the repertoire were original material written for the Swedish market, a large share of the genre was made up of Swedish-language cover versions of recent songs from the United Kingdom, the United States, and other parts of the world. Standard music-industry practice of the time consisted in obtaining licensing for a foreign song for Sweden (or Scandinavia), writing Swedish lyrics for the song, and recording it for the Swedish market with one of the popular *svensktopp* artists. The most prolific music-industry operator in this line of production was publisher, lyricist, and record producer Stig "Stikkan" Anderson, who wrote Swedish lyrics for some 3,000 foreign songs and subsequently used his extensive international music-industry contact network as one of the bases for his successful managing of ABBA's career in the 1970s (see Smith-Siversten 2007, 90ff). If much of its musical material, as well as its stylistic models for domestic pop production, thus were foreign, *Svensktoppen* still also provided a convenient media platform for those mainstream-pop composers, lyricists, and artists who formed the basis for Swedish ESC participation.

One factor forming part of the explanation for this synergy is the well-established pattern of personal connections between the popular-music industry and public-service media (both radio and television) in Sweden: for a considerable time, several producers and anchormen in public-service broadcasting had backgrounds as popular musicians, publishers, composers, or authors, rather than academics or journalists. In comparison to the situation in, for instance, the United Kingdom or Denmark, this seems to have been a characteristic which was specific for Sweden at least well into the 1970s.[1] Examples include, among others, actor/director/lyricist Stig Olin, composers/pianists/bandleaders Stig Holm, Stig Rybrant, and Willard Ringstrand, bass player/accordionist Hasse Tellemar, and composer/guitar player Sten Carlberg.[2]

THE 1960s: SWEDISH VS. "CONTINENTAL" POP

As already hinted at, several different phases may be identified in the general musical-stylistic makeup of Swedish ESC entries and entries in the Swedish ESC preliminaries. To some extent the boundaries of these phases can be aligned with decade boundaries, but on closer examination these boundaries are not clear-cut delimitations; rather, the various phases form tendencies which appear and fade away gradually.

The first stylistic phase in Swedish ESC history, lasting roughly until the early 1970s, can be characterized as one of "Continental" aspirations. The first Swedish ESC entry, "Lilla stjärna" in 1958, was a fairly sophisticated slow waltz in interwar Viennese style, and the following year, Sweden participated with "Augustin," a tango song in an unmistakeably German march-like tango style. Another stylistic influence was noticeable in those songs of the Swedish preliminaries of this early period which were perceived to be situated on the somewhat more "sophisticated" side: these were often modeled on the big-band swing arrangements written by Nelson Riddle for Frank Sinatra, thus keeping alive the Swedish tradition, dating back to the years of World War II, of popular songs in a big-band dance-music swing style; a good example of this is the 1960 ESC entry "Alla andra får varann."

This stylistic makeup is rendered more complicated in the period 1963–1966, which in retrospect stands out as quite exceptional in Swedish ESC history. These years saw the peak of ambitions on the part of the organizers of the Swedish preliminaries to "enhance the quality" of popular song, an enhancement which was to be realized on terms derived from the popular end of contemporary art music and the sophisticated end of orchestral entertainment music. To accomplish this, some entries in the preliminaries—in 1965, all six entries—were commissioned from invited professional composers representing both of these fields.[3] Perhaps the most explicit manifestation of this tendency was the 1965 ESC entry "Annorstädes vals," which was written by popular neoclassicist composer Dag Wirén and sung by professional opera/operetta singer Ingvar Wixell.[4]

Continental influences continued to be in effect throughout the second half of the 1960s; for instance, both "Vad har jag kvar" (1966) and the 1967 ESC entry "Som en dröm" featured a slow 12/8 ballad style, at the time perceived in Sweden as specifically "Italian." Another stylistic strand was gospel pop, represented, for instance, by "Härliga söndag" (1966), composed on the basis of models such as Horace Silver's "The Preacher" and Bill Cook's "You Can Have Her," which were national pop hits in Swedish-language versions in 1959 and 1961, respectively; the 1962 ESC entry "Sol och vår" also belonged to this category. The most prominent influence in this period, however, came from British 1960s orchestral pop, with which several songs in the Swedish preliminaries were stylistically aligned, some even being more or less modeled on easily recognizable individual British hit songs. Examples include "Alla har glömt" (1967) and "Du vet var jag finns" (1968; modeled on Petula Clark's "Don't Sleep in the Subway"), the Tom Jones–inspired "Du är en vårvind i april" (1968) and "Gång på gång" (1969; modeled on Jones's "Help Yourself"), "Du ser mej inte" and "Du skänker mening åt mitt liv" (both in 1969; the latter possibly modeled on Chris Andrews's 1965 hit "Yesterday Man"). The Swedish ESC entries in 1968 ("Det börjar verka kärlek, banne mej") and 1969 ("Judy min vän") were also composed in this vein, although not modeled on individual British pop songs. As already mentioned, similar stylistic influences were noticeable well into the early 1970s.[5]

It may be argued that in this period and within the stylistic framework outlined thus far, in their ESC and MF entries, Swedish mainstream-pop songwriters, arrangers, and artists demonstrated a significant degree of craftsmanship in songwriting, performance, and production. In spite of this, in the public reception of Swedish ESC music, it was often characterized as provincial and amateurish in comparison to Continental models. For instance, in 1961 a tabloid commentator described the songs of the preliminaries as "domestic horrors in an international competition," and in 1967, the composers of the Swedish ESC entry stated that their song is "a speculation in the type of popular song which appeals to the Latin countries."[6] In 1973, a commentator asks rhetorically: "should we let ourselves be represented internationally by hummable ditties of the most blue-and-yellow everyday kind—or by a song of more Continental complications?"[7] The expression of sentiments like these seems to be a common pattern for those European nations whose national self-esteem involves a view of the national culture in question as somehow "marginal" compared to the cultural centers of the continent.[8] In Sweden, this view of the state of things was prevailing well into the 1980s, although it was gradually modified after the successes of ABBA in 1974 and Herreys in 1984.

THE 1970s: THE "COMMERCIAL/PROGRESSIVE" DICHOTOMY

From the late 1960s and throughout the 1970s, the popular music scene in Sweden was to a large extent shaped by the antagonistic opposition between "commercial" and "progressive" music. In partial distinction to British and Continental "progressive rock," in Sweden the designation "progressive" was conceived in political rather than aesthetic terms. The so-called "progressive music movement" grew out of actions and manifestations such as the protests against a commercial "Teenage Fair" held in 1968 and the open-air music festivals arranged in Stockholm 1970–1972. The movement had roots in the youth revolts of 1968 and associations with international solidarity movements and the new left-wing political parties formed around 1970. It developed during the first half of the 1970s in a variety of organizations and activities. Local music societies, "music forums," were organized all over the country and cooperated in the national organization *Kontaktnätet*. Independent record companies owned by musicians or music activists were established, and the movement also included the record-distribution organizations *SAM-distribution* and *Plattlangarna*, as well as the journal *Musikens makt*.

On the "commercial" side of the dichotomy, a popular-musical category emerging around 1970 and gaining in import throughout the decade was the genre of *dansband* ("dance band"). As the term indicates, the genre was centered on groups playing music for dancing; some of these groups had been formed as early as around 1960, when groups with an electric-guitar-based lineup had started replacing the jazz-combo dance bands of the 1950s. New record companies were established, almost exclusively aimed at the dance-band market, the most important of these being Mariann Records, founded in 1972 by prolific entrepreneur Bert Karlsson. *Dansband*, as mainstream pop with Swedish song lyrics, was perceived as a subgenre of *svensktopp*, although stylistically, the subgenre was rather more well-defined than *svensktopp* in general, combining stylistic traits from nineteenth-century broadsheet ballads, 1950s New Orleans rhythm and blues, early 1960s high-school pop, and country music.

ABBA's victory in the 1974 ESC launched their international career, but, as has already been noted, one important prerequisite for this was the purposeful building up of an international musical-industrial contact network in the course of the 1960s.[9] In terms of musical style, ABBA to a large extent built on the same musical foundations as the dance bands, although "Waterloo" featured a rougher sound and a heavier beat than any previous song in the Swedish ESC preliminaries. The group also combined this with a stylistically more wide-ranging eclectic approach to songwriting and, more significantly, sophisticated recording-studio production at a level previously unrivaled in Swedish popular music. These characteristics, in combination with the group's glamorous on-stage visual image and the blatantly displayed concern of their manager Anderson for the profit-generating aspects of producing pop music, resulted in ABBA functioning as an emblematic representative of "commercial" music in the heavily polarized cultural-political climate of Sweden in the mid-1970s. At the time, the "progressive music movement" played a prominent part in public discourse on cultural policy, and although not necessarily sharing its political views, virtually all publicly subsidized musical organizations in Sweden joined forces with the movement in the struggle against musical "commercialism." Simultaneously with the 1975 ESC finals, hosted by the SR, several "Alternative Festivals" were arranged all over the nation as a joint manifestation of protest against the event and the commercial music industry it was taken to represent. One immediate consequence of this was the public-service broadcaster's withdrawal from further participation in the ESC:

> After this year's round of the European Cup of Eurovision popular song, the SR will say "thank you and good-bye" and back out for good (. . .) there are more important things to put one's money on.[10]

However, SR's abstention only lasted for one year; already in 1977, the broadcaster was back in the ESC (and, as it appears some thirty years later, "for good").

Another consequence of the "progressive" protests against commercialism was the change in _Svensktoppen_ rules, introduced in 1974, whereby only songs with music and lyrics created by Swedish citizens were allowed on the list. This effectively put an end to the music-industry practice, described above, of providing imported songs with lyrics in Swedish for the Swedish market. One motivation for this change may have been an ambition to make way in mainstream music media for some of the more commercially oriented "progressive" artists; the result, however, was the paving of the way for the emblematically commercial domestic genre of dance-band music.[11]

In terms of musical style, several Swedish ESC and MF entries in the second half of the 1970s demonstrated rock-music influences to a previously unprecedented degree, thus following ABBA's example. Examples include "Rockin' and reelin'" (1975), "Bang en boomerang" (1975), "Michelangelo" (1975), "Nattmara" (1978), "Satellit" (1979), and "Just nu" (1980).[12] A few songs from the dance-band genre also appeared, such as "Beatles" (1977), "Miss Decibel" (1978), and "Mycke' mycke' mer" (1980). However, not unexpectedly, throughout the 1970s, there were no traces of contemporary "progressive" music in the Swedish ESC preliminaries. Also, despite ABBA's victory in 1974, there were still few high expectations of good results in the ESC. ABBA's success seems to have been perceived as a one-off affair or the exception to prove the rule; as one commentator complained in 1978, "Sweden doesn't have much to make a show of after ABBA and the victory with 'Waterloo.'"[13]

THE 1980s: THE APOLITICAL BACKLASH

Public criticism of "commercial" music on the basis of cultural-political standpoints was rather rapidly dying away in Sweden at the beginning of the 1980s. Concomitantly, the 1980s Swedish ESC and MF entries were mostly dominated by music deriving from the straightforwardly commercial genre of dance-band music. Examples include "God morgon" (1981), "Dag efter dag" (1982), "Främling" (1983), "Diggi-loo diggi-ley" (1984), "Bra vibrationer" (1985), "Är det de' här du kallar kärlek" (1986), "Fyra Bugg och en Coca-Cola" (1987), and "100%" (1988). Here, it may be noted that of the songs mentioned, six (those from 1982–1987) won the Swedish preliminaries and went on to represent Sweden in the ESC. It also deserves mentioning that all six of them were produced by Mariann Records, the dominating company in the dance-band music scene. To some extent this style appears to have set a pattern for ESC entries from the neighboring Scandinavian countries as well. Danish examples in a similar stylistic vein include "Det' lige det" (1984), "Ka' du se hva' jeg sa'" (1988), "Vi maler byen rød" (1989), and "Hallo, hallo" (1990); a prominent Norwegian example is Norway's first ESC winner, "La det swinge" in 1985.

In terms of perceived anchorage in a specific national cultural situation, if not in terms of musical "origins," it may be argued that this 1980s dance-band music constitutes the most "genuinely Swedish" musical style representing Sweden in the ESC throughout the history of the event. That this style also possessed some international potential was demonstrated by Sweden's second, and rather unexpected, ESC win in 1984 with "Diggi-loo diggi-ley." In addition to dance-band music, the two main musical styles represented in the Swedish 1980s preliminaries were, on the one hand, a rock/pop-ballad style and, on the other, a danceable up-tempo synth-disco style. On the whole, however, the 1980s were a period characterized by a low degree of diversity; in fact it may be argued that Swedish ESC songs of the decade displayed a degree of stylistic homogeneity never attained before nor since.

The 1980s were also the decade of the first growth of what in the 1990s was to be termed "the Swedish music-export miracle": in the wake of ABBA, this decade saw the international breakthroughs of soft-metal group Europe in 1986 and pop/rock duo Roxette in 1989. So far, however, these emerging success stories left few traces in the music of Swedish ESC entries or in the public expectations accompanying these entries in the international contest—none of these artists participated in the competition in the 1980s, although Per Gessle of Roxette wrote (but did not perform) one song for the 1980 preliminaries. A representative

tabloid comment after the 1986 preliminaries stated "I like the song
(. . .) very much, but I don't think it stands a chance in Bergen."[14] Sweden's third ESC winner, "Fångad av en stormvind" in 1991, was still
situated in the musical, cultural, and musical-industrial landscape of
dance-band music.

THE 1990s: SWEDEN IN THE NEW EUROPE

The post-1989 developments within the ESC, representing what Bohlman
(2004) has termed "the New Europeanness," involved a steadily growing
number of nations participating in the contest and, concomitantly, an
increasing presence of stylistic hybrids, combining elements from various
local musical traditions with structures from Western mainstream-pop
music. The latter applies to Sweden as well: in the course of the 1990s,
the stylistic makeup of the Swedish ESC and MF repertoire established
in the previous decade was expanded by a number of examples of "self-
consciously 'ethnic' styles" (Solomon 2007, 142; Björnberg 2007, 21).
Examples include "Långt härifrån" in 1992, a march-like song with a
"medieval ballad" structure, including short repeated refrain lines, the
"Celtic New Age" song "Den vilda" in 1996, combining archaic-sounding
lyrics with music inspired by the sound of Irish singer Enya, the hurdy-
gurdy-based folk-rock song "En gång ska han gråta" in 1997, and the
modally flavored folk-song pastiche "Som av is" in 1999.[15] Of these songs,
however, only "Den vilda" won the preliminaries and went on to represent Sweden in the ESC. The artists performing these songs were previously not particularly associated with "ethnic" music, with the exception
of Garmarna (who performed "En gång ska han gråta"), an established
Swedish modern folk music/world music group.

In Sweden, however, "New Europeanness" was also coincident with an
increasing public awareness of the Swedish music industry being a significant international actor in the popular-music field. The success stories
of Europe and Roxette were followed by the international breakthrough
of pop group Ace of Base in 1993. The same year, the interest organization Export Music Sweden was formed, and at about the same time, the
first public reports appeared specifying the economic importance of the
Swedish music industry in terms of export income. This growing awareness was also reflected in 1990s press comments on Sweden's chances in
the ESC, where a new confidence in the potential of Swedish ESC entries
was clearly discernible:

> . . . a song with the type of qualities which makes it able to give a certain echo
> internationally (. . .) It is this kind of innocent boy-pop which tends to be a
> hit on the continent.[16]

Tonight we'll get a new topic for conversation. Maybe also a new international Swedish star.[17]

Ten years after Abba's victory, 1984, Sweden won its second international
contest (. . .) and in 1991 we were third time lucky (. . .) Perhaps we'll see a
new star being born on Saturday?[18]

Sweden's fourth ESC win in 1999 could thus be perceived as a definite
confirmation of the degree of professional know-how which by this time
had been acquired by the Swedish music industry. In terms of musical
style, however, the song, "Tusen och en natt" (English title: "Take Me
to Your Heaven"), with its straightforward diatonic-major tonality, up-
tempo shuffle rhythm, and pentatonic-major second-line riffs, was still
largely situated in the musical landscape of 1980s dance-band music. It
thus constituted the latest (and, possibly, the last?) of a number of successful ESC entries to emerge from the musical environment of Swedish
dance-band culture.

2000 AND BEYOND: PROFESSIONAL PASTICHE

In 2002, the format of the Swedish ESC preliminaries, the MF, was considerably expanded, from a one-night show featuring ten competing
songs to a process spread out over six consecutive weekend prime-time
shows and presenting in all thirty-two competing songs. The basic rationale behind this change seems to have been the ambition to keep up
audience ratings in the face of increasing competition from commercial
broadcasters in the recently deregulated Swedish mediascape. The effect
was also one of rendering the preliminaries an event in its own right, as
a showcase for both Swedish public-service and Swedish music-industry
professionalism, to some extent more independent of the ESC finals than
before, although the latter still provided the nominal justification for the
entire selection procedure.

These developments were accompanied by growing expectations, on
the part of both audience and critics, of professionalism as regards songwriting, performances, and TV-program production. In terms of musical
style, however, Swedish professionalism in the ESC of the 2000s has been
manifested in a quite particular way. Several of the last few years' Swedish ESC entries can be characterized as "musical pastiches," reconstruc-
tions of recognizable musical styles previously not represented in this
context, rather than "musical hybrids" (attempts at syntheses of preexist-
ing styles, which, it may be argued, constitute a more regular popular
music practice). Typical examples of this are the 2005 ESC entry "Las
Vegas," a U.S.-style big-band show number, the 2006 entry "Evighet"
(English title: "Invincible"), a sort of pastiche of dance-band drama,

seemingly aspiring at a passion which the style does not appear fully able to support, and the 2007 entry "The Worrying Kind," musically as well as visually a reconstruction of 1970s glam rock.[19]

Although not very visible in the Swedish ESC entries, in the preliminaries "ethnic" tendencies have been persistent into the new millennium. Among these, several constitute attempts at a construction of musical "Swedishness"; examples include the 2000 ESC entry "När vindarna viskar mitt namn" (English title: "When Spirits Are Calling My Name"), as well as, in the preliminaries, "Genom eld och vatten" in 2003, "Här stannar jag kvar" in 2004, "Ödet var min väg" in 2005 and "I lågornas sken" in 2008. A new phenomenon, however, is the appearance of "foreign ethnic styles" in the Swedish preliminaries, represented by songs such as the Ricky-Martinesque latin-pop song "Adrenaline" in 2002, the downhome-bluegrass tune "Mama Take Me Home" in 2006, the Balkan brass-ensemble piece "Kebabpizza Slivovitza" in 2008 and the percussion-heavy Greek-pop song "Alla" in 2009. Thus, there is a noticeably increasing presence of "multiculturalism" in the Swedish preliminaries, if yet not so much so in the winning ESC entries. This raises questions of possible changes in the significance of multiculturalism in the ESC. In a text published in 2002, Bohlman summed up the cultural climate of the ESC in this respect, stating that:

> [t]he nations of the stage of the Eurovision Song Contest have, with few exceptions, been primarily monocultural, not least because multiculturalism would initially have to be a statement by the competing nation about its identity. (Bohlman 2002, 92)

His conclusion is that "[i]t is still the case that, in order to win, a song must be unobtrusive, musically and ideologically" (Bohlman 2004, 289). This may have been true to a considerable extent throughout most of the history of the contest, but the last few years' developments within the ESC may indicate that things are changing. Lutgard Mutsaers has recently claimed that:

> [i]t is common knowledge among ESC aficionados and general audiences alike that national references in the form of particular folk sounds or costumes influence the song's winning chances considerably—for a long time in a completely negative way, but in recent years in a much more positive way. (Mutsaers 2007, 70)

From the perspective of Swedish audiences and critics, however, the multiculturalism represented in the Swedish ESC preliminaries seems rather to have been construed as yet another facet of professionalism: a manifestation of the ability of Swedish songwriters and artists to write and perform songs in a wide variety of musical styles.[20] Accordingly, in press comments in the 2000s, Swedish success in the ESC seems almost to have been taken for granted. When such success has failed to appear, this has increasingly been explained in terms of conspiracy theories of Eastern European "bloc voting," often termed "buddy voting" in Swedish media.[21] And in the last few years, success has been scarce: none of the entries "Las Vegas" in 2005, "The Worrying Kind" in 2007, or "Hero" in 2008 managed to reach a higher position than the eighteenth in the ESC finals, despite the fact that the latter song—in a dance-band-cum-euro-disco style—was performed by 1999 ESC winner Charlotte Perrelli (then Charlotte Nilsson). Before the 2009 ESC, expectations were once again high, as Sweden was represented by "La voix," a bilingual hybrid of europop and Pucciniesque opera-aria pastiche performed by Malena Ernman, a *bona fide* opera diva, but once again disappointment ensued, as the song ended up twenty-first in the finals.[22] When asked on the evening of defeat how to change this negative trend, Christer Björkman, head of the Swedish ESC delegation, was quoted answering:

> . . . I believe we'll have to talk at this very moment to publishers and song-writers and really ask them to challenge themselves. But right now, I don't know.[23]

Thus, the solution seemingly lying closest at hand once again amounted to the reliance on Swedish music-industry professionalism, by this time an integrated aspect of the self-understanding of Swedish audiences, critics, and public-service media officials. However, the following year's result was perceived as a disastrous all-time low in the history of Swedish ESC performance, as the 2010 entry "This Is My Life" even failed to advance from the semifinals. Relief was finally brought in the 2011 ESC, where the Swedish entry "Popular" ended up third after an unusually even voting process, where the result hung in the balance until the last few nations had cast their votes. The performer, Eric Saade, was quoted in the tabloids claiming to have finally "recovered Sweden's honour."[24] However, while celebrating this success-at-last, press critics devoted equal amounts of energy to arguing that the Azerbaijanian ESC victory in reality should be regarded as a Swedish triumph, as the Azerbaijanian entry involved Swedish songwriters, Swedish background singers, a Swedish choreographer, and a Swedish stylist—yet another case of Swedish music-industry professionals lending a helping hand.

CONCLUSION

In a sense, the history of the ESC is one of a steadily increasing problematization of the notion of national identity being represented by specific national styles. From a Swedish perspective, this process has been characterized by a particular kind of professionalization. Rather than being represented by distinctive musical-stylistic features, a Swedish identity in the field of popular music has increasingly been perceived in terms of, and represented by, the nation's music-industrial know-how, a gradually increasing professionalism with regard to the production of popular music. This, rather than some perceivable cultural significance within Swedish national culture, seems to be what is at stake in the skillfully worked-out but perhaps not very culturally significant musical pastiches constituting recent Swedish ESC entries. Although these developments have had a particular resonance for the Swedish situation, due to the particular circumstances forming the Swedish popular-music industry throughout the last decades, it appears that they may to a large extent be common to large parts of "Western" (in cultural rather than geographical terms) Europe.

NOTES

1. From the start of Swedish ESC participation, public critique was leveled at the connections between public-service media and the music industry, regarding, for instance, the multiple roles of show-biz veteran Thore Ehrling as music publisher, band leader, and emcee in the 1959 ESC preliminaries.

2. Carlberg, who had been employed in public-service broadcasting since the late 1940s, made an on-stage reappearance as a guitar player in the 1986 ESC finals, where he performed a remarkable bare-chested heavy-metal solo in the Swedish entry "Är det de' här du kallar kärlek," astonishing those European colleagues who only knew him as a TV producer and leader of the Swedish ESC delegation.

3. In 1963, the invited composers were those who had achieved good results in the previous years' preliminaries, rather than being selected according to extrinsic quality criteria. However, also this year these invited composers (as well as the arrangers of the orchestral backgrounds) seem to have aspired at increased sophistication.

4. In order to minimize the influence of the individual artist on the judgment of jurors, Wixell sang all six entries in the 1965 preliminaries. The same rationale lay behind the practice in the preliminaries in the years 1960–1963 to let each song be sung twice in the broadcast show by different artists and in different arrangements, for a large entertainment orchestra and a small dance combo, respectively.

5. The last attempt to reduce the influence of the individual artist (see previous note) appeared in 1971, when the preliminaries were held on six consecutive Saturday evenings, where on each of the five first occasions three songs were performed by the same artists, the singers Tommy Körberg and Sylvia Vrethammar and the vocal group Family Four. The five winners of these heats then competed in national finals. Ironically, the "influence of the artist" was clearly demonstrated by the fact that the song performed by Family Four won each of the five heats. The group also performed the Swedish ESC entry in 1972.

Invincible Heroes   217

w6. Bengt Melin, "Ingen chans i Cannes med den melodin," *Aftonbladet*, February 7, 1961, 11; Hans Fridlund, "Vi vann, sa Marcus," *Aftonbladet*, February 25, 1967, 8.

7. Hans Fridlund, "Rätt låt vann", *Expressen*, February 11, 1973, 8.

8. For analyses of similar sentiments in Finland, Turkey, and Yugoslavia, respectively, see Pajala 2007; Solomon 2007; Vuletic 2007.

9. ABBA's first attempt occurred in the 1973 preliminaries with "Ring ring." The song ended up third, this comparative failure allegedly due to a jury of "experts" rather than "laymen," although it is difficult to ascertain how significant this distinction was in reality.

10. Suzy Persson, "Punkt och slut för schlager-SM," *GT*, February 15, 1975, 34. The expression "European Cup of Eurovision popular song" is a rough translation of one of several unofficial designations for the event used by the Swedish press at the time.

11. This rule was changed in 1978, when Swedish-language cover versions of foreign songs were again allowed; still, at least half the songs tested for the list had to be created by Swedes.

12. Here, the "internationally marketable" character of several of these song titles may be noted; to some extent, this may also be attributed to ABBA, although previous examples of such song titles may be found in the Swedish preliminaries.

13. Christer Faleij, "Jag tror inte Björn har en chans i Paris," *Aftonbladet*, February 12, 1978, 25.

14. Richard Herrey, "Style borde ha vunnit," *Aftonbladet*, March 23, 1986, 40.

15. Nonetheless, these were not the first examples of such musical hybrids in the MF. Previous examples of "self-conscious ethnicity" include the national-romanticist entertainment-orchestral "Svart-Olas polska" in 1967 and the peculiar "folksy" hybrid "Ola mä fiola" in 1977, mixing traditional musical elements of diverse origins in a way perceived as clearly incoherent.

16. Olle Berggren, "Schlagkraftigt—folkets röst slår an tonen för framtidens melodi," *iDag*, March 6, 1993, B1.

17. Olle Berggren, "Ladda med kaffe till EM i kitsch," *iDag*, May 13, 1995, 15.

18. Ulrika Bremberg, "Glittrig festival en modern rit," *Metro*, March 6, 1997, 15.

19. Another aspect of Swedish professionalism which has attracted some media attention has been the provision by public-service broadcaster SVT as well as Swedish private-company professionals of technical support for the production of several of the ESC finals in recent years (Tallinn 2002, Riga 2003, Istanbul 2004, Kyiv 2005, and Belgrade 2008).

20. Here, questions obviously arise concerning the complicated relationship between, on the one hand, such music-industry professionalism and, on the other, the cultural background of the individual artists performing these and similar songs, questions which deserve a more elaborate discussion than can be undertaken in the present context.

21. See Pajala 2007, 80ff. For analyses of bloc voting patterns in the ESC see Björnberg 1992; Le Guern 200. In 2007, the German broadcaster NDR presented a rough analysis of bloc-voting patterns in that year's ESC: in a division of the voting nations into a Western European and an Eastern European half, the four nations which could be demonstrated to have benefited most from "bloc" voting

were Belarus, Macedonia, and Slovenia (supported by the Eastern "bloc") and Sweden (supported by the Western). (The analysis was published on www.eurovision.de on May 14, 2007; the Web page was no longer accessible in May 2009.)

22. The obvious resemblance between the chorus of "La voix" and Puccini's aria "Nessun dorma" has been much commented upon in the Swedish press. In this connection, it may be noted that the composer of the former, Fredrik Kempe, had a national hit in 2002 with a euro-disco version of the latter, entitled "Vincero."

23. Anon., "Malena tillbaka till operan—och tvättstugan," *Metro*, May 18, 2009, 46.

24. Sofia Persson, "Saades treumf," *Expressen*, May 15, 2011, 35.

REFERENCES

Björnberg, Alf. 1992. "Musical Spectacle as Ritual: The Eurovision Song Contest." 373–82 in *1789–1989: Musique, Histoire, Démocratie*, vol. II, edited by Antoine Hennion. Paris: Editions de la Maison des Sciences de l'Homme.

———. 2007. "Return to Ethnicity: The Cultural Significance of Musical Change in the Eurovision Song Contest." 13–23 in *A Song for Europe: Popular Music and Politics in the Eurovision Song Contest*, edited by Ivan Raykoff and Robert Deam Tobin. Aldershot: Ashgate.

———. 2009. "The Soundtrack of Sales: Music in Swedish Radio Commercials." 223–36 in *Music in Advertising: Commercial Sounds in Media Communication and Other Settings*, edited by Nicolai Graakjær and Christian Jantzen. Aalborg: Aalborg University Press.

Bohlman, Philip V. 2002. *World Music: A Very Short Introduction*. Oxford: Oxford University Press.

———. 2004. *The Music of European Nationalism: Cultural Identity and Modern History*. Santa Barbara, Calif.: ABC-CLIO.

Le Guern, Philippe. "From National Pride to Global Kitsch: the Eurovision Song Contest." *The Web Journal of French Media Studies* 3(1): 2000. wjfms.ncl.ac.uk/enframes.htm (April 24, 2009).

Mutsaers, Lutgard. 2007. "Fernando, Filippo, and Milly: Bringing Blackness to the Eurovision Stage." 61–70 in *A Song for Europe: Popular Music and Politics in the Eurovision Song Contest*, edited by Ivan Raykoff and Robert Deam Tobin. Aldershot: Ashgate.

Pajala, Mari. 2007. "Finland, Zero Points: Nationality, Failure, and Shame in the Finnish Media." 71–82 in *A Song for Europe: Popular Music and Politics in the Eurovision Song Contest*, edited by Ivan Raykoff and Robert Deam Tobin. Aldershot: Ashgate.

Raykoff, Ivan. 2007. "Camping on the Borders of Europe." 1–12 in *A Song for Europe: Popular Music and Politics in the Eurovision Song Contest*, edited by Ivan Raykoff and Robert Deam Tobin. Aldershot: Ashgate.

Smith-Sivertsen, Henrik. 2007. *Kylling med soft ice og pølser: Populærmusikalske versioneringspraksisser i forbindelse med danske versioner af udenlandske sange i perioden 1945–2007*. Diss., Copenhagen: Copenhagen University.

Solomon, Thomas. 2007. "Articulating the Historical Moment: Turkey, Europe, and Eurovision 2003." 135–45 in *A Song for Europe: Popular Music and Politics in the Eurovision Song Contest*, edited by Ivan Raykoff and Robert Deam Tobin. Aldershot: Ashgate.

Vuletic, Dean. 2007. "The Socialist Star: Yugoslavia, Cold War Politics and the Eurovision Song Contest." 83–97 in *A Song for Europe: Popular Music and Politics in the Eurovision Song Contest*, edited by Ivan Raykoff and Robert Deam Tobin. Aldershot: Ashgate.

Chapter 9

"And After Love . . ."

Eurovision, Portuguese Popular Culture, and the Carnation Revolution

LUISA PINTO TEIXEIRA
AND MARTIN STOKES

The question of Europe has often, in recent years, taken the shape of a question about the possibility of transnational civility. Sociologist Ulrich Beck put the argument in earnest terms in an article published in *The Guardian* in 2008 entitled "Europe's Last Political Utopia." The separation of church and state with the Peace of Westphalia, he argued, is echoed in modern times by the separation of nation and state with the birth of the European Union. The purpose of this separation was similar: to put an end to the causes of Europe's (and by extension, the world's) wars. It has taken political catastrophe, Beck suggested, to bring out the best in Europe. "The traditions from which colonial, nationalist and genocidal horror originated were clearly European. But so were the legal standards against which those acts were condemned and convicted in the spotlight of world publicity. At this formative moment in its history, Europe mobilised its traditions to produce something new." The political evolution of the state system is not at an end, he claimed. Utopia is still thinkable, and, he suggests, it is Europe's task to lead the way there. At the same time, this possibility means that "we must radically rethink the conventional categories of social and political analysis."

The article is striking for its almost feverishly anxious tone. But this is not surprising. Racial and islamophobic violence steadily increases across Europe. Full-scale wars over Balkan borders continue to be a real possibility. EU membership and Eurozone integration are incendiary political issues in the Western European heartlands. Washington rather than Brussels continues to set both the political and the economic terms that actually matter, especially to the smaller nations. Anxiety about dependence on a gas-rich Russia grows steadily. The debt crisis of 2012—and its mishandling by the EU—seems likely, at the time of writing, to push Greece out of the Eurozone. The frailty of Beck's vision is plain to see, and the recourse to "belief" symptomatic. To engage questions of "belief" in public is to shift political discourse in the direction of faith rather than reason and the practical engagement with, or contestation of, politically concrete projects and issues. In this we would argue that Beck's article is not only symptomatic of Europe's predicament, but, more generally, a sign of our late-liberal times.

Beck's questions reverberate in Eurovision, and have throughout its history. They do so in a complex way. For Eurovision has also staged and spectacularized doubt, irony, cynicism, and disbelief. Cynicism about Eurovision hardly needs illustrating. Consider only the long history of Eurovision "spoof" acts, such as Ireland's "Dustin the Turkey" entry in 2008. Ireland, as is well known, has been a Eurovision success story, with a disproportionate number of winning entries and runners-up. But 1999, a moment of increased Eastern European participation, marked a sudden and precipitous drop in Ireland's fortunes: nonqualification for the finals in 2005 and, perhaps even more painfully, last place with a mere five points in 2007 for a traditional music group, Dervish, and nonparticipation in the finals of 2009. A turkey glove puppet representing a dodgy North Dublin builder represented some uncomfortable truths about life in the Celtic Tiger economy, and a more general disillusionment with Euro-civility in general.

Satire, irony, camp, the staging of cynicism, as we know, are part of Eurovision's fun, the compelling ingredients of a competition that succeeds in dragging millions to their television sets each May, year after year. As Žižek pointed out in *The Sublime Object of Ideology* (1989), cynicism and belief are the coconstituent and mutually sustaining—if unstable and compensatory—dynamics of public life in the late-liberal West. This perspective allows us to see the connections between Beck's earnest vision of Euro-civility and the irony, cynicism, and camp of Eurovision. The Beckian vision, one might say, is *sustained* by Eurovision. Even as its inverse is acknowledged, a fundamental structure of belief in the Beckian vision is affirmed and maintained. No better illustration of this could be found than the terms in which long-standing U.K. Eurovision commentator Terry Wogan resigned in 2008. His stock in trade was a mischievous, genteel cynicism. And yet he resigned because, he claimed, he could no longer take the competition *seriously*.

The juncture marked by Dustin the Turkey in 2008 was one of a Western Europe that no longer seemed to take the competition seriously, and an Eastern Europe that did. Cynicism and earnestness have an apparently simple geopolitical distribution across Eurovision's landscape, and tell a familiar story: of a Western Europe that is now experiencing the downside of European integration, and an Eastern Europe that still feels it has everything to gain from the prospect of further integration. Of a Western Europe where many people feel cosmopolitan civility is under pressure from migrants—nominally European, but speaking incomprehensible languages, carrying unfamiliar cultural baggage—and an Eastern Europe where many continue to see in the European project realistic prospects of a liberal, civil, and, above all, prosperous future for their own countries. This picture owes much to the Beckian vision of cosmopolitanism and Euro-civility with which we started, though acknowledging imbalances, time lag, and disequilibrium. A common Eurovision narrative underscores this picture, claiming Eurovision as a means of welcoming eager new Europeans into the fold, and accustoming the old and jaded to their exuberant and energetic presence.

Our project in this chapter is to trouble this picture, with its rather self-satisfied assumption of Western Europe's civilizing mission. We aim to do so by focusing on a moment of Eurovision history that is either now forgotten in Eurovision's own discursive circles, or remembered only as a joke, an oddity. This concerns the Portuguese entries of the early 1970s, and with them the broader question of Eurovision's relations with the Iberian dictatorships, that of Franco in Spain and Salazar in Portugal. In Portugal, our more specific focus, these broader questions are still very much in play, and do much to condition participation in the competition, and the pleasures Portuguese audiences derive from it. So, in part, this chapter contributes to a broader picture of Eurovision by reminding readers of the richness and multiplicity of local music histories intersecting with this competition, a richness and multiplicity that cannot simply be aligned to the dominant narrative, sketched above, of a cynical (but civil) West and an earnest (but, as yet, uncivil) east. Our weightier claim, put in simple terms, is that Eurovision's accommodation of the Spanish and Portuguese entries in the 1970s serves as an uncomfortable reminder of the deeply persistent conservative/religious authoritarianisms of *Western* European political experience in the latter half of the twentieth century, their accommodation by the Western European democracies and their cultural legacy. The story is worth telling, then, for a variety of reasons.

PORTUGAL'S EUROVISION DEBUT

We start with a photograph from the Danish press, taken during the final in Copenhagen at the Tivoli Gardens in 1964, the first year of Portugal's participation in the Eurovision contest, and Spain's fourth (*Berlingske Tidende* March 22, 1964).[1] To the left we see the national hostess of the event, Lotte Waever, a well-known Danish television personality of the time. To the right, the frozen, blurred choreography of a protestor on stage being wrestled to the ground. The photograph has been taken close to the front of the stage, and we see another photographer and his camera immediately to our left. The period details are striking: the antiquated camera, the ball gown worn by Waever, the tails worn by the balding, bespectacled middle-aged man confronting the protestor. This respectable figure seems, somewhat improbably, to have managed to wrestle the vigorous young protestor into submission. At least, the young man seems to have lost his balance, and his placard—which, we learn, reads "Boycott Franco and Salazar"—has disappeared from view in the struggle.

One's immediate sense of choreography is not entirely misplaced. The protestor, a young cartoonist and illustrator, represented a group known as "Group 61," a youth splinter group of the Socialist Folk Party in Denmark. Protests marking the thirtieth anniversary of Franco's rule in Spain had long been expected. The moment coincided with the thirty-second anniversary of Salazar's *Estado Novo* regime, and a brutal turn in Portugal's colonial wars. Group 61 had demanded Portugal's exclusion from Eurovision (Spain's inclusion now, presumably, being an established, if not accepted, fact). The group threatened to bomb the Tivoli Concert Hall if their demands were not met. The protest took place, but had clearly been anticipated by police and security. The Danish television cameras turned away, apparently, but other nations' camera crews caught the

Figure 9.1. Demonstration during the Copenhagen Eurovision Song Contest in 1964 protesting Portugal's and Spain's participation. Source: PA Photos Ltd. (used with permission).

event, and pictures of the protest found their way across Europe. Portugal's entry that year, António Calvário's "Oração" ("Prayer"), came last.

What does the picture tell us? From a northern perspective, it documents the continued galvanization of the European Left by the entrenched Iberian dictatorships. It also represents a moment of recognition by the European left of the power of mass media and popular culture (particularly television) as a space of political struggle. The speed with which this opportunity was perceived and acted on is striking. It also tells us something about the growing internationalization of Europe's social movements, an internationalism that would culminate on the streets of Paris four years later, in 1968. And, perhaps, it captures an embarrassment, as the Cold War gathered momentum and divided East and West, at the persistence of these profoundly illiberal regimes, and their accommodation by the Western European democracies.

The picture says much, too, through what it does *not* represent. The Portuguese musicians are absent from the scene. Little is remembered, outside Portugal, about the song in question, apart from the fact that it came last. This points to a persistent problem. Portuguese Eurovision entries are, indeed, often remembered in Eurovision lore for various things, but rarely their music. Ten years later, another Portuguese entry, Paulo de Carvalho's "E Depois do Adeus" ("And After the Farewell"), signaled the start of the so-called Carnation Revolution, which brought the Estado Novo to an end on April 25, 1974. It, too, came last, and it, too, continues to be remembered only as a quirky and humorous footnote in Eurovision history. Remembering Portugal's Eurovision entries only as mute political signs, remembered as humorous anecdotes, seems to be one way in which metropolitan northwestern Europe has kept these uncomfortable memories at bay.

Our intention in what remains of this essay is to remember Portugal's Eurovision entries as *songs*, as experienced in Portugal's lively and energetic popular musical culture during these years. This is not, of course, an attempt to depoliticize them. Precisely by suggesting that they were not, simply, mute ciphers expressing resistance or accommodation to the Salazar and Caetano regimes, we hope to arrive at a more subtle and nuanced picture of the cultural politics of the moment. Poulantzas, for instance, distinguished the "cultural" and the "political" revolutions of 1968, a distinction, essentially, between northern and southern Europe (he was interested, specifically, in Greece, Portugal, and Spain in this latter category, see Poulantzas 1976). This understanding of the "southern" revolutions of the late 1960s and 1970s persists. The cultural dynamics of the Carnation Revolution of April 25, 1974, bear consideration in this broader context. Poulantzas's distinction may have been drawn too emphatically, and there was certainly more "culture" in the Carnation Revolution than Poulantzas might have recognized.

CULTURAL POLITICS IN THE ESTADO NOVO

In Portugal, the role of "E Depois do Adeus" in acting as the signal for the Carnation Revolution is still celebrated. But it is intimately linked with another song, Zeca Afonso's "Grândola, Vila Morena" (Grândola, Swarthy Town). "E Depois do Adeus," broadcast at 10:55 p.m. on April 23 by the radio Emissores Associados de Lisboa, sent a standby message to the revolutionary commanders of the Movimento das Forças Armadas (MFA, the Armed Forces Movement). The next day, at 12:25 p.m., Rádio Renascença broadcast Zeca Afonso's "Grândola, Vila Morena." This was the signal for the MFA to actually take over strategic points of power in the country (Ferreira 1994). Consequently, the one song is rarely remembered in Portugal today without the other song instantly coming to mind.

The two songs are a study in contrast. "E Depois do Adeus" is a sentimental ballad, narrating the end of an affair. "Grândola, Vila Morena" is a revolutionary ballad, narrating workers struggle in the downtrodden south of the country, the Alentejo. "E Depois do Adeus" is a piece of popular musical cosmopolitanism, a Southern European *chanson* or *canzona*, known through a sophisticated studio arrangement. "Grândola, Vila Morena" is rendered as a folk song, usually sung in unison or parallel thirds harmony, associated with a particular locality. Paulo de Carvalho, the singer of "E Depois do Adeus," was a figure the Portuguese regime thought it could trust. Zeca Afonso, by contrast, was a radical, a communist. After being forbidden to teach in 1968 and under close surveillance, Afonso focused on songwriting and singing, while remaining politically active. His albums of this latter period were recorded in studios in London and Paris.

Before exploring this contrast further, and considering its significance in Portuguese song culture, we should explain some of the circumstances of the Carnation Revolution. By 3:00 a.m. of April 25, 1974, the forces of the MFA had occupied the television and radio studios of RTP (Rádio e Televisão de Portugal), the Rádio Clube Português (Portuguese Radio Club), and the Emissora Nacional (National Radio). At 4:30 a.m. they occupied the military general headquarters in Lisbon. Later that morning, at Ribeira das Naus in Lisbon, militia lieutenant Maia Loureiro signaled V for Victory from the top of the first of ten tanks belonging to the Escola Prática de Cavalaria (Cavalry Training School), indicating that the military coup to overthrow the longest dictatorship in Europe had succeeded. The tanks followed the jeep where the most famous of the so-called "Captains of April," Salgueiro Maia, rode. These stopped at Terreiro do Paço (Palace Square), a symbolic location of power in Lisbon. In the meantime, people turning on the radio in the morning realized that something was wrong. Short but detailed reports gradually informed people about the evolution of the events, while songs long forbidden were played on national radio. Despite these clear efforts to keep people at home listening to the radio, Lisbonites began their morning commute. Rumors circulated in the trains and buses. Instead of going to their offices and factories, they made their way to the Terreiro do Paço, following the growing crowds. Flower sellers who traditionally gathered at Rossio, a nearby plaza, realized there was no business to be done that day, and started distributing red carnations, the symbolic flower of Socialism and Communism, to all and sundry.

The action at Terreiro do Paço was soon over. Salgueiro Maia, confronted by four tanks belonging to the Seventh Cavalry regiment, had a white handkerchief in his hands signifying peaceful intentions. The Seventh Cavalry was under the command of Junqueira Reis, faithful to Caetano's regime. Junqueira Reis ordered his men to fire, but they refused, and with that refusal the battle with the Caetano regime was effectively over. Red carnations, by this moment, had filtered their way through the crowds and found their way into the muzzles of the MFA's rifles. The future of the country, in the symbology of the Carnation Revolution today, was decided at that moment. The Guarda Nacional Republicana (Republican National Guard) headquarters in Largo do Carmo, the main Lisbon military police station where Marcelo Caetano had taken refuge, was then occupied. Once again Salgueiro Maia was instrumental in this most emblematic moment of the revolution, the surrender of the dictator.[2]

The regime was, then, brought down in a military coup d'état, but what ensued was a full-blown social and cultural revolution that totally transformed the identity of Portugal. For nearly half a century, Portugal had been subjected to a fascist dictatorship, which rested on an aggressive politics of colonial exploitation and internal repression. A military coup in 1926 paved the way to Antonio Salazar's rise to power in 1928. The coup brought an end to a long period of chaos following the collapse of the Portuguese monarchy and the establishment of the Republic in 1910. Salazar had been a professor of law in Coimbra, a conservative institution, where he cultivated a close relationship with the Catholic Church. In 1928 he became finance minister, and in 1930 he established the União Nacional (National Union)—not a political party but rather a civilian-political association that was to become instrumental during the dictatorship acting as a *de facto* party. In 1933 he promulgated the so-called Estado Novo, the "New State," becoming president of the Council of Ministers (i.e., prime minister). The Estado Novo was an authoritarian regime, which controlled the metropolis together with the Atlantic islands and its colonies in Africa, India, Macau, and East-Timor (see Rosas 1992).

Historians divide the Estado Novo into three periods. The first, lasting up to the 1940s, was characterized by an economic state of emergency, managed by a *de facto* one-party state, legitimized by a sham democracy when the Estado Novo established the political and legal foundations that enforced its powers. The second, up to 1961, was characterized by repression, as resistance began to take shape (increasingly organized by the Portuguese Communist party whose first, illegal, congress had taken place in 1943). That repression is intimately associated with PIDE (Polícia Internacional e de Defesa do Estado [State Security Forces]), the notorious political police whose primary charge was the elimination of all opposition (see Pimentel 2011). It is also associated with the Direcção Geral dos Serviços de Censura (Department of Censorship), which was established in 1933. This censorship body operated at one national level, three regional levels, and in twenty-two branches in the Atlantic islands, the colonies, and across Portugal itself. Censorship became a powerful organ of repression and state terrorism, profoundly affecting several generations of Portuguese (see Pimentel 2007; Tengarrinha 2006). The years of 1958 to 1961 may be regarded as the beginning of the end of the Estado Novo. In 1958, General Humberto Delgado stood against the regime's presidential candidate, Américo Tomás, refusing to withdraw from the run. Tomás won the election but amidst claims of electoral fraud. In 1961 the war began in northern Angola and in December the army of the Indian Union overtook the Portuguese enclaves of Goa, Daman, and Diu, thus deleting the traces of the First Portuguese Empire.

The third period began with Primavera Marcelista (Marcello's Spring) in 1968. Salazar fell off a chair while relaxing on his terrace, and had a stroke. Marcello Caetano, another former Coimbra law professor, took power. Caetano had advocated a liberalization of the Estado Novo, which was why his first two years in power were understood as a "spring," by analogy with the Prague Spring. Writers, editors, and journalists opposing the regime felt able to express themselves in print. It also made room for the consolidation of an *ala liberal* (liberal wing) of dissidents who opposed the dictatorship. But this moment of freedom was short lived. By 1970 the repression had begun again. This time it was worse (Fernandes 2006, Pinto 2011).

The reason for this relates to the regime's colonial policy. The Colonial Act of 1930 established an aggressive capitalism in the colonies, a regressive labor code for workers, and an indigenous people's statute defining a variety of categories of colonial status. This system enabled systematic labor exploitation that triggered opposition to the regime in the Portuguese colonies of Mozambique, Angola, Guinea-Bissau, San Tome, and Principe. Lisbon, in the grip of a deep financial crisis, was reliant on the colonies for cash. Politically and ideologically the overseas empire was also a matter of national interest, as the regime regarded the maintenance of a colonial empire necessary to continued national power and influence. The metropolis's policies generated an intense sense of exploitation amongst Portuguese and African intellectuals and workers. Such feelings flowed into the emerging liberation movements, FRELIMO in Mozambique; MPLA, FNLA, and UNITA in Angola; and PAIGC in Guinea-Bissau.[3]

In 1961 a guerrilla war began in northern Angola, launching the Angolan liberation movement. This marked the beginning of what, in Portugal, continues to be known as the "Colonial War." As Portuguese colonial fortunes degenerated in 1964 (after the beginning of the war in Guinea and Mozambique), enforced drafts resulted in widespread, but silent, disaffection in Lisbon. Those who were able to do so left the country, to escape drafting, or imprisonment and torture by PIDE, especially if they had been identified as left-wing students and antiwar activists. The empire and the colonial wars became increasingly an issue, costing Portugal 48 percent of its annual budget and thousands of lives. Dissent grew within the armed forces too, becoming explicit in 1971. The "Captains of April," the leaders of the Carnation Revolution, emerged from this increasingly mutinous milieu. By 1973 it was clear that the wars were unwinnable, and in that summer the *Movimento dos Capitães* (Captains' Movement), a committed group within the military, became seriously devoted to the overthrow of the regime. Though a coup attempt failed on March 16, 1974, a month later this group of military and members of the media were able to stage a coup that met virtually no resistance.

António Costa Pinto, one of the leading historians of this period, emphasizes the significance of the Colonial War in defining resistance to the Caetano regime, stressing significant conflicts within the military itself.

> The decolonization process was the main reason for the conflict that broke out between some conservative generals and the Armed Forces Movement (MFA)—which had planned and executed the coup—in the immediate wake of the regime's collapse: a conflict that was also at the root of the military's active intervention in political life following the dictatorship's overthrow. (Pinto 2011: 259)

The ongoing colonial wars shaped the growing revolt within the military, which was unwilling to fight them. This mood of disaffection was voiced by one of the highest-ranking officers in the army, General António Spínola, in his book *Portugal and the Future*, published in February 1974, where he advocated Portuguese withdrawal from Africa.[4] The colonial wars also provoked a profound economic and social crisis, becoming a major cause of dissent and a focus for antigovernment forces in Portuguese society, paving the way for a split not only in the ranks of the ruling class but also within the Portuguese Catholic church.

In cultural terms, the Carnation Revolution involved a profound transformation of society.[5] Salazar and Caetano had presided over a desperately poor country in which the reproduction of a conservative social order could be left to what Portuguese people today refer to as "The Three

'F's," *Fátima, Futebol,* and *Fado*—that is to say, popular religion, sport, and music. Caetano was sufficiently media-savvy to understand that the new mass media, television in particular, could support the regime's grip on the metropolis.[6] Television broadcasting, at that point, only occupied a few carefully controlled hours each evening. His Sunday "Family Conversations," broadcast on RTP 1, were legendary. An older generation today still remembers his wooden and paternalistic style in these broadcasts. Their primary concern was to communicate the healthy state of the nation and the colonies. However implausible and unsympathetic, his message was, to a degree, heard and internalized by large sections of both the urban and the rural population who would gather to watch television in village cafés.

Though strictly controlled, popular musical *cançonetistas* (singers of popular *canções,* the Portuguese-language version of internationally circulating French *chanson* and Italian *canzone*) were permitted airtime. In this sparse and drab media environment, the RTP Song Festival—the national competition to select a Eurovision song—and Eurovision itself, became *the* major national media event. Though it is hard to impute motives, it seems clear that the regime regarded the song competition as a harmless distraction internally and, at the same time, good propaganda externally. (The same seems to have been true in Franco's Spain.)

But song culture in Portugal was not so easily controlled. Fado had been permitted by the regime. In fact, a more populist version was promoted by the state to counterbalance the growing song movement led by singers such as Zeca Afonso, Adriano Correia de Oliveira, José Jorge Letria, and Manuel Freire, among others.[7] Its fatalism, melancholy, and nostalgia posed no conceivable threat. But a star culture had emerged in fado, with its own dynamics. Taking advantage of the brief window of opportunity represented by "Marcello's Spring," Amália Rodrigues linked up with Ary dos Santos, a poet already known for his ability to tread a cautious, but distinctly critical line in his poetry and song lyrics. Amália Rodrigues was famous far beyond the Lusophone world. She had toured regularly in Latin America and Europe, had made highly popular films, and had recorded with EMI. The "Amália sound" had become more or less synonymous with fado itself (Vernon 1998, 32–6). She was, by this point, untouchable. Her fado, and that of those who followed her, assumed subtly, but persistently critical dimensions.

Folk music during this period mainly flourished at saint's days' festivities in rural Portugal. Since all kinds of public performance were subject to the censorship laws of the country, folk music was easily harnessed to regime ends. In the south of the country, though, in the Alentejo region, Portugal's principal wheat, olive, and cork-growing area, conditions were somewhat different. Its social and economic conditions were dominated by latifundism, that is to say, agricultural production in large estates farmed by landless laborers, rather than property-owning peasants. The Communist movement channeled agrarian unrest, and quickly established deep roots in the region. The folk music of the Alentejo soon came to function, for radicals in Lisbon and elsewhere in Portugal, as a sign of leftist resistance.

Eurovision was, of course, subject to regime surveillance, as was everything else. Explicit critique of the regime was entirely impossible. Songs had to be in Portuguese (a fact that, on its own, meant that most early Portuguese entries received very few votes). Women had to dress modestly on stage. Performances had to conform to the regime's notion of national propriety and decorum, even as they acknowledged the cosmopolitan musical values of *chanson* and *canzona*. But quietly radical elements had infiltrated the system. Ary dos Santos, already mentioned in relation to Amália Rodrigues and by now a major national figure, wrote many of the lyrics for the early Portuguese Eurovision entries. His "Desfolhada" of 1969, sung by Simone de Oliveira, is a typical example. The title means picked, or plucked, or stripped, with reference to foliage, or, more specifically, corn. But the sexual *double entendre* (*desfolhada* also meaning "deflowered") could not have been more obvious. The sly humor was only increased by Simone's conservative dress sense and poker-faced delivery. In no obvious sense was this song "political," but urbane viewers realized, through Simone's performance, that the regime's grip on the media was far from complete. The absurdity of a sexually repressive country making a display of the very apparatus of this repression on the largest international stage was to be relished.

"AFTER THE FAREWELL" AND "GRÂNDOLA, SWARTHY TOWN"

Paulo de Carvalho was born in Lisbon in 1947. He played football for the Benfica juniors, and founded a number of successful bands in the early 1960s (notably The Sheiks). He made his name in the Festival Rádio e Televisão de Portugal da Canção ("Festival RTP" for short) in the 1970s, qualifying him to represent Portugal in Eurovision in 1974. "E Depois do Adeus," the song chosen that year, was composed by José Calvário to lyrics by José Niza.

In most regards it is a typical mid-1970s *chanson*: a midtempo ballad, elaborately orchestrated, delivered by Paulo de Carvalho in a style recalling Johnny Halliday, Julio Iglesias, Engelbert Humperdinck, or Enrico Macias. Its hook is a rising major triad (1-3-6), the last note of which descends (6 to 5) to a dotted rhythm. Verse one is in a major tonality. The tune is repeated, in verse two, in the same key, but in its minor version. A change in orchestration also marks this shift; in the first verse the voice has a full strings counterpoint, in the second, a contrapuntal line in octaves on the piano. Verses three and four repeat the opening verse, though the last line of the last verse is extended by a mini-cadenza (*"Tua paz que perdi, minha dor que aprendi / De novo vieste em flor, te desfolhei"*; Your peace that I lost, my sorrow that I learned / Again you came as a flower, and I "picked" you). The opening words of verse four, the song title, are then repeated in a final cadential flourish. The major/minor alternation seems to underline one of the points of the song: that the lonely lover, getting over the affair, swings between optimism and melancholy. The cadenza draws attention to an odd line, with unmistakable sexual overtones: "Again you came as a flower that I picked"; the singer asserts his mastery of grief, melancholy, and the absent lover.

Listening to the song three decades later, political interpretations are inescapable. The beloved is vicious and manipulative, the lover weak and vulnerable. But the former has disappeared, unaccountably, and the lover must now find his feet. This daunting task is met with emotional ambivalence. How to manage without her? At the same time, this is a moment of rebirth. At the cadenza, the power relationship is emphatically reversed. He, the lover, asserts his power to turn the beloved from manipulator to manipulated object: she is "picked," like a flower. The expression "te desfolhei" directly recalls Ary dos Santos's lyrics for Simone's "Desfolhada" of 1969. A sentimental psychodrama representing the Carnation Revolution in symbolic terms, one might say: Caetano the "beloved," the revolutionary forces the lover.

Paulo de Carvalho's own recollections are colored, of course, by hindsight. And also, perhaps, by a certain anxiety about the way this cosmopolitan song repertory might still be entangled with the regime they were intended to be propaganda for. Some years later he turned to fado, a more "Portuguese" style, whose critical credentials had been firmly established by Amália Rodrigues in the late 1960s. But his recollections of this Eurovision moment also support the view that Portuguese participants were thoroughly aware of, and implicated, a complex game being played with the censors.[8]

> Quis saber quem sou, o que faço aqui
> quem me abandonou, de quem me esqueci
> Perguntei por mim, quis saber de nós
> Mas o mar não me traz tua voz
>
> Em silêncio, amor, em tristeza enfim
> Eu te sinto em flor, eu te sofro em mim
> Eu te lembro assim, partir é morrer
> Como amar é ganhar e perder

Tu vieste em flor, eu te desfolhei
Tu te deste em amor, eu nada te dei
Em teu corpo, amor, eu adormeci
Morri nele e ao morrer renasci

E depois do amor, e depois de nós
O dizer adeus, o ficarmos sós
Teu lugar a mais, tua ausência em mim
Tua paz que perdi, minha dor que aprendi
De novo vieste em flor, te desfolhei

E depois do amor, e depois do nós
O adeus, o ficarmos sós

(Translation of lyrics)
I wanted to know who I am, what I'm doing here
Who has abandoned me, whom I forgot
I asked about myself, I wanted to know about us
But the sea doesn't bring me your voice

In silence, my love, in sadness at last
I feel you like a flower, I feel you hurting in me
I remember you as such, leaving is dying
Like loving is winning and losing

You came as a flower, and I picked you
You gave yourself in love, I gave you nothing
In your body, my love, I fell asleep
I've died in it and in dying I was reborn

And after love, and after us
Saying goodbye, staying alone
Your empty place, your absence in me
Your peace that I lost, my sorrow that I learned
Again you came as a flower, and I picked you

And after love, and after us
Saying goodbye, staying alone

Zeca Afonso, born José Manuel Cerqueira Afonso dos Santos in 1929, was, at first glance, a very different figure. He spent his formative years in the colonies, firstly Angola, and later Mozambique. He returned in 1938 to the conservative environment of Belmonte, and then Coimbra. He emerged as an anti-regime activist in the 1960s, joining a variety of groups and making a name as a singer-songwriter with a particular following among youth and labor movements. By the 1970s, a time of increasing radicalism,

Zeca, under close surveillance by PIDE, traveled the country singing just about everywhere. By this time his albums were being recorded in studios in Paris and London. A trip to Grândola, in the Alentejo, in 1964, resulted in the composition of "Grândola, Vila Morena." The song quickly became an icon of the labor movement, and an unambiguous signal, when it was broadcast on Portuguese radio in 1974, that the Carnation Revolution had succeeded. Shortly before the coup, on March 29, Zeca Afonso, Adriano Correia de Oliveira, José Jorge Letria, Fernando Tordo, José Barata Moura, and others had given a concert at Coliseu in Lisbon. The concert ended with all singers singing "Grândola, Vila Morena." In the audience there were some military belonging to the MFA, who then chose "Grândola" as the signal for the revolution. Earlier that day the censors had provided the list of songs forbidden at the concert; surprisingly, the singing of "Grândola" had been permitted (see Almeida and Almeida 1998).

"Grândola, Vila Morena" is often sung unaccompanied, with simple counterpoint in thirds and descants. It comprises three verses, each of which is a double quatrain where the second constitutes a textual and musical variant of the first. The text celebrates democracy, equality, and socialism as the ancient heritage of this marginal, "swarthy" region. The ancient holm oak is where the singer swears his companionship and solidarity. The music indexes the folk song of the Alentejo in its dialect and lyrics, while at the same time evoking liberty, justice, and fraternity in its emphatic dotted rhythms.[9]

Its most striking feature, on the well-known recordings made by Zeca Afonso himself, is the sound of marching feet. The song belongs to what is unanimously considered Zeca's best album, *Cantigas de Maio*, recorded in 1971 in Paris at Michel Magne's Strawberry Studio. José Mario Branco, responsible for the musical arrangements, suggested the marching feet as accompaniment of "Grândola," in order to illustrate the song's Alentejano cadenza. The sound was recorded at night, by eight microphones strategically placed in an area with gravel close to the Chateau d'Herouville, where Strawberry Studio was located.

> *Grândola, vila morena*
> *Terra da fraternidade*
> *O povo é quem mais ordena*
> *Dentro de ti, ó cidade*
> *Dentro de ti, ó cidade*
> *O povo é quem mais ordena*
> *Terra da fraternidade*
> *Grândola, vila morena*
>
> *Em cada esquina um amigo*
> *Em cada rosto igualdade*

Grândola, vila morena
Terra da fraternidade
Terra da fraternidade
Grândola, vila morena
Em cada rosto igualdade
O povo é quem mais ordena

À sombra duma azinheira
Que já não sabia a idade
Jurei ter por companheira
Grândola a tua vontade
Grândola a tua vontade
Jurei ter por companheira
À sombra duma azinheira
Que já não sabia a idade

Grândola, swarthy town
Land of brotherhood
It is the people who command the most
Inside of you, oh city
Inside of you, oh city
It is the people who command the most
Land of brotherhood
Grândola, swarthy town

On every corner, a friend
In every face, equality
Grândola, swarthy town
Land of brotherhood
Land of brotherhood
Grândola, swarthy town
In every face, equality
It is the people who command the most

In the shadow of a holm oak
Whose age it no longer knew
I swore to have as my companion
Grândola, your will
Grândola, your will
I swore to have as my companion
In the shadow of a holm oak
Whose age it no longer knew

The two songs and the two singers were linked by the circumstances of the Carnation Revolution. They constitute a studied set of contrasts in musical style and revolutionary emotion: cosmopolitanism vs. folksiness, ambivalence vs. earnestness, sentimentalism vs. fraternity. And yet, as we have seen, both songs exploited mass-mediated spaces of dissent to a certain extent enabled by the Caetano regime, and the two singers moved in musical worlds that often overlapped. Both songs circulated in a political climate in which the tiniest musical signs could indicate resistance. Over time, memory of the songs became fused, and they became as much symbols of the Carnation Revolution as did pictures of Maia Loureiro entering Lisbon in his tank in his trademark Ray-Bans, and images of carnations in rifle muzzles on Lisbon's streets. Portugal's Eurovision entries, always defiantly in Portuguese, continue to reverberate to the events of 1974, and the fusion, in popular memory, of these two remarkable songs.

CONCLUSIONS

Portugal has been marginal to Eurovision, having no major successes. Popular written accounts of Eurovision have, perhaps as a consequence, generally treated Portugal as a humorous footnote. The accommodation of Portugal and Spain's entries during the dictatorships (including the vote-fixing in Spain's favor that supposedly denied Cliff Richard a Eurovision triumph in 1968) is a topic of embarrassment, only now being aired in the press. Some of this evasiveness and embarrassment is captured in the picture in the Danish press, showing the anti-Franco and Salazar protestor, with which we started.

This marginalization is, we suggest, a product of a more recent Eurovision narrative, a narrative largely authored by fans, journalists, and the institution itself. This narrative maintains a certain horizon of seriousness, of belief. This is counterintuitive, on the surface. Light-heartedness and playful cynicism might be described as Eurovision's official narrative, after all. Nobody—or, at least, not many—expect serious music at Eurovision, and the voting system is commonly understood as a vehicle for amusement and spectacle rather than sound judgment. Portugal's marginalization in this official narrative has two dimensions. On the one hand, Portugal has ignored—even, perhaps, defied—well-worn recipes for success: singing in English, elements of auto-exoticism, the self-conscious parading, according to well-worn formulae, of the nation's subcultural, cosmopolitan, or multicultural capital. There is a price to be paid for this. On the other, its Eurovision history has been—embarrassingly—entangled with serious political and historical events. Eurovision must, above all, banish historical and political earnestness. Those who fail to play this game, or those whose histories simply do not permit them to play it, have stepped beyond the bounds of a certain kind of civility.

In Portugal, meanwhile, the competition continues to be taken seriously. We hope that this chapter will have indicated some of the reasons why. Nostalgia for the Eurovision entries of the last years of the Caetano regime, of the Carnation Revolution, and of the democratic regime that followed entails an important, and deeply emotional, reckoning with the past. We have tried to show in this chapter how memories of "E Depois do Adeus" and "Grândola, Vila Morena" provide a resource for thinking about the dictatorship and the revolution, about relations between city and countryside, about relations between Portugal and its colonies. We have tried to show how two very different songs, in two very different styles, carrying very different political meanings, constituted mutually intertwined practices of resistance to the Portuguese regime, a resistance, as we have shown, that is underrecognized in studies of the Iberian dictatorships, and trivialized in Eurovision lore.

A great deal of historical work on the democratization of Portugal remains to be done, but the power of these popular musical memories keep the Portuguese intelligentsia engaged by that moment, and its contemporary reverberations.[10] For these ramifications have a European dimension. Portugal in the late 1960s and early 1970s may, from a North West European perspective, have been a remote and impoverished country. But events in both Spain and Portugal galvanized the European left, played an important role in the social foment of North Western Europe in the late 1960s, and continue to raise unsettling questions about Europe's democratic traditions and histories. And, of course, its futures.

NOTES

1. We are indebted to Annemette Kirkegaard for alerting us to the Danish press's coverage of Portugal's first Eurovision entry and for references to various *Belingske Tidende* articles during the course of the festival detailing this story.

2. Caetano surrendered, ceding power to General Spínola. Marcelo Caetano and the president, Américo Tomás, fled to Brazil. Caetano remained in Brazil, but Tomás returned to Portugal a few years later.

3. Respectively, the *Frente de Libertação de Moçambique*, the *Movimento Popular de Libertação de Angola*, the *Frente Nacional de Libertação de Angola*, the *União Nacional para a Independência Total de Angola*, and the *Partido Africano da Independência da Guiné e Cabo Verde*. Together FRELIMO, the PAIGC, and the MPLA constituted the *Conferência das Organizações Nacionalistas das Colónias Portuguesas* in 1961.

4. The book earned Spínola the reputation as a liberal, especially after he was dismissed from the army by Caetano. Spínola, who wrote his book as a result of his mission in Guinea, became one of the leaders of the MFA in 1973. The other was General Costa Gomes. On May 15, 1974, Spínola became the president, empowered by the Junta de Salvação National, which was established late in the night of April 25.

5. After the coup there followed a two-year transitional period known as the PREC, or the *Processo Revolucionário em Curso* (Ongoing Revolutionary Process),

characterized by social turmoil and power dispute between the left- and the right-wing political forces. During the PREC the country lived under a state of political, social, and financial turmoil. The most immediate issues were decolonization and the independence of the African colonies in 1975 with the immediate consequence of hundreds of thousands of Portuguese citizens, the so-called *retornados*, returning to Portugal, forcing the country to adjust to a new social and racial dimension. The agrarian revolution involved the expropriations of estates in Alentejo and the establishment of collective farms. Family structures collapsed as a direct consequence of the legalization of divorce. The chaos that ensued in the universities and schools were also to have long-lasting repercussions (see Gomes and Castanheira 2006).

6. Television could not be seen, of course, in the colonies, where the radio was also controlled. Nevertheless, control and censorship was not as effective in the colonies, where radio broadcasted from neighboring countries could be heard on short wave. In Mozambique, for example, radio played a significant role.

7. Vernon notes that censorship of Fado dates back to the 1920s (Vernon 1998, 20); family themes were encouraged, though little, interestingly, was done to prohibit sung representations of poverty or prostitution. A generation of stars following Ercília Costa (1902–1986) in the mid-1930s, and associated with the Retiro da Severa (a review that had contracts with noted fadistas such as Berta Cardosa, Maria Emilia Ferreira, and Adelina Fenandes) carefully toed the government line, presenting a Fado, as Vernon notes, "authentically and typically Portuguese, inextricably tied to a vaguely rustic-folkloric background, and shorn of any vestige of a Rabelasian mentality" (Vernon 1998: 29). This constituted the Fado "mainstream" throughout both the Caetano and Salazar period.

8. Personal communication with Paulo de Carvalho (Luisa Pinto Teixeira, April 2009).

9. On dotted rhythms in the European classical tradition, and its associations with "the popular voice," the "Marseillaise," and so forth, see Middleton 2006.

10. "The Democratization of Portugal, 1961–1982" workshop, celebrating the thirty-fifth anniversary of April 25, 1974, took place at the University of Oxford, May 11, 2009, with the participation of some of the players of this period, and of international scholars. The academic reckoning of this period is well under way.

REFERENCES

Almeida, Luis Pinheiro, and João Pinheiro de Almeida, ed. 1998. *Enciclopédia da Música Ligeira Portuguesa*. Lisbon: Círculo de Leitores.
Beck, Ulrich, 2008. "Nation-State Politics Can Only Fail the Problems of the Modern World." *The Guardian*, January 15. Accessed June 5, 2009. http://www.guardian.co.uk/commentisfree/2008/jan/15/politics.eu.
Fernandes, Tiago. 2006. *Nem Ditadura, nem Revolução. A Ala Liberal e o Marcelismo (1968–1974)*. Lisbon: Assembleia da República/Publicações D. Quixote.
Ferreira, José Medeiros. 1994. "Portugal em transe (1974–1985)." In *História de Portugal*, vol. VIII, edited by José Mattoso, 17–33. Lisbon: Círculo de Leitores.

Gomes, Adelino, and José Pedro Castanheira. 2006. *Os dias loucos do PREC*. Lisbon: Expresso/Público.

Middleton, Richard. 2006. *Voicing the Popular: On the Subjects of Popular Music*. New York: Routledge.

Pimentel, Irene Flunser. 2011. *A História da Pide*. Lisbon: Temas e Debates.

———. 2007. "A censura." In *Vitimas de Salazar. Estado Novo e Violência Política*, edited by João Madeira, Irene Pimental, and Luisa Farinha, 33–72. Lisbon: A Esfera dos Livros.

Pinto, António Costa, ed. 2011. *Contemporary Portugal: Politics, Society and Culture*, 2nd Edition. Boulder: Social Science Monographs.

Pinto, António Costa, and Pedro Tavares de Almeida. 2009. "'The Primacy of 'Independents'? Party Politics and Political Elite in Portuguese Democracy." In *The Selection of Ministers in Europe: Hiring and Firing*, edited by Keith Dowding and Patrick Dumont, 147–58. London: Routledge.

Poulantzas, Nikos. 1976. *The Crisis of the Dictatorships: Portugal, Greece, Spain*. London: New Left Books.

Rosas, Fernando, ed. 1992. *Portugal e o Estado Novo (1930–1960)*. Lisbon: Editorial Presença.

Tengarrinha, José. 2006. *Imprensa e Opinião Pública em Portugal*. Coimbra: Minerva.

Vernon, Paul. 1998. *A History of the Portuguese Fado*. Aldershot: Ashgate.

Žižek, Slavoj. 1989. *The Sublime Object of Ideology*. London: Verso.

Chapter 10

The Monsters' Dream
Fantasies of the Empire Within
DAFNI TRAGAKI

And now what shall become of us without any barbarians?
Those people were some kind of solution

(*Waiting for the Barbarians*, Konstantinos Kavafis, 1908)

In 2006, Rovaniemi, a town perhaps best known as the birthplace of the benevolent and kindhearted Santa Claus, also became popular as the homeland of the self-described, "Unholy Overlord of All Tremors," Mr. Lordi, whose "Hard Rock Hallelujah" won the Eurovision Song Contest that year. The official Rovaniemi Santa Claus did not seem to be overly concerned about the apparent victory of evil. On the contrary, with the proper kindness of the white-bearded Christmas hero, he marveled at the band's "hard work and belief" in their own abilities, belief which can make "even the greatest dreams come true."[1] Lordi's dream indeed came true; Finland's too, especially after the embittering years of *null points*. The more complex question, however, concerned the extent to which they contributed to the realization of another dream. That is the Europeanization of Europe, one of the European Broadcasting Union's visions, which the phantasmagoria of the Eurovision Song Contest (the ESC) aspires to bring to life.

The crowning of the monsters as the Eurovision kings was largely discussed as a kind of diversion from the proper Eurovision aesthetic. Lordi were depicted by the media as subversives, as wild winners. Their success was commented on as a heavy-metal "miracle," or as a sign of change that brought a whiff of hell into the realm of so-called "bubble-gum pop." "Europe, be afraid, be very afraid" warned the journalist of the *Metal Hammer* magazine, while for the *Times* columnist, the so-called

241

"consternation" that their performance caused was to be attributed to "the surreal world of Eurovision, where an air of Benetton-bright positivity seems mandatory."[2] Indeed, the "extraordinary" success of the horror rock band gave the impetus for interpretations of what was thus far thought to be the "ordinary" character of the Eurovision song: "cheesy," "ultra-safe," "catchy" pop, "the world's biggest celebration of kitsch." Lordi themselves enthusiastically declared that it was "a victory for rock music, not only for Finland and not only for Lordi," as well as "a victory for open-mindedness."[3] This "open-mindedness" was connected to the growing diversity of genres, "beyond pop and ballad," as Mr. Lordi put it, increasingly recognized on the ESC stage. Thanks to the Finnish monsters, heavy metal had managed to make it. "Hard Rock Hallelujah" became one of the most memorable moments in ESC history, alongside Cliff Richard, ABBA, and Dana International.

The question of "openness" raises the question of belonging in the pantheon of Eurovision song. It also evoked the issue of pluralism, one of the enduring myths of European identity, on which subject Lordi were optimistic. They believed that theirs was a victory of a "minority" in the world of Eurovision, which will hopefully now attract fans of various genres. Soon after its victory, the Lordi "minority" attracted majorities.[4] Not surprisingly, the tour in Europe that took place a few months after the 2006 ESC was named "Bringing Back the Balls to Europe." And it is tempting to interpret Mr. Lordi's enthusiasm about the triumph of the "minority" in association, perhaps, with his Saami origins, and, furthermore, with the way their victory was received back home.[5]

For Finland had been waiting for this victory for years. Its Eurovision life was full of shame, despair, and disappointment (see Pajala 2007). It has finished last eight times. Participating in ESC has been a traumatic experience for the nation. Assuming that the country would be represented by a group of "Satanic" monsters, local religious leaders tried to persuade the president Tarja Halonen to withdraw the entry as dangerous to the morals of Finnish youth.[6] When Lordi lifted the ESC trophy, however, they became national celebrities, almost a Finnish trademark—next to reindeers, Sibelius, and Nokia—that fed the local sense of national pride. To celebrate their victory a free concert was organized in Helsinki. Ninety thousand people are reported to have attended the biggest public event in the city so far. Even more impressive is that the collective singing of "Hard Rock Hallelujah" was supposed to have broken the *Guinness Book of Records* world record for the largest karaoke event.[7] The Rovaniemi officials renamed a large central square after Lordi, while the Finnish postal services announced the launching of a Lordi postage stamp. Soon, the country was swept by a kind of Lordi-mania. Lordi could be bought as action figures, and local magazines printed monster masks for children. Pepsi-Cola transformed the title of their song to make its slogan "Hard

Drink Hallelujah," while the brand "Lordi Cola" was launched with labels designed by Mr. Lordi. Lordi became the heroes of a comic series and in 2008 the horror movie *Dark Floors — The Lordi Motion Picture*, funded by the Finnish government, was released featuring the band members playing—what else—the monsters. And for those really hungry for a monstrous delicacy, there was the *Rocktaurant*, a Lordi-themed restaurant.[8]

Monstrosity was thus displaced from its supposed musical marginality and eccentricity. It became pop, cool and hip, and rapidly conquered almost every domain of Finnish popular culture. It also became a vehicle for reasserting Finnishness in the European/global context. Being proud to be Finnish became a way to forget, at least for a while, the so-called national "inferiority complex," often attributed to the country's years of oppression and its historically liminal position in between Eastern and Western Europe (see Pajala 2007, 72–73). The hitherto questionable "Europeanness" of Finland could now become a matter of the past.[9] As the Finnish member of the European Parliament, Alex Stubb, commented, "We are now seen as the miracle of the north . . . one of the most competitive economies in the world and a country that is rocking and rolling."[10] Even the prime minister, Matti Vanhanen, paid his homage to the miraculous monsters and was photographed with the band forming a heavy-metal gesture with his fingers.

With their charming deviance the monsters entered what has been described as the "meta-language of allegories" featuring institutional Europe.[11] Lordi's show became part of the figurative language of European symbols—of the invented histories and rites (such as ESC) that serve to allegorically represent the complex we-ness of the European institution. As a musical allegory of Europe, "Hard Rock Hallelujah" was supposed to inspire a shared sense of belonging to a European project made in Finland, as well as a hard-rock trope for being Finnish/European. They continue to challenge, it would seem, various European truisms concerning "European history" and "identity" that feature the idea of "Europe" per se. Rather than being civilized, cultivated human beings practicing the noble art of music, they are inhabitants of the dark ages; they are savage, they perform barbaric sounds, they are monsters, they are supernatural and, most definitely, evil.[12] At the same time, though, these are the very qualities of their phantasmagoria and uncanniness, or, at least, the qualities that made for an amusing difference in the ESC mediascape in 2006.

NEOMEDIEVALISM AND MUSIC

Lordi, following the tradition of Scandinavian metal rock, wished to be experienced as supernatural creatures living in a mythical cosmos popularly associated with a mysterious and timeless European antiquity imagined as gothic fairy tale. Their icons are the heroes of medieval fantasy fiction such as, for instance, those of *The Lord of the Rings* by J. R. R. Tolkien, or those of "B-movie" horror films and online role-playing games, such as *World of Warcraft* or *Dungeons and Dragons*. Their music is the sound of a wrathful era of European history envisioned as the age of dark magnificence featuring bloodthirsty warriors, supernatural species, plunders, and endless battles between the forces of the good and the forces of the evil. Lordi, our self-styled freaks from the Arctic Circle, wished to playfully animate an era of European history commonly juxtaposed to the Age of Reason, the age that entertained the enlightened idea of "universal" Europe—a vision of Europe that is also sustained by the Eurovision Song Contest. Yet, following Michael Camille, nothing created during the Middle Ages could be as medieval as the "medieval" imagined by modernity and its afterlives experienced in the context of postindustrial capitalism (see Camille 2009, 357). With Lordi, stereotypical perceptions of the mysterious, thrilling, and otherworldly medieval times, already proliferating in other domains of popular culture (such as literature, comics, film, and computer games) entered the universe of the Eurovision song.[13] This spectacle of neomedieval horror-glam rock fed a fantasy of a Europe that could also be obscurely majestic, dramatic, and eternal.

It may thus be seen as a phenomenon of what Eco described, a while ago, as "fantastic neomedievalism" (Eco 1986, 63). For Eco, the Middle Ages were the era in which "all the problems of the Western world emerged" (*ibid.*, 64); he mentioned, among other things, debates surrounding the Common Market, the organizational ancestor of the contemporary European Union. Even if this perhaps sounds as an overstatement, Lordi's victory reminds us of how we like dreaming about the Middle Ages, as Eco stressed, whether in the science-fiction spectacle of *Xena: Warrior Princess* or of *Conan the Barbarian*, at least as a way to escape from everyday ennui.[14] This fantasy of the Middle Ages satisfies a continuous need for return to the origins of Europe, alongside a need for reaffirmation of the irrational and the intuitive (see Eco 1986, 65). It is a desire for the wonderous and wondrous that has been lost, a desire to imagine a "larger, brighter, bitterer, more dangerous world than ours."[15] The Middle Ages are, therefore, constantly reinvented as an alterity, an era located at a safe distance from what is perceived as our ordinary reality, "to make us less inclined to apply our ordinary standards of plausibility and probability to it" (Cawelti 1976, 19). Friedman and Spiegel described a "shift over the last twenty years from a Middle Ages represented as being in tune with modernity—indeed, the very seed-bed and parent civilization of the modern West—to a more vivid and disturbing image of medieval civilization as West's quintessential 'other'" (Freedman and Spiegel 1998,

677). Michael Camille, for instance, in his detailed discussion of the construction of the gargoyles of Notre-Dame during the nineteenth century explores the making of the "gothic" by modernity tracing the ways "they transformed, as all monsters must, to become the abject chimeras of modernity: the Jew, the revolutionary worker, the prostitute, the hysterical woman and the homosexual" (Camille 2009, xiv). The "gothic" in the modern imagination symbolized an imagined past that was recalled as a sign of despair with the present; it was a product of modernity. Gothic monsters, Camille argues, became compelling "as emblems of loss" (*ibid.*, xiii). Gargoyles' recent Disney-inspired, for the author, restoration makes Notre-Dame de Paris "*not* a medieval monument but one that thinks it is medieval through its fantasy of the gargoyle" (*ibid.*, 362). This "new Notre-Dame" that was restored, as Camille argued, in the shadow of the Walt Disney animation blockbuster film *The Hunchback of Notre Dame* (1996) "is haunted by gargoyles who have returned to reclaim one of their original functions—to scare people—embodying the monsters of global capitalism" (*ibid.*, 352). For Camille, these are the chimeras of contemporary American cultural imperialism; the contemporary gothic that is reappropriated and remade in the very birthplace of gothicness, Europe, in accordance with the dominant trend of the American/global gothic (*ibid.*, 350).

This ever-present medieval is, nonetheless, a familiar and entertaining alterity that pleasantly fulfills our expectations of the fantastic. Besides, this fantasy of the "barbaric" Dark Ages, enacted here by Lordi, became one of the lasting myths of modernity; a myth that defined modernity by being thought of as its exact opposite, or as what modernity had supposedly left behind. The reinvention of the Middle Ages as modernity's "other"—and Lordi were broadly perceived as ESC's "other"—suggests that neomedievalism provides a getaway from the everydayness of global capitalism, if not a trope of resistance exercising a powerful critique against it. Ironically, this deeply rooted fascination with the medieval has legitimized neomedievalism as a European master narrative. What interests me in this chapter is the fact that this new medievalism was initiated in such spectacular fashion on the ESC stage.

Eco's formulation of "a hypothesis of the Middle Ages" (Eco 1986, 74) is of interest in this context. He imaginatively traced several parallels between now and then that are intended to exemplify his argument that "our age is neomedieval" (*ibid.*, 73–85). What is required to make "a good Middle Ages" (*ibid.*, 74)? We need a great international power that collapses, and "barbarians" invading the borders, bringing with them new morals and modes of living, faiths, and ideas. The decadence of the empire initiates an era of economic crisis and power instability, a mess that is pregnant with change, cultural, political, social (*ibid.*, 74–85). "Our

own Middle Ages, it has been said, will be an age of 'permanent transition,'" Eco argued in a rather prophetic tone, "for which new methods of
adjustment will have to be employed. . . . There will be born—it is already
coming into existence—a culture of constant readjustment, fed on utopia
. . . The Middle Ages preserved in its way the heritage of the past but not
through hibernation, rather through a constant retranslation and reuse; it
was an immense work of bricolage, balanced among nostalgia, hope and
despair" (*ibid.*, 84).

Similar arguments describing "the New Middle Ages" have also been
expressed by scholars and commentators in the field of international politics who spoke of a world with numerous centers of power, a multipolar
global order.[16] Drezner, for instance, argued that the escalating interest in
the specter of the living dead from the 1990s onward in popular media
"provides a window into the subliminal or unstated fears of citizens"
(Drezner 2011, 4) that represents an important puzzle for scholars of
international relations.[17] At the same time, there has been an increasing
concern with the contemporary inventions of the medieval in medieval
studies, comparative literature, and cultural studies. Camille associated
the ongoing fascination with the medieval with the "inherent hybridity
and confusion" of the Middle Ages. "America is a very Medieval country,
far more Medieval than Western Europe. In the Middle Ages, it [Western
Europe] was a pioneer culture. There was a sense of newness moving
forward, evangelical, full of weird and wonderful mixtures, ultra-reli-
gious, and yet at the same time, ultra-decadent. . . . I think that's one of
the reasons why we're so fascinated in America with the Middle Ages.
Because we're living it."[18] It is challenging, therefore, to place Lordi's
neomedievalism alongside recent discussions of post-enlargement EU as
an empire whose increasing determination to exercise power and control
seems to threaten the authority of the nation-state, all the while becoming
more and more obviously uncertain and insecure about its own project.

Regardless of whether "the New Middle Ages" describes the emerging
European polity or not, the triumph of Lordi in the ESC brought to our
attention, among other things, the persistence of the medieval in contemporary popular music culture and invited us to think about the ways
history is experienced, fabricated, and reappropriated in the realm of
music.[19] Why do we enjoy the medieval, and, as Brown puts it, "what are
we doing when we go there?" (Brown 2000, 548). The medieval fantasy
performed by Lordi "call(s) us to . . . learn to live *in the middle*, between familiar categories of past and present, subject and object, 'self' and 'other'"
(*ibid.*). It generated new senses of history, ways of connecting ourselves
with the past that dissolves into the present, ways of forming our subjectivities and collectivities in the ESC mediascape, ways which have the
power to thrill us. We have constantly been revisiting the medieval partly

because, as Camille suggested, "although we like to imagine ourselves as obsolete, we also like to dream that our subjectivity exists in the light of something eternal, something that was before and will exist beyond us" (Camille 2009, 364).

Perhaps even more thrilling was Lordi's desire for recreational anachronism, for disturbing established arrangements of time, a desire that damaged the notion of linear progress and fed our imagination with new memories of bygone times. Mythology can do that. It can supply the lived universe of music with fantasies—invented, in this case, by Lordi themselves—about the origins and adventures of every musical creature of the band. Amen, for instance, the guitar player, was the Egyptian god of gods, Amen Ra. After death, Amen was mummified, and thousands of years later he was woken up to play in Lordi. He also had various other names, such as "The Ruler of the Annubis Dynasty," "The Unstoppable Avenger," or "The Ancient Assassin." Awa, the keyboard player, also known as "The Possessed Sorceress," "The She-Devil," "The Snake-Eyed Feminine Specter," "Miss Madness," "The Origin of Be AWAre," was a vampire countess and a ghost witch from Victorian times, says the Lordi mythology. Kita, the drummer, was a mix of samurai and demon stemming from an alien ancient race who was sent to earth for unknown purposes. Rumors say that Kita's race was linked with the Mi-go of the Cthulhu mythos recounted by the master of gothic fiction, H. P. Lovecraft. Mr. Lordi, says the myth, found Kita in the mountains of Himalaya. The Minotaur-like Egyptian-Finnish horn-head OX, the drummer, half-man, half-bull, used to be the loyal servant of a magus living on an island in the Aegean Sea and later the leader of the brotherhood that inhabited the fortress built in the dark realm between dimensions. He has also been addressed as the "Smashquatched," "The Giant Powerhouse on Hooves," "The Hell Bull." Yet "The Most Fearsome Khan of All" is Mr. Lordi, "The Biomechanical Man." Having received supernatural powers, the bastard son of a goblin and a demon, he was reanimated over the centuries in the figures of Genghis Khan and Vlad the Impaler, until he became the Lord of Lapland. He now controls the whole planet. Together with the other band members, they are all engaged in a transdimensional war against their enemies. In 2006 they defeated all their enemies in the Eurovision Song Contest, gaining the hitherto unprecedented score of 292 points.

Mr. Lordi, Kita, Awa, and OX are all time travelers, transported from one historical regime to another, and producing their musical subjectivities through an assemblage of historical referents. All together, these are the pasts—displaced and entextualized in the narrative of the Lordi mythology—that constitute their gothicness. Walser describes this interference of historical signifiers in heavy metal as "the loss of history," which apparently damages the "historical specificity" of "hegemonic history" (Walser 1993, 160). Or, perhaps, it suggests a counterhistory that is more attractive, as it is subversive, which reinvests the very historical referents employed with power and horror, conjoining them—in the case of Lordi—in the narrative of a new medieval fantasy[20]: a fantasy that manipulates time by taking place *simultaneously* in the various heroic and mythical sometimes and somewheres of bygone centuries.[21]

MONSTROUS DE-MONSTRATION

Lordi belongs to the species of Homo Monstrous. They are creatures deprived of the spirituality, the civility, the reason, the cultured nature, the nobility, the intelligence featuring the superior of all of the races, Homo Europaeus. Homo Europaeus makes civilized music, a higher art that overarches the mundane, has its own unquestionable canon of masterpieces, which require a disciplinary knowledge in order to be analyzed. The embodied, harsh, and wild music of the monsters thus apparently inverts the vision of Europe and its popular song encapsulated in the noble art of Homo Europaeus. Their gothic/horror/glam take on Eurovision questions the idea of a gifted and privileged humanity made in Europe, destined to conquer the world, offering civilization, prosperity, and welfare. Moreover, set against the monsters, we appear to have something common on a basic, biological level: we belong to the human species, we are European humans, we share a naturalized Europeanness. This is, of course, hardly new (see Shore 2000, 63). Europe has been defined, and continues to be defined, by excluding what is not European (and exclusion becomes a way of manipulating and reinventing), whether it is barbaric sounds, Islam, magic, or totalitarian regimes.

Lordi therefore seems to embody one of the many counternarratives to hegemonic conceptualizations of Europeanness that has been invented and recounted now and then in opposition to its religious, cultural, and political inner and external "others," whether it is superstitious primitives, noble savages, blood-thirsty cannibals, Untermenschen, Islamic fundamentalists, backward Eastern Europeans, dangerous migrants, or corrupt nation-states. Yet the poetics of all these "others"—as well as shifting ideations of "Europe"—either in the shadow of Europe's imperial expansion or in the present of its postcolonial enlargement, is itself a project of the European imagination that is not confined to Europeans.[22] Gothic monsters, too. Coming from the dark past of the Old Continent, they are a fiction made *in* Europe that is entertaining at least *for* Europe and for everyone in pursuit of a sense of a wild Europeanness.[23] Rather than identifying them as threatening aliens of the human species, we cherish the Eurovision monsters as the cuddly beasts of our own making.

Seen in those terms, Lordi's performance invites us to think of the monsters as a metaphor for Europe; the monstrous, enlarged Europe greedy for power, yet troubled, if not frightened, by its own monstrosity.[24] It is a metaphor that one may primarily sense in the grain of the monster's voice, the sense of "the body in the voice as it sings" (Barthes 1977, 182). The scream coming from the depth of the creature's innards, passing through its lungs, carrying its breath into a burst of wrathful "Hallelujah" blasting in the cavity of its voracious mouth, sonifies its monstrous ontology. The overwhelming materiality of this monstrous voice makes a new world by its very presence. The grain gathers its bearer's life and world within itself (see Frith 1981, 165).[25] From a psychoanalytic perspective, the voice becomes the interface between the body and the language, the monster and the spectator, the internal of the beast and the external of human realities. It is what Lacan described as the "object voice," the voice that functions as a surplus exceeding the meaning of the words and acquiring a force by itself. It is part "neither of the language nor of the body" (Dolar 2006, 73). The monstrous voice as a source of desire, a fetish object, is both "the flesh of the soul, its ineradicable materiality, by which the soul can never be rid of the body" and an object "by the virtue of which the body can also never quite simply be the body, it is a truncated body" (*ibid.*, 71). "One is too exposed to the voice and the voice exposes too much" (*ibid.*, 81). This savage *objet petit a* stemming from the beast's bowels violently grasps the body of the listener who takes pleasure in the sonic avalanche of its power.

It is an indulging power also felt in the aggressive waves of sounds made of heavy metal, the loudness and amplitude of Lordi's monstrous art of music. Described as an "onslaught of sound" (Weinstein 2000, 23), "an important contributor to the heaviness of heavy metal" (Walser 1993, 45), loudness in heavy metal sonifies a musical ontology that is charged with hallucinations of dominance, virile muscular strength, and madness that are supposed to cause fear (see Walser 1993). Walser also comments upon the technological sound effects used to amplify the sonically driven sense of space "making the music's power seem to extend infinitely" (Walser 1993, 45). High volume sounds the anger of the Arctic wilderness, effervescent in the distorted sounds of Lordi, the sculptural, overdriven qualities of the guitar arrangements, the stormy drone of the bass guitar, the ferocity of the drumbeats. Next to its sonification, this monstrous ontology is spectacularly visualized. Mr. Lordi performs himself as an angry prophet with red eyes, who preaches on his platform shoes holding out a martial double axe at the end of which he has attached the microphone— the worldly technological device necessary to mediate his monstrosity. His face is despicably disfigured, he has horns on his head, and his fangs are sharp; his beastly body is covered with a shiny metal warrior's panoply embedded with apotropaic figures, leaving out his long raptorial nail that points toward the spectatorship.[26] The only worldly part of his costume is the high hat featuring the Finnish flag: the sign of the national that perhaps demystifies the supernatural and/or of the national that is being elevated to the supernatural, the subliminal national.

The three-minute storm of Lordi's wild high-volume energy intruded into the ESC, occupying spectatorial space, and amplifying our sensorium by employing some of the most influential features of the "stadium anthem metal" musical discourse. The song is introduced with the thunderous drumbeats that rhythmically alternate with the howling of the three words announcing the song's title. The second "Hallelujah" moves to a higher register, with a toxic scream of insanity, supposedly to warn about the war of sounds yet to come. The monumental sonorities of the chorus and refrain sections are underpinned by the electric shocks of the bass/guitar chords played with gestures of rage that transform the string instruments to sonic weapons. Solid patterns of epic, in-synch-played passages link one verse to the next, leading to the explosion of a repetitive refrain that is destined to captivate the memory of its listeners. Adrenaline also builds at the traditionally more relaxed sonic dynamics of the bridge, the "site of difference" and thus, "the site of politics," as suggested by Bohlman (see Bohlman, this volume).

It is there where the beast decides to demonstrate the whole of its phantasmagoric monstrosity: he unfolds a pair of black, gigantic bat wings on his back that transform him to a flying demon bathed in bloody red lightning.

> Wings on my back
> I got horns on my head
> My fangs are sharp
> And my eyes are red
> Not quite an angel
> Or the one that fell
> Now choose to join us
> Or go straight to Hell

"Hell" becomes the site of a fervent escalation of intensity that leads to the triumph of the "rock 'n' roll angels" glorified in the dazzling lights of a cataclysm of pyrotechnics. The stage is flooded by jets of fire. It's the Arockalypse, after all; a moment of Eurovision spectacle which, faithful to its neomedieval aesthetics, could hardly be more plethoric[27]: a spectacle of *horror vacui* that is intended to suppress anything else heard and seen before or after them. All that is left for the spectators is to enjoy having been captivated by its power to overflow their bodies, to own them. This is Eurovision in the age of excess of affect, Eurovision as a musical world suspended by a surfeit of affects that saturate our mediatic everydayness (see Massumi 2002, 27). Lordi's hard-rock prayer emanating from the liquid crystals of our TV screens projects a passionate Europe constituting Europe as a postcolonial empire of late modernity.

Moreover, the bridge as a political site of extreme de-monstration challenges us to bear in mind that "monsters have the same root as to demonstrate; monsters signify" (Harraway 1992, 333). Because they are demonstrated, "they have no life outside of a constitutive cultural gaze" (Cohen 1999, xiv). When, for instance, a Finnish tabloid magazine published a ten-year-old photo of Tomi Putaansuu (Mr. Lordi), Finns reacted with fury.[28] More than an offense against a "sacred" symbol of Finnishness, the unmasking of their monster undermined the existence of the national self that was regenerated through the monstrous victory; and it undermined the monstrous as a regime of truth—a regime also safeguarded by the band members themselves, who were united in the promise of never taking their masks off.[29] It was an attempt that, however marketable and scandalous, brought forward the idea that there are no monsters: there are subjective ways of seeing someone as a monster, a curiosity, a natural anomaly, a marvel, a grotesque creature, an error of nature. Monsters, of course, do not preexist as bounded biological entities, they emerge from a discursive process. It takes a kind of engagement with them, and a kind of display, in order to bring them to life (see Harraway 1992, 298). They resemble what Benjamin described as "dialectical images" which "in the now of [their] recognizability" bear to "the highest degree the imprint of the perilous critical moment on which all reading is founded" (Benjamin 1999, 463).

The discursive and performative process through which Lordi comes to life here is intensified in the bridge. In the bridge they are fully constituted as musical alien objects that beyond calling for a reflection upon what we are and we are not, they also entertain us by violating the perceived natural order, by challenging established ways of making sense of the world. Because, as Žižek puts it, "the alien's form of life is (just, merely, simply) life, life as such: it is not so much a particular species as the essence of what it means to be a species." Žižek goes on to describe the alien as "a kind of limit image": "the image to cancel all images, the image that endeavors to stretch the imagination to the very border of the irrepresentable" that dissolves all identities.[30]

The bridge thus ultimately encapsulates our aesthetic fascination and curiosity for artifactual deformity, our scopophilia for the "inappropriate(d) others" (Harraway 1992, 299). Mr. Lordi feeds our appetite for the bizarre by exhibiting (and singing) a horrific "ontological fusion" that transgresses categorical distinctions such as human/animal voice, normal/uncanny, Eurovision/anti-Eurovision song, animal/bat/man, man/machine, gothic/ancient/futuristic, terrestrial/alien, Nordic/Egyptian/European (Noël Carol quoted in Gilmore 2003, 9; see also Braidotti 1994).[31] In psychoanalytic terms, the display of the endearing monsters becomes an "acoustic mirror" of our modern European subjectivity: the "auditory double" through which we can hear ourselves (see Silverman 1988, 80).[32] The encounter with the uncanny "double" undermines the wholeness of a modern subjectivity that is eternally split, incomplete.[33] With Lordi, we indulge in the play of recognizing ourselves in the otherness of the double (see Inoue 2003). As a source of both attraction and repulsion, monsters can stimulate desire.

AROCKALYPSE FOR THE "PEOPLE'S EUROPE"

Overall, Lordi's performance invites us to forge a transitory togetherness directed at least toward one particular end: on the level of the spectacle of our Europeanness. Because, in the end, regardless of how the millions of viewers experience the monster's show, our subjectivities are temporarily united via a common reference, the fact that we are there, in front of our TV screens, to watch it. After all, this is entertainment. Lordi knows that their monstrosity is, as the singer himself has stressed, "horror for fun," the same way it is for splatter movies or for horror comics. By enacting a gothic horror fiction that is attractive to the European imagination, the beasts are welcomed and adored as playful primates coming from the frozen borders of the continent. Their violently childish dream-world infantilizes the Eurovision mediascape, at the same time that it becomes a quality of their monstrosity, their infantile monstrosity. Besides, they are aware that they perform a difference that wishes to make the European musical media-topos more amusingly thrilling and that Eurovision dismantles their monstrosity from its supposed power to cause fear, if it ever was fearsome. For, as Braidotti argues, in a rather pessimistic tone, we live in the "age of the commodification of freaks."[34] "The whole rock 'n' roll scene," she writes, "is a huge theatre of the grotesque, combining freaks, androgynies, satanics, ugliness, and insanity, as well as violence." The popularity of the freaky in contemporary popular culture, according to Braidotti, displaces "the dimension of the 'fantastic,' causing a shift in the level of representation, in the cultural imagery." "The 'becoming freaks' of monsters both deflates the fantastic projections that have surrounded them and expands them to a wider cultural field. The whole of contemporary popular culture is about freaks, just as the last of the physical freaks have disappeared. The last metaphorical shift in the status of monsters—their becoming freaks—coincides with their elimination" (Braidotti 1994, 75). Derrida also discussed the process of normalization that begins once one perceives the "monster *as* monster" (see Derrida 1994, 387).

By performing on the Euro-stage, the monsters are fully domesticated; in terms of the European Union's political discourse, they are integrated. So is heavy metal, a musical style once criticized as responsible for youth alienation, reckless behavior, suicidal tendencies, or denounced as a propagator of Satanism, perverted sexuality, or dangerous eccentricity (see Walser 1993). Lordi gentrifies heavy metal. Its hellishness weakens as it is infused by the Eurovision aura. By competing with the standard soft, sensitive, sensual, sexy, and groovy sounds of a euphoric and sentimental europop, its difference is stripped of its power. It becomes a token of difference.

Thus integrated, our freaks howl in favor of Europe. Their song is a prophecy for Europe. They scream for Apocalypse, or, better, Arockalypse.[35] The "rock 'n' roll angels," according to Mr. Lordi, are going "to strike down the prophets of false." On "the day of 'Rockoning'" "the true believers shall be saved"; this will be the day when "demons and angels all in one will arrive" "in God's creation supernatural high." The day of Arockalypse—Mr. Lordi is warning us—wins the one "who dares," so "brothers and sisters keep stronging the faith," because "all we need is lightning, with power and light." Arockalypse, therefore, becomes the sound of the emerging, new Europe, envisioned here as a Land of Promise. Not everyone is welcome there. Mr. Lordi is threatening: the enemies of this paradise will be punished: "now choose to join us or go straight to hell!" Arockalypse becomes the hymn for a "fortress Europe," as advocated in current neoliberal discourse that celebrates democracy, integration, multiculturalism, "unity in diversity" *on its own terms*. It is a hard rock anthem for the Europe of the Day After, the dawn of a cosmos of "believers" and "sinners," "brothers" and "sisters," "demons" and "angels," who can become the nationless inhabitants of the kingdom that will rise in the name of God; a kingdom like the "people's Europe" envisaged by the European Union.[36]

This sounds a little like democracy after Ragnarok, the battle between order and chaos in the Nordic eschatological myth—or, it is the heroic/dystopic metamorphosis of a Christian-inspired utopia.[37] More than anything else, Lordi's Arockalypse is a song for the end of history; a song imbued with endism. Endism, for Bohlman, is "a product of an anxiety about encounter," "a fear for the unknown that lies ahead" that music has the power to mediate and deflect not least because music may arrest and represent time, that is, it can sustain history (Bohlman 2002, 6). The arockalyptic song negotiates the anxiety that New Europe experiences at a moment at which euphoria at its enlargement and discomfort at its fragility coincide. "Hard Rock Hallelujah" sings Europe in a state of aporia, if not crisis, as it faces its own return: Europe as a rehabilitated whole anxious to scream its wholeness. This to-be-Europeanized Europe loves singing the Arockalypse, withdrawing itself in a hard rock prayer that exorcises the Devil while he is knocking at the door.

After their victory in the ESC the Nordic supernatural creatures became supranational too. Even as they are attached to their Finnish locality, they are welcomed into the pantheon of European popular culture, and the colorful assembly of musical icons that constitutes the ESC collective memory. How powerful is their song, though, to transform the several "imagined communities" singing for the nation-state into one "imagined community" singing for a united Europe? Perhaps it does both. Eurovision is a musical *contest* loaded with the sentiments of a grand-prix competition, an annual experiment for musical Europeanness that takes place in the interface of moments of national conflicts, embarrassment and rejection, of stress and curiosity, with moments of bitterness and escalating hope, moments of success and supranational joyful togetherness. As such, it embodies the tensions between a fragmented Europe and a European wholeness (see Bohlman 2004, 7–9). In the end, Lordi's utopian religious prophecies seem to converge with the current discourses of a secular EU-topianism and an ongoing quest for "rapprochement" among the "peoples of Europe." What is mutually desired, albeit in a different modality, is a common European destiny according to the European "standards of civilization."[38] This is the fascinating, transient encounter of the passionate Eurovision song's arockalyptic discourse with the normative, bureaucratic discourse of Brussels officials. They both love to dream of the colonization of Europe by itself, of the empire within. Instead of representing an antithesis—"monsters/civilization" or "barbarians/Europe"—the monster and the empire coexist as interrelated intensities that interlock in the hegemonic formation of "the new global form of sovereignty" (Hardt and Negri 2000, xi). To return to Kavafy's famous poem, *Waiting for the Barbarians* (quoted at the beginning), the barbarians will never come to the city, the emperor and his people are waiting for them in vain, because "there are no barbarians any longer."[39]

NOTES

1. See http://news.bbc.co.uk/2/hi/europe/5006286.stm.

2. Pete Paphides, writing a day before the final (May 19, 2006). See *The Times Online* http://entertainment.timesonline.co.uk/tol/arts_and_entertainment/music/article720914.ece. Accessed June 10, 2011.

3. The winner's press conference at http://www.youtube.com/watch?v=ezdIDHz0Hzg. Accessed May 12, 2012.

4. "Hard Rock Hallelujah" remained for eleven weeks at the Finnish top charts. Their album *Arockalypse* reached the top ten in Germany, Austria, and Sweden. In 2006, Mr. Lordi was invited to present the award for "the best rock song" at MTV Europe Music Awards. They also performed at the TV show *Eurovision: Making Your Mind Up* in the United Kingdom. In 2006, Bill Aucoin, the original manager of their beloved group Kiss, became their manager. In 2007 they toured in Japan, the Baltic countries, and North America, where they performed at the heavy-metal festival *Ozzfest*. No wonder, their album *Deadache*, released in 2008, was marketed internationally. They are currently signed with Sony Music Entertainment. For further information on the band's discography, concerts, and ongoing activities visit Lordi's official website at http://www.lordi.fi/.

5. For an exhaustive study of Finnish folk music, identity, and nationalism in the shifting realities between national imagination and the global market networks see Ramnarine 2003.

6. The then head of the Greek Orthodox Church, Archbishop Christodoulos, was also said to have accused Lordi of Satanism (see http://www.topix.com/forum/religion/orthodox/TP3O6G2EE6S6DJQ3N, accessed June 10, 2011). There was also a public plea by the head of the Greek bar and restaurant owners union against Lordi's performance in the Athens ESC, also on the basis that they are Satanists. Mr. Lordi rejected the accusations: "We have absolutely nothing to do with devil worship," he replied. "I mean, 'Hard Rock Hallelujah'! Would a satanic band write a song title like that? No. Our second single was called 'The Devil Is a Loser.' Although we are not a gospel band, either." (*The Guardian*, April 25, 2006. Accessed June 11, 2012. http://www.guardian.co.uk/music/2006/apr/25/1). In the same article it is mentioned that a group named Hellenes publicly expressed their objection to the participation of the "evil" and "satanic" band at the Athens contest. Nonetheless, Greece awarded twelve points to Lordi. Walser also discusses the conservative discourse around heavy metal in the North American context (see Walser 1993, 141–44).

7. The video is available at http://video.google.com/videoplay?docid=343737760800366549#.

8. See http://www.rocktaurant.com/.

9. Finland was ruled by Sweden until 1809 and then from Russia until 1917, when it became an independent state. During the Cold War era it was under the political control of the Soviet Union. Finland participated both in the Eurovision and the Intervision Song Contests (see Pajala 2007, 73).

10. Bilefsky, Dan. 2006. "No Longer Embarrassed, Finland Embraces Its Monster Band." August 12, 2006. Accessed June 12, 2012. http://query.nytimes.com/gst/fullpage.html?res=9500E1DA163EF931A2575BC0A9609C8B63.

11. For McElvoy, "institutional Europe has its own meta-language of allegories, euphemisms and omissions" (McElvoy quoted in Shore 2000, 62).

12. The idea of Europe and the invention of Europeanness have been discussed in numerous accounts in the field of humanities, the social sciences, political theory, and philosophy. For anthropological accounts of the European Union see, among others, the various publications by Marc Abélès, Irene Bellier, Douglas Holmes, Maryon MacDonald, John Borneman, Verena Stolcke, and Chris Shore (see also the various publications, the journal, and conferences organized by the

Society for the Anthropology of Europe). Michael Herzfeld in his seminal study *Anthropology through the Looking Glass: Critical Ethnography in the Margins of Europe* (Cambridge: Cambridge University Press, 1989) explores the ambiguities featuring the discursive constructs of the "European identity" "from the margins" based on his ethnographic research in Greece.

13. Fantasies of Europe's supposedly wild tribal past were also enacted in the performance of the Ukrainian entry "Wild Dances" performed by Ruslana Lyzhichko, winner of the ESC 2004 held in Turkey.

14. Donna Buchanan discusses the soundtrack of the *Xena: Warrior Princess* television show as one that associates Bulgarian music "with an amorphous, remote past and equally nebulous 'Eastern' place" (Buchanan 2007, 255).

15. C. S. Lewis, quoted in Cantor 1991: 213.

16. The term "new medievalism" was coined by the political scientist Hedley Bull in *The Anarchical Society. A Study of Order in World Politics* (Columbia University Press, 1977). Bull uses the term in order to describe the multiple and overlapping sources of power, as well as the increasing control of organizations such as the European Union that challenge the exclusive sovereignty of the state.

17. Thomas Jones recalls Drezner's thesis in his discussion of the zombie craze in the review of Colson Whitehead's book *Zone One*. See *London Review of Books*, 34(2), January 26, 2012, pp. 27–28. I would like to thank Martin Stokes for bringing this to my attention.

18. The interview was part of Public Radio International's broadcast "Simulated Worlds," where the host, Ira Glass, visited together with the author the theme park Medieval Times in Chicago. It was aired on November 10, 1996. See the transcript of the interview at http://www.thisamericanlife.org/radio archives/episode/38/transcript. I am indebted to Martin Stokes for bringing Camille's ideas to my attention.

19. Medievalism may be seen as a phenomenon of music revival and acquires various musical forms described either as "new age," "neotraditional," "gothic metal," and so on.

20. For music as a language of European counterhistory see Bohlman 2002.

21. To that extent, my interpretation here slightly deviates from that provided by Walser, who adopts a rather Marxist, à la Marshal Berman, approach, in his interpretation of this "loss of history" in heavy-metal music as a form of resistance against the "monovocal, hegemonic history" and suggests its examination in the context "of the bourgeois ideals that are supposedly being resisted" (Walser 1993, 160). While I concur with his argument that "heavy metal is intimately related to the fundamental contradictions of its historical moment," that is a way "to make sense of the . . . tensions that drive and limit their lives" (*ibid.*, 162; 171), I think that it is also necessary to consider it as more than a medium of critique against late capitalism, more than a musical trope of surviving the maelstrom of modernity. The case of Lordi may perhaps point toward this dimension of heavy-metal music, suggesting an understanding of the genre in association with cultural institutions, such as the ESC, its global popularity, and its ongoing commodification in the network of music industries and technologies.

22. See, for instance, Dipesh Chakrabarty's *Provincialising Europe: Postcolonial Thought and Historical Difference* (Princeton and Oxford: Princeton University

Press, 2000) for a critique of the mythical figure of Europe as a universal paradigm of modernity. In the area of music studies, Erlmann examines the mutual transatlantic invention of "Europe," "Africa," and the "West" by the musical worlds of both the colonizers and the colonized and the reciprocal formation of modernity's global imagination in the process of intercultural encounters (see Veit Erlmann, *Music and the Global Imagination: South Africa and the West*. Oxford: Oxford University Press, 1999). See also Georgina Born and David Hesmondhalgh, *Western Music and Its Others: Difference, Representation and Appropriation in Music* (Berkeley and Los Angeles: University of California Press, 2000); Timothy Taylor, *Beyond Exoticism: Western Music and the World* (Durham and London: Duke University Press, 2007).

23. Gothicness has thrived in the United States throughout the twentieth century up to today (see, for instance, Camille 2009, 323–39). The so-called "American Gothic" has been reimported in Europe and has highly influenced current forms and meanings of gothicness in the European popular context.

24. Žižek, recalling Gramsci, uses a similar analogy describing our age as "the age of monsters." See, for instance, Žižek 2010. Also, the video of the lecture he gave at the Polytechnic School in Athens, Greece, in 2010 is available at http://www.egs.edu/faculty/slavoj-zizek/videos/living-in-the-age-of-monsters/. Accessed July 3, 2011.

25. Frith here is inspired by Barthes.

26. Lordi's Eurovision costume was bought by a Finnish entrepreneur at an auction organized by the Finnish TV channel YLE.

27. *Arockalypse* is the title of the studio album featuring the hit "Hard Rock Hallelujah." In 2006 a special edition including a DVD was rereleased in Finland. *Arockalypse* was the first Lordi album to be released in the United States.

28. Read the report published at *Helsinki Sanomat* at http://www.hs.fi/english/article/Lordi+fans+furious+at+outing+by+gossip+magazine/1135220038344. Accessed July 3, 2012.

29. In October 2010 Kita, Lordi's drummer, was fired for taking his mask off. Lordi explained that Kita's actions were "in direct conflict with one of the cornerstones of Lordi's image." See http://www.metalhammer.co.uk/news/lordi-sack-their-drummer/. Accessed July 15, 2012.

30. Slavoj Žižek, "Troubles with the Real: Lacan as a Viewer of *Alien*," in *How to Read Lacan*, available at http://www.lacan.com/zizalien.htm.

31. Braidotti in her discussion of the monster's own ambivalence and in-betweenness mentions the ancient meaning of the Greek word for monster, "teras," "which means both horrible and wonderful, object of aberration and adoration" (Braidotti 1994, 62). Her ideas on the monstrous are situated within the feminist theory and her interest in the status of difference within European rational thought, especially in relation to contemporary biotechnology and the procreation process.

32. Her discussion of the term "acoustic mirror" is grounded in Guy Rosolato's *La Voix, Entre Corps et Language. Revue Française de Psychanalyse*, 38 (January 1974): 8.

33. For Camille, "this music is also about pouring industrial loud noise into the silent spaces, screaming with the gargoyle's mouth . . . Goth-punk music videos play on metaphors of the fragile human body, which becomes the abode of

gargoylike parasites, disgorging what is inside to the outside, ultimately being about the fragmentation of human identity" (Camille 2009, 336).

34. It is noteworthy that several of the scholars referred to in the present chapter who come from various disciplinary backgrounds (medieval studies, anthropology, philosophy, and psychoanalysis) are keen in describing our age as either "the age of monsters," or the "age of the commodification of monsters," or the "New Middle Ages."

35. Biblical references are common in heavy metal (see Walser 1993). Interestingly, visual representations of the Revelation are often full of mammals, birds, reptiles, or various imaginary beings.

36. See the lyrics at http://www.metrolyrics.com/hard-rock-hallelujah-lyrics-lordi.html. Accessed February 28, 2012.

37. J. R. R. Tolkien's gothic fiction *The Silmarillion* was heavily influenced by the Finnish *Kalevala* myth, as well as by ancient Greek mythology.

38. Jacques Delors in his first speech as a commission president to the European Parliament in 1985 stressed that "We have to build a powerful European culture industry that will enable us to be in control of both the medium and its content, maintaining our standards of civilization and encouraging the creative people amongst us" (quoted in Shore 2000, 46). Since the 1980s—especially after the Maastricht Treaty in 1992, which introduced the category of "European citizenship"—EU officials have placed a growing emphasis on the so-called "cultural sector," "in anticipation of the creation of a European cultural area" (Commission of the European Communities, 1988b, 37; quoted in Shore 2000, 53). By "culture" EU officials' discourses usually refer to art, heritage, information, sports, audiovisual policy, education, and information. No wonder, during the 1990s ESC both as a media event and a cultural institution enjoyed escalating interest by the mass media across Europe and beyond. It became a more and more high-tech, high-budget spectacle, a mega-event of sophisticated production.

39. For a political and philosophical reading of the poem in the context of European history see Tziovas 1986. Tziovas argues that "the new barbarism would be different from the original one since the people would enjoy freedom and power which their ancestors never enjoyed before" (Tziovas 1986, 173–74). See also Arampatzidou 2011.

REFERENCES

Arampatzidou, Lena. 2011. "Between the Barbarians and the Empire: Mapping Routes toward the Nomadic Text." Σύγκριση/*Comparaison* 22: 68–86.

Barthes, Ronald. 1977. *Image, Music, Text*. London: Fontana Press.

Benjamin, Walter. 1999. *The Arcades Project*. Edited and translated by Rolf Tiedemann. Cambridge, Mass., and London, England: Harvard University Press.

Bohlman, Philip V. 2002. "World Music at the End of History." *Ethnomusicology* 46(1): 1–32.

———. 2004. *The Music of European Nationalism: Cultural Identity and Modern History*. Santa Barbara, Calif.: ABC CLIO.

Braidotti, Rossi. 1994. *Nomadic Subjects: Embodiment and Sexual Difference in Contemporary Feminist Theory*. New York: Columbia University Press.

Brown, Catherine. 2000. "In the Middle." *Journal of Medieval and Early Modern Studies* 30(3): 547–74.

Buchanan, Donna. 2007. "Bulgarian Ethnopop along the Old Via Militaris: Ottomanism, Orientalism, or Balkan Cosmopolitanism?" In *Balkan Popular Culture and the Ottoman Ecumene: Music, Image and Regional Political Discourse* edited by Donna Buchanan, 225–67. Lanham, Md., Toronto, Plymouth: Scarecrow Press.

Camille, Michael. 2009. *The Gargoyles of Notre-Dame. Medievalism and the Monsters of Modernity*. Chicago and London: The University of Chicago Press.

Cantor, Norman F. 1991. *Inventing the Middle Ages: Lives, Works and Ideas of the Great Medievalists of the Twentieth Century*. New York: William Morrow.

Cawelti, John G. 1976. *Adventure, Mystery and Romance: Formula Stories as Art and Popular Culture*. Chicago: University of Chicago Press.

Cohen, Jeffrey, J. 1999. *Of Giants, Sex, Monsters and the Middle Ages*. Minnesota: Minnesota University Press.

Derrida, Jacques. 1994. *Specters of Marx. The State of the Debt, the Work of Mourning, and the New International*. Translated by Peggy Kamuf. London: Routledge.

Dolar, Mladen. 2006. *A Voice and Nothing More*. Cambridge, Mass.: MIT Press.

Drezner, Daniel. 2011. *Theories of International Politics and Zombies*. Princeton University Press.

Eco, Umberto. 1986. *Travels in Hyperreality*. Translated by William Weaver. San Diego, New York, London: Harcourt Brace.

Freedman, Paul, and Gabriele Spiegel. 1998. "Medievalisms Old and New. The Rediscovery of Alterity in North American Medieval Studies." *The American Historical Review* 103(3): 677–704.

Frith, Simon. 1981. *Sound Effects: Youth, Leisure, and the Politics of Rock 'n' Roll*. New York: Pantheon Books.

Gilmore, David D. 2003. *Monsters: Evil Beings, Mythical Beasts, and All Manner of Imaginary Terrors*. Philadelphia: University of Pennsylvania Press.

Hardt, Michael, and Antonio Negri. 2000. *Empire*. Cambridge, Mass., and London, England: Harvard University Press.

Harraway, Donna. 1992. "The Promises of Monsters. A Regenerative Politics for Inappropriate/d Others." In *Cultural Studies* edited by Lawrence Grossberg, Gary Nelson, and Paula A. Treichler, 295–337. New York: Routledge.

Inoue, Miyako. 2003. "The Listening Subject of Japanese Modernity and his Auditory Double: Citing, Sighting, and Siting the Modern Japanese Woman." *Cultural Anthropology* 18(2): 156–93.

Massumi, Brian. 2002. *Parables for the Virtual. Movement, Affect, Sensation*. Durham: Duke University Press.

Pajala, Mari. 2007. "Finland Zero Points. Nationality, Failure and the Shame in the Finnish Media." In *A Song for Europe: Popular Music and Politics in the Eurovision Song Contest*, edited by Ivan Raykoff and Robert Dean Tobin, 71–82. Aldershot: Ashgate.

Ramnarine, Tina K. 2003. *Ilmatar's Inspirations: Nationalism, Globalization and the Changing Soundscapes of Finnish Folk Music*. Chicago: Chicago University Press.

Shore, Chris. 2000. *Building Europe: The Cultural Politics of European Integration.* London, New York: Routledge.

Silverman, Kaja. 1988. *The Acoustic Mirror: The Female Voice in Psychoanalysis and Cinema.* Indiana: Indiana University Press.

Tziovas, Dimitris. 1986. "Cavafy's Barbarians and their Western Genealogy." *Byzantine and Modern Greek Studies* 10: 161–78.

Walser, Robert. 1993. *Running with the Devil: Power, Gender and Madness in Heavy Metal Music.* Middletown, Conn.: Wesleyan University Press.

Weinstein, Deena. 2000. *Heavy Metal: The Music and its Culture.* London: Da Capo.

Žižek, Slavoj. 2010. "A Permanent Economic Emergency." *New Left Review* (July–August) 64: 85–95. Accessed March 9, 2012. http://www.newleftreview.org/?view=2853.

———. "Troubles with the Real: Lacan as a Viewer of *Alien*." In *How to Read Lacan*. Accessed March 10, 2012. http://www.lacan.com/zizalien.htm.

Chapter 11

The Rise and Fall of the Singing Tiger

Ireland and Eurovision

Tony Langlois

"The best chance Ireland has of winning it again is to take it seriously. We have to prove ourselves again, and we can't presume that just because we're Irish that everybody loves us. Those days are gone."

—Johnny Logan, *The Irish Times Weekend Review.* August 8, 2009: 9

INTRODUCTION

The dramatic transformation of the Irish economy which took place between 1993 and 2008—the so-called "Celtic Tiger" era—brought about a number of unprecedented sociocultural changes, and this chapter explores possible correlations between these developments and Ireland's success, or otherwise, at the Eurovision Song Contest. The impact of the economic boom was profound at every level. In demographic terms alone, it reversed the centuries-long trend of out-migration of young adults toward diasporic nodes in the anglophone world. For the first time since seventeenth-century British plantations, Ireland attracted numbers of international economic migrants, largely from the new Eastern member states of the European Union.

Economic success, important breakthroughs toward resolving the political deadlock in North Ireland, and the assumption of a prominent role in the EU power structure not only brought substantial material benefits, but altered the ways in which Ireland was perceived internationally. Likewise, within Ireland, well-established conceptions of national identity itself were called into question and gradually (if sometimes reluctantly) reconfigured. In order to accommodate new demographic realities, wider

261

regional perspectives, and greater economic aspirations, "Irishness" itself was beginning to be conceived as having a political rather than an ethnic basis. In the last twenty years of the millennium representations of Ireland had evolved from an impoverished, monocultural, and quintessentially Catholic European fringe into a modern, rapidly secularizing state with a technologically advanced industrial base.

While these radical transformations were taking place, Ireland's fortunes in the Eurovision Song Contest were changing just as dramatically. Between 1980 and 1998, Ireland had become the most successful competitor in the history of the competition, winning first place six times and second place twice. In the subsequent decade, however, just as the economic boom peaked, its competitive fortunes slumped, and recently it has failed to even qualify beyond the semifinal stage.

In this chapter I will investigate the contextual circumstances which frame these seemingly unconnected developments. I will posit an explanation which suggests they are linked by factors which include demographic changes, but also by European responses to Ireland's initial rejections of the Nice and Lisbon European treaties. While accepting that the quantitative expansion of the ESC and resulting bloc voting changes (see Yair 1995; Raykoff 2007) have contributed to Ireland's isolation from powerful regional groupings, it is also possible to make a positive correlation between success in the competition with fundamental changes in discursive relations between Ireland and Europe. I will argue that since the 1970s, Irish entries to the Eurovision Song Contest have themselves played a part in broader negotiations of discourses of cultural identity, constructed as these are within a shifting European context. Irish songs have resonated less convincingly with an ever-broadening Eurovision electorate, to whom established Western European narratives of Irishness (or in a broader sense, "Celtitude") have little capital.[1] These songs, selected as they were by the Irish public during a period when an end to the economic boom was unthinkable, reflect a period of disenchantment with its relations to Europe.

STRATEGIC DILEMMAS WITHIN
THE EUROVISION SONG CONTEST

As my previous remarks make clear, I do not consider that success in the ESC is solely, or even mostly, due to a song's musical excellence. The competition is a technologically interactive event which in principle invites participation from as many as forty-three participating countries, many of which are likely to have historical enmities or alliances with their neighbors. It is quite reasonable then to expect that voting choices are just as likely to be influenced by national or ethnic biases as they are by individual or regional musical preferences. Technically this system serves to benefit countries which have a large expatriate population who are in a position (i.e., working elsewhere in Europe) to televote from abroad for their home nation. Germany's consistently strong support for Turkish songs is arguably evidence for just this kind of relationship. This "émigré vote" will therefore enhance the prospects of songs from relatively poor but demographicaly mobile countries such as those who have most recently joined the European Union. Since the late 1990s, Ireland had been a recipient of a substantial number of Eastern European migrants, creating potential for émigré voting for specific countries.[2] Generations of Irish migrants, on the other hand, have tended to move to English-speaking countries, and although the United Kingdom has been reliably supportive of Irish entries for many years, there is little potential to benefit from this kind of relationship elsewhere in Europe.

The aesthetic parameters of a pan-cultural competition of this scale will inevitably reduce the creative options of composers regardless of the sway of voting patterns. The challenge facing any competitor is to appeal to the diverse tastes of 400 million possible voters in just three minutes, a demand which is bound to encourage the adoption of common formulaic structures at the cost of musical innovation. In a context which effectively rewards musical conservatism, success in one year with a certain stylistic approach tends to stimulate emulation in subsequent competitions.[3]

The strategic dilemma facing composers is that while closely adhering to the most universally accessible musical language, they must still find a way of rendering their entry distinctive among dozens of other contenders. The pressure to conform is therefore in conflict with the need to be memorable for at least the length of the competition. This contradiction is often resolved by concentrating innovation into the visual aspects of performance rather than the music. This is, after all, a multimedia event, not a radio broadcast, and its live performative context adds both an opportunity to dazzle and a genuine degree of risk. The combination of these opposing imperatives creates a competition in which spectacular performances tend to accompany highly standardized music. Extravagant dance routines, glamorous costumes, exaggerated sexuality and emotionality, and just plain gimmicks are the hallmark of Eurovision, whether the spectacle is considered attractive or repugnant.[4]

In the decades since the first festival in 1956 the performative and musical criteria have diverged stylistically from mainstream popular music in many participating countries, to the point where its aesthetic parameters are almost unique to itself. Even without the broader political and cultural factors which, I would argue, eventually determine success in the competition, the context is such that it is irrelevant to evaluate the music of the ESC according to criteria outside the competition. Somewhat like the Esperanto language, Eurovision music is an outworking of grand, even noble cultural aspirations, but its level of signification should not be compared to the dense polysemy of musical traditions enjoyed in any other context.[5]

A second inherent contradiction within the ESC, which Philip Bohlman has highlighted (see Bohlman 2004), is the conflict between the essence of the festival as a celebration of "collective" identity while remaining a competition between nation-states (and, perhaps, European regions). Merely participating on this most visible of stages can be a matter of considerable national pride, not because of the possibility of winning, but because it presents that country as an equal member of an international cultural community. The smallest nation, or perhaps, like Croatia, a young one, has just the same three minutes of limelight as the rich and powerful countries of "Old Europe"; the same opportunity to assert a cultural presence. The fact that the music they play might sound more "pan-European" than "local" may only strengthen the implication that they share common ground with this international milieu.

For nations which have recently joined the European Union, or which aspire to do so, the ESC provides a tangible sign of international recognition. As a highly structured annual event with established rules, procedures, and technologies, it could be argued that the competition embodies, however briefly, a representation of shared utopian values. Such values are rarely spelled out explicitly, although discourses concerning youth and beauty, reciprocal respect, democracy, modernity, and tradition are gesturally evoked throughout the event's spectacle and pageantry. Occasionally these ideals actually break through to the surface, as when Toto Cutungo's song "Insieme" (Together) won the competition for Italy in 1992.[6] In much the same way that international sporting competitions such as the Olympic Games invoke an ethos of communitarianism, equality, and fair play, so the ESC serves as a potent representation of shared values, even if, in practice, the reality does not match up to them. If, as Adams (1992) suggests, we have good reasons to consider television as a "geographical space," which allows the experience of belonging to a bounded community, then visible participation in the contest is much more significant than mere symbolism. It is the ritualized sphere within which mass viewing itself validates the legitimacy and equality of participating nations, their right to be accepted in a common, virtual community. For nations considered politically peripheral in European terms, participation in the ESC is of considerable symbolic value. To actually *win* the competition through the free votes of the greater European viewing public would amount to a highly potent acknowledgment of a country's existence as a distinct political entity. For nations which have recently gained independence, wealth, or democracy, or which aspire to EU membership, such affirmation may be of great significance, and consequently the ESC is taken very seriously.

If the kudos to be gained from participation is most symbolic to those on the European periphery, then it stands to reason that attitudes toward the festival may change as a nation becomes more established and confident of its place within the international community. In Ireland's case, attitudes toward the festival have shifted, from a early innocent enthusiasm toward an increasingly cynical viewpoint, and this shift is reflected in the songs which were chosen over the period in question.

As a nation's opinions of the ESC may change over time, so established tropes relating to competing countries may also fluctuate in the light of contemporary events (see also Gatherer 2006; Raykoff 2007). While competing nations strive to keep aggressive political messages out of their songs, ordinary citizens may nevertheless register affirmation or criticism of other competing nations through their voting behavior. Once again this aspect of voting has almost nothing to do with the music itself, but rather reflects value judgments relating to the actions of a member state. For example, while Britain's 2003 entry "Cry Baby" (performed by Jemini) may not have been the most memorable of songs, historical voting patterns would have predicted that it at least received a number of "courtesy" votes from neighboring countries. The United Kingdom can usually rely on high points from Ireland, Austria, and Belgium, and singing in English is itself considered to be advantageous. On this occasion, however, the entry received a humiliating "zero" score—the worst ever for the United Kingdom. A possible explanation for such markedly dire results is that the competition took place very shortly after the invasion of Iraq, a war which the United Kingdom supported against the views of the overwhelming majority of European Union members. I am not suggesting that participants in the ESC actively coordinated a protest vote against the Gulf War in this way, but it is plausible that previously sympathetic or neutral attitudes toward the United Kingdom had shifted because of this unpopular act of foreign policy. As the ESC adopts both the appearance and structures of an organized, democratic forum (with judges, regulations, equality of suffrage, and ritualized procedures), so widely held negative attitudes toward one of its members are quite likely to be manifested as votes of disapproval.

It is my opinion that over the period of the "Celtic Tiger" boom, popular European discourses *about* Ireland were similarly altered. Likewise, Ireland's attitudes also changed toward both the European Union and the song contest itself as prosperity forced a rethinking of its national culture and international relations. In order to support this hypothesis it will be

Table 11.1. Final Placings of Irish ESC Entries

Year	Artist	Song	Place	Contestants
1965	Butch Moore	"Walking the Streets in the Rain"	6	18
†1966	Dickie Rock	"Come Back to Stay"	4	18
†1967	Sean Dunphy	"If I Could Choose"	2	17
†1968	Pat McGeegan	"Chance of a Lifetime"	4	17
1969	Muriel Day	"The Wages of Love"	7	16
*1970	Dana	"All Kinds of Everything"	1	12
‡1971	Angela Farrell	"One Day Love"	11	18
‡1972	Sandie Jones	"Ceol an Ghrá"	15	18
‡1973	Maxi	"Do I Dream"	10	17
1974	Tina Reynolds	"Cross Your Heart"	7	17
1975	The Swarbriggs	"That's What Friends Are For"	9	19
1976	Red Vincent Hurley	"When"	10	18
†1977	The Swarbriggs + 2	"It's Nice to Be in Love Again"	3	18
1978	Colm T. Wilkinson	"Born to Sing"	5	20
1979	Cathal Dunne	"Happy Man"	5	19
*1980	Johnny Logan	"What's Another Year?"	1	19
1981	Sheeba	"Horoscopes"	5	20
‡1982	The Duskeys	"Here Today Gone Tomorrow"	11	18
†1984	Linda Martin	"Terminal 3"	2	19
1985	Maria Christian	"Wait Until the Weekend Comes	6	19
†1986	Luv Bug	"You Can Count on Me"	4	20
*1987	Johnny Logan	"Hold Me Now"	1	22
1988	Jump the Gun	"Take Him Home"	8	21
‡1989	Kiev Connolly & The Missing Passengers	"The Real Me"	18	22
†1990	Liam Reilly	"Somewhere in Europe"	2	22
1991	Kim Jackson	"Could It Be That I'm in Love"	10	22
*1992	Linda Martin	"Why Me?"	1	23
*1993	Niamh Kavanagh	"In Your Eyes"	1	25
*1994	Paul Harrington & Charlie McGettigan	"Rock 'n' Roll Kids"	1	25
‡1995	Eddie Friel	"Dreamin'"	14	23
*1996	Eimear Quinn	"The Voice"	1	23
†1997	Marc Roberts	"Mysterious Woman"	2	25
1998	Dawn Martin	"Is Always Over Now?"	9	25
‡1999	The Mullans	"When You Need Me"	17	23
2000	Eamonn Toal	"Millennium of Love"	6	24
‡2001	Gary O'Shaughnessy	"Without Your Love"	21	23
2003	Mickey Harte	"We've Got the World"	11	26
‡2004	Chris Doran	"If My World Stopped Turning"	23	36
‡2005	Donna & Joe	"Love?"	X	39
2006	Brian Kennedy	"Every Song Is a Cry for Love"	10	37
‡2007	Dervish	"They Can't Stop the Spring"	24	42
‡2008	Dustin the Turkey	"Irelande Douze Pointe"	X	43
‡2009	Sinéad Mulvey & Black Daisy	"Et Cetera"		42

* 1st Place
† Top 4 places
‡ Bottom half of results table

useful to consider the changing fortunes of Irish ESC entries alongside some other relevant statistics.

IRISH CULTURE IN THE "TIGER" YEARS

Considering all forty-four Irish entries together, it is clear that the period of the greatest success came between 1980 and 1997, after which time results tailed off rapidly. Since 2004 the number of competing entries in the ESC has risen sharply, which, if all other factors had been equal, would inevitably reduce the statistical chances of any one country's victory. However, since 2000 there has also been a distinct Northern and Eastward shift among the winning songs, which suggests that Ireland's recent demise has been due to more than simply a numerical increase in the competition.[7] It is my view that the dramatic decline in Ireland's success is largely due to three linked factors: the demographic shifts of émigré voters (which has favored the Northern and Eastern countries), a change in cultural discourses *about* Ireland within Europe, and a corresponding shift of Irish attitudes toward greater Europe and the EU in particular. Hard proof for such broad *attitudinal* changes over such a wide field is admittedly hard to come by, especially with hindsight, but some exisiting statistics do provide compelling circumstantial evidence.[8]

It is apparent, for example, that during the period of the "Celtic Tiger" boom, a positive correlation exists between the growth of Irish gross domestic product and inward migration. See figures 11.1 and 11.2.

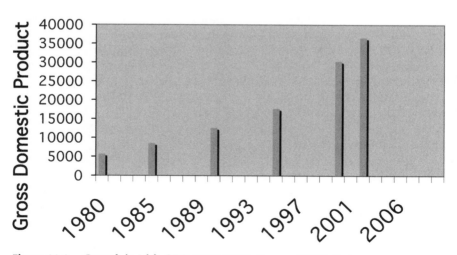

Figure 11.1.   Growth in Irish GDP, 1980–2006. *Source:* OECD.Stat

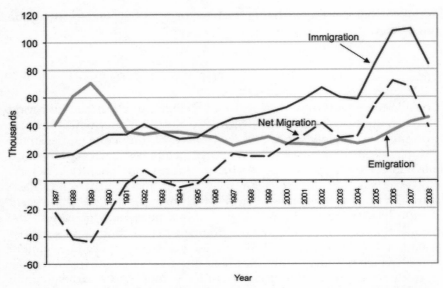

Figure 11.2.   Reverse Migration Trends. *Source:* **Central Statistics Office. Population and Migration Estimates.**

Although a significant proportion of net immigration during the Celtic Tiger years may be explained by Irish citizens returning home from their own economic diaspora, Ireland's newfound prosperity also attracted a large number of migrants from new members of the European Union, and for the first time since the Second World War, asylum seekers.[9] It had been centuries since such a significant influx of "foreigners" came to Ireland, and although their participation in the less-well-paid economic sectors helped sustain the Celtic Tiger boom, some sections of Irish society were wary of the cultural impact this trend might have in the long term. In particular, the education of Irish-born children with non-Irish parents drew attention to the need, for the first time, to seriously consider the implications of a culturally diverse population.[10]

Besides the subtle but significant influence of immigration upon Irish national culture, such an unprecedented economic boom in itself had effects upon cultural practices and beliefs. O'Toole (2009) considers that the apparently successful policy of light state regulation of the economy had fostered an unquestioning belief in market forces and private enterprise. O'Toole claims that this not only encouraged a somewhat less communitarian governmental approach (allowing the gap between rich and poor to widen considerably), but in a more generalized sense, material self-interest became a more pronounced feature of Irish cultural life than it had during previous lean decades. Membership in the European Union, with its agenda for expansion of territory and influence, itself precipitated considerable changes in national culture. Harmonizing Irish legislation with those common in the EU, homosexuality was legalized in 1993 (after cases were taken to the European Court), and divorce (after a referendum) in 1995. The economic boom also coincided with revelations of widespread child abuse within schools run by the Catholic religious orders. Roman Catholicism had been a central pillar of national identity since Irish independence and an active opponent against the above reforms.[11] As a consequence of these and many economic and technological developments, over one short decade Irish society had become considerably more ethnically cosmopolitan, more secularized and (arguably) materialistic than it ever had been before. The adoption of a common currency (2002), the receipt of billions of euros in structural funds,[12] and the Irish presidency of the council of the EU (in 1990, 1996, and 2004) made closer political and economic alliance with continental Europe an attractive proposition, at least until the referendum campaign for the Nice Treaty in 2001.

The combination of all of these changes have obliged Irish people to revisit established discourses of national identity and Ireland's place in the world. Prior to EEC membership in 1973 Ireland had been one of the poorest countries in Europe, embroiled in postcolonial political disputes and economically dependent upon its own migrants. Twentieth-century representations of Ireland centered on traditional rural culture; a fervent, patriotic religiosity; and in military terms at least, political neutrality.[13] Still living in the shadow of its ex-colonial power, pre-EU Ireland looked

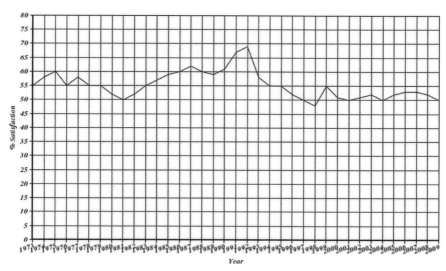

Figure 11.3.   Ireland's declining success at ESC.

to its wide diasporic community for political and financial support. By the early 2000s, as Ireland became Europe's fastest-growing economy, these discourses and attitudes could not be easily sustained, even for the sake of the tourism industry. No longer the poor man of Europe, nor the political underdog, and making its cultural influence felt internationally through successes in music, sport, and literature, these long-established tropes gradually came to incorporate a more complex and perhaps a less innocent conception of national identity.

FROM DANA TO DUSTIN

Alongside this dramatic sociocultural transformation, Ireland's best run of successes in the Eurovision Song Contest came during the early Celtic Tiger years and declined as steadily as gross domestic product continued to rise (see figure 11.4). While the increasing size and demographic of the competition led to regional voting patterns which militated against Irish success, I suggest that Ireland's changing international image was another significant factor in its demise. Before the boom years Europeans may have been inclined toward sympathy for Ireland "as a brand" for a number of reasons. Firstly, Ireland was, until the 1990s, considered a peripheral underdog in Europe, both economically and politically. Images of the conflict in Northern Ireland had, since the 1970s, presented Ireland as a war zone, and thus well deserving of such symbolic support as neighbors could offer. Tropes relating to a rich traditional culture set in preindustrial rurality were a mainstay of both film and touristic representations, and Ireland's claim to political neutrality was as appealing internationally as it remains important within the country itself.[14]

It was also probably an advantage that the Irish could sing in English, a language which already had a strong presence in the international popular music industry. Between 1977 and 1997 Eurovision entries were possibly handicapped by an obligation to use their national language, while Ireland was able to communicate directly in the most widely understood language in Europe. To European tourists, Ireland represented itself as un unspoiled rural idyll at the Atlantic edge of the continent, where a traditional life had been eked out for generations despite colonization and conflict. Ireland, then, was "sold" as charming in its rusticity, as unthreatening and friendly. Morover, as it was important to break its trade dependency upon Britain, the Irish government was keen to join the Common market, and became an enthusiastic member of the EEC project in 1973. It is understandable in light of these circumstances that Europeans may have adopted something of a paternalistic attitude toward Ireland in this period.

Ireland's first Eurovision major success managed to embody, both musically and performatively, this "Irish" simplicity and innocence. Dana sang "All Kinds of Everything" (1970) when she was eighteen years old but appeared even younger. The song itself, a gentle waltz, had the mood of a lullaby and words which evoked naïve uncritical acceptance.

> *Seagulls and aeroplanes, things of the sky*
> *Winds that go howling, breezes that sigh*
> *City sights, neon lights, grey skies or blue*
> *All kinds of everything reminds me of you*
>
> *Summer time, winter time, spring and autumn too*
> *Monday, Tuesday, every day I think of you.*

(Music and lyrics: Derry Lindsay & Jackie Smith)

Figure 11.4. Dana in 1970. Photograph: Daily Mail Newspapers

"All Kinds of Everything" bore an affective correspondence with discursive evocations of a childlike innocence and vulnerability. However, Ireland's most productive Eurovision phase came between 1980 and 1997, with a particularly strong run from 1990 onward. By then Ireland was experiencing a period of unprecedented growth in both prosperity and national confidence, which was boosted by its presidency of the EU Council and even success in the 1990 World Cup finals. Coincidentally the Irish group U2 had emerged as one of the most popular rock acts in the world, and chains of "Irish-themed pubs" were attracting business on a global scale.[15] Even before the Celtic Tiger boom had peaked, "Brand Ireland" had become international hot property. In 1994 the ESC was held in Dublin, and its intermission entertainment, a spectacular dance act called *Riverdance*, proved to be so popular that it became an international success in its own right. Irish culture (or a particular globalized version of it) had never been so popular nor so profitable as in this period. The country was presented as energetic, proud, and youthful, while drawing upon the resource of its traditional culture. Above all, this Ireland was a European success story—a nation which had been rescued from impoverished marginality to become a dynamic cultural force in the world. If Dana's Ireland was childlike and passive, the 1990s version was confident, enthusiastic, and expressive.

Between 1992 and 1997 Ireland won first position in the ESC for a record four times and came in second once. The songs of this period were both more musically sophisticated and emotionally "adult" than "All Kinds of Everything" had been. They might be broadly categorized as "torch songs": slow-paced, dramatic ballads which increased in emotive expression as the songs progressed. Most songs treated adult love with a tendency toward bittersweet romance.[16] Johnny Logan, the singer who won the competition twice with his own performances, also composed 1992's winning entry in a style which typified the introspective emotionalism of his writing.

> *Sometimes I lie awake and watch you sleeping*
> *And listen to the beating of your heart*
> *And sometimes, when you're lying there*
> *You take my breath away*
> *And I wanna say*
>
> *Why me?*
> *I look at you and I get to feeling*
> *Why me?*
> *I know it's true but I can't believe that it's me*
> *Who's gonna be holdin' you in my arms tonight*
> *And why it's me*

> Who's gonna be the one to make you feel all right
> Tonight
>
> ("Why Me?" Sung by Linda Martin, 1992
> Music and lyrics by Johnny Logan)

Although the most successful songs were technically effective, and had the "English language" advantage, none were particularly markable in comparison to other entries of the period. Ireland's "edge" is very likely to have been the country's prominence as an international "brand" throughout this period. Ireland was a model success story of the European project and (unlike its neighbors in the United Kingdom) an enthusiastic member of the EU.[17] European countries came to embrace Irish "Celtic" culture as a regional exotic, which unlike the Basques, Sami, or Bretons did not challenge their own national hegemonies. It was not long, however, before this tide turned, and once again the ESC served as something of a barometer of popularity among European nations.

The end of the 1990s saw a falling away of support for Irish entries to the ESC. A warning sign of decline came in 2001, when Gary O'Shaughnessy received a total of only six points for "Without Your Love," a song which adhered closely to the previously effective "Johnny Logan" formula. According to the prevailing regulations, Ireland was consequently excluded from the 2002 competition altogether. It is unlikely that musical tastes would have changed that radically across Europe between 1997 and 2001, and I consider it no coincidence that this was also the year that the Irish voted against the Nice Treaty in a national referendum. The treaty, which, among other provisions, enabled the accession of a further twelve EU member states, had been rejected in Ireland for a complex, sometimes contradictory mixture of reasons, which included concerns about the maintenance of Irish military neutrality within a closer administrative union. Within Europe, however, this decision was viewed very negatively—not only was Ireland the first country to go against the clear will of the European majority on this matter, but it was widely regarded as refusing to allow the benefits it had enjoyed for over twenty years to be offered to other deserving nations. The following year, Ireland did approve a lightly amended Nice Treaty, but its reputation as a nation of grateful Europhiles had been undermined. In Eurovision terms considerable cultural capital had been squandered. The once-appealing extramusical discourses about Ireland had withered, and it proved impossible to reverse this change.

The Nice Treaty was a watershed in Ireland's Eurovision fortunes for another reason. Once implemented, the Irish labor market was opened to migrant workers from the new EU members, principally from eastern European states. This influx of "New Irish"[18] was more likely to vote for their

home countries in the ESC than for the contestants Ireland had traditionally "exchanged" votes with, so deestablishing an established balance of
influence.[19] Secondly, and most importantly, the national cultures of new
EU states had never shared the same conceptions of "Irishness" as those
cherished so recently in "Old Europe." To eastern Europeans Ireland was
a very wealthy country worth emigrating to, and its political hardships
may have seemed rather insignificant when compared to their own recent histories. Ireland's romantic "rural" and "Celtic" associations were
perhaps less apparent from the perspective of a *gastarbeiter* on a building
site. The new Europeans were probably too busy negotiating their own
postcolonial identities to see Ireland as deserving of particular sympathy.
Perhaps they also recalled their initial rejection of the Nice Treaty.

Following a disheartening string of failures, Irish attitudes toward the
Eurovision Song Contest hardened. A survey carried out by the Lansd-
owne market research company in 2005 discovered that 46 percent considered the Eurovision Song Contest not worthwhile and 25 percent even
wanted it abolished.[20] Perhaps, poised at the very apex of an economic
boom, the Irish public felt less gratitude for the European project than
they once had. The European Commission's "Eurobarometer" surveys
of attitudes toward the EU show that while the Irish recognized that
they benefited enormously from membership, they have never been very
supportive of expansion or political integration. In summer 2008 Ireland
again went to referendum to ratify the Lisbon Treaty, which, if implemented, would have greatly streamlined central administration, at the

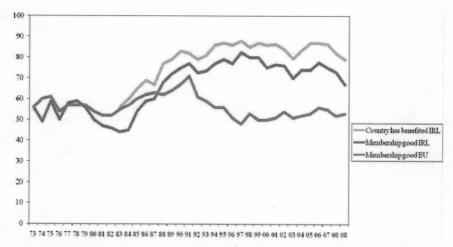

**Figure 11.5. Trends in support for European integration. Ireland and the EU: 1973–
2008 (%).**[21]

cost of slightly reducing the number of Irish commissioners, and central-
izing greater authority in Brussels. Although most EU members were not
given the opportunity to vote, Ireland was the only country to actually
reject the treaty, leaving the EU without an agreed consitution.[22]

The same year as the Lisbon referendum, Ireland's Eurovision entry
was a spectacular expression of Irish disenchantement. The "performer,"
Dustin the Turkey, was a hand-puppet character, familiar to Irish television
viewers for acerbic observations and dark humor. Dustin's song, "Irlanda
Douze Points," was explicitly intended to undermine those discourses relating to Irish identity which had served the country so well in the previous
decade, and it poked fun at the ESC itself. Set to a hard electro dance beat
and surrounded by lightly clad dancers, Dustin performed from inside a
supermarket trolley. The song also parodied the common "Eurovision"
song characteristic of including a list of other places in Europe, but did so
inaccurately, and even ridiculed Michael Flatley, the star of *Riverdance*, on
the grounds that he was a "yank"; that is, not a genuine Irishman.

> Oh, I come from a nation
> What knows how to write a song
> Oh Europe, where oh where did it all go wrong?
> Come on!
> . . .
> Give us another chance, we're sorry for Riverdance
> Sure Flatley he's a yank and the Danube flows through France
> Block voting, shock voting, give your 12 today
> You're all invited to Dublin Ireland and we'll
> party the shamrock way
> Irelande Douze points
> Irelande Douze points
> Irelande Douze points . . .
>
> (Music and lyrics by Darren Smith, Simon Fine,
> and Dustin the Turkey)

The song was received terribly in the contest; achieving only fifteenth
place out of nineteen in the semifinal and failing to proceed to the final
competition. What is remarkable about Dustin the Turkey's song is not so
much that it didn't perform well in the competition, as recent "straight"
songs had not fared very much better, but given the history of Ireland's
cultural relations with its European neighbors, it is surprising that such
a song could have been chosen by popular vote to represent the country.
The selection itself was highly controversial and received criticism at the
time from none other than Dana, of "All Kinds of Everything" fame.[23]

*Dana Rosemary Scallon expressed her disdain at the inclusion of the puppet in the
competition. Prior to the announcement of Dustin's victory, the former Eurovision*

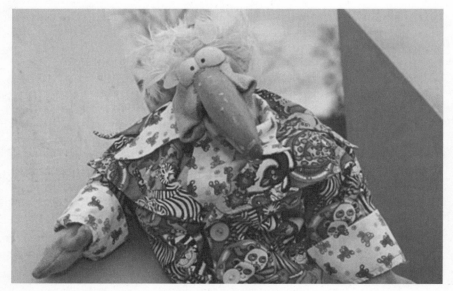

Figure 11.6.   Dustin the Turkey. *Source:* Guardian Newspapers.

winner said, "if it's the turkey, I think we're better not to go into the Eurovision again." Upon hearing the result she said, "the people have spoken, but I think it's a foul decision."
    —Andrea Byrne, *Irish Independent* newspaper. February 24, 2008

Whatever had motivated Irish voters in their choice, frustration with recent results, lack of belief toward their own national tropes, or simply the view that a kitsch parody might be a popular novelty song, the view was clearly not shared in greater Europe. Recently incorporated nations tend to take the competition at face value and, precisely as Ireland had ten years earlier, consider success a matter of national pride.

Ireland's musical approach to the ESC had consequently shifted from an early phase of naïve enthusiasm to a successful middle period of mature professionalism, finally resorting to an expression of cynical humor targeting both the event itself and its own national representations. That this progression coincided with radical economic and demographic shifts, and changing attitudes toward the European Union, is unlikely to be accidental, and it would be valuable to discover whether similar long-term patterns can be discerned among other competing nations.

It will also be interesting to observe Ireland's cultural relations with the rest of Europe now that its long financial bubble has burst and the Celtic Tiger has come to a jarring end. The global financial downturn which began in 2007 has had a particularly deleterious impact upon the Irish economy, as it emerged that much of the later stages of the boom had been based upon inflated real estate speculation. In the ensuing turmoil the European Union, and the common euro currency, has become a source of ontological security for many states, and when Ireland came to vote a second time for the Lisbon Treaty it was supported with a 67 percent vote of approval. For the 2009 competition, Ireland's public service broadcaster, RTE, amended its song selection process to involve a jury alongside the public vote and chose a straightforward pop-rock song, performed by an all-female group, Black Daisy. The song didn't progress beyond the semifinal, and it remains to be seen if, in subsequent years, Ireland will be able to regain the cultural capital which had served it so well in the 1990s.

NOTES

1. For a discussion of this cultural phenomenon in the context of Irish and Breton traditional musics see Wilkinson 2003.

2. In 2008 Ireland awarded eight points to the United Kingdom, ten to Poland, and twelve to Latvia.

3. For example, I have observed that if a ballad wins the competition one year its success will influence the choices of national selectors in the next.

4. The unusual combination of high glamour with relatively mundane music provides the grounds for the "kitsch" label often attached to the ESC. Ironic readings of the event deliberately valorize the contradiction of "good taste" tropes. Although some entries occasionally seek to benefit from the popularity of kitsch or camp readings, this viewing community is probably not significant enough on its own to bring a song overall success.

5. Despite (or even because) of the internationalism of the "Eurovision Style," this shared musical vocabulary does effectively delineate a bounded territory. European pop is still very distinguishable from Arab or Asian genres, and the standardization found in the ESC only serves to confirm these differences.

6. The song celebrated the completion of the Maastricht Treaty, which allowed a much greater degree of European political integration and the introduction of EU citizenship.

7. Recent winners include Denmark (2000); Estonia (2001); Latvia (2002); Turkey (2003); Ukraine (2004); Greece (2005); Finland (2006); Serbia (2007); Russia (2008); Norway (2009).

8. The European Commission's "Eurobarometer" publications do, however, regularly investigate attitudes of member states toward the EU, and a database of ESC voting patterns is readily available online at http://www.songcontestvoting .com/e/.

9. In 2000, foreign nationals resident in Ireland amounted to 3.33 percent of the population, 4.02 percent in 2001, and 5.58 percent by 2003. Source: OECD.

10. Such cultural considerations are evident in a number of policy documents produced between 2000 and 2010. See, for example, Titley et al. 2010.

11. The Ryan Report on clerical child abuse in Ireland (2009) found that for decades the church had such a standing in Irish political culture that it was effectively impervious to legal investigation.

12. Because of Ireland's historical impoverishment, and the deleterious economic effects of the "troubles" in Northern Ireland, the state qualified as a disadvantaged European region and received structural funding of IR£ 8.6 from the EC between 1987 and 1998.

13. These associations were fostered by Ireland's first independent governments, which promoted Catholicism and rural culture as distinguishing features of national identity.

14. While Ireland may have been understood to be suffering from its own conflicts, it had no history of aggression against neighboring countries in Western Europe. The "Troubles" were in any case represented by some protagonists as a war against a colonial oppressor, and therefore a cause many "left of center" Europeans may have sympathized with.

15. 1985's Live Aid charity concerts were the result of the tenacity of another Irishman, Bob Geldof, a fact which may have also contributed to global perceptions of a "national character."

16. The exception being Eimear Quinn's "The Voice," which drew upon the "neo-Celtic" traditions, which by 1996 had become so marketable that it was subsequently emulated by other ESC competitors.

17. By contrast, the United Kingdom's relationship with the European Union was marked by scepticism and wariness. Unlike Ireland, the United Kingdom was a net financial contributor to Europe throughout this period and sought to maintain its independent currency.

18. A term which refers to immigrants who choose to settle permanently in Ireland.

19. One of the longest-standing examples of reciprocal high voting in the competition is between Ireland and the United Kingdom. Sweden and Norway also have a strong tendency to "exchange" votes with Ireland.

20. As reported by the *Irish Examiner Newspaper*, May 12, 2005.

21. Source: http://ec.europa.eu/public_opinion/archives/eb/eb70/eb70_ie_nat.pdf. "The European Union does not endorse changes, if any, made to the original data and, in general terms to the original survey, and such changes are the sole responsibility of the author and not the EU."

22. Any changes to the Irish constitution require a full national referendum. In most other EU states it was successfully argued that the responsibility for such decisions had been devolved to the government in national elections.

23. Since her Eurovision success, Dana had become a politician, espousing a largely traditional Catholic moral agenda, and served as a member of the European Parliament from 1999 to 2004.

REFERENCES

Adams, Paul C. 1992. "Television as Gathering Place." *Annals of the Association of American Geographers*, 82(1): 117–35.

Bohlman, Philip V. 2004. *The Music of European Nationalism: Cultural Identity and Modern History*. Santa Barbara, Calif.: ABC-CLIO.

Eurobarometer 70. Public Opinion in the European Union. National Report: Ireland. Autumn 2008, European Commission. http://ec.europa.eu/public_opinion/archives/eb/eb70/eb70_ie_nat.pdf.

Flash Eurobarometer 245. Post-Referendum Survey in Ireland: Preliminary Results. European Commission, June 2008. http://ec.europa.eu/public_opinion/flash/fl_245_en.pdf.

Gatherer, Derek. 2006. "Comparison of Eurovision Song Contest Simulation with Actual Results Reveals Shifting Patterns of Collusive Voting Alliances." *Journal of Artificial Societies and Social Simulation* 9 (2)1. http://jasss.soc.surrey.ac.uk/9/2/1.html.

O'Toole, Fintan. 2009. *Ship of Fools: How Stupidity and Corruption Sank the Celtic Tiger*. London: Faber and Faber.

Raykoff, Ivan, and Robert D. Tobin, eds. 2007. *A Song for Europe: Popular Music and Politics in the Eurovision Song Contest*. Aldershot: Ashgate.

Titley, Gavan, Aphra Kerr, and Rebecca King O'Riain. 2010. *Broadcasting in the New Ireland—Mapping and Envisioning Cultural Diversity*. BAI/NIU: Maynooth Policy Report.

Wilkinson, Desmond. 2003. "Celtitude, Professionalism, and the Fest Noz in Traditional Music in Brittany." In *Celtic Modern: Music at the Global Fringe*, edited by Martin Stokes and Philip V. Bohlman, 219–56. Lanham, Md.: Scarecrow Press.

Yair, Gad. 1995. "'Unite Unite Europe' The Political and Cultural Structures of Europe As Reflected in the Eurovision Song Contest." *Social Networks* 17: 147–61.

Yair, Gad, and Daniel Maman. 1996. "The Persistent Structure of Hegemony in the Eurovision Song Contest." *Acta Sociologica* 39: 309–25.

WEB SOURCES

Central Statistics Office Ireland: http://www.cso.ie/en/releasesandpublications/population/. Accessed March 2011.

Irish Eurovision Fan Website: http://www.allkindsofeverything.ie/. Accessed May 2011.

Chapter 12

Doing the
European Two-Step

ANDREA F. BOHLMAN
AND ALEXANDER REHDING

Has the United States woken up to the Eurovision Song Contest? In the run-up to the 2009 contest, an unprecedented four articles in the *New York Times* reported on the event.[1] Numerous factors could, of course, have contributed to such coverage: there is, for one, the circumstance that the 2009 contest took place in Moscow, the center of Cold War politics, as well as the disaffection on the part of many Western European countries with the "bloc" voting of the more recently admitted Central and Eastern European countries that broadly replicates historical geopolitical affiliations. But what is more, the 2009 contest became explicitly, indeed unabashedly, political. Two songs stand out: for its entry, "We Don't Wanna Put In," whose not-too-subtle pun reflected the political tensions after the short war between Georgia and Russia during the 2008 Olympics, Georgia was told by the organizers to revise its lyrics and withdrew from the contest in protest; and Israel's entry by the Jewish-Arab duo Noa (Achinoam Nini) and Mira Awad, "There Must Be Another Way," was lambasted both by the political right and, more surprisingly perhaps, by the left, who felt that at a time of renewed aggression between Israeli and Palestinian forces this song would send an overly harmonious, propagandistic picture to Moscow.[2]

This is far from the first time that politics has made an entry into the Eurovision Song Contest. Despite annual assertions by Svante Stockselius, the former executive supervisor of the competition, that there is no place for politics on this musical stage, performers are often all too aware of the political impact of the event.[3] We need only to think of the celebrated and much-discussed victory of the transgender Israeli singer Dana International in 1998, whose political repercussions were clear to everybody.[4]

Even Dana International acknowledged, in accepting her trophy, "this is a bad night for the Orthodox" (Feddersen 2002, 324).[5] But it seems that in the case of the 2009 contest an invisible line had been crossed, so much so that the contest's political undertones called the attention of the international media. Over many years, the Eurovision Song Contest had honed the subtle art of soft politics—to borrow from Joseph Nye's concept of "soft power" (see Nye 2004): a politics that operates on the basis of persuasion rather than confrontation, suggestiveness rather than explicitness, a politics that is read between the lines.

This soft politics is by no means a simple process, since it requires a high degree of cultural attunement to the situation of the various constituencies—multiple national audiences—involved.[6] Given the two-tiered structure of the Eurovision Song Contest, with both national selections and international competitions, these constituencies can have very different interests and predilections. For example, an Icelandic voter may imagine Iceland's representative on the European stage differently than a Maltese voter. Often national audiences can appreciate subtleties that are lost on an international audience, while on the international platform implications can come to the fore that were irrelevant to the domestic audience. In other words, while the model on which the contest is designed follows a binary structure with distinct levels of national and international competition, it is the complexities of the interactions at the interstices between these two levels that we are interested in. As we shall see, the specifics of the national level can be productive or counterproductive in the popular reception of each song on the European stage.

The underlying mechanism is relatively straightforward: each song needs to pass through two stages, one after the other: the national selections and the transnational finals. The goals of these two stages are not mutually exclusive, but they often do not have a unified vision for a successful Eurovision song. Conventional pairs of binaries that are commonly employed in scholarship—for example, local/global, national/international—do not quite capture the double set of requirements that each song encounters from its own national community and the European community at large, in part because the songs, as three-minute acts conforming to rigorous Eurovision guidelines, bridge the gap between the stages of national selection and transnational broadcast. What we are interested in are the multivalent qualities that allow a song to be read, and valorized, at two levels, corresponding to the two stages. Producers and artists may have their eyes on an international prize but, as one observes in the great variety of winning songs, there remains no key to Eurovision success. In some cases, the appeal to national and European voters may be straightforward and in line with the expectations of the producers of a given song, but on occasion each set of requirements highlights the difference in expectation, leading the performer away from European acclaim. By focusing our attention on the relation between the national level and the European finals, we are hoping to build on the rich literature on Eurovision within different individual national contexts, and to contribute to the study of Eurovision at the transnational level.

Take as an example the singer and comedian Guildo Horn (Horst Köhler), who represented Germany in the 1998 contest in Birmingham. Before a domestic audience, the song, "Guildo hat euch lieb" (which translates roughly as "Guildo Cares for You"), had a satirical purpose whose targets were clear: written by Alf Igel (a pseudonym for the comedian Stefan Raab, in reference to the ubiquitous Eurovision songwriter Ralph Siegel) and performed by a balding, middle-aged singer in a velvet costume, the song was a parody of the German *Schlager* tradition with its easy-listening sound and its penchant for romantic-nostalgic subject matters (see Hinrichs 2007). The references had a specific significance to the German contest and its own traditions, but they could only be vaguely understood as humorous and ironic by viewers unfamiliar with the culture of that national contest: non-German audiences were bemused by his odd looks and his clownish antics on stage, without assigning it any specific meaning. What came to the fore in Britain, instead, was the stage name Guildo Horn—whose phallic connotations arguably work better in an English-language context.[7]

We can broaden our scope and generalize these issues of multivalent signification, since the areas of friction between the national and the European levels are an integral component of the annual rituals of Eurovision. The crux, in many ways, is that national decisions try to accomplish two things at once: first, the task at hand is to choose a song that is relevant to—and represents in an exemplary fashion—the domestic market. Or, to put it in less explicitly economic terms, the task is to choose an act that embodies the salient values of the domestic musical culture. Such salient values may, for instance, draw on ethnic musical traditions, or they may take up musical tropes that have been associated with previous popular songs, such as the "ABBA sound" that has become a staple of numerous Eurovision entries—not only from Sweden. And second, it is hoped that the chosen song will at the same time do well on the international level, garnering a victory for its country. That is, national selection involves "imagining the nation" as well as visions of European success. Ultimately, it is an issue of how voting, pop-music-consuming members of each country wish to see their nation represented on the international stage, in such a way that would earn them the largest possible number of votes.

Put simply, this could mean two things: at the national selections domestic audiences could vote for a song that they like best, or that they hope would speak to a transnational audience—through musical, topical, and further choices. (The category of "further choices" allows for the possibility of sending a "message in a song" to the international community, as did, for instance, Georgia in "We Don't Wanna Put In.") Many countries are only too aware that these goals are not always coterminous. Jan Feddersen, a regular host on German Eurovision broadcasts, outlines the problem of competing interests:

> Offerings of pop music that would omit *Volksmusik* and *Schlager* [German folk music and easy listening]—in order to increase their market appeal on the international scene—would get nowhere in Germany, even though it is Europe's largest TV market. The question of whether or not a German pop-music production would have any chances for success abroad seems generally irrelevant. (Feddersen 2002 in Wolther 2006, 136)[8]

While the problem is structurally similar in most participating countries—especially among non-English-speaking nations, who will always have to choose whether to adopt their national language or opt for a "cosmopolitan" English song—each country solves it in a different way. Germany, to stick with our example, generally shifts the balance toward domestic interests: in the interest of *Anspruch* (high cultural standards), German entries often emphasize lofty ideals and international peace. Irving Wolther notes perceptively that, despite Guildo Horn's irreverence, his song effectively continues in this tradition (see Wolther 2006, 135).

Such international complexities overshadow the specific national discourses that contributed to the song's initial selection once the act reaches the Eurovision stage. Often, the resulting dissonance between the national and European levels leads to the performance's failure to achieve a high ranking. Satirical entries trading on national humor, such as Ireland's irreverent puppet Dustin the Turkey (2008), flop as do songs whose national context becomes invisible, for example Norway's glam-rock 2005 song "In My Dreams," which too-subtly traded on the popularity of its genre in Scandinavia.[9] "Guildo hat euch lieb" provides an important counterexample to this trend, since his act gained new significance through the interpretation of a transnational public. Even though most audience members in Birmingham and at the European TV screens in 1998 cannot have been aware of the cultural complexities behind Guildo Horn's song, his titillating, multivalent appearance on the Eurovision stage may have worked to Germany's advantage, which resulted in a respectable seventh place.

Here, we shall examine three examples from the 1990s and 2000s: (1) Amina Annabi's "Le dernier qui a parlé" (France 1991); (2) Lior Narkis's "Words for Love" (Israel 2003); and (3) Sürpriz's "Reise nach Jerusalem" (Germany 1999). In choosing these brief case studies, we explore the complex interactions between the two levels described above and the inherent potential for what are varying—and sometimes radically different—interpretations of the same audiovisual spectacle. All three songs focus on specific questions of subordinate groups—national, sexual, and racial minorities—within a broader national culture and examine how these minorities connect by musical means with their international audiences.

We will be probing the potential of these three songs to appeal to different audiences at different levels and to play with multivalent modes of signification. As each of these cases is historical and since we are interested in the widest transnational response, ethnographic methodologies do not best address our question here, since we cannot ask informants for their immediate responses. Instead, we will rely on a relative crude measure: popularity. In this, we are not necessarily looking for the winning entries—the fact that a song garnered *more* votes than another one and carried off a victory is relatively unimportant here. (In fact, one of our three case studies is distinguished by its relative *lack* of success.) We will not conduct statistical analyses, nor will we factor in the peculiarities of voter behavior, such as the much-maligned "bloc voting." Rather, we are interested in general popularity—or lack thereof—as a measure of the appeal of a song to the televised final's audience, who may not be attuned to the cultural specifics that may have characterized the song in its national context.

1991: AMINA ANNABI (FRANCE)—146 POINTS, SECOND PLACE

The French-Tunisian singer Amina Annabi entered the history of the Eurovision Song Contest as one of the most tragic nonwinners. Her song, "Le dernier qui a parlé," was tied with "Fångad Av En Stormvind," sung by Sweden's Carola. According to the rules at the time, the tie-breaker was determined by adding up the number of times a song received the proverbial *douze points* (see O'Connor 2005, 127). Both songs were tied on that count as well, at four times twelve points each. When the number of times both songs received ten points was compared, Sweden led France—five times against two times—and was declared the overall winner by the slimmest margin of victory in Eurovision history.[10]

What is particularly interesting for our purposes, however, is that the song was an early example of incorporating non-Western musical styles into a Eurovision pop song, at a time when the world music phenomenon was still a novelty in Europe, and clashed significantly with the prevalent pop music aesthetic there (see Bohlman 2002). The Eurovision broadcasters seemed oblivious to Amina's prominence in world music media, such as Radio Nova, when they introduced her to their audiences: British Eurovision commentator Ken Bruce opined in his introduction to this song that it had "a bit of an Eastern feel to it," and his German counterpart, Max Schautzer, concurred that this song was "pleasantly out of the ordinary." We need not worry at this stage how much the expressive hand gestures and vocal techniques Amina employed during her performance owed to "genuine" North African traditions, since what mattered for the European audiences was the mere fact that it was broadly perceived as exotic and attractively different (especially as compared with the boppy post-ABBA sound that enjoyed great popularity at the time).

The wider European audiences may have delighted in the unwonted exotic freshness of the song as a welcome departure from standard Europop, but for the French audiences the Maghreb question presented a very topical reality related to France's colonial history (see Hargreaves and Mark McKinney 1997; Killian 2006).[11] Having a Maghrebi female singer representing France held a certain political explosive potential.[12] For Amina's French-speaking audiences, meanwhile, the song had a whole other dimension that would have resonated with domestic politics and brought specificity to the difference outlined above. The song, whose full title runs "C'est le dernier qui a parlé qui a raison dans ta maison" ("It's he who has spoken last who is right in your house"— which is later varied as "who has spoken the loudest"), was meant as a clarion call for women's rights all over the world.[13] Its verbal message aims to transcend the exotic origin of its musical language and to reach out to universalize its appeal.

It is of course not difficult to explain the strong affinities between the discourses of feminism and those of the foreigner: both are often figured as lesser citizens who are expected to play by the rules set by their (male/indigenous) hosts. The philosopher and feminist Julia Kristeva has particularly emphasized the interchangeability of the stranger and woman consistently through European history (see Kristeva 1991; Clark 1995). But rather than interpreting the discursive analogies in detail, what matters here is the fact that the same musical object allows different constituencies to relate to it, and identify with it, coming from very different perspectives. Amina's performance is multiply liminal, and the convergence of nationally, musically, historically, and gender-inspired interpretations of difference explains, to a certain extent, her Eurovision success.

Amina's choreographed femininity, as in the delicate hand gestures that accompany her performance, connects the exotic and feminist meanings of her song.[14] We may pause to question whether the sweeping gesture, graceful arching all the way down her torso, with which Amina concludes her performance is an all-embracing arabesque or a hand sign indicating pregnancy. But it is precisely the ambivalence of the gesture that beautifully summarizes the two messages that "Le dernier qui a parlé" embodies.

2003: LIOR NARKIS (ISRAEL)—SEVENTEEN POINTS, NINETEENTH PLACE

On the surface, there was no political message in Lior Narkis's carefree performance of "Words for Love" in Riga. However, this declaration of love, sung in French, English, Greek, and Hebrew by Narkis as he danced with five backup dancers, subtly responds to strained undercurrents of nationalism in local popular music history as well as the more prominent controversies surrounding sexuality after Dana International's afore-mentioned victory. Since 1948, popular song has been a forum in which genres and styles, often associated with specific Jewish ethnic groups, have competed to represent the nation as "the true Israeli music" (see Re-gev and Seroussi 2004, 2). In the limelight because of her sexuality, Dana International's victory staged tensions of representation and identity with an eye on the transnational audience.[15] Interpreted in both of these con-texts, Narkis's selection for Eurovision represents a calculated balance of national values that remained inaudible and invisible on the international stage, as we shall show.

Israel's participation in the Eurovision Song Contest has long itself been interpreted as a political statement. Though membership in the European Broadcasting Union is not limited to countries in Europe, either New or as defined by the European Union, Israel was the first non-European coun-try to participate in the competition (1973) and the first to win (1978).[16] Israel's interest in participating in the Eurovision Song Contest may be explained with the strong national tradition of song competitions in Israel and the captive audience of European Jews living in Israel, who followed the competition from the initial broadcasts.[17] Early appearances at Euro-vision connected the winners of hotly contested national song competi-tions to the international scene. The Israeli Song Contest, founded in 1960 and hosted by the Israeli Broadcasting Authority, promoted a Hebrew interpretation of the French *chanson* tradition (*zemer ivry*), excluding the increasingly commercially successful popular music genre that incor-porated Middle Eastern musical elements sung by Arab and Sephardic Jews (*musica mizrakhit*, or "Eastern" music, see Regev and Seroussi 2004, 112–18). In the 1970s, this competition briefly served as the national finals for Eurovision, so that no Middle Eastern–influenced musicians could represent Israel (see Wolther 2006, 47). Antagonism within the popular music scene in Israel excluded sections of this local music scene from participating in Eurovision by excluding them from the national selection processes.

The national friction inherent in defining a song's Israeliness receded before Eurovision performances, as is evident from a survey of the Israeli entries from the 1970s and 1980s. The 1979 ESC winners, Gali Atari with

Milk and Honey, sang in Hebrew but punctuated their verse with re-
frains of the internationally comprehensible and inoffensive "Hallelujah."
"Chai," the big-band-inflected 1983 entry by Yemenite singer Ofra Haza,
later famous for her recordings and remixes of Yemenite songs (notably
"Nin' Alu," recently covered by Madonna), has no trace of the 7/8 me-
ter and major-minor mode-switching characteristic of her other performances' orientalist inflections. In the Israeli case, then, the importance of
the competition for local popular music culture has meant that national
political tensions relate significantly to the demographic to which the
singers belong as well as the musical market in which they work and the
performance decisions they make.[18] In order to progress to the Eurovision
stage, they must first negotiate their home market very carefully. Even
though the stigma against *musica mizrakhit* singers has diminished significantly since the 1980s in Israel, the genre distinction remains significant in the case of Lior Narkis. His performance both recalls these earlier
avoidances of musical markers of Eastern-ness and responds to Dana's
powerful-yet-threatening transgender performance.

The profile of Israel in the context of Eurovision radically shifted with
Dana International's ascent to Eurovision fame, as gender became a focus
of Israel's musical discourse at the competition and at home.[19] The explosive popularity of her 1998 act and the grace with which she handled the
media attention is one of the landmark events in the competition's history (see Feddersen 2002, 310). Her alluring disco-trance overshadowed
the poor performances by Israeli entries in the Song Contest in the years
that followed. She became a point of comparison for every subsequent
Israeli entry, even when her influence was negative. First, the disco-pop
"Happy Birthday," the 1999 entry sung in Jerusalem by the all-male
quartet Eden, contained no trace of the driving techno-pulse nor the epic
synthesized strings. Second, while Dana constantly asserted her desire
to represent even her fiercest opponents by waving the Israeli flag as an
act of inclusion,[20] subsequent entries wielded the standard to articulate
dissatisfaction with national politics, much to the discontent of national
organizers.[21] In 2000, Israel's musical entry was overshadowed by the
political uproar the group caused in the national and international press.
PingPong, a group fronted by an uncharismatic blond woman with a
tendency to sing below pitch, repeatedly shouted the conclusion of their
refrain, "Be Happy!" while waving Syrian and Israeli flags through the
last twenty seconds of their performance. Opposing this critical stance
toward Syria-Israeli relations, the Israeli Broadcasting Corporation pulled
their sponsorship of the act.[22]

On a national level, the soft politics of Lior Narkis negotiated a balance of the internal and gender politics that had tested the limits of the
competition's supposedly apolitical discourse. Significantly, his selection

was calculated; we can consider his performance a result of exercised control on the part of the Israeli delegation. Instead of holding a traditional "Kdam Eurovision," a nationally televised competition whose protocol mirrored that of Eurovision, the Israeli Broadcasting Authority selected Narkis in advance.[23] His biography alone supplies justification for his selection. In the tradition of many Israeli pop music stars, he joined a band as part of his military service, establishing his credibility within the traditional Israeli popular music scene. His prolific output—seven albums between the ages of sixteen and twenty-six—reflected his popularity, but also labeled him as a *mizrakhi* singer, since this music appeared on that genre's labels. But Narkis was a logical decision for reasons beyond his popularity. Unlike his female *mizrakhi* predecessor at the 2002 competition, Sarit Hadad, his appearance and performance aesthetic exuded masculinity in counterpoint to the challenge of traditional gender expression by Dana International (see Jaman-Ivens 2007). Dressed in casual urban attire, Narkis appeared with a flock of women in all of his press photos, the preview postcard broadcast during the contest, and on stage during his performance.

"Words of Love" is an exuberant expression of adoration. Overwhelmed by his joy, the narrator grasps for words to articulate his elation. The refrain repeats "I love you" in English, French, Spanish, Greek, and Hebrew. Thus, the song is marked as simultaneously Mediterranean and European, for he sings in the contest's two official languages. This multilingual appeal seems to have worked on some level, since Spain (1), Greece (3), and France (8) account for all but five of his points, with the remaining from Russia. Musically, only the brief interjection of a synthesized double-reed instrument in the introduction and dizzying chromatic scales in the brass at the borders between verse and refrain recall *musica mizrakhit*. The tune is otherwise a Latin-inflected high-energy big-band number reminiscent of the live orchestras of Eurovision's past, with much of the energy derived from tom-tom off beats and a brassy musical dialogue between the backup singers and synthesized horns.

The performance relies upon Narkis's pretty, but not effeminate, complexion and his charisma. He hardly dances, thrusting his pelvis along with the catchy rhythm and moving around the stage so that his adoring women can follow him. In contrast to Dana International's performance, there is little original or challenging about this performance's physicality. As Terry Wogan sardonically reflected over the final chord in the British broadcast, "Do you think everybody's got the same choreographer?" A prefacing comment by the German broadcaster reiterates the consensus that there is little Israeliness in this entry; instead it seems to be predictably Eurovisionesque. In the broadcast, the girls chase Narkis through the streets of Riga in the introductory postcard, ripping off his jacket in motions foreboding their own repeated removal of clothing onstage. The commentator explains, "This time no musical appeal for peace from Israel. Instead, lighter entertainment."

On the stage in Riga, Narkis failed to garner attention precisely because he projects heteronormativity so constantly and his main cultural references are in the Western pop music sphere—even the schoolgirl outfits in which his backup singers begin the song only mildly attempt to disguise the reference to Britney Spears's famous midriff-bearing video for "Hit Me, Baby, One More Time."[24] Together, these elements buried Narkis's roots in the Israeli popular music scene, so integral to his handpicked selection, from prominence on the stage in Riga, contributing to his rather tepid showing. It is perhaps ironic that the winner in 2003 was Turkey's Sertab Erener, who, unlike Narkis, actively signified the musical culture of her nation and orientalism in her belly-dance-driven "Every Way That I Can."

1999: SÜRPRIZ (GERMANY), 140 POINTS, THIRD PLACE

The German national contest of 1999 was another highly dramatic event. The winner, Corinna May, was disqualified since her song was not original: it had already been recorded before under a different text and by a different group. (Corinna May went on to represent Germany in Estonia in 2002, though without much success.) The surprise winner of the night was the aptly named group Sürpriz.

What makes Sürpriz's unexpected rise so interesting is the fact that nothing was left up to chance. Sürpriz was a group carefully put together by the influential composer and producer Ralph Siegel, who has sent no fewer than eighteen songs to Eurovision. While ostensibly the group Sürpriz is comprised of Turkish-German musicians and may seem to represent a new, multicultural Germany that embraces its major immigrant population and has a harmonious relationship with Islam, it is almost completely the product of hard-nosed economic calculation. The then-recent lifting of language restrictions (1999) opened up new possibilities: Sürpriz's song "Reise nach Jerusalem—Kudüs'e seyahat" was sung in four languages: German, English, Turkish, and the last line—for the host audience—in Hebrew. It made the most out of an appeal to the broad European audience.

Siegel had already fared well with multilingual songs: when his 1982 composition, Nicole's "Ein bißchen Frieden," had won the contest, the singer repeated her musical plea for international peace in Dutch, English, French, and German to rapturous applause. In 1999, Siegel's calculation added up again: Sürpriz was rewarded with points from all the participating nations except Lithuania, Cyprus, and Ireland, landing in a solid third place with 140 points. Turkey and Israel (as well as Portugal and Germany's neighbors Poland and the Netherlands) gave full marks to the song—as was no doubt hoped for by the production team.[25] And again, the lyricist Bernd Meinunger foregrounded international peace: riffing on the multiple meanings of "Die Reise nach Jerusalem"—which not only means "the journey to Jerusalem" but is also the German name for the party game "musical chairs"—the song admonished that "peace is more than a game in which only one person wins."

The musical language of the song worked with the markers of near-Eastern music, or rather what may seem like it to European ears. The refrain of the song worked in elements that trod a fine line between the domestic and the exotic, and that could be interpreted as either Western or non-Western: it adhered to the harmonic minor mode, incorporated syncopated lombardic rhythms, and stepwise predominantly descending melodies. The accompaniment foregrounds low (düm) and high (tek) rhythmic patterns; a *saz* player and a synthesizer are visible on stage. During the bridge, the orientalist elements suddenly cease, the percussion section stops, and gives way to a new symphonic texture to highlight the song's central message: "We walk hand in hand to a peaceful land." The English version is sung in calm, simple rhythms and in the major mode, stripped of any elements that could be marked as "ethnic," while the Turkish response, sung in a smokier voice, gradually slips into a more exotic sound, evading harmonically to the flat second and ending her performance with a vocal melisma that prominently displays the "oriental" augmented second (see Bellman 1998). This emblematic moment is followed by a solo section during which the orientalist texture intensifies, with undulating melodic arabesques and long melismata over a pedal, during which the *saz* sound comes to the fore. The pedal, supporting the exotic highpoint of the song, turns out to be a very Western expediency: it serves as the dominant of the key and allows easy return to the short refrain, which is repeated eight times in various languages, culminating in the final Hebrew, "Shalom 'al ha-olam mi-Yerushalaim."

In many ways, "Reise nach Jerusalem—Kudüs'e seyahat" beautifully represents the well-oiled Eurovision machine. In its musical expression, its blend of the familiar with the exotic, it offers an irresistible mixture of elements that make up the New Europe. Its multilingual message of peace and harmony represents, arguably, the lofty goal that the Eurovision Song Contest aspires to. That the mechanisms behind this song, which plays so carefully with difference and sameness, are the very same that have produced song after song for the Eurovision Song Contest industry is the proverbial fly in the ointment.

After the "Alf Igel" scandal of the previous year, Ralph Siegel, who had shaped and determined the German Eurovision sound like no one else, had perhaps emerged stronger. On one level it seems that he had turned over a new leaf, in response to Guildo Horn's departure from the more traditional songs that usually represent Germany. The sound world that Siegel explores here in "Reise nach Jerusalem—Küdus'e seyahat" is unprecedented in his Eurovision music and in that of the major sponsoring countries, the Big Four. On the other hand, below the exotically shimmering surface, everything was what the traditional German audiences had come to expect from a Eurovision song: the messages of international peace and happiness continue to rule. After the initial blip—the fact that Sürpriz did not win the national contest in the first place—all the signs were set for a highly successful Eurovision song.[26]

These three case studies offer a glimpse into the complexities at work in the Eurovision Song Contest. As we have seen, the reasons a song is popular and garners success on the national level are not always the same reasons a song may do well at the final, televised spectacle. The often different exigencies of the national selection and the international finals make it necessary to dance a veritable "two-step" in navigating the two levels simultaneously. At the same time, these very same complexities also allow for the representative potential of the "soft politics" that is so characteristic of the Eurovision Song Contest—and, by extension, the New Europe.

This is particularly true for the signification of minority and under-represented groups within the New Europe. As we have seen, each of the groups or singers examined above plays with elements pertaining to a liminal group within the country they represent. Each of them, however, employs the markers of their difference on the transnational level in different ways: all but imperceptibly in the case of Narkis, self-consciously in the case of Amina, and profit-oriented in the case of Sürpriz. Likewise, it appears that in each case a supplemental focus is foregrounded that interacts in complex ways with the peripheral status of the singer: Narkis's heteronormativity sets a powerful symbolic mark; Amina thematizes the role of women in society, while Süpriz underlines a larger, perhaps global, community exemplarily.

Understanding this European "two-step," understanding the semiotic intricacies of the "soft politics" of Eurovision, which often require a detailed knowledge of the peculiarities of the national politics and specific histories of the participating countries, may also help explain why non-European media, such as the *New York Times*, have by and large ignored this event up until recently. The question is not whether the nature of the Eurovision has suddenly changed to an out-and-out political battlefield where musical content is irrelevant: the Eurovision Song Contest, obviously, has always already been political. The national success of our three case studies—which, in the case of Narkis, did not translate to international popularity—results from a musical negotiation of political difference. The 2009 case of Georgia contrasts because the entry's explicit attack on Putin responded musically to the military conflict of the previous autumn, and it articulated this attack on the competition's host country.[27]

An act's maneuvers between national and European levels invariably enmesh it in politics. Seen and heard from this perspective, soft politics are not a cop-out for Eurovision success, they anchor a performer's relationship to diverse audiences. Is Eurovision to remain hopeful of a New Europeanness? Between the national and transnational, political musicians must tread lightly, dancing their way toward their neighbors' *douze points*.

NOTES

1. Bronner, Ethan. 2009. "In Israel, Jew and Arab Sing, But Political Chorus Is Heard." *New York Times*, February 25, A5(N); Schwirtz, Michael. 2009. "Georgia Withdraws from Music Contest," *New York Times*, March 12, A8; "Russia Serves as a Musical Muse for Europeans with an Itch." *New York Times*, April 21, 2009, A8; Widdicombe, Ben. 2009. "Imported Cheese." *New York Times Online*, April 6. Accessed November 22, 2011. http://themoment.blogs.nytimes.com/2009/04/06/imported-cheese-eurovision-contest/.

2. See Belkind 2010.

3. See for example the assertions with direct reference to the 2009 Georgian entry, http://www.esctoday.com/news/read/12223 (August 25, 2008; accessed November 22, 2011). He similarly denied the political nature of Russia's 2008 victory when questioned about the exorbitant production costs of the entry in the winner's press conference on the twentieth of May, 2008.

4. Dana International has been a *cause célèbre* for Eurovision studies and has been discussed at length. See, for instance, Lemish 2007, 131–34; Middleton 2006, 131–34.

5. Indeed, Orthodox leaders threatened public protests in wake of her victory. (See *BBC News*. May 13, 1999. Accessed November 22, 2011. http://news.bbc.co.uk/1/hi/entertainment/342857.stm.)

6. Philip Bohlman has explored the role of the Eurovision Song Contest in the forging of a New Europe. See Bohlman 2010, 1–9.

7. German audiences were by and large indifferent to any sexual connotations of the name Guildo Horn. Difficult as it is to prove a negative, German online dictionaries of swearwords—www.rindvieh.com (Austria) and schimpfwort-station.de (Germany)—do not offer sexual explanations for the entry "Horn" (a word that only tends to appear in the compound "Hornorchse"; accessed November 22,

2011). The explicit entry "Dildo Horn" was not entered into the German website www.stupidedia.org until July 24, 2007, that is, nine years after the contest.

8. "Mit einem pop-musikalischen Angebot, das aus Gründen internationaler Marktfähigkeit ohne Volksmusik und Schlager auskommen wollte, ist in Deutschland, Europas größtem TV-Markt, kein Blumenpott zu gewinnen. Ob eine deutsche Pop-Produktion im Ausland reüssieren könnte oder nicht, scheint einerlei." Feddersen's comment comes across as outdated in the wake of Lena's 2010 victory. Germany's revamped national selection process, which mixes aggressive European marketing online and a reconfigured German television competition, provides another model of negotiating the two Eurovision stages and might even be read as itself an acknowledgment of the phenomenon Feddersen describes.

9. Wolther reflects similarly upon the failure of national markers that are not read as such by an international audience: "At the same time, that which is interpreted as a typically national element within the national audience is not necessarily perceived as such by other constituencies" ("Dabei muss das, was innerhalb der nationalen Gemeinschaft als typisch nationales Element empfunden wird, von den Angehoerigen anderer Gemeinschaften nicht zwangsläufig als solches erkannt werden," Wolter 2006, 85). In the Israeli context, Motti Regev and Edwin Seroussi insist that international ambition does not diminish local tensions' relevance for song selection. In fact, they argue that the global-pop industry "increases the efforts of local pop-music communities to redefine and insist on the existence of their own national styles" (Regev and Seroussi 2004, 10).

10. The background anecdotes to this dramatic event live on in Eurovision lore. See, for instance, Feddersen 2002, 258–61.

11. Robert J. C. Young brings the discussion to bear on the emergence of *rai* music (see Young 2003, 69–79).

12. Race relations in France have a very different tradition from those in English-speaking countries. In 1972 France introduced antiracism laws that form the basis of its color-blind policies, which was confirmed and expanded in a set of laws passed in 1990. Legal thinking in this area is significantly concerned with hate speech.

13. The song, composed by Senegalese musician Wasis Diop, was recorded for her debut album, *Yalil* (Night). Her song's success at Eurovision and within France paved the way for Amina's involvement with global popular music politics; her selection as Best Female Musician of the Year at "Prix de Piaf" led to her collaboration with Peter Gabriel on his Gulf War peace project. She also recorded a cover of John Lennon's "Give Peace a Chance" that same year.

14. "I am very attracted to the idea of the woman as an irrecuperable foreigner [. . .] I see the role of women as a sort of vigilance, a strangeness as always to be on guard and contestatory," in an interview with Suzanne Clark and Katherine Hudley (Kristeva and Guberman 1996, 45).

15. According to Yossi Maurey, "Dana disputes and resists Israel's national fixation with its borders; in particular, she engages provocatively with the tensions between Israel's geographical location in the Arab and Muslim Middle-East, and its self-perception as a European nation" (Maurey 2009, 100).

16. Ivan Raykoff and Robert D. Tobin go so far as to claim that "Israel presents the most celebrated and complicated case for marginality and camp in Eurovision" (Raykoff and Tobin 2007, 11). With thirty-four entries and eighteen top-ten finishes under their belts, Israel's "marginality" refers not to their musical success, but to their position at the boundaries of Europe. The contest began moving east in 1961, when Yugoslavia participated for the first time. Following Israel's involvement, Turkey entered for the first time in 1975, while Morocco, entering with the only song in Arabic, briefly took part for one year in 1980.

17. It is also part of a general trend to look to Europe within entertainment culture, as seen in Israel's participation in the Union of European Leagues of Basketball, for example.

18. It is important to note here that although Dana International has Sephardic origins, her music does not fall into the category of *musica mizrakhit*. See Maurey 2009, 102; n. 18.

19. Maurey turns to the Israeli context of Dana's entire career (see Maurey 2009).

20. At the same time, Dana's flag-waving must appear like an act of provocation when viewed from the perspective of the homophobic right. Similarly, it is noticeable that Israeli GLBT groups, above all Agudah, promote a consciously nationalist, self-inclusive image, in response to attempts to brand them as "un-Israeli."

21. Israeli newspapers quoted her as saying, "I don't represent only myself. I represent the flag that sent me, and I need to respect it. I remember feeling the highest sense of pride" (quoted in Maurey 2009, 98).

22. Goldenberg, Suzanne. 2000. "Outraged Israel Disowns Daring Eurovision Entry." *The Guardian*, May 12. Accessed November 22, 2011. http://www.guardian .co.uk/world/2000/may/12/israel. This article suggests the band provoked the authorities further with its preview video in which two male band members kiss. On the stage in Stockholm, the love affair between an Israeli woman and a Syrian man that is the subject of this tongue-in-cheek performance is enacted by modest petting of the lead singer during the bridge.

23. Notably, none of Israel's Eurovision winners were selected in this national competition. The televised competition still happened, but only the song was at stake. At the Kdam Eurovision, Narkis performed four songs from which "Milliam L'ahava/Words of Love" was declared the victor.

24. Theories of heteronormativity bring the question of representation to the fore. Michael Warner writes that "heteronormativity has a totalizing tendency," referring to "heterosexual culture's exclusive ability to interpret itself as society" (Warner 1991: 8).

25. Neighbors' votes are notoriously difficult to interpret. Since the rise of cell phones in the late nineties, it has become easier to circumvent the rule that audiences cannot vote for the song representing their own country. It has become standard practice for audiences near national borders to cross over to another country and to vote for their home country from there. The results from the Netherlands and Poland—not traditionally the closest of Germany's neighbors in musical or political terms—can probably be explained by "vote-hopping."

26. There were allegations that Sürpriz's song was not wholly original either, but the German commission decided that the song was sufficiently original to abide by the rules (see Feddersen 2002, 328).

27. By contrast, explicitly political attacks against non-European nations do not constitute a problem: When Ukraine's 2005 entry, Greenjolly, rapped that "Lies be the weapons of mass destruction," the protest against the Bush administration's Middle Eastern politics could not have been more explicit. Unlike Georgia, however, Ukraine's musical invective expressed futile frustration rather than direct provocation of a national audience within Europe, threatening the stability of the contest.

REFERENCES

Bellman, Jonathan. 1998. *The Exotic in Western Music*. Boston: Northeastern University Press.

Belkind, Nili. 2010. "A Message for Peace or a Tool for Oppression? Israeli Jewish-Arab Duo Achinoam Nini and Mira Awad's Representation of Israel at Eurovision 2009." *Current Musicology* 89: 7–35.

Bohlman, Philip V. 2010. *Music, Nationalism, and the Making of the New Europe*. New York: Routledge.

———. 2002. *World Music: A Very Short Introduction*. New York: Oxford University Press.

Clark, Suzanne. 1995. "Julia Kristeva: Rhetoric and the Woman as Stranger." In *Reclaiming Rhetorica: Women in the Rhetorical Tradition*, edited by Andrea A. Lunsford, 305–18. Pittsburgh: University of Pittsburgh Press.

Feddersen, Jan. 2002. *"Ein Lied kann eine Brücke sein": Die deutsche und internationale Geschichte des Grand Prix Eurovision*. Hamburg: Hoffmann und Campe.

Hargreaves, Alex G., and Mark McKinney, eds. 1997. *Post-Colonial Cultures in France*. London and New York: Routledge.

Hinrichs, Thorsten. 2007. "Chasing the 'Magic Formula' for Success: Ralph Siegel and the Grand Prix de la Chanson." In *A Song for Europe: Popular Music and Politics in the Eurovision Song Contest*, edited by Ivan Raykoff and Robert D. Tobin, 49–69. Aldershot: Ashgate.

Jaman-Ivens, Freya, ed. 2007. *Oh Boy!: Masculinities and Popular Music*. New York: Routledge.

Killian, Caitlin. 2006. *North African Women in France: Gender, Culture and Identity*. Stanford: Stanford University Press.

Kristeva, Julia. 1991. *Strangers to Ourselves*. Translated by Leon S. Roudier. New York: Columbia University Press.

———. and Guberman, Ross Mitchell, eds. 1996. *Julia Kristeva: Interviews*. New York: Columbia Press.

Lemish, Dafna. 2007. "Gay Brotherhood: Israeli Gay Men and the Eurovision Song Contest." In *A Song for Europe: Popular Music and Politics in the Eurovision Song Contest*, edited by Ivan Raykoff and Robert D. Tobin, 123–34. Aldershot: Ashgate.

Maurey, Yossi. 2009. "Dana International and the Politics of Nostalgia." *Popular Music* 28(1): 85–103.

Middleton, Richard. 2006. *Voicing the Popular: On the Subjects of Popular Music.* New York: Routledge.

Nye, Joseph. 2004. *Soft Power: The Means to Success in World Politics.* New York: Public Affairs.

O'Connor, John Kennedy. 2005. *The Eurovision Song Contest 50 Years: The Official History.* London: Carlton Books.

Raykoff, Ivan, and Robert Deam Tobin, eds. 2007. *A Song for Europe. Popular Music and Politics in the Eurovision Song Contest.* Aldershot: Ashgate.

Regev, Motti, and Edwin Seroussi. 2004. *Popular Music and National Culture in Israel.* Berkeley: University of California.

Warner, Michael. 1991. "Introduction: Fear of a Queer Planet." *Social Text* 29: 3–17.

Wolther, Irving. 2006. *"Kampf der Kulturen": Der Eurovision Song Contest als Mittel national-kultureller Repräsentation.* Würzburg: Königshausen und Neumann.

Young, Robert C. 2003. *Postcolonialism: A Very Short Introduction.* Oxford: Oxford University Press.

Index

de Oliveira, Simone, 231
Derrida, Jacques, 252
Desfolhada (song), 231, 232
Det börjar verka kärlek, banne mej (song), 208
Det' lige det (song), 211
dialectical images, 251
dictatorship, 112, 225, 226, 227. *See also* authoritarian state; fascism
difference, 3, 8, 9, 12, 20, 27n29, 36, 42, 43, 44, 87, 88, 89, 90, 194, 243, 250, 252, 253, 286, 291, 292. *See also* otherness; monster
Diggi-loo diggi-ley (song), 149n8, 211
disco, 99, 211, 215, 218n22, 288
Disco Tango (song), 93
distinction, 4, 5, 7, 8, 82
Diva (song), 45, 98
Divać, Vlade, 64
Dizionario dei film Morandini, 115
Don't Sleep in the Subway (song), 208
dos Santos, Ary, 230, 231, 232, 233
douze points, 7, 74n20, 76n39, 93, 285, 293
Drama Queen (song), 96
Drezner, Daniel, 246, 256n17, 259
Du är en vårvind i april (song), 208
Du ser mej inte (song), 208
Du skänker mening åt mitt liv (song), 208
Du vet var jag finns (song), 208
Dublin, 88, 94, 222, 272, 275
Dungeons and Dragons (game), 244
Dustin the Turkey (singer / puppet), 19, 222, 266, 275, 276, 284
Dutch national broadcaster, 156

East and West, 82, 217n21, 223, 225, 243, 291
Eden (band), 288
E Depois do Adeus (song), 6, 18, 225, 226, 231, 237
E dimmi che non vuoi morire. Un thriller sanremese (novel), 133, 119
Ein bißchen Frieden (song), 45, 84, 89, 98, 290
Ell/Niki (band), 9, 10
Emissora Nacional, 226

Emissores Associados de Lisboa (radio station), 226
emotion, 15, 66, 74n19, 92, 93, 101, 137, 141, 142, 147, 232, 235, 237, 263, 272. *See also* affect; sentiment
empire, 2, 4, 8, 18, 23, 29n57, 175, 177, 228, 229, 245, 246, 251, 254. *See also* imperialism
endism, 49, 253. *See also* eschatology
En gång ska han (song), 212
Enigma (band), 90
Enya (singer), 212
Erçetin, Candan, 179
Erener, Sertab, 16, 17, 27n32, 98, 103n19, 173, 174, 179, 180, 181, 184, 185, 186, 187, 188, 189, 190, 191, 192, 193, 194, 195n2, 196n25, 196n30, 197n31–34, 290
Erlmann, Veit, 90, 91, 106, 257n22
Ernman, Malena, 5, 25n12, 26n27, 215
erotic, 15, 96, 142, 183, 186, 188. *See also* kiss, on ESC stage
escapism, 148
eschatology, 253. *See also* endism
ESC song: and historical moment, 3, 7, 18, 20, 45, 46, 50, 72, 256n21; and historical narrative, 39, 44, 53; as a site of history and politics, 3; identity, 41, 42, 45, 48, 49. *See also* temporality and song; bridge
essentialism, 12, 92, 190
Estado Novo, cultural politics, 225–226, 228–233, 224, 239
Estonia, 35, 75n31, 290
ethnic entries, 7, 8, 53, 148, 203, 217n15, 283. *See also* world music
ethnicity, 20, 90, 95, 96, 190. *See also* ethnic turn; ethnic entries
ethnic turn, 17, 46, 26n23, 80, 90, 101, 139
ethnography, 61, 74n26, 75n29, 285
ethnophobia, 96
Eurasia, 9, 11, 23
Euro Neuro (song), 9, 28n45
Eurobarometer, 274, 277n8, 279
Eurobody. *See* body
Eurocity, 9, 14, 27n34, 59, 62, 63, 64, 67, 69, 73n13

About the Contributors

Alf Björnberg is professor in musicology at the Department of Cultural Sciences, University of Gothenburg, Sweden, where he received his Ph.D. in 1987 for a dissertation analyzing the songs in the Swedish preliminaries of the Eurovision Song Contest. His research interests include popular music, music and the media, and music analysis. He has published work on music video, the history of music broadcasting in Sweden, the cultural politics of the Eurovision Song Contest, and the history of popular music in the Scandinavian area.

Andrea F. Bohlman is assistant professor in music at the University of North Carolina, Chapel Hill. After receiving an MMus from Royal Holloway, University of London, she earned her doctorate in historical musicology at Harvard University in 2012 with a dissertation that examined intersections between political activism and music in Poland at the end of the Cold War. She studies the recent past, in particular the musical cultures of East Central Europe from the final decades of the twentieth century through the present. Through a long-standing concern with music and politics, she considers diverse musical genres together in her archival and ethnographic work on soundscapes of political protest, musico-socialist idealism, and the musical media of oppositional cultures. Her current project, "The Documentary Impulse: A History of Sound Media in Twentieth-Century Poland," engages with amateur music-making practices and "old" media, such as magnetic tape and radio, to reframe the vantage point from which twentieth-century music history is written.

Philip V. Bohlman is the Mary Werkman Distinguished Service Professor of Music and the Humanities at the University of Chicago and Honorarprofessor at the Hochschule für Musik, Theatre und Medien Hannover. A pianist, he is the artistic director of the New Budapest Orpheum Society, a cabaret troupe and ensemble-in-residence at the University of Chicago, as well as the 2011 recipient of the Noah Greenberg Award for Historical Performance from the American Musicological Society. Among his most recent publications are *Jüdische Volksmusik—Eine mitteleuropäische Geistesgeschichte* (Böhlau, 2005), *Jewish Music and Modernity* (Oxford, 2008), and *Focus: Music, Modernity, and the Making of the New Europe* (Routledge, 2011). *Revival and Reconciliation: Sacred Music in the Making of European Modernity* appears in the series "Europea: Ethnomusicologies and Modernities," which he coedits with Martin Stokes. His current research includes ethnographic studies of religion and the arts in India and of the Eurovision Song Contest.

Annemette Kirkegaard is associate professor in musicology at the University of Copenhagen. Working as an ethnomusicologist, her present research is on popular music in Zanzibar, East Africa, and the patterns of change resulting from the historical and contemporary exchange with music cultures globally, and she is leading a NordForsk-funded researcher's network on music censorship. Annemette Kirkegaard has coedited the book *Playing with Identities in Contemporary Music in Africa* (Gidlunds förlag, Uppsala 2002), and recent publications include "Censoring Music through Race—The Struggle between African and Arab Values and Politics in the Music in Zanzibar," *Danish Yearbook for Musicology*, volume 36, 2009, and with Steven Feld, "Entangled Complicities in the Prehistory of 'World Music': Poul Rovsing Olsen and Jean Jenkins Encounter Brian Eno and David Byrne in the Bush of Ghosts," in *Popular Musicology Online*, volume 4, 2010.

Apostolos Lampropoulos is associate professor of literary theory at the Department of French Studies and Modern Languages of the University of Cyprus. He has also taught at the Université Paris Ouest, the University of Patras, and at the Freie Universität Berlin. His research focuses on literary and cultural theory, as well as body and film studies. He has published the monograph *Le Pari de la description. L'effet d'une figure déjà lue* (L'Harmattan 2002) and the Greek translations of A. Compagnon's *Le Démon de la théorie* (Metaichmio, 2003) and J. Culler's *On Deconstruction* (Metaichmio, 2006). He has also coedited the volume *States of Theory: History and Geography of Critical Narratives* (in Greek, with A. Balasopoulos, Metaichmio, 2010), a special issue of the journal *Synthesis* on "Configurations of Cultural Amnesia" (with V. Markidou, 2010), and the volume

AutoBioPhagies (with M. Chehab, Peter Lang, 2011). Currently he prepares the volume *Textual Layering: Contact, Historicity, Critique* (with M. Margaroni and C. Hadjichristos, Lexington Books, 2012).

Tony Langlois lectures in media and communication at Mary Immaculate College, University of Limerick. With a background in ethnomusicology, his research interests include the popular music of Algeria and Morocco, film sound, the experimental music scenes of Ireland and Iceland. Recent and forthcoming publications include an edited volume on non-Western popular music (Ashgate Press); the Jewish musicians of colonial Algeria; frame drums of the Maghreb; and neo-Sufism and music in Morocco. Further details of his research and nonacademic activities can be found at http://zelloloid.org/.

Goffredo Plastino is reader in ethnomusicology at the International Centre for Music Studies, Newcastle University (United Kingdom). He has been editor of the series *Italian Treasury* (Rounder Records), from the 1954–1955 Italian field recordings by Alan Lomax and Diego Carpitella. He is coeditor (with Franco Fabbri) of the *Routledge Global Popular Music Series*. Among his publications: *Lira. Uno strumento musicale tradizionale calabrese* (Monteleone, 1994); *Mappa delle voci. Rap, raggamuffin e tradizione in Italia* (Meltemi, 1996); *Mediterranean Mosaic; Popular Music and Global Sounds* (as editor, Routledge, 2003); *Cosa Nostra Social Club. Mafia, malavita e musica in Italia* (il Saggiatore, 2013); *Jazz Worlds/World Jazz* (coedited with Philip V. Bohlman, University of Chicago Press, forthcoming); *Neapolitan Postcards: The* Canzone Napoletana *as Transnational Subject* (coedited with Joseph Sciorra, Scarecrow Press, forthcoming).

Ioannis Polychronakis is an ethnomusicologist and pianist. He completed his undergraduate studies in music at the University of Athens, Greece, and he earned a diploma in piano performance from the "Philippos Nakas" Conservatoire of Athens. He was then awarded an MSt in Music at Christ Church Oxford, focused on the aesthetics and philosophy of music, and an MMus from Royal Holloway University of London with a binary specialization in popular music studies and the performance of twentieth-century piano music. In 2012 he completed his doctoral degree at the University of Oxford, St. Hugh's College. His thesis, titled *Song Odyssey: Negotiating Identities in Greek Popular Music,* is a historically informed ethnography of Greek popular song. It examines the ways in which Greek popular music has responded to globalization from the 1990s to the present, with specific attention to issues of nationalism, gender, and cultural politics. It argues that there is significant fragmentation in present-day Greek society, which is most evident in popular music where the idea of the individual and the legitimacy of individual ideas about the nation have become prominent in the last couple of decades.

Alexander Rehding is Fanny Peabody Professor of Music and chair of the Department of Music at Harvard University. He was editor of *Acta musicologica* 2006–2010 and is editor-in-chief of the Oxford Research Reviews in the field of music. His research has been supported by the ACLS, Guggenheim, Humboldt, and Mellon Foundations. His research is located at the intersection between history and theory, focusing on the long nineteenth century, but his interests range from the music of Ancient Greece to the Eurovision Song Contest. Recent publications include *Music and Monumentality* (2009) and *The Oxford Handbook of Neo-Riemannian Music Theories* (2011).

Thomas Solomon is associate professor in the Grieg Academy-Department of Music at the University of Bergen. He has previously taught at New York University, University of Minnesota, and Istanbul Technical University. He has done field research in Bolivia on musical imaginations of ecology, place, and identity, and in Istanbul on place and identity in Turkish hip-hop. His publications include articles in the journals *Ethnomusicology, Popular Music, European Journal of Cultural Studies,* and *Yearbook for Traditional Music,* as well as numerous papers in edited volumes. He is also editor of *Music and Identity in Norway and Beyond: Essays Commemorating Edvard Grieg the Humanist* (Bergen: Fagbokforlaget, 2011) and coeditor of *Ethnomusicology in East Africa: Perspectives from Uganda and Beyond* (Kampala: Fountain Publishers, 2012).

Martin Stokes is King Edward Professor of Music at King's College, London. He is the author of *The Arabesk Debate: Music and Musicians in Modern Turkey* (Clarendon 1992) and *Ethnicity, Identity and Music: The Musical Construction of Place* (Berg 1994). *The Republic of Love: Cultural Intimacy in Turkish Popular Music* was published by the University of Chicago Press in 2010. His research interests continue to revolve around Turkey, Egypt, and the Mediterranean.

Karin Strand is a scholar and archivist at Svenskt visarkiv (Centre for Swedish Folk Music and Jazz Research) in Stockholm. Her doctoral dissertation from 2003, *Känsliga bitar: Text- och kontextstudier i sentimental populärsång* (Emotional Songs: Text- and Context Studies of the Sentimental Schlager) was a study of crooner repertoires within the Swedish *schlager* from the early days of radio up to the 1950s. Her research interests concern lyrics and mediation of folk songs and early popular music, such as handwritten songbooks, broadsheet ballads, chapbook songs, and *schlager* from the early twentieth century. Presently she is working on a project on beggar verses and "blind man songs" in broadsheets.

Luisa Pinto Teixeira is director of the Instituto Camões Centre for Portuguese Language and Fellow of St. John's College, Oxford. She is the author of *Railways of Mozambique: 100 Years* (Manica & CFM, 1995). She is currently writing about the Goanese community of Sao Paulo and Rio de Janeiro. Her research interests comprise migrations in the lusophone world, the Third Portuguese Empire, and colonialism.

Dafni Tragaki is a lecturer in anthropology of music at the Department of History, Archaeology and Social Anthropology, University of Thessaly, Greece. She is the author of *Rebetiko Worlds: Ethnomusicology and Ethnography in the City* (Cambridge Scholars Publishing, 2007). Her recent research focuses on music and cultural theory, popular music and politics, sound, senses, and the city. She collaborates with the project De.Mu.Ci.V.: Designing the Museum for the City of Volos—Historical Research and the Development of Innovative Interactive Environments for the Distribution of Scientific Knowledge of the research program Thalis, financed by the Ministry of Education and the European Union. She is currently editing a collection of essays on popular music in Greece.